The
Transforming
WORD

VOLUME 3

The Prophets
From Isaiah to Malachi

The
Transforming
WORD
Revised Edition

Mark W. Hamilton
General Editor

Kenneth L. Cukrowski
Nancy Wilhite Shankle
James W. Thompson
John T. Willis
Associate Editors

Abilene Christian University Press

THE TRANSFORMING WORD
Volume 3: The Prophets: From Isaiah to Malachi

ACU
PRESS

ACU Box 29138
Abilene, Texas 79699
www.acupressbooks.com | www.transformingwordcommentary.com
1-877-816-4455 toll free

Copyright © 2022 Mark W. Hamilton
ISBN 978-1-68426-052-2 | LCCN 2021050986

LIBRARY OF CONGRESS CATALOGING-IN-PUBLICATION DATA
Names: Hamilton, Mark W., editor. | Cukrowski, Kenneth L. (Kenneth Larry),editor. |
  Shankle, Nancy Wilhite, 1956- | Thompson, James W. (James Weldon), 1942- editor. |
  Willis, John T., 1933- editor. | Abilene Christian University.
Title: The transforming word / Mark Hamilton, general editor ; Kenneth L. Cukrowski,
Nancy Wilhite Shankle, James W. Thompson, John T. Willis, associate editors.
Description: Revised edition. | Abilene, Texas : ACU Press, 2022. | Includes
  bibliographical references.
Identifiers: LCCN 2021050986 (print) | LCCN 2021050987 (ebook) |
  ISBN 9781684262311 (v. 1 : hardcover) | ISBN 9781684260423 (v. 2 : hardcover) |
  ISBN 9781684260522 (v. 3 : hardcover) | ISBN 9781684260621 (v. 4 : hardcover) |
  ISBN 9781684260720 (v. 5 : hardcover) | ISBN 9781684269518 (v. 1 : epub) |
  ISBN 9781684269006 (v. 2 : epub) | ISBN 9781684268993 (v. 3 : epub) |
  ISBN 9781684268986 (v. 4 : epub) | ISBN 9781684268979 (v. 5 : epub) |
Subjects: LCSH: Bible—Commentaries. | Bible—Criticism, interpretation, etc.
Classification: LCC BS491.3 .T73 2022 (print) | LCC BS491.3 (ebook) | DDC 220.7—dc23
LC record available at https://lccn.loc.gov/2021050986
LC ebook record available at https://lccn.loc.gov/2021050987

Original Dust Jacket Design · Nicole Weaver, Zeal Design Studio
Original Book Design and Typesetting · William Rankin
Maps & graphics · William Rankin with Lawson Soward

22 23 24 25 26 27 28 / 10 9 8 7 6 5 4 3 2 1

Contents

To faithful students of the Bible

past, present, & future

Contributors

Philip G. Camp   PhD, Union Theological Seminary and Presbyterian School of Christian Education; Professor of Old Testament, Hazelip School of Theology, Lipscomb University; Nashville, Tennessee.

Brandon L. Fredenburg   PhD, University of Denver/Iliff School of Theology; Professor of Biblical Studies, Lubbock Christian University; Lubbock, Texas.

Mark W. Hamilton   PhD, Harvard University; Robert & Kay Onstead Professor of Biblical Studies, Abilene Christian University; Abilene, Texas.

Nathaniel D. Lollar   MA, Abilene Christian University; Inventory Control Specialist & Materials Analyst, Happy Family Organics; Boise, Idaho.

Keith N. Schoville   PhD, University of Wisconsin; Professor Emeritus of Hebrew and Semitic Studies, University of Wisconsin-Madison; Madison, Wisconsin.

Tim Sensing   PhD, University of North Carolina at Greensboro; Associate Dean and Professor of Ministry and Homiletics, Abilene Christian University; Abilene, Texas.

Nancy Wilhite Shankle   PhD, Texas A&M University; Provost and Associate Vice Chancellor, Texas A&M RELLIS Academic Alliance; Bryan, Texas.

David I. Shaw   JD, Baylor University; MA, Abilene Christian University; Assistant City Attorney; Waco, Texas.

Jonathan Wade   PhD, University of Texas at Dallas; Senior Educational Technologist, Western Carolina University; Cullowhee, North Carolina.

Paul L. Watson   PhD, Yale University; Professor Emeritus of Bible and Ministry, Graduate School of Theology, Amridge University; Montgomery, Alabama.

John T. Willis   PhD, Vanderbilt University; Burton & Sissy Coffman Distinguished Chair of Biblical Studies, Emeritus, Abilene Christian University; Abilene, Texas.

Preface

The book you are holding primarily concerns another book, the Bible. The editors and authors of this book, in their fervent belief that the Bible reveals to human beings the path to God and thus to meaningful human existence, offer this commentary on the church's central texts. In doing so, we stand in a long tradition of interpreters of Scripture going back to ancient times, as readers sought to understand the stories, prophecies, songs, prayers, and letters making up the great anthology that is the Bible. More than that, they—and we—seek to hear afresh transforming words that will quicken the life of the church as it shares in God's redeeming work in the world.

The authors and editors of this book share a common history. They are all members of churches that emerged in the nineteenth century in North America following the direction of such great leaders as Barton Stone, Walter Scott, Alexander Campbell, and others. Their "present Reformation," as they named it, began as an effort to purify the Christianity they had inherited of its divisions and corruptions. By returning to the Bible as the only rule in faith and practice, they believed they could restore primitive Christianity and thus help welcome God's in-breaking kingdom.

For these men and women of faith, the Bible offered a picture of a healed world in which God's will was done on earth as it was in heaven. Thus teaching the Bible was an act of redemption, not merely a technical exercise. As Thomas Campbell put it in 1809,

> [A]ll that are enabled, thro' grace, to make such a profession, and to manifest the reality of it in their tempers and conduct, should consider each other as the precious saints of God, should love each other as brethren, children of the same family and father, temples of the same spirit, members of the same body, subjects of the same grace, objects of the same divine love, bought with the same price, and joint heirs of the same inheritance. Whom God hath thus joined together, no man should dare to put asunder.

This commentary thus has a past. It is one of reform and division and now hopeful reconnections. We trust that it will also have a future as a source of healing for all who read the Bible as what Alexander Campbell called "the living oracles of God." We thus offer this volume as a gift to all God's people in the Stone-Campbell tradition and far beyond. And we pray that it will be a source of enlightenment for all who use it.

THE METHODS OF THIS WORK

Contemporary biblical scholarship offers a wide range of methods and conclusions on some points of the ancient texts, while producing broadly agreed upon understandings on others. In this commentary, the editors have imposed no method on authors, nor have we censored their interpretative conclusions, which range across the broad mainstream of current biblical interpretation. Everyone whose work appears here has received advanced training in biblical studies, which includes command of the original languages and a deep awareness of the literary shape and flow of the Bible, the relevant archaeological and textual evidence from the ancient Near East or Greco-Roman worlds, and the history of biblical interpretation, ancient, medieval, and modern. Authors drew upon such bodies of knowledge for their comments, but their works have differing emphases. In every case, however, the reader should expect to gain an understanding of the organization and arguments of each biblical book, the main historical issues bearing on its interpretation, and the theological meaning of each book and part thereof. A five-volume work cannot hope to include every relevant issue or fact, but we have written with the reader in mind, to help him or her encounter the biblical text with greater understanding and commitment.

Alongside their work as scholars, each author of this volume lives as an active Christian. Many of them teach in Christian seminaries or universities. Thus their interest in the Bible is not merely theoretical but connects to an active faith working to bear the good news of God's redeeming work in Christ to the world.

Each author uses the best available editions of the original Hebrew, Aramaic, or Greek texts of the Bible, but comments refer to several English translations—and frequently to the translations of the authors themselves.

THE LAYOUT OF THIS WORK

This volume includes a commentary on each biblical book as well as additional articles on the background of the Old and New Testaments. The commentaries include a chapter outline, a discussion of the contexts of the biblical book, a detailed commentary, a brief essay on the book's theological implications, a list of texts for further study, and a list of works cited. The reader may dip in wherever he or she likes or read straight through. The supplementary essays at the beginning of this book are designed for continuous reading.

Each chapter may also includes maps, graphics, and sidebars. Rather than collecting this material in one place, we have sought to locate it where readers will need it most. An index of these special supplementary materials appears at the end of this volume. Most of these materials are the responsibility of the editors and may not reflect the precise point of view of the authors of the commentary in which they appear.

ABBREVIATIONS & ATTESTATION

In the interest of readability, this work avoids most abbreviations—even those common in biblical scholarship. However, a few abbreviations do appear, including:

JB/NJB	Jerusalem Bible/New Jerusalem Bible
JPS	Tanakh: The Jewish Publication Society Translation
KJV	King James Version
LXX	Septuagint
NAB	New American Bible
NASB	New American Standard Bible
NIV	New International Version
NJPS	Tanakh: The New Jewish Publication Society Translation
NLT	New Living Translation
NRSV	New Revised Standard Version
REB	Revised English Bible
RSV	Revised Standard Version
BCE	Before the Common Era (formerly called BC)
CE	Common Era (formerly called AD)

In addition, the names of biblical books are abbreviated in parentheses accordingly:

GEN	Genesis		**ECCL**	Ecclesiastes
EXOD	Exodus		**SONG**	Song of Solomon
LEV	Leviticus		**ISA**	Isaiah
NUM	Numbers		**JER**	Jeremiah
DEUT	Deuteronomy		**LAM**	Lamentations
JOSH	Joshua		**EZEK**	Ezekiel
JUDG	Judges		**DAN**	Daniel
RUTH	Ruth		**HOS**	Hosea
1 SAM	1 Samuel		**JOEL**	Joel
2 SAM	2 Samuel		**AMOS**	Amos
1 KGS	1 Kings		**OBAD**	Obadiah
2 KGS	2 Kings		**JONAH**	Jonah
1 CHRON	1 Chronicles		**MIC**	Micah
2 CHRON	2 Chronicles		**NAH**	Nahum
EZRA	Ezra		**HAB**	Habakkuk
NEH	Nehemiah		**ZEPH**	Zephaniah
ESTH	Esther		**HAG**	Haggai
JOB	Job		**ZECH**	Zechariah
PS/PSS	Psalms		**MAL**	Malachi
PROV	Proverbs		**MATT**	Matthew

MARK	Mark	**1 TIM**	1 Timothy
LUKE	Luke	**2 TIM**	2 Timothy
JOHN	John	**TITUS**	Titus
ACTS	Acts	**PHLM**	Philemon
ROM	Romans	**HEB**	Hebrews
1 COR	1 Corinthians	**JAS**	James
2 COR	2 Corinthians	**1 PET**	1 Peter
GAL	Galatians	**2 PET**	2 Peter
EPH	Ephesians	**1 JOHN**	1 John
PHIL	Philippians	**2 JOHN**	2 John
COL	Colossians	**3 JOHN**	3 John
1 THESS	1 Thessalonians	**JUDE**	Jude
2 THESS	2 Thessalonians	**REV**	Revelation

THE LANGUAGES OF THE BIBLE

Although this volume assumes no knowledge of the Bible's original languages on the part of readers, words in those languages occasionally appear here when the biblical author's use of wordplay—a very prominent feature in both the Old and New Testaments—would otherwise be lost. Readers interested in a more detailed look at the original languages may consult the texts listed in the chapter's bibliographical entries.

A brief note about the languages of the Bible and our representation of them may be in order. Most of the Bible was written in Hebrew over about a millennium. During this time, Hebrew developed (as every language does), so that the Hebrew of, say, old poems like Judges 5 or Exodus 15 differs significantly from that of a later book, such as Chronicles. The Bible contains several dialects of Hebrew and three basic stages of the language (Early, Classical, and Late). Ancient Hebrew is otherwise attested in inscriptions, letters, seals and seal impressions.

A few parts of the Old Testament survive in Aramaic (Ezra 4:8–7:26; Jer 10:11; and Dan 2:4b–7:28). Like Hebrew, Aramaic is a language in the Northwest Semitic family, a group that also included Phoenician, Moabite, Ammonite, Edomite, and other languages. Hebrew and Aramaic were not mutually intelligible (though Phoenician and Hebrew probably were), but many ancient Jews probably spoke both.

This volume transliterates Hebrew and Aramaic words following an informal system. Scholars may easily recognize the original behind the transliteration, so we have made no effort at reproducing a fully scientific system. Spirantized consonants (consonants spoken with a continuous expulsion of breath) are not represented except with ב and פ (v and f respectively), following modern Israeli conventions. The correspondences are as follows:

א '	ב *b* (v after vowels)	ג *g*	ד *d*	ה *h*	ו *w*	ז *z*
ח *ch* (as in "choir")	ט *t*	י *y* or *i*	כ *k*	ל *l*	מ *m*	נ *n*
ס *s*	ע '	פ *p* (f after vowels)	צ *ts*	ק *q*	ר *r*	שׁ *s* or *sh*
ת *t*						

Originally the writing systems for these languages did not include signs for vowels. Scribes added vowel signs below and above the consonants long after the biblical period. The vowels for these languages differ from those in English, and include short and long *a* (like the second *a* in *garage*), short and long *i* (like the *i* in *machine*), *o* (as in *long*), short and long *e* (as in *bet* and *beta* respectively), and short and long *u* (as in *umbrella* and *parachute* respectively). A schwa sound (like the first *a* in *garage* or *barrage* as Americans pronounce those words) also exists, represented here by *e*. When the consonants represented by ch, ts, or sh are doubled in Hebrew, we have indicated the letter only once (thus *matsevot*, not *matstsevot*) in order to avoid confusion.

While the Old Testament is written in two Semitic languages, the New Testament is written primarily (with the exception of a few Latin and Aramaic words) in one Indo-European language: Greek. During the first century CE, Greek language and culture dominated the eastern Mediterranean world. The upper classes even in Rome spoke and wrote in Greek. The Greek of the New Testament closely resembles that used by non-Christians at the same time. The authors use the language with varying degrees of sophistication, from the marketplace level of Mark to the educated language of Paul to the highly sophisticated text of Hebrews.

Again, as with Hebrew, this commentary uses Greek words only when necessary for explaining the argument of the biblical author. Readers should consult the bibliography for further references. Here we follow a transliteration system closely resembling that of the *SBL Handbook of Style* (Hendrickson, 2014).

α *a*	β *b*	γ *g*	δ *d*	ε *e*	ζ *z*	η *e*
θ *th*	ι *i*	κ *k*	λ *l*	μ *m*	ν *n*	
ξ *x*	ο *o*	π *p*	ρ *r*	σ *s*	τ *t*	υ *u*
φ *f*	χ *ch* (as in "choir")	ψ *ps*	ω *o*			

ACKNOWLEDGMENTS

The production of a book as large as this requires many hands and eyes. The editors wish to thank the following colleagues, in addition to their fellow contributors to this book: from ACU Press, to Thom Lemmons and Karen Cukrowski, who worked with us at the beginning stages of this work, and especially Leonard Allen who materially aided its completion; from friends who read earlier drafts of parts of the book, to Kris Southward, Dan Brannan, David Shaw, Gerardo Lara, Eddie Sharp, Jack Reese, Dwayne VanRheenen, and members of the Highland Church of Christ, University Church of Christ, and the Hillcrest Church of Christ; to Hannah Nielsen, Sandra Armstrong, Crystal Perry, and Diane Vanderford for their valuable proofreading, typesetting, and corrections; to Bill Rankin and Sherry Rankin, whose skills as typesetter and proofreader only begin the list of their accomplishments; to Harry Conner, Kelly Shearon, and David Skelton, Mark Hamilton's assistants, who worked diligently on turning editorial marks into typescript; and most of all to our families, who saw us through to the end. For bringing this revised edition to fruition, we thank Jason Fikes, Duane Anderson, and Mary Hardegree. Without the help of these many colleagues, this volume would not exist at all.

AN INVITATION

Finally, we wish to invite our readers to join us in the study of the words of Scripture. As the apostle Paul put it when connecting the Old Testament to the Christian message, *whatever was previously written was written for our instruction, so that through endurance and encouragement from the Scriptures we might have hope* (Rom 15:4). We pray that this book may contribute in some measure to the life of hope that its readers seek. Such a result will justify our labors.

The Editors

Reading the Prophets

Mark W. Hamilton

For many readers, the prophetic books present the most difficult challenges. Isaiah–Malachi all weave together poem after poem, oracle after oracle to create an effect. They do not so much make an argument as explore a set of ideas from many angles. The prophets were social critics and preachers, religious thinkers and rethinkers, but most of all they were poets speaking in ways that sometimes excited and transformed their hearers, but just as often alienated them. Their books still do all those things.

To be more specific, the prophetic books we have are all anthologies of varying sorts of literature. In three cases, the collection bears a single name (Isaiah, Jeremiah, Ezekiel), and in one the coexistence of multiple voices comes out front and center (the Book of the Twelve Minor Prophets). Even Daniel, which Christians count as a prophetic book and Jews place among the Writings, combines two very different sorts of material (stories about life at the royal court and dramatic visions of an apocalyptic future). All these works privilege the multivoiced nature of prophecy. This fact makes them harder to read, but more powerful once we understand how to read them.

Take, for example, the famous text of Isaiah 2:2–4:

> In later days, Yhwh's mountain will be secure,
>> the highest mountain, elevated above the hills.
> And all nations will stream to it.
> Many peoples will go and say,
> "Come on, let's go to Yhwh's mountain,
>> to the temple of Jacob's God.
> He will teach us his paths,
>> and we will go down his roads."
> For instruction (torah) will go forth from Zion,
>> Yhwh's word from Jerusalem.
> He will judge among the nations,
>> resolve problems for many peoples.
> Then they will beat their swords into plowshares
>> and their spears into pruning tools.
> Nation will not bear sword against nation,
>> nor will they learn the arts of war again.

This poem has enjoyed a long afterlife, with its vision of a world free of both human strife and the human structures that force strife underground. In this imagined world, the causes of strife will find peaceful resolution and the skills of war will be a lost art.

Yet the poem does not come to us by itself as a sound bite for us to hope for or reject as hopelessly overoptimistic. It comes in a context, or rather a series of contexts.

The first context is the opening of the book of Isaiah. Prior to this vision of the future, the book has given two long poems criticizing the injustices of the people of Judah and Jerusalem (Isa 1:1–9, 10–23). Following the vision comes a sustained description of the calamities now facing Judah, probably a description of one of the Assyrian invasions of the late eighth century BCE (Isa 2:5–22). Given the dangers of the time, both in the real world and in the world of the text, readers of Isaiah 2:2–4 should recall the opening words of the oracle: "in later days." The vision has not yet come to pass.

A second context exists because, also unusual in the biblical prophetic books, this oracle appears elsewhere as well. The almost identical text of Micah 4:1–5 likewise sits among long descriptions of the dangers and sins of Judah, but intensifies even more the hopefulness for a different future. So Micah 4:4 adds to the oracle in Isaiah a vision of sitting under vines and fig trees, an image of peace and prosperity, and Micah 4:5 contrasts Israel's potential for honoring God with the nations' tendency not to do so. The wished-for future must include a radical reorientation of the prophet's audience away from its faithlessness toward an alternative lifestyle of faithfulness.

These versions of the vision of the peaceable kingdom do not exhaust the list, however. Back in the book of Isaiah, several elements of chapter 2 play out in different places. Isaiah 42:4, 9, and 26 speak of Yhwh's *torah* spreading to the furthest reaches of the known world, which would lead to the rebuilding of Jerusalem during the Persian Empire. Isaiah 49:22–26 speaks of Yhwh summoning the Gentiles and their rulers to bring back the captives from Babylonian exile, returning them to Jerusalem. In other words, the "later days" come about, at least partially, during the period of restoration at the end of the sixth century BCE.

Partially, but not completely. Isaiah 66:18–24 ends the book by describing the final defeat of the hostile Gentiles (not all Gentiles, to be clear). The universal peace longed for in the beginning of the prophetic book can only happen after bitter conflict, according to its end.

There are many other ways this vision plays out in Isaiah, but we should notice one more example of its influence. The phrase "nations will stream" (Hebrew: *naharu haggoyim*) appears in Isaiah 2:2, and the synonymous phrase "people will stream" (Hebrew: *naharu ammim*) shows up in Micah 4:1, but the verb "to stream" (*nahar*) occurs only one other time in the Old Testament. Jeremiah 51:44 says about Babylon that "nations will never again stream to it." That is, the Babylonian Empire will fall, and the peoples subjected to its cruel dominion will see better days. The line appears as part of a very long oracle denouncing the abusive practices of the empire and predicting its imminent demise. But the relevant point is that Jeremiah is clearly alluding to Isaiah 2 and setting up a surprising contrast between Babylon and Jerusalem. It is surprising because Jeremiah has not exactly been complimentary of Jerusalem in his many speeches about the city and its inhabitants. But like his predecessor a century earlier, Jeremiah expects a world in which God will reign and, therefore, justice will flourish. In that world, the covenant people will also flourish because they will be faithful.

Now all these interconnections simply provide one example among a myriad. However, they illustrate several important points about the prophetic books.

- These books do not operate in a linear, sequential fashion like lists of laws or collections of stories. Rather, a short speech in one place will not only bounce off those surrounding it, but also will reverberate much further afield.
- Because the prophetic books anthologize many different sorts of material, it is important both to savor each individual section in detail and to see which themes also appear elsewhere.
- The multiple appearances of a theme need not simply repeat each other. Rather, they take an idea or an image and look at it from a series of angles. They may modify or even contradict an earlier appearance of the theme, at least on the surface.
- This is because the prophets do not strive for coherence in a narrow sense. They may use an image or idea one way in one place and a different way in another. They are not writing philosophy or science. They are trying to capture the uncapturable.
- All this means, finally, that the prophets explore the limits of language. To speak of the ways of God, as they seek to do, always challenges human capacities. We can go so far and not further. But even knowing that limit and bumping up against it repeatedly has meaning. Because beyond that limit lies God.

FOR FURTHER READING
Couey, J. Blake. *Reading the Poetry of First Isaiah: The Most Perfect Model of the Prophetic Poetry*. Oxford: Oxford University Press, 2015.
Sharp, Carolyn J. *The Prophetic Literature*. Nashville: Abingdon, 2019.

Old Testament Prophecy

John T. Willis

A prophet is Yahweh's spokesperson to a designated audience, as three lines of study show. First, the Old Testament states that a prophet *speaks for* God. When Moses tries to avoid accepting Yahweh's charge at the burning bush to return to Egypt to lead Israel out of bondage, Yahweh replies: *[Aaron] will speak for you to the people; he shall serve as a mouth for you, and you shall serve as God for him* (Exod 4:16). Later, in Egypt, when Moses tries to avoid speaking to Pharaoh, Yahweh responds: *I have made you like God to Pharaoh, and your brother Aaron shall be your prophet* (Exod 7:1). Since Aaron speaks for and is a mouth for Moses, he is Moses' prophet. Likewise, Amaziah, priest of Bethel, prohibits Amos from declaring Yahweh's word in Israel, saying: *Do not prophesy against Israel, and do not preach against the house of Isaac* (Amos 7:16). To "prophesy" is to "preach," or to "speak for" God. When Yahweh tells Jeremiah: *I appointed you a prophet to the nations*, Jeremiah responds: *Ah, Lord God! Truly I do not know how to speak* (Jer 1:5–6; compare 15:19; 1 Cor 14:3).

Second, the Old Testament uses terms for prophet derived from four realms of ancient Israelite life, all of which indicate that a prophet is Yahweh's spokesperson to a designated audience. Four terms (council, servant, man, and messenger) come from the royal court. To begin, a prophet belongs to Yahweh's council, analogous to royal cabinets. Ancient Near Eastern kings gathered a few trusted people, the king's council, before them early each day to assign them tasks, often carrying a message from the king to some person or group. Yahweh condemns false prophets with these words in Jeremiah 23:21–22b:

> *I did not send the [false] prophets, yet they ran; I did not speak to them, yet they prophesied. But if they had stood in my council, then they would have proclaimed my words to my people.*

As a member of Yahweh the King's council, a prophet speaks Yahweh's words to the audience Yahweh designates. Moreover, a prophet is a servant who does the King's (Yahweh's) bidding. "My (His) servants the prophets" is a common Old Testament expression (Amos 3:7; Jer 7:25; 26:5). Also, a prophet is the King's special "man" (or woman) commissioned to declare a certain message to some audience.

The Old Testament frequently calls a prophet a *man of God* (1 Sam 9:6–10; 1 Kgs 17:18, 24; 2 Kgs 4:9, 16, 21, 25, 40; 5:13–15). Then again, a prophet is the King's "messenger." Second Chronicles 36:15–16 says: *The Lord . . . sent persistently to them by his messengers . . .; but they kept mocking the messengers of God, despising his words, and scoffing at his prophets. . . .*

Divination

Any of a set of practices (such as reading the entrails of sacrificed animals) by which ancient persons sought to discover the future or determine the will of the gods is known as divination.

One term comes from a means of protecting walled cities. Ancient peoples posted sentinels on walls to watch for signs of danger on the horizon and to warn the proper authorities or the people within by shouting out or blowing a trumpet. Second Samuel 18:19–32 reports that when Ahimaaz approached the walled city of Mahanaim, *the sentinel . . . looked up, [and] he saw a man running alone. The sentinel shouted and told the king . . .* (vv. 24–25; compare Isa 21:6, 8, 11–12). Drawing from this familiar sight, Yahweh charges Ezekiel to be a *sentinel [watchman] for the house of Israel* and thus warn his hearers of impending punishment (Ezek 3:16–21; 33:1–9).

One term comes from divination. Micah 3:6c–7b says: *The sun shall go down upon the prophets, and the day shall be black over them; the seers shall be disgraced, and the diviners put to shame.* "Prophets," "seers," and "diviners" stand in synonymous parallelism here. Apparently, composers of the Old Testament borrowed the term "seer" from divination, which was popular in the ancient world, including Israel (Deut 18:10, 14; 1 Sam 9:9; 28:8; Isa 29:10; Jer 29:8; Ezek 21:21–29; Mic 3:11). A prophet is like a diviner in that he/she communicates with the unseen world to receive information helpful to those he or she addresses (see 1 Sam 9:6; Isa 37:1–7).

One term derives from the ancient method of refining metals. Ore dug from the ground was impure. Assayers heated it in a furnace, which melted the alloys at different temperatures, leaving the metal much purer than when mined. Jeremiah 6:27–30 compares a prophet's task with refining metals. His or her message removes corruption from the heart as Yahweh's purifying process (compare Isa 1:21–26).

Third, a careful oracle-by-oracle study of relevant Old Testament prophetic texts verifies that their presenters understood a prophet to be a *speaker* or *mouthpiece* for God to some audience. As Yahweh's spokesperson to a designated audience, the prophet often refers to past events and teachings (Isa 1:9–10; Hos 11:1–4; Amos 3:1–2; 4:6–11; Mic 6:3–5), present situations (Isa 8:16–20; Jer 5:1–6; Hos 5:1–7; Amos 5:4–17), and future activities of Yahweh (Isa 28:16–22; 40:1–11;

Amos 6:11–14; Hos 11:5–11). In all cases, the prophet aims to change or guide the hearts and lives of audiences. Most prophetic predictions announce events to occur in the near future. The few proclamations of distant forthcoming events reassure the hearers that Yahweh controls nations and individuals throughout human history. There is no unequivocal specific prediction of the coming of Jesus Christ and/or the church in the Old Testament. New Testament speakers reinterpreted and reapplied Old Testament texts to Christ and/or the church.

FUNCTIONS OF ISRAELITE PROPHETS

Israelite prophetism arose with Samuel. Scattered texts refer to Abraham (Gen 20:7), Miriam (Exod 15:20), Aaron (Exod 7:1), Moses (Deut 18:15–22), Eldad, Medad and seventy elders (Num 11:16–30), Deborah (Judg 4:4), and an anonymous man in the days of Gideon (Judg 6:7–10) as prophets. However, these individuals were not "prophets" in the sense of those succeeding Samuel. For example, Genesis 20:7 calls Abraham a prophet because he prayed for Abimelech king of Gerar, since one function of a prophet is to intercede for others (for example, Jer 7:16; 11:14; 14:11; Amos 7:2, 5). Exodus 7:1 calls Aaron a "prophet" of Moses, because he speaks for Moses to Pharaoh or to the people of Israel.

Prophets arose as a divine check on kings. Yahweh was the true king of Israel, with the earthly king as Yahweh's representative. Prophets also anointed kings. Yahweh charges Samuel to anoint Saul (1 Sam 9:15–16; 10:1) and David (1 Sam 16:1–13) as prince (not king) over Yahweh's (not the earthly king's) people; David commissions Nathan (in conjunction with Zadok the priest and Benaiah) to anoint Solomon king in his place (1 Kgs 1:32–39). Yahweh instructs Elijah (1 Kgs 19:16), whose mantle empowered Elisha (2 Kgs 2:1–15), who in turn tells a young prophet in his prophetic group to anoint Jehu king over the northern kingdom of Israel (2 Kgs 9:1–6).

Non-Israelite Ancient Near-Eastern Prophets
Prophets were common in ancient Near Eastern societies. The Old Testament refers to Balaam the Mesopotamian prophet (Num 22–24; 31:8, 15–16; Deut 23:4–5; Josh 13:22; 24:9–10; Neh 13:2; Mic 6:5; compare 2 Pet 2:15–16; Jude 11; Rev 2:14) and the prophets of Baal (1 Kgs 18:17–40; 19:1–14; 2 Kgs 10:19). Extrabiblical texts from Tell Deir 'Alla east of the Jordan in the region inhabited by the ancient Ammonites (eighth century BCE), Mari in northern Mesopotamia (eighteenth century BCE), and Assyria in northern Mesopotamia (eighth–seventh centuries BCE) extensively corroborate the existence of prophets throughout the ancient Near East. These prophets worked in ways similar to those reported of Israelite prophets in the Bible.

Moreover, prophets denounced kings who sinned against Yahweh. Thus Samuel reproves Saul for not waiting until he arrived to offer the sacrifice at Gilgal (1 Sam 10:8; 13:8–15) and for not utterly destroying the Amalekites (1 Sam 15). Nathan condemns David for committing adultery with Bathsheba and having Uriah murdered (2 Sam 12:1–15). Elijah rebukes Ahab for having Naboth murdered and seizing his vineyard (1 Kgs 21).

On the other hand, prophets encouraged kings to be faithful to Yahweh. For example, Azariah urges Asa to be courageous; thus Asa destroys foreign idols in Judah and restores the worship of Yahweh (2 Chron 15). Isaiah assures Hezekiah that Yahweh will deliver Jerusalem from the Assyrians who had been deployed by Sennacherib to capture the city (Isa 37:21–35).

Prophets even announced Yahweh's rejection of kings when they turned against Yahweh. Samuel informs Saul that Yahweh has rejected him from being king because of his disobedience (1 Sam 13:13–14; 15:22–23, 28–29).

In sum, prophets addressed God's chosen people, charging them to be faithful to or return to Yahweh, who had acted on their behalf in various ways in the past by giving instructions about how they should live in the law at Sinai and by continuing to work for the good of the people. The prophets did not establish a new religion but used Israel's traditions to call their hearers to God. They often referred to Yahweh's bringing Israel out of Egypt at the exodus, leading them through the wilderness forty years, and giving them the land of Canaan (Isa 43:14–21; Jer 2:4–7; Hos 2:14–15; 12:9; 13:4–5; Amos 2:9–11). They appealed to specific laws, including the Ten Commandments, to support their message (Jer 7:8–11; 17:19–27; Hos 4:1–3).

Prophets could pray for nations or individuals. Biblical writers cite the prophet Samuel as a model of a praying person (1 Sam 7:8–9; 12:19, 23; Ps 99:6). Jeroboam I begs a prophet to pray for him that Yahweh restore his withered hand (1 Kgs 13:6). Amos prays that Yahweh would not destroy north Israel (Amos 7:2, 5). Jeremiah prays for his enemies (Jer 18:20). King Zedekiah asks Jeremiah to pray for the Judeans as Babylon threatens Jerusalem (Jer 37:3), and Johanan and his associates implore Jeremiah to pray for them (Jer 42:2, 20).

Prophets & Foreigners

Prophets proclaimed Yahweh's words to foreign nations (Isa 13–23; Jer 46–51; Ezek 25–32; Amos 1–2; Obadiah; Nahum). Sometimes they announced forthcoming doom to a nation, such as Assyria (Isa 14:24–27; 17:12–14) or Babylon (Isa 13:1–14:23; 46–48; Jer 50–51); and sometimes they declared hope to a nation, such as Egypt (Isa 19:18–25) or Phoenicia (Isa 23:17–18).

MATERIALS IN PROPHETIC BOOKS

Prophetic books contain various types of material: narratives (Isa 36–39; Jer 40–44); descriptions of symbolic (sign) acts, usually with an explanation of the meaning (Isa 20; Jer 13:1–11; 27–28; Ezek 4–5; 37:15–28); reports of prophetic calls (Isa 6; Jer 1; Ezek 1–3); visions (Amos 7–9; Jer 1:11–19; Ezek 1; 8); oracles of doom (announcing punishment on a nation or an individual, often with reasons) (Isa 2:6–22; Amos 3:9–15), including woe oracles (Isa 5:8–30; 28–33; Amos 5:18–20; 6:1–7); covenant lawsuits (Isa 1:2–20; Mic 6:1–8); laments (Jer 8:18–9:1; Amos 5:1–2; Mic 1:8–16); songs (Isa 5:1–7); allegories (Ezek 17:1–21); acrostics (Nah 1:2–8); and oracles of hope announcing deliverance of a nation or individual from distress or oppression (Isa 40–55; Jer 29–33; Ezek 33–48; Amos 9:10–15;

Mic 2:12–13; 4–5; 7:7–20). Usually, hope oracles depict a complete reversal of the present negative situation.

DEVELOPMENT & ARRANGEMENT OF PROPHETIC BOOKS

Old Testament prophetic books are the final product of a long process of development, as generations of prophetic groups reapplied, revised, rearranged, and reinterpreted earlier materials and added oracles, explanations, modifications, and grammatical links of their own. The book of Jeremiah mentions at least three stages in its growth: a collection of prophetic oracles from 627 to 605 BCE (Jer 36); the insertion of prophetic materials from 605 to 587 BCE (Jer 1:1–3); and the insertion of prophetic materials from 587 to 550 BCE (Jer 52:31–34). Prophetic authors did not simply add later materials to earlier collections—for example, several passages in Jeremiah 1–35 date after the event related in Jeremiah 36 (605 BCE); Jeremiah 21, 32, and 34:8–22 (588 BCE), or chapters 24 and 29 (597 BCE). Rather, they interwove earlier and later materials, creating a new work.

Composers of prophetic books arranged their materials coherently for effective use in oral proclamation or performance at festivals of faith communities and other occasions, using repetition, or juxtaposing doom and hope oracles, for example.

FALSE PROPHETS

The Old Testament often denounces Israelite prophets (for example, 1 Kgs 22:1–28; Isa 28:1–8; 29:9–10; Jer 23:9–40; 27–28; Ezek 13; Mic 3:5–12). Audiences who heard messages by prophets had no obvious way to know whether God sent these spokespersons. When Jeremiah announces the Jews will be in Babylonian captivity seventy years, but Hananiah declares they will be there only two years, Jeremiah says to Hananiah: *The prophets who preceded you and me from ancient times prophesied war, famine, and pestilence against many countries and great kingdoms. As for the prophet who prophesies peace, when the word of that prophet comes true, then it will be known that the Lord has truly sent the prophet.* Jeremiah's two criteria for determining a true prophet are: the typical messenger proclaims impending punishment; and if a spokesperson announces hope and it comes to pass (see Deut 18:15–22), that person is a true prophet. However, these general principles do not always apply.

> **Performance & the Prophets**
>
> *The structure of prophetic books seems designed in part to help people remember their content for performance or recitation. To take one typical case, the book of Amos falls into three structural sections after the superscription (1:1):*
>
> - *Eight similarly structured doom oracles against the nations (1:2–2:16).*
> - *Three sections, each beginning with* Hear this word *(3:–5:17), followed by two sections beginning with* Woe *(5:18–6:14).*
> - *Five visions announcing that Yahweh will soon punish the sinful people (7:1–3 and 7:4–6; 7:7–9 and 8:1–3; and 9:1–10).*
>
> *A related section follows each of the last three visions: a dispute between Amos and Amaziah (7:10–17), an oracle against injustice (8:4–14), and a hope oracle (9:10–15).*

For example, Jeremiah announces a bright future for God's people in Jeremiah 29–33, yet his declarations that the northern kingdom of Israel would return to Yahweh (Jer 31:15–20) never happen.

RELIGIOUS TEACHINGS OF THE PROPHETS

Various prophets spoke at different times to many audiences, but certain religious themes permeate the prophetic books. First, Yahweh is creator and sustainer of everything (Isa 42:5; 45:12; Amos 4:13). God is more powerful than all nations, who are like *a drop [hanging] from a bucket, dust on the scales, grasshoppers,* and *less than nothing* in his sight (Isa 40:15, 17, 22). As *king of the nations, the true God, the living God,* and *the everlasting King* (Jer 10:7, 10), Yahweh exerts power over all earthly kings, so that Cyrus of Persia is his *shepherd* and *anointed one* (Hebrew *meshiach,* "messiah") (Isa 44:28–45:1), and Nebuchadrezzar II of Babylon is his *servant* (Jer 25:9).

Second, Yahweh entered into an intimate relationship with Israel at the exodus (Jer 2:1–8; Hos 2:14–15; 11:1; 12:9; 13:5; Amos 3:1–2), like that of a husband and wife (Hos 2:2–15), parent and child (Hos 11:1–9), gardener and vineyard (Isa 5:1–7), shepherd and flock (Isa 40:11), doctor and patient (Jer 30:12–17), and potter and clay (Jer 18:1–11). Yahweh instructed Israel how to be religiously faithful and how to treat other human beings (Jer 7:8–11; Ezek 18:5–10; Hos 4:1–3).

Third, Yahweh will soon punish a foreign nation (Isa 13:1–14:23) or the chosen people (Isa 1:2–20; Hos 8; Amos 3:9–15; 6:11–14) because of their sins (Isa 1:4, 16–17; 13:19; 14:4, 11–14; Hos 8:1, 3, 7; Amos 5:10–12). Sin is a heart problem (Jer 3:10; 4:3–4; 9:25–26; 17:9–10). The primary sin of the heart is pride or self-centeredness or ingratitude (Isa 2:6–22; 10:5–19; 13:19; 16:6; 23:9; Obad 3–4). The prophets denounce those who forsake Yahweh to serve other gods (Isa 44:9–20; Jer 10:1–16; Ezek 8; 20:1–31; Hos 2:2–13) and those who oppress and manipulate their fellows (Isa 58; Jer 9:2–9; Amos 8:4–6; Mic 2:1–11).

Fourth and finally, Yahweh's ultimate purpose in punishing sinners is not to destroy but to refine and redeem. As a doctor inflicts pain on a sick patient in order to heal, so Yahweh punishes those who are unfaithful in order to bring them to repentance and save them. Isaiah 30:26 speaks of *the day when the Lord binds up the injuries of Israel, and heals the wounds inflicted by his blow* (compare Jer 30:12–17). So the prophets announce hope for the penitent *remnant* of God's people (Isa 10:20–23; Jer 31:7–9; Mic 2:12–13; 4:6–8). Yahweh will overthrow the people's captors (Isa 44:24–45:7; Jer 51), gather the remnant of Israel from captivity and return them to Zion (that is, Jerusalem; Isa 52:7–12; 54:4–17); reunite Israel and Judah as in the days of David and Solomon (Jer 30:1–3; 31:10–14; Ezek 37:15–28); place a *new David* over them (Jer 23:5–8; 30:9; 33:14–16; Ezek 37:24), namely, Zerubbabel (Zech 3; 6:9–14); remarry the divorced wife Israel (Jer 3:6–11; 31:31–34; Hos 2:2, 14–16) because she will love her divine husband from the heart rather than with mere external religion (Deut 6:6–9; Jer 31:31–34; 32:36–41;

Ezek 36:22–32); and restore her spiritual health (Jer 30:12–17). The prophets thus provide readers even today with a bold vision of God's redeeming work in a broken world. As such, they deserve our close attention.

FOR FURTHER STUDY

Clements, Ronald E. *Old Testament Prophecy: From Oracles to Canon.* Louisville: Westminster John Knox, 1996.

Couey, J. Blake. *Reading the Poetry of First Isaiah: The Most Perfect Model of the Prophetic Poetry.* Oxford: Oxford University Press, 2015.

Davis, Ellen F. *Biblical Prophecy: Perspectives for Christian Theology, Discipleship and Ministry.* Louisville: Westminster John Knox, 2014.

Rofé, A. *Introduction to Prophetic Literature.* Sheffield: Sheffield Academic Press, 1997.

Sharp, Carolyn J. *The Prophetic Literature.* Nashville: Abingdon, 2019.

Steck, Odil Hannes. *The Prophetic Books and their Theological Witness.* Translated by James D. Nogalski. St. Louis: Chalice, 2000.

The Bible & Literature

Jonathan Wade & Nancy Wilhite Shankle

CHAPTER CONTENTS

FEATURES

The Bible is still the best-selling and most reprinted book in the world. Numerous writers in varying fields, in various forms, and in multiple languages have used the Bible as inspiration for their own creative works. It is quoted in titles, in text, and in song. In English, the cadence and rhythm of the King James Version of the Bible still influences the way we speak and write.

THE BIBLE IN LITERATURE

Many stories adapt the biblical text or retell it in a different way. Others attempt to illuminate biblical principles by allegory. There are also allusions to the Bible in numerous texts. Examples include "the mark of Cain," "the Ten Commandments," "love your neighbor," and "the gifts of the magi."

There are also quite a few extrabiblical texts with biblical themes. Some examples from the Middle Ages include the stories of King Arthur and his knights and Dante's *Divine Comedy*. The "Matter of Arthur," as it has been called, has been told in numerous ways. In almost every case, the stories share the idea of Arthur as a bringer of goodness, civilization, and perhaps salvation, who is ultimately betrayed by his wayward bride and faithless friends. This tale clearly echoes the Christian story of a savior betrayed by a faithless humanity. Of course, in many of the stories, the connection is less clear because Arthur is portrayed less sympathetically while Lancelot and Guinevere are made more sympathetic.

In his *Divine Comedy*, Dante, the great medieval Italian poet, writes about a journey from Earth through hell, purgatory, and heaven. Dante appears to have been attempting to adapt the Greek and Roman myths of journeys to the underworld to a Christian conception of the nature of reality. This journey illustrates much about the medieval conception of the afterlife, about the nature of God's relationship with humankind, and about the political situation in Italy in Dante's time. It is worth noting that the *Divine Comedy* tries to explain and explore an idea that the biblical text did not adequately explain. So in these poems, Dante attempts to explore the possibilities at which the Bible only hints.

Later works like John Milton's *Paradise Lost* continue in the same vein. In *Paradise Lost*, Milton describes the war in heaven between the forces of Lucifer and the forces of God. He describes the event where Lucifer and his minions are cast into hell, and he depicts the fall of humanity as yet another skirmish in the war that Satan wages against the works of God. In telling this story in poetic form, Milton, whether he meant to or not, depicts a Satan who is more vivid, comprehensible, and perhaps more sympathetic than the sketchy depictions of him in some biblical texts. At the very least, Milton makes it more possible to understand how Satan might have justified to himself his rebellion against God. *Paradise Lost* remains one of the central and most valuable texts in English.

Another text worth considering is John Bunyan's *A Pilgrim's Progress*. In this short work, Bunyan tells the story of Christian as he tries to make his way from the City of Destruction to the Celestial City. On his way, he encounters obstacles like the Slough of Despond and Vanity Fair. Eventually, by the grace of God (and with a good bit of work on his own), he accomplishes his goal. This book is a superb example of religious allegory. From a modern perspective it is, perhaps, a bit morally heavy-handed and not particularly subtle, but it is a beautiful and touching work, nonetheless.

A good bit of short poetry on biblical themes also exists. Some poets, like Alfred Lord Tennyson in his *In Memoriam*, use poetry as a way to question and praise God. The prelude to *In Memoriam* is a plaintive prayer from a person saddened by the sudden and untimely death of a loved one:

> Strong Son of God, immortal love,
> Whom we, that have not seen Thy face,

The Bible & Literature
The Bible has had a great effect in shaping the character and form of Western literature. It has served as a template, an encouragement, an inspiration, and a source to be contested for many authors and traditions. Biblical phrases still linger in the popular mind and in the literary record. Biblical cadences still echo in our poems and our songs. Whatever one's belief stance, the Bible is an important piece of the knowledge of humankind. Even discounting its great literary importance, for those who believe, the Bible is a gift from a God who seeks to embrace humanity with all its weaknesses. It is a message from beyond that can connect humankind to that which is truly real and truly beautiful.

By faith, and faith alone, embrace,
Believing where we cannot prove.

Thou wilt not leave us in the dust;
Thou madest man, he knows not why,
He thinks he was not made to die:
And Thou hast made him: Thou art just.

Thou seemest human and divine,
The highest, holiest manhood, Thou.
Our wills are ours, we know not how;
Our wills are ours, to make them Thine.

Our little systems have their day;
They have their day and cease to be;
They are but broken lights of Thee,
And Thou, O Lord, art more than they.

We have but faith: we cannot know;
For knowledge is of things we see;
And yet we trust it comes from Thee,
A beam in darkness: let it grow.

Let knowledge grow from more to more,
But more of reverence in us dwell;
That mind and soul, according well,
May make one music as before.

But vaster. We are fools and slight;
We mock Thee when we do not fear;
But help Thy foolish ones to bear—
Help Thy vain worlds to bear Thy light.

In this poem, Tennyson echoes the odd mixture of faith and doubt that is produced even in those with the strongest belief in times of trouble. He sounds very much like the prophet Habakkuk in Habakkuk 1:1–4:

> *The oracle that Habakkuk the prophet received. How long, O Lord, must I call for help, but you do not listen? Or cry out to you, "Violence!" but you do not save? Why do you make me look at injustice? Why do you tolerate wrong? Destruction and violence are before me; there is strife, and conflict abounds. Therefore the law is paralyzed, and justice never prevails. The wicked hem in the righteous, so that justice is perverted.*

In reading the Psalms, one is often struck by the way that the writers explore the goodness of God while still acknowledging or even questioning the power

Sin Depicted in Literature

Literature as a whole does not depict fools, hypocrites, or the cruel in a positive light. It is therefore no surprise that the literature of western civilization, steeped as it is in Christian history and tradition, has no qualms about pointing out the sins of those who claim to be righteous. In the English language, one can look as far back as Chaucer's Canterbury Tales *and find numerous examples of hypocrisy. Chaucer illustrates the fleshly sins of the Pardoner, the Summoner, and the Friar who are all employed in some way by the church. In continental literature, we have works like Voltaire's* Candide *in which the reader meets many churchmen but finds them all to be horrible people. In Jane Austen's* Pride and Prejudice, *the character Mr. Collins depicts the churchman as a boring social climber. In Leo Tolstoy's* Anna Karenina, *Karenin, the title character's husband, is "religious" but unbelieving and cold. In Dostoevsky's* The Brothers Karamazov, *Rakitin, the student of religion, is a calculating and godless person.*

of wickedness in the world. The Victorian poet Gerard Manley Hopkins, often praised for his innovative poetic form, explores both God's greatness and humanity's suffering in his poetry. In poems like "The Windhover," Hopkins explores the beauty of nature as it reflects the goodness of God. In another group of poems, called his "terrible sonnets," Hopkins explores the worst experiences of humanity. For example, in his "Carrion Comfort," the speaker of the poem is struggling with depression but eventually realizes—by defying his dark thoughts—that God is seeking him.

Lately, many of the adaptations have served as criticism of the Bible. For example, Oscar Wilde's *Salome* is a play that attempts to get at the aesthetic beauty behind the story of John the Baptist's beheading. The play attempts to fill in the gaps in the biblical story by expanding the characters of Salome and John the Baptist. Wilde's explicit text still condemns Salome, but implicitly he also condemns John as a man too proud to love. Another more recent example might be *Job: A Comedy of Justice* written by Robert A. Heinlein. In this book, a modern retelling of Job, Satan becomes one of the heroes and God figures as the one who torments Job.

There are, however, some positive depictions of Christians and Christianity in literature. Chaucer gives us the Parson, an honest and caring man. Victor Hugo gives us the Bishop of Digne who rescues the hero of his *Les Misérables* from a life of sin and dissipation. Even Voltaire, who opposed Christianity for several reasons, shows us in the character of the kind Anabaptist in *Candide* that some people do actually live the Christian ethic. Finally, also in his *The Brothers Karamazov*, Dostoevsky gives us positive examples of both otherworldly Christianity (in the person of the elder Zossima) and concrete day-to-day Christianity (in the person of Alyosha).

In recent times, there has been a shift toward allocating all explicitly Christian fiction to publishers who cater specifically to Christian audiences. In fact, Christian fiction has become as much a separate genre as science fiction or young adult fiction. However, there are two possible problems with sequestering most Christian works in a specifically Christian genre. The first is that authors and readers have to choose between secular and religious works. Although this approach has given us such best-selling fiction as the *Left Behind* series, the audience for such works are usually self-selected Christians. This leads us to the second problem: whenever a group sequesters itself from the world, it automatically excludes the majority of people who do not at least partially agree with its precepts. The current Christian fiction market is predominantly white, middle-class, evangelical, and Protestant. This leaves out people from other Christian traditions, ethnicities, and classes, as well as those who do not believe. This market, then, mainly centers on encouraging and reinforcing a worldview rather than spreading it. Christians should support great Christian writers like Calvin Miller or Stephen Lawhead whether their books are published by Christian presses or not, but they should also seek out good writing from Christians who are publishing in the mainstream presses. There are many contemporary writers who explore the reality of life from a Christian perspective and are being published by mainstream publishers. Some worth noting are Walker Percy, Frederick Buechner, Annie Dillard, and Anne Lamott.

Before the Christian book market became a separate entity, mainstream works often dealt with Christian themes. One example of explicitly Christian themes that are buried in a work intended for all people is C. S. Lewis' *The Chronicles of Narnia*. In this seven-book series, intended for grade-school children, Lewis crafts a beautiful world that is parallel to our own. In doing so, he creates stories that stand on their own but still point to central Christian beliefs. This series is beautiful and encouraging for people of all ages.

J. R. R. Tolkien, a friend of Lewis, in his *Lord of the Rings* trilogy, creates a world that is less specifically related to Christianity but which clearly shows the struggle between good and evil. One could argue that Tolkien's legacy has shaped the entire genre of fantasy, so even today one can still find books like J. K. Rowling's *Harry Potter* series that, while not specifically Christian, do support the idea that the forces of good and the forces of evil are constantly battling each other.

CHRISTIAN APPROACHES TO READING

When Christians approach any text, we should carefully attempt to discern the immediate aesthetic effect, the author's intent, and the possible implications of the text. We should be able to examine texts logically and appreciate them for their quality, their stance, and their truthfulness. We can consider the effects of a text on ourselves and on others. We can also look at the historical, social, artistic, and even religious context of the work.

Fantasy & the Young Adult

Some Christians are concerned with the "occult" references in popular books like the Harry Potter *series by J. K. Rowling. Others have even condemned C. S. Lewis for portraying witchcraft or Tolkien for writing about wizards and sorcerers. Often the condemnation of such writing is based, not on a well-formulated critique, but instead on a general dislike for fantastic literature or, perhaps, for fiction in general. It is important for Christian leaders to realize that Jesus explicitly condoned fiction in his use of parables, and he, to some extent, seems to have condoned fantasy in his description of the woman married to many brothers and in the story of the rich man and Lazarus. Even if one decides that fiction is permissible but fantasy is not, one still has to face the facts that the literature is very popular, and that censoring works without thought or persuasive argument usually compels young people to want to read them. In the case of popular series, parents can choose three paths. They can ignore the issue, which avoids responsibility. They can attempt to completely separate their children from all outside influences. Or they can logically and prayerfully encounter the texts and discuss them with their children. The third way seems preferable.*

If one examines the Harry Potter series logically, it is very difficult to find much to condemn. The "sorcery" in Harry Potter is obviously fanciful and quite different from the depictions of witchcraft in historical accounts and even the rhetoric of modern self-proclaimed witches. In most cases, the spells and magical creatures are loosely influenced by earlier works of fantasy but are primarily products of the author's imagination. They are light, enjoyable books that center on adolescent issues of growing up and the battle of good versus evil. Parents should be more concerned with works that are explicitly occult oriented. Many books classified as Teen Horror books portray occult activities in a positive manner, but are not nearly as popular as the Harry Potter series. If a parent cannot steer his or her children to less troublesome books, he or she should read the book and use it as a starting point for discussion.

One fantasy series that might be treated as an opportunity for discussion is Phillip Pullman's His Dark Materials trilogy. These three books are exceedingly well-written and interesting. They are also part of Pullman's effort to deconstruct and criticize the Christian worldview. They subtly undermine the Christian tradition while weaving a captivating story. Even in this case, however, parents and youth workers would be best advised to logically analyze Pullman's arguments against Christianity and to discuss them critically with any child who decides to read (or who is assigned) this series. In this way, a work that is aesthetically beautiful can be appreciated as a work of art and as a persuasive argument. Once Pullman's argument is unmasked, it is easily countered, and in the encounter between his arguments and the reader's counterarguments comes an opportunity for growth in both mind and spirit.

It is not the genre (fantasy, science fiction, or even horror) that makes a work anti-Christian. It is the intent and the effect. Careful reading and honest and prayerful critique are important weapons in the arsenal of good.

It may be that we encounter a text with which we already agree, but we will also, almost certainly, encounter texts with which we do not agree. In the latter case, we should not allow our dogmatism to override the opportunity to understand the perspective of another human being. Censorship should be the last resort. The Bible gives us an example of the value of candid reporting. If God had censored the Bible, we would not have the stories of Abraham's attempted deceit, of Jacob's successful deceit, of David's indiscretion with Bathsheba, or of Peter's denial. All of these stories, though negative in one sense, illuminate the power and love of God.

LITERATURE'S POWER TO INFLUENCE

The children's rhyme "Sticks and stones may break my bones, but names will never hurt me" belies the power of language to shape our ideas, build our moral consciousness, or tear down our fragile beliefs. Most people can easily recall a book they read as a child or young adult that shaped their development in powerful ways. For many famous writers, it was more than simply one book; it was the amazing world of books. For example, Eudora Welty, in her autobiography *One Writer's Beginnings*, wrote about her trips to the library as a child. Mrs. Calloway, the librarian, had strict rules; she allowed only two books to be checked out at a time and patrons could not return the books on the same day they were checked out. As a result, young Eudora pedaled her bicycle back and forth to the library reading her books two by two. She had an eclectic, impressionable, and insatiable appetite for reading. As an adult, she reported that she had lived a sheltered life in Jackson, Mississippi, but it was nonetheless a "daring life" because "all serious daring starts from within" (Welty 104). Welty began an intense, sustained life of the mind with her countless bicycle trips to the library as a child. In the same way, people today continue to prosper from a rich habit of reading.

Gene Edward Veith Jr. argues that "the habit of reading is absolutely critical today, particularly for Christians" (Veith xiii). In a time of increasing influence of pop culture, habits of reading reinforce important skills of thinking—analyzing, evaluating, exploring, questioning. Moreover, Christians are heirs to a rich tradition of literature that examines our faith and nurtures our beliefs (read, for example, Milton's *Paradise Lost* or Flannery O'Connor's short stories).

Throughout the Bible, the Word figured prominently. John reminds us: *In the beginning was the Word, and the Word was with God, and the Word was God* (John 1:1). God spoke our world into existence and gave us a revelation in written word. We remember the biblical narratives told to us as children long after we are grown, for *the word of God is living and active* (Heb 4:12).

Still more evidence of the power of language is the frequency with which some books are banned. Book banning has a long history, and Christians have often led the call for censorship of reading. Famously censored great works of literature include: Shakespeare's *Othello*, Mark Twain's *Huckleberry Finn*, and

Harriet Beecher Stowe's *Uncle Tom's Cabin* for their racial themes; James Joyce's *Ulysses* and Walt Whitman's *Leaves of Grass* for sexuality; or even Grimm's *Fairy Tales* for violence. Christians usually have good motives—to protect others from dangerous ideas—yet banning books deprives everyone of the opportunity to examine ideas and form independent opinions on their content. Ironically, the Bible itself is frequently banned.

There is no doubt that literature can be a positive, sustaining influence for Christian readers, yet some books can lead to what Veith describes as "vicarious sin"; that is, through reading, people vicariously experience the events being depicted in the work. In this way, a Christian can be led to sin—through titillating sexual fantasies, violent disregard for humanity, or other immoral subjects. The goal of good literature is to entertain and to instruct. The problem with bad literature is that bad books are simply bad—they have predictable plots, undeveloped characters, and they pander to prurient interests. There is a market for bad books; smut sells. However, even books judged as good literature may prove to be harmful if the content leads to vicarious sin.

How then, should a Christian judge a work of literature with questionable content? First of all, simply depicting a sordid element of life does not automatically lead to vicarious sin. There are many biblical stories that depict sin—from the sexual sin of David and Bathsheba to the violence of the passion of Christ. Reading these stories should inspire us to live better lives, not to sin vicariously or, more dangerously, to duplicate the portrayed sins in our own lives. In the same way, many literary stories reinforce biblical themes because they do show the dangers of sin. We can vicariously experience the temptation, the guilt of having committed sin, and perhaps even the release that comes from confession and redemption.

Regular reading sharpens our abilities to read critically; thus, an inexperienced reader may not understand the aesthetic technique or purpose that generates a powerful response to a work from a more experienced reader. Too often, Christian critics will attack a work for its use of profanity, sexuality, or violence, without considering the real message of the book. In its goal to instruct, literature must often challenge us, asking us to question our unstated assumptions about life. For example, Frederick Douglass was born a slave, taught himself to read and write, and escaped from slavery. Once

Personal Reactions to Literature

We should also recognize that our past experiences influence our responses to literature individually. One woman I know who experienced a sexual assault as a young woman cannot read any passage depicting sexual violence without the painful memories returning in a flood of emotion. Anyone who has watched a loved one die knows the emotion behind Dylan Thomas' lament "Do not go gentle into that good night" or the measured acceptance of Alfred Tennyson's "'Tis better to have loved and lost than never to have loved at all." However, young people who have not yet lived through the depths of grief rarely find similar comfort from Tennyson or Thomas.

freed, he wrote a narrative of his life as a corrective to the commonplace arguments of many pro-slavery men and women who declared the black slaves to be
little more than animals—incapable of normal emotional ties to family, unable to
live independently, and in need of constant discipline. Douglass chronicles the
beatings, the humiliations, the sexual abuse of female slaves by their owners, and
the tearing apart of slave families. His story has been criticized for its violence,
and the book is violent. It is a difficult book to read. However, Douglass' truth
telling was influential in bringing people of his day to acknowledge truths about
slavery and thus to bring public opinion toward the side of the abolitionists.
Christian readers of the book today learn that many Christians in Douglass'
time supported slavery, either through willful blindness to the inhumanity of
slavery or through twisting Scripture to support the institution of slavery. We
must learn always to be on guard against the dangers of popular opinion, even
(or especially) in a democratic society.

UNDERSTANDING THE CHRISTIAN WORLDVIEW

Our worldview is most easily explained as the lens through which we view the
world. However, it is far more complex than a simple lens. Our worldview contains our core values and beliefs, especially beliefs about what happens in the
world and why. These core values and beliefs explain the world to us and thus
shape our image of the world. They drive our behavior and actions in the world
and our interactions with others. Our worldview gives us our purpose in life. It
guides us as we set priorities.

Throughout time, believers in God have had conflict with other people whose
explanations of God contrasted sharply with our own. Arthur F. Holmes
describes the development of a monotheistic worldview among the Israelites.
When Abraham left Chaldea for the promised land, the journey was an "act of
faith in a God who called him to a markedly differ-
ent view and way of life" (Holmes 7). Similarly, the
Israelites' flight from Egypt was more than an economic or political act; the migration sought to
preserve their monotheistic view. Holmes notes
that in the Greco-Roman world of the New
Testament, Paul confronted mystics who "tried to
find salvation by escape from physical and earthly
involvements" (Holmes 8). This error led to "the
dualism of flesh and spirit" that "confused the
meaning of good and evil" and affected "attitudes
toward marriage, toward work, and toward social
relationships in general" (Holmes 8). Our beliefs
about the world will influence our actions today as
surely as in past centuries.

Christians & Cultural Influence

*Christians should acknowl-
edge the ways their lives are
affected by their culture's beliefs
regarding children, education,
politics, marriage, economics,
art, and more. Furthermore,
our worldview may change over
time as we mature through life
experiences, reflect on national
events or technological change,
and practice a spiritual lifestyle.*

A worldview is rarely static. It is the product of many influences—our life experience, our culture, our family, our ethnicity, and our national politics. Worldview is the result of many influences, especially culture. Brian J. Walsh and Richard Middleton assert that cultural life is "not only *rooted* in the dominant world view; it also *orients* life in terms of that world view" (Walsh and Middleton 33).

Differences in how one worldview compares with another can be subtle until one looks carefully at underlying beliefs. For example, conservative Christians and conservative Muslims share many assumptions about modesty, alcohol consumption, and dating, even though our beliefs about sacred texts differ radically. Thus, I could count on the family of one of my son's friends, members of the Ba'hai faith, to share our family rules about restrictions on movies our son was allowed to watch because of their conservative values. Our local zoo has an exhibit explaining the work being done to protect the environment and save endangered species. I, too, support most environmental issues. However, the language of the exhibit demonstrates that while the zoo and I have a shared response to the environment, our motives are completely different. The zoo exhibit argues that all species are equal and thus no one has a right to exploit one species for the benefit of another. In contrast, the underlying cause for my environmentalist attitudes is due to biblical teachings that God created our world for us to be stewards. As in the parable of the vineyard, one day I will be held accountable for how I treated the creation. Thus we share similar responses to the problems of the environment, but from vastly different assumptions about the purpose of my work.

How does our worldview influence our reading? Our worldview drives our understanding of a text. In one of my college classes on multicultural literature, I start with a short story by a Native American author, Leslie Marmon Silko, called "Yellow Woman." In the story, a contemporary woman, married, with a baby and extended family, leaves her home (voluntarily or under duress?) to spend three days with a stranger on the mountain in an adulterous relationship. At the end of the story, she returns to her family. For most of my students with a strong Christian worldview and little experience with non-Christian literature, the story makes no sense. They perceive little motive for Yellow Woman's behavior, nor do they comprehend the resolution at the end of the story. In class, we read about Native American legends, however, and discuss how the main character is reenacting the

Literature & Its Influence

How does our reading influence our worldview? Everything we read adds a layer to it. At times, our reading so transforms our ideas that it causes us to exchange one idea or layer of our worldview for another. We should never accept the idea that what we read is unimportant. However, limiting our reading to texts that we know in advance support our worldview will limit our development of a critical apparatus necessary to read with understanding. In other words, we must learn to be effective judges of what we read because reading is an essential element in developing our worldview.

legend of Yellow Woman. In doing so, she reconnects to her past heritage and returns to her family with a renewed commitment to family tradition. The story shows my students the significance of our worldview in interpreting events, and that our assumptions of the world may vary considerably from other worldviews.

The first step in reading is to adopt Alan Jacobs' "hermeneutics of love" through "charitable reading." Jacobs posits that Christ's great commandment to love God and love your neighbor as yourself influences every human interaction, including reading. If we are to love our neighbor as God commands, then we must be willing to hear what our neighbor has to say and to understand who our neighbor is. Jacobs says, "the hermeneutics of love requires that books and authors, however alien to the beliefs and practices of the Christian life, be understood and treated as neighbors" (Jacobs 13). Further, Jacobs warns us that we should be humble when approaching a text because we are not gifted in the same way as the author nor have we had the same experiences as the author: thus, we must understand "the role that humility—or, to be more specific, an honest recognition of another's gifts—can play in reading. Surely such honesty and humility are necessary in a reader who would love God and her neighbor through the act of reading" (Jacobs 75). When we read literature in this way, we may be able to grow in our understanding of the gospel itself.

FOR FURTHER STUDY

Cavill, Paul, and Heather Ward, eds. *The Christian Tradition in English Literature*. Grand Rapids: Zondervan, 2007.

Hamlin, Hannibal. *Psalm Culture and Early Modern English Literature*. Cambridge, UK: Cambridge University Press, 2004.

Tippens, Darryl, Stephen Weathers, and Jeanne Murray Walker, eds. *Shadow and Light: Literature and the Life of Faith*. 3rd ed. Abilene, TX: ACU Press, 2012.

WORKS CITED

Holmes, Arthur F. *Contours of a World View*. Grand Rapids: Eerdmans, 1983.

Jacobs, Alan. *A Theology of Reading: The Hermeneutics of Love*. Boulder, CO: Westview, 2001.

Silko, Leslie Marmon. *"Yellow Woman,"* edited by Melody Graulich. New Brunswick, NJ: Rutgers University Press, 1993.

Veith, Gene Edward, Jr. *Reading between the Lines: A Christian Guide to Literature*. Wheaton, IL: Crossway, 1990.

Walsh, Brian J., and J. Richard Middleton.*The Transforming Vision: Shaping a Christian Worldview*. Downers Grove, IL: InterVarsity, 1984.

Welty, Eudora. *One Writer's Beginnings*. Cambridge, MA: Harvard University Press, 1984.

Isaiah

John T. Willis

CHAPTER CONTENTS

MAPS, TABLES, & FEATURES

The book of Isaiah contains materials originating over four centuries. Several specific, datable historical events are referenced in Isaiah and provide the framework for the book: the year King Uzziah of Judah died (742 BCE; 6:1); the Syro-Ephraimite War (734–732 BCE; 7:1–9:7; 17:1–11); the fall of Samaria (721 BCE; 10:9–11); the siege of Ashdod (711 BCE; 20:1–6); Sennacherib's invasion of Judah and siege of Jerusalem (701 BCE; 1:2–20; 28–33; 36–39); the Babylonian conquest of Judah and subsequent exile of the Judeans (587 BCE; 40:1–2; 47:6; 48:3–6); the rise of Cyrus, king of Persia, and his capture of Babylon (540–539 BCE; 44:24–45:7; 46:11–13; 48:14–15); the Jewish return from Babylon and the rebuilding of the temple (536–516 BCE; 60:11–14; 62:9); and the rebuilding of the walls of Jerusalem (445 BCE; 58:12; 60:18; 62:6).

CONTEXTS

The book's composer uses a variety of specific events and God's message derived from them to present relevant truths to his contemporaries in Jerusalem at the end of the fifth century BCE. He assumes that what God has done in the past God can and will do again, and God's centuries-old messages still speak to contemporary audiences.

The composer did not construct the book to be read silently in isolated settings but to be performed orally by trained readers or dramatic actors before assembled audiences. Accordingly, he used many traditional "oral transmission" techniques, giving special attention to structure, rhetoric, repetition, plays on words and phrases, dialogue, quotations, sign acts, symbolic names, allegories, gestures, and other means of communication to assure that those responsible expressed God's message clearly and effectively.

Like all the prophetic books, Isaiah contains a great deal of Hebrew poetry, which relies on parallelism, or some form of repetition, for its overall effect.

COMMENTARY

SUPERSCRIPTION · 1:1

The contents of Isaiah extend far beyond the chronological limits of the four Judean kings mentioned in Isaiah 1:1. Since there are superscriptions at 2:1 and 13:1, perhaps 1:1 is not intended as a superscription for the whole book, but only for 1:2–31 or 1:2–12:6 (compare Jer 1:1–3, which clearly does not cover all the contents of Jeremiah). *Vision* here does not refer to a particular type of divine revelation, but is a very broad term for all kinds of divine messages. *Judah and Jerusalem* does not adequately describe the intended audience for the contents of Isaiah, which also contains oracles for north Israel (9:8–10:4) and several other nations (13–23; 46–48).

Chiasmus

A way of structuring texts so that the first and last parts are parallel, the second and next-to-last are parallel, and so on, chiasmus is very common in the Bible and seems to reflect how Israelites thought texts should be written to be most compelling. In citing a chiasmus, the first and last parts are referred to as A and A′, respectively, the second and next-to-last, B and B′, and so on.

DOOM & HOPE FOR JUDAH & JERUSALEM · 1:2–12:6

The first major section of the book consists of four parts (1:2–5:30; 6:1–9:7; 9:8–10:4; 10:5–12:6) that together portray Israel under threat and promise. Isaiah 1:2–5:30 forms a chiasmus. The outer sections (1:2–31 and 5:1–30) emphasize justice and righteousness, while the center section (2:1–4:6) calls humans to be humble and praise God.

1:2–31 This section uses three metaphors for Yahweh's relationship to Judah: parent-child (vv. 2–4), doctor-patient (vv. 5–6), and husband-wife (v. 21). The wealthy and powerful oppress orphan, widow, and the helpless for personal gain, but scrupulously observe rituals at the temple (vv. 11–15). The prophet declares Yahweh's punishment for this injustice but redemption for the penitent (vv. 5–9, 18–20, 24–31).

For the Lord has spoken (v. 2b) and *for the mouth of the Lord has spoken* (v. 20c) form an inclusio. In this covenant lawsuit, Yahweh is plaintiff; the prophet, Yahweh's lawyer; Israel, the defendant; and heavens and earth, witnesses to the validity of Yahweh's claims (Wildberger 12). Although Yahweh lovingly raised children as a parent, operated on the patient as a doctor, and besieged Jerusalem like an enemy army, Israel continues to rebel. Publicly they present large numbers of sacrifices, festivals, and prayers, but privately they oppress the defenseless. Hence they are sick, desolate, and threatened with the sword. Their only hope is that Yahweh has left them a few survivors and beckons them to be willing and obedient in order to wash their sins clean and make them like snow and wool.

Not know, not understand (v. 3cd) parallels *rebel* (v. 2d), *forsake, spurn, turn...backs on* (v. 4e–g), but contrasts with *the ox knows his master* (v. 3a), which refers not to intellectual information, but to a personal relationship. *The Holy One of Israel* (v. 4f) is a major title for Yahweh in Isaiah (twenty-eight times), along with affirmations that Yahweh is "holy" (for example, 6:3; 57:15), indicating one significant theme in this work. Yahweh inflicts the people with *wounds* (v. 6c) to motivate them to repent in order to heal them (see Jer 30:12–17), but they refuse to return.

Descriptions of the *desolate country*, *cities burned with fire*, hostile *foreigners* (*strangers*) in the land, Jerusalem *like a city under siege*, and *some survivors* point to Sennacherib's invasion of Jerusalem in 701 BCE (Isaiah 36–37), when he conquered forty-six Judean towns and exiled 200,150 prisoners (Pritchard 288). *Remnant*, a term prominent in Isaiah, here means those remaining after invasion.

Lex Talionis

Biblical law states a principle of reciprocity in punishment: "an eye for an eye, and a tooth for a tooth." Such a law fits punishment to the crime but also insists on punishment.

Yahweh punishes the people as he did *Sodom* and *Gomorrah* (v. 9) because they sin like those cities (v. 10). The verse assumes the *lex talionis* (Gen 18:16–19:29). Isaiah uses terms like *multitude* (v. 11a), *more than enough* (v. 11c), *trampling* (v. 12c), *burden* (v. 14c), and *many* (v. 15c), to show God's people assuming that if they bring large quantities of sacrifices in public worship, Yahweh will ignore their unjust treatment of others. Yahweh *hates* those who hide their sins under elaborate worship. Uplifted palms and eyes are common in prayer throughout Scripture (1 Kgs 8:22, 54; Ps 28:2; Lam 3:41; 1 Tim 2:8).

Justice, especially toward the *oppressed*, *fatherless*, and *widow*, is central to godliness (Jas 1:27). Legal decisions favoring the powerful above the weak contradict justice (Isa 10:1–2).

The lament in verses 21–31 expresses Yahweh's frustration with the unfaithful wife, Jerusalem. She who formerly practiced *justice* and *righteousness* now teems with *murderers*, *rebels*, and *thieves* who oppress the *fatherless* and the *widow*. These oppressors are Yahweh's *enemies*, whom God will *remove* and replace with righteous *judges* and *counselors*. God's people fall into two groups: the *penitent*, whom Yahweh will *redeem*, and *rebels*, whom Yahweh will destroy. Foreign idols and worship practices provide little help for the unfaithful.

Verses 21–26 are chiastic. Yahweh will transform his wife, the *harlot*, who abandoned *justice* and *righteousness* (A—v. 21), into a *City of Righteousness*, a *Faithful City* (A'—v. 26), like one eliminates the *dross* that adulterates *silver* (B—v. 22; B'—v. 25). On Judah's *rulers*, who oppress the *fatherless* and *widows* for selfish gain (C—v. 23), he will *avenge* misdeeds (C'—v. 24). NIV's *the Lord Almighty* inadequately translates the Hebrew *Yahweh tseva'ot* (NRSV: *the Lord of hosts*); "hosts" may refer either to angels (Ps 103:20–21), Israel's armies (1 Sam 17:45), or foreign armies (Jer 25:8–9); the latter option seems most likely here (Wildberger 29–30).

Scripture frequently distinguishes between professed and true believers (vv. 27–28; Rom 2:17–29). Yahweh will punish his people who practice foreign cults under *oaks* (57:5) and in *gardens* (65:3; 66:17).

2:1–4:6 This section is chiastic, with the following structure:

> A Zion's Mission to the Nations (2:1–5)
>
> B Humbling arrogant people (2:6–22)
>
> B' Humbling arrogant leaders (3:1–15)
>
> B" Humbling arrogant women (3:16–4:1)
>
> A' Exaltation of Zion's penitent remnant (4:2–6).

In 2:1–5, the prophet quotes a "Song of Zion" (Ps 137:3): Yahweh will exalt abased Zion and the temple. A faithful people will go out from Zion proclaiming God's redeeming message to the nations, who will respond enthusiastically, make pilgrimages to Zion, and learn Yahweh's word more fully. Yahweh will mediate among them, bringing peace. This vision can become reality if God's people walk in Yahweh's light.

In the last days (v. 2a) means "sometime in the future" (Gen 49:1; Deut 31:29). *Law* (v. 3f) is Yahweh's "teaching," as the synonymous parallelism with *word* (v. 3g) shows.

In 2:6–22, alternating recurring refrains (vv. 9, 11, 17 and vv. 10, 19, 21) emphasize that Yahweh will humble the arrogant, including Judah, and they will flee in terror. Because God's people trust in foreign cult practices and the pursuit of wealth and military strength (vv. 6–8, 12–18, 20), the *day of Yahweh* will come (vv. 11, 12, 17, 20), when Yahweh will punish them for their infidelity.

In verses 6–9, the prophet addresses Yahweh concerning the people's misplaced trust, which fuels arrogance, and beseeches Yahweh not to forgive them. In verses 10–22, the prophet urges the people to hide from the *day of Yahweh*, when Yahweh will humble human arrogance in all its manifestations.

As 3:1–15 points out, corruption abounds among the leaders of God's people. Soon, all strata of society will oppress people indiscriminately. Conditions will become so chaotic that the populace will allow anyone to rule. Sin is everywhere; Jerusalem is *like Sodom* (v. 9). Yahweh will punish *the wicked* but sustain *the righteous* (vv. 10–11). God will bring a "covenant lawsuit" against the wicked *elders and leaders* of the people, because they oppress *the poor*. God does not call all Judah *my people*, but only the faithful ones (vv. 14–15).

According to verses 1–7, all Judah's leaders, whether military, political, judicial, religious, moral, or practical, are corrupt (vv. 2–4).

In verses 8–12, Jerusalem *staggers*; Judah *is falling* like a drunkard (v. 8). *They have brought disaster upon themselves* (v. 9). Yahweh will deliver the righteous remnant but punish his people as a whole (vv. 10–11); their leaders have misled them (v. 12).

> **The Day of the Lord**
> *In the Old Testament, the theme of Day of the Lord appears frequently. It does not refer to the end of time, but to a period of God's dramatic intervention in human history to right wrongs. See, for example, Amos 5:18–20.*

The "covenant lawsuit" in verses 13–15 is similar to 1:2–20: Yahweh accuses the rich and powerful of oppressing the poor and defenseless. God's true *vineyard* is not Israel or Judah as a whole, but only those faithful to him, who practice justice and righteousness (5:1–7).

According to 3:16–4:1, influential women in Judah and Jerusalem are *haughty*, parading their beauty, clothing, ornaments, perfumes, and accessories in public, extolling their importance and wealth. Yahweh has a *day* (3:18; 4:1) when he will make these women repulsive eyesores, with the accompanying hideous smells, garments, sounds, and social conditions.

In 4:2–6, Yahweh punishes the arrogant not to destroy, but to refine. Yahweh's *fire* will *wash away the filth of the women of Zion* and *cleanse* the *bloodstains* of the oppressed *from Jerusalem*. He will *create* for *the survivors in Israel, who remain in Jerusalem*, a *shelter* from *heat* and a *refuge* from *storm and rain*.

5:1–30 Isaiah 5 contains three parts: the parable of a disappointing vineyard (vv. 1–7); six "woes" against injustice (vv. 8–23); and an announcement that Yahweh will punish the unjust (vv. 24–30).

In verses 1–7, probably playing a lyre or harp (Ps 33:2–3), Isaiah appears before an audience as a minstrel and sings about his best friend and his vineyard. His friend expended much time and energy preparing the ground for a vineyard and a vat for its fruit. His expectations of bountiful good grapes are very high. But the vineyard produces *wild grapes*. His friend's disappointment is immeasurable. He resolves to demolish his vineyard. The audience empathizes with the vinedresser. Then the prophet declares: "You are that vineyard!". . . and Yahweh is the vinedresser. Using Hebrew wordplays, the prophet declares that the good grapes are *justice* (*mishpat*) and *righteousness* (*tsedaqah*); but the wild grapes, *bloodshed* (*mispach*) and *a cry* (*tse'aqah*, NRSV).

Isaiah 5:8–23 pronounces six "woes" against injustice, examples of the sin condemned in the song of the vineyard. The first woe denounces the rich and powerful for endless property expansion (removing a neighbor's boundary marker; see Deut 19:14) and home improvement. As just punishment, Yahweh will despoil *the great houses* and deplete the crops of the rich. The second woe rebukes powerful, rich leaders of God's people who try to escape impending punishment for their sins by becoming absorbed in drunkenness and salving music; these individuals show *no respect* for Yahweh's *deeds* or *work* of humbling the people (see 2:11, 17) by sending powerful armies to overthrow them and carry them into *exile*, demonstrating that God is *holy* by *justice* and *righteousness*. The third woe reproaches Isaiah's opponents who mock his announcement that Yahweh has a *plan* to send enemies to punish his people for their sins, asking, "If Yahweh really plans to do this, why hasn't it happened yet?"

In verse 20, context suggests that the fourth woe censures those who proclaim all is well in Judah although God's people are approaching calamity (compare v. 30); yet it may also condemn people who reverse God's moral standards.

In verse 21, the fifth woe rebukes those who assume they can live by norms derived from their own wisdom apart from Yahweh's guidance. In verses 22–23, the sixth woe condemns indulgence in drunkenness (compare v. 11) and undermining justice in court by giving and receiving *bribes* (compare Exod 23:8; Deut 16:19), thereby refusing *justice to the innocent* (1:17, 23).

According to 5:24–30, Yahweh will punish his people as *fire* consumes *straw* or *dry grass* because they have ignored *instruction* (or his *word*). Prophets did not establish a new religion but evaluated people by God's existing law, as these six "woes" illustrate. Yahweh unleashes *anger* once and again, because the people persist in sin (v. 25e–f recurs in 9:12, 17, 21; 10:4). As army commander, Yahweh *lifts up a banner* (11:12; 13:2; 18:3; 31:9; 49:22; 62:10) to and *whistles for* (7:18) a distant *nation* (NRSV), Assyria, summoning its soldiers to move against Judah. The army advances *swiftly*, refreshed, well-equipped, deafening, and swarming, making the land appear *darkened* (8:21–22).

6:1–9:7 This large subsection begins with a theophany and ends with visions of a deliverer. In between, stories and oracles of conflict and salvation appear.

Theophany
A divine being's appearance to a human is known as theophany. Israelites believed that seeing God would lead to death, but that did not occur for Isaiah in this text. Isaiah 6 marks the beginning of the prophet's career.

6:1–13 Isaiah 6:1–9:7 addresses the question: Who is king? Within that section, chapter 6 relates Yahweh's commission to Isaiah (742 BCE), while 7:1–9:7 recounts four "son" oracles bearing on the Syro-Ephraimite War (734–732 BCE).

Isaiah worships at the Jerusalem *temple* (vv. 1, 4), Yahweh appears as *King* (vv. 1, 5), *the Lord of hosts* (vv. 3, 5 NRSV), that is, the heavenly hosts of seraphim and attending angels (1 Kgs 21:19; Ps 103:20–21) under a universal sovereign (v. 3). Yahweh strongly contrasts with the earthly *King Uzziah* who has just died (742 BCE). Angelic beings, *seraphs*, attend him, proclaiming to all that he is *holy*,

holy, holy (Ps 99:3, 5, 9; Rev 4:8), which manifests itself in *glory* disseminated throughout *the whole earth*.

Immediately, Isaiah realizes he is a spiritual leper among leprous people. For public protection, lepers covered their upper lip and warned anyone approaching: *Unclean, unclean* (Lev 13:45–46), in contrast to the seraphs' cries to God: *Holy, holy, holy* (v. 3). Yahweh sends a seraph with a *live coal* to touch the prophet's *lips*, inflicting pain as punishment but granting forgiveness in mercy.

Yahweh must send someone to expose his people's spiritual disease: *calloused heart, dull ears, closed eyes*. The choice falls on Isaiah, one formerly with the same disease but now recovered. Although the Judeans' infirmity is chronic, the Great Physician yearns for them to *turn* to him and *be healed* (1:5–6), as Isaiah has been (vv. 6–7). The prophet asks *how long* he must preach to this hardened people; Yahweh replies: *Until* the land is completely devastated and only *the holy seed* remains (4:3), a small group of penitent believers surviving the fall of Samaria (721 BCE), Sennacherib's invasion (701 BCE), the overthrow of Jerusalem and Babylonian exile (587 BCE).

7:1–9 Isaiah 7:1 (which parallels 2 Kgs 16:5) sketches circumstances surrounding the Syro-Ephraimite war (734–732 BCE), preparing the hearer for 7:2–9:7. *Rezin, king of Aram* (Syria) and *Pekah, king of Israel* (or *Ephraim*), rebelled against Tiglath-Pileser III of Assyria (2 Kgs 16:7), who controlled the small western states along the Mediterranean. They invited *Ahaz, king of Judah*, to join, but he refused. So they *marched . . . against Jerusalem* to dethrone Ahaz and put *the son of Tabeel* (perhaps an offspring of Uzziah or Jotham by a Syrian woman from Tabeel in Syria) on the throne, because he would join them.

Ahaz and the Judeans greatly fear Pekah and Rezin. Yahweh sends Isaiah to Ahaz with this message: *Don't be afraid. Do not lose heart*. To encourage Ahaz, Isaiah presents a *son* as a *sign* (Isa 8:18) and an illustration.

The *son* is Isaiah's own *son Shear-Jashub*, "a remnant shall return," here apparently meaning: "[Only] a remnant [of the armies of Syria and Ephraim] shall return [from this attack on Jerusalem]," implying: "If you [Ahaz and the Judeans] trust Yahweh to overthrow Syria and Ephraim, you will not ask Tiglath-Pileser III and the Assyrians for help, but will trust Yahweh to act." The "illustration" supports this interpretation: Rezin and Pekah are merely *two smoldering stubs of firewood*, able to harm no one. Briefly they burn brightly like two large pieces of wood used to start a new fire, but Yahweh will quench their power so that they cannot execute their plan against Judah. Syria and Ephraim will fail because each has the wrong *head*, or king: Rezin and Pekah, respectively. Ahaz and the Judeans (*you* in verse 9c–d is plural) must decide whether they will accept the prophet's message with trust: *If you do not stand firm in your faith, you will not stand at all*. Ahaz and the Judeans must believe this *sign* will occur before it happens (Exod 3:12; 1 Sam 2:34).

7:10–25 Yahweh sends Isaiah to Ahaz again to tell the king to ask for a miraculous *sign*. Ahaz refuses, asserting he would never *put the Lord to the test* by demanding a sign. Isaiah replies that Ahaz is *trying God's patience* with his religious hypocrisy, since he was considering sending to Tiglath-Pileser III for help rather than trusting in Yahweh (2 Kgs 16:7–9).

Who Is Immanuel?

Throughout history, readers of Isaiah have identified Immanuel with several figures, including Hezekiah, Maher-Shalal-Hash-Baz, and others. In the context of the original events of Isaiah 7, the child must have been someone living in Isaiah's lifetime, since otherwise Ahaz could not see the sign. Early Christians understandably connected the verse to the boy who was most fully "God with us," Jesus.

Upon Ahaz's refusal, Yahweh gives him a *sign*, again involving a *son*, then an illustration (v. 20). Gesturing toward or pointing at an unnamed young woman nearby (Tucker 112), perhaps one of Ahaz's wives (Watts 99; Wildberger 306–12) or Isaiah's wife (Clements 86, 88). The young woman does not refer to Mary (see Motyer 84–87). Isaiah declares: *Look, the young woman is with child* (NRSV, Masoretic text) *and will give birth to a son* (not twins or a daughter) *and will call him Immanuel* [with us (Judeans) is God, so we have nothing to fear]; baby Immanuel *will eat curds and honey* (when his mother weans him, the only food available; verses 21–22); but before little Immanuel *knows how to refuse the evil and choose the good* (NRSV) food, *the land of the two kings* (Rezin and Pekah) *you* (the singular pronoun refers to Ahaz) *dread will be laid waste*. If Ahaz and the Judeans believe this, Yahweh will deliver them. But if they make a treaty with Tiglath-Pileser III, *the king of Assyria*, after he subdues Syria and Israel, he will oppress Ahaz and the Judeans, bringing devastation worse than had been experienced *since Ephraim broke away from Judah* after Solomon's death (1 Kgs 12–14).

Here four oracles, each beginning with *in that day*, announce devastating conditions threatening Judah because Ahaz and his advisors refuse Isaiah's pleas to trust in Yahweh. First, Yahweh, king of the nations (Jer 10:7), will *whistle for* (that is, summon, 5:26) *Assyria* (*Egypt* parallels Assyria in Hos 9:3; 11:5, 11) to decimate Judah (vv. 18–19). Second, the prophet uses an illustration to convey the same message as the Immanuel sign. Yahweh, the barber, will use his *razor, the king of Assyria* (Tiglath-Pileser III), to *shave the head* (Rezin), *the hair of the feet* (Pekah), and *the beard* (Ahaz; v. 20 NRSV), because Ahaz and Judah reject trust in Yahweh (2 Kgs 16:5–18). Third, the Assyrians will reduce Judah's population so drastically that *a young cow and two goats* can supply sufficient food for them. All remaining in Judah will eat *curds and honey* (including little Immanuel, v. 15), since this will be the only food available (vv. 21–22). Fourth, the small size of the population will make cultivation impossible, allowing *briers and thorns* to engulf the land. People will hunt game in the fields, and let their livestock run free, searching for pasture.

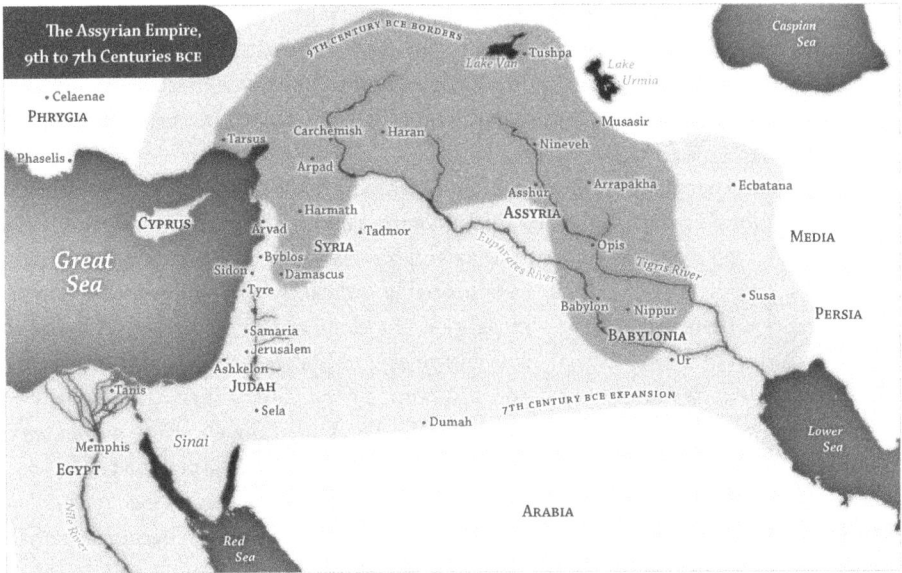

The Assyrian Empire, 9th to 7th Centuries BCE

8:1–15 For the third time, to encourage Ahaz not to fear Rezin and Pekah but to trust Yahweh, Isaiah gives Ahaz a *son* as a *sign* (8:18) and an illustration.

Yahweh instructs Isaiah to *write* on a *large scroll* the words *This scroll stands for Maher-Shalal-Hash-Baz*, and to certify it legally using *reliable witnesses*. Isaiah is to put it in a public place for all to read.

Further, Isaiah goes to *the prophetess* (his wife), and she *conceived* and *gave birth to a son*. Yahweh instructs him to name him *Maher-Shalal-Hash-Baz*, which means, "The Spoil Speeds, The Prey Hastens." Yahweh tells Isaiah: *Before the boy knows how to say* "Dada" *or* "Mama," *the wealth of Damascus and the plunder of Samaria will be carried off by the king of Assyria*. The details and point of this "sign" are identical with the "sign" of Immanuel (7:14–17), occurring approximately a year later. By the time little *Maher-Shalal-Hash-Baz* says his first words (at about one year), Syria and Ephraim will no longer threaten Judah. Hence, it is unnecessary to send to Assyria for help.

The illustration accompanying this sign involves two rivers (vv. 5–10). One is *the gently flowing waters of Shiloah*, a channel supplying water to Jerusalem during siege (7:3; 36:2), symbolizing trust in Yahweh (28:16; 30:15). Ahaz and his advisors (*this people*) rejected this river because they *melt in fear* (NRSV) before Rezin and Pekah. Therefore, Yahweh will bring against them *the mighty flood waters of the River . . . the king of Assyria*, which will *overflow all its channels* (into Syria), and *run over all its banks* (that is, destroy Israel, or Ephraim), and it will *sweep on into Judah*, as well. Judah's alliance with Assyria (2 Kgs 16:7–9) will backfire: after Tiglath-Pileser III overthrows Syria and Ephraim, he will subjugate Judah (2 Kgs 16:10–18; 2 Chron 28:16–25). While making this declaration, Isaiah holds the year-old *Immanuel* in his arms, representing the small population that will survive (7:21–22), addressing him by name (v. 8c). In verses 9–10, Isaiah proclaims to Syria and Ephraim his message to Ahaz in 7:7–9: their *plan* to dethrone Ahaz and replace him with *the son of Tabeel will not stand* (7:6).

Next, the prophet tells an audience (imperatives in verses 12–13 are plural) what Yahweh said to him (v. 11). His audience is different from *this people* (vv. 11–12 NRSV), which usually refers to Ahaz and his associates (7:2, 17; 8:6), but in this case probably indicates Isaiah's comrades. God's message is the same as that to Ahaz and his advisors in the *sign* of Shear-Jashub: *do not fear* Syria and Ephraim; *let the Lord of hosts* (NRSV) *be your fear*; trust God (7:4, 9). Yahweh *will be a sanctuary* from the Syro-Ephraimite alliance for those who trust in him, but *a stone that causes men to stumble for both houses of Israel*: Ephraim, because she has joined Syria against Assyria; and Judah, because she has not trusted in Yahweh but asked Tiglath-Pileser III for help against the Syro-Ephraimite invaders (2 Kgs 16:7–9). This political maneuvering will cripple Ephraim and Judah.

> **Necromancy & Divination**
>
> *In the ancient world, it was common to consult the gods or the dead ancestors about the future. Techniques for doing so included reading entrails of sacrificed animals, studying stellar movements, looking for unusual behaviors of animals or persons, and digging holes into the ground to induce ghosts to rise from the netherworld. Israel's prophets forbade all these practices as incompatible with worshiping the God of life.*

8:16–20   Ahaz, his advisors, and most Judeans refuse to accept Isaiah's advice to trust in Yahweh. Isaiah decides to quit preaching until his announcements occur, but he leaves two witnesses. First, he instructs one of his associates (imperatives in v. 16 are singular) to *bind up the testimony* and *seal the teaching* (NRSV) among his *disciples*, to write his oracles now preserved in Isaiah 7:3–8:15 and keep them among Judeans who share his trust in Yahweh. When the events Isaiah has announced occur, the Judeans will *consult mediums and spiritists* (NRSV *ghosts* and *familiar spirits*), seeking in vain explanations for them from *their gods* (NRSV). Then they must resort to the *teaching* (NRSV) *and to the testimony!* (v. 20; v. 16); at that point, it will be time to read Isaiah's oracles written on the little scroll his disciples preserved. Second, Isaiah and *the children the Lord has given* him (*Shear-Jashub* [7:3], *Immanuel* [7:14; 8:8, 10], and *Maher-Shalal-Hash-Baz* [8:3]) will be *signs and symbols in Israel*. Whenever Judeans see Isaiah or these *children*, their symbolic names will recall Isaiah's message.

8:21–9:7   The placement and content of 8:21–9:7 date this oracle near the beginning of Hezekiah's reign (715 BCE; 2 Kgs 18:13). It contains four contrasts between Judah's devastation at the end of Ahaz's reign and the renewal Hezekiah brings: where Ahaz's reign brought distress (8:21, 22; 9:1), Hezekiah's brings joy (9:1, 3); where Ahaz's brought defeat (9:1, 4), Hezekiah's brings victory (9:4–5);

where Ahaz was an evil king (8:21), Hezekiah is a good king (9:6–7); and where Ahaz brought darkness (8:22; 9:2), Hezekiah brings light (9:2).

Judeans remaining after Assyrian subjugations live in chaos and despair. They *curse their king* (Ahaz), in whom they had great confidence; and *their gods* (NRSV), whom they adopted from the nations (2 Kgs 16:3–4, 10–18; 2 Chron 28:2–4, 22–25) and whom they trusted instead of Yahweh. Tiglath-Pileser III overran *the land of Zebulun and the land of Naphtali*, that is, *Galilee of the Gentiles*, in Ephraim west of the Jordan, and Gilead in Ephraim east of the Jordan (2 Kgs 15:29); so only Samaria in southern Ephraim west of the Jordan remained.

According to 9:2–5, as Yahweh miraculously defeated the large Midianite army with 300 poorly equipped, inexperienced soldiers under Gideon on *the day of Midian* (NRSV; Judg 6:2–6; 7:1–25), so Yahweh, through his angel, will defeat the large Assyrian army with a much smaller Judean army under Hezekiah (Isa 37:36). Isaiah likens God's people's ensuing *joy* with joy *at the harvest* (Ps 126:6) and the joy an army experiences *when dividing the plunder* (Hebrew *shalal*, recalling the name *Maher-Shalal-Hash-Baz*, 8:1, 3) of its defeated enemy (Judg 5:28–30; 1 Sam 30:16–20).

In verses 6–7, the statements *for a child has been born for us, a son given to us* (NRSV) refer not to physical birth of a royal prince (Wildberger 398–402; Blenkinsopp, *Isaiah 1–39*, 248–49), but to a king's accession, which has already occurred when the prophet utters this (Clements 107; Hayes and Irvine 180–81). This *son* is Hezekiah, Ahaz's successor. The king of Israel is Yahweh's *son* (2 Sam 7:14; Pss 2:7; 89:26–27). His accession is his *begettal* (Ps 2:7) or *birth* (Isa 9:6). As *son*, the king is *heir* of Yahweh's estate (Ps 2:8), the world, and its nations. Yahweh gives his *son* victory and rule over all nations through Yahweh's universal rule (Pss 47:1–3, 8–9; 99:1–2).

Hezekiah's *name* (v. 6b) is symbolic, consisting of four parts: *Wonderful Counselor* (Hebrew *pele' yo 'ets*), who acts wisely, as Solomon did (1 Kgs 3:3–14); *Godly Hero* (or "mighty warrior") (Hebrew *'el gibbor*), who derives his strength from Yahweh, enabling him to lead his people against their enemies (Wildberger 403–4); *Father of Eternity* (Hebrew *'abi 'ad*), one responsible for the king's public and private affairs and estate (see 22:21; Gen 45:8), whose durability Yahweh assures; and *Prince of Peace* (Hebrew *sar shalom*), promoting peace by submitting himself to Yahweh and promoting *justice and righteousness* among Yahweh's people (Isa 1:17; 5:7).

9:8–10:4 As in Leviticus 26:14–24 and Amos 4:6–11, Isaiah 9:8–10:4 declares that Yahweh has smitten the people repeatedly to bring them to repentance, but they persist in sin. This section contains four oracles, each ending with: *For all this, his anger is not turned away; his hand is stretched out still* (9:12, 17, 21; 10:4 NRSV).

Yahweh delivered Israel from Egypt *with an outstretched arm* (Exod 6:6) and now *stretches out his hand* against his own people, who refuse to repent. The prophet addresses Ephraim in the first three oracles, Judah in the fourth. The first three oracles describe what Yahweh has done recently.

Yahweh punished *Ephraim* and her capital *Samaria* because of *pride and arrogance*. A possible reconstruction of the setting of this oracle is that the anti-Assyrian Pekah, incited by Syrians and Philistines, murdered the pro-Assyrian Pekahiah, but the Ephraimites confidently resolve they will *rebuild* and *replace* their losses (2 Chron 28:5–6, 18). Yahweh's "hand is stretched out still" (NRSV) to punish Ephraim more severely by sending the Assyrians under Tiglath-Pileser III against them and their allies.

> **The "Outstretched Hand" of the Lord**
> *Yahweh cut off Ephraim's religious leaders, elders and* prominent men (the head), *and* prophets (the tail), *because they "led this people . . . astray," so that "everyone was godless and an evildoer" (Isa 19:15 NRSV). Perhaps this refers to murders of Ephraimite kings between 746 and 737 BCE (Hos 7:3–7). His "hand is stretched out still" to punish Ephraim's rulers and people for not returning to him.*

According to 9:18–21, Yahweh consumed Ephraim like *fuel for the fire*, because her *wickedness burned like a fire* (NRSV). Northern Israelites opposed each other (*Manasseh devoured Ephraim, and Ephraim Manasseh*): one group after another murdering the reigning king and enthroning its own candidate (2 Kgs 15:8–26); and, *together*, they fought against Judah: they joined Syria and attacked Jerusalem to dethrone Ahaz and enthrone *the son of Tabeel* (2 Kgs 15:37; 16:5; Isa 7:1–6). *His* [Yahweh's] *hand is stretched out still* to punish the Ephraimites, because they did not repent when Yahweh punished them previously.

Isaiah's announcement (10:1–4) that Yahweh will punish the rich, powerful, influential leaders of Yahweh's people for oppressing the *poor, oppressed, widows,* and *fatherless* recalls Isaiah 1:10–17 and 5:8–23, oracles addressed to Judah, so it is likely that the prophet is addressing Judah here. Authorities made laws allowing them to oppress the helpless legally (29:20–21). *Their spoil* (v. 2c) is *shelalam,* and *make their prey* (v. 2d) is, in Hebrew, *yabozzu,* both recalling the name *Maher-Shalal-Hash-Baz* (8:1, 3). Yahweh has a *day of punishment* (NRSV) which they cannot avoid, when they will become *captives* or *slain. His hand is stretched out still* to punish the powerful for oppressing the defenseless.

10:5–12:6 Just as most of 7:1–10:4 concerns the Syro-Ephraimite War, 10:5–12:6 fits Sennacherib's invasion of Judah in 701 BCE, reapplied to the Jews' return from Babylonian exile in 536 BCE and afterward. This section falls into two parts: Yahweh will overthrow Assyria after using that nation to punish Judah (10:5–32); and Yahweh will then restore the remnant of the people under a *new David* (10:33–12:6).

Isaiah 10:5–32 is a woe oracle (compare 5:8–23) against Assyria (see 33:1). It reflects a conflict in purposes between Yahweh and Assyria regarding Assyria's invasion of Judah. Yahweh intends to use Assyria to punish Judah (vv. 6, 12), then to restore a faithful remnant (vv. 20–25); Assyria intends only to *destroy* Judah (vv. 7, 11).

Yahweh sends Assyria against Judah because the latter is *a godless nation*, a *people who angers* him, intending for Assyria to *take spoil* (Hebrew *lishlol shalal*) and *seize plunder* (Hebrew *laboz baz*), once again recalling the name *Maher-Shalal-Hash-Baz* (8:1, 3). Yahweh is like a lumberjack wielding an *ax* (Assyria) to fell a tree (Judah), a carpenter handling a *saw* (Assyria) to cut a board (Judah, v. 15), and a parent using a *rod* (Assyria) to discipline a child (Judah, vv. 5, 15). As the lumberjack controls the ax, not the ax the lumberjack, so Yahweh controls Assyria, not Assyria Yahweh.

The king of Assyria brags in his *arrogant boasting* and *haughty pride* (v. 12 NRSV) that he will destroy *Jerusalem and her images* as Assyria has destroyed other cities and their idols, including *Samaria* (vv. 8–11), which Assyria overthrew after a three-year siege under Shalmaneser V and Sargon II (724– 721 BCE).

Yahweh, the *Light* and *Holy One of Israel*, will overthrow Assyria like a deadly illness suffocates an invalid (v. 18c) or like a rapidly spreading *fire* destroys fields of *thorns* and *briers* (7:23–25) and *forests* (vv. 16c-18b), leaving only a few trees (v. 19). The *wasting disease upon* Assyria's *sturdy warriors* (v. 16b) refers to Yahweh's angel killing 185,000 Assyrian soldiers (Isa 37:36).

Yahweh *decreed* the *destruction* of Judah by Assyria, so *only a remnant will return* (vv. 20–22), a clause recalling the Hebrew name *Shear-Jashub* (7:3). But the remnant will not *rely on him who struck them down* (the Assyrians), as Ahaz relied on Tiglath-Pileser III (2 Kgs 16:7–9), but on Yahweh (7:9; 31:1; 36:4–7). Hebrew *'el gibbor* in verse 21b refers to Yahweh and means *Mighty God*, recalling Hezekiah's throne name (9:6).

According to 24–27b, since Yahweh is punishing Judah, she must *not be afraid of* the Assyrians whom Yahweh is using to do this. When Yahweh finishes using the Assyrians, he will overthrow them as he did the Egyptians at the Red Sea (Exod 3:7–10; 14:26–31) and the Midianites when they oppressed Israel in the time of Gideon (Judg 7:24–25; Ps 83:9–12; Isa 9:4), thus breaking *the yoke* on Judah's neck.

The prophet's intensely dramatic rhetoric in verses 27c-32 enables his audience to envision and hear the Assyrians (*he* in vv. 28, 32 [NRSV]; *they* in v. 29) tramping methodically and irrepressibly from *Rimmon* (NRSV) southward through *Aiath*, then *Migron*, then *Michmash* (NRSV), onward, until *he* reaches the village of *Nob*

Assyrian Propaganda
According to Isaiah, the king of Assyria exalts his own strength and wisdom (vv. 13–14), boasting he is so terrifying that he vanquishes enemies like one gathering eggs out of nests mother birds feared to protect: not one flapped a wing or opened its mouth to chirp. *This simile resembles Sennacherib's boast that he made Hezekiah "a prisoner in Jerusalem, his royal residence, like a bird in a cage" (Pritchard 288). Indeed, the book of Isaiah knows a great deal about Assyrian propaganda and quotes it several times.*

about a mile and a half north of Jerusalem on Mount Scopus overlooking the city, where he shakes his fist at Jerusalem, signifying his imminent attack on the city. Sennacherib's annals do not mention an approach from the north. Micah 1:10–16 describes a similar approach of this army from the west, which Sennacherib's annals corroborate. This sets the stage for the second part of Isaiah 10:5–12:6.

Isaiah 10:33–12:6 completes the picture begun in 10:5–32, reapplying the aftermath of Sennacherib's invasion in 701 BCE to the Jews in Babylonian exile after 587 BCE. This section falls into three parts: Yahweh will devastate Judah, then restore justice, righteousness, and peace to Judah through a *new David* (10:33–11:9); Yahweh will work through the *new David* to restore his faithful remnant to their land (11:10–16); and the remnant will praise Yahweh (12:1–6).

10:33–11:9 Using Assyria as an *ax* (10:15), Yahweh fells the *lofty trees* and *forest thickets* of *Lebanon*. The mention of *Lebanon* indicates that 10:33–34 announces Yahweh's devastation of Judah, not Assyria. The situation looks bleak for Judah. But Yahweh will cause a *shoot* to come forth from the *stump of Jesse*, a *new David* (1 Sam 16:1–13; 2 Sam 23:1–2), infused with ample *wisdom and understanding* to restore and maintain *righteousness* and *justice* in the land by slaying the *wicked* and vindicating the *needy* and *poor*. Yahweh will establish peace between former enemies. Some scholars understand verses 6–9 literally, reasoning that human sin produces enemies in the animal kingdom (Genesis 3), and these verses announce that Yahweh will end that hostility by enacting peace among human beings (Brueggemann, *Isaiah 1–39*, 102). However, "context suggests that the talk of harmony in the animal world is a metaphor for harmony in the human world. The strong and powerful live together with the weak and powerless because the latter can believe that the former are no longer seeking to devour them" (Goldingay 85; see Seitz, *Isaiah 1–39*, 96, 106–7).

The New David

Isaiah 10 does not identify the "new David." He might be Hezekiah or Josiah, but the promise of return from exile as a "second exodus" (11:12, 15–16) indicates that most likely he is Zerubbabel, or perhaps an ideal future ruler.

The setting of 11:10–16 comes near the end of the Babylonian exile (550–536 BCE). The prophet announces that Yahweh will do four things. First, God will duplicate the mighty act of delivering Israel from slavery to Pharaoh at *the Egyptian sea*. He will send *a scorching wind* to part the waters of *the Euphrates River* so the remnant may *cross over* on dry land and escape from foreign bondage, effecting a "second exodus" (vv. 15–16; Exod 14:21–22). Second, God will *gather the remnant* from their various habitations in exile (vv. 10–12) and lead them along a *highway* back to their land, thus repeating the entrance of Israel into the promised land (vv. 11–12; Exod 15:13, 17). Third, Yahweh will remove the *jealousy* of Ephraim over Judah, and the *hostility* of Judah against Ephraim (v. 13). The hope that Yahweh will end the animosity between Ephraim and Judah, which dates at least to the time of David (2 Sam 2:12–3:39; 19:41–43), is prominent in late preexilic and exilic texts (Jer 30:1–3; 31:1–14, 31–34; Ezek 37:15–28), suggesting that Isaiah 11:10–16 (and probably all of 10:33–12:6) originated in that era. Fourth, Yahweh will use the reunited people to overthrow their enemies, *Philistia, Edom, Moab*, and *the Ammonites* (v. 14), essentially the same peoples who trembled upon learning that Yahweh delivered Israel from Egypt (Exod 15:14–15). The phrase *they will plunder* (Hebrew *yabozzu*) recalls the name *Maher-Shalal-Hash-Baz* (8:1, 3).

As 12:1–6 points out, after Yahweh delivered Israel from Egypt (Exod 14:21–31), Moses and the Israelites sang praises (Exod 15:1–18). Similarly, after Yahweh delivers the Jews from Babylonian exile in a "second exodus" (Isa 11:10–16), they will sing praises (Isa 12:1–6). *You* is singular (referring to Israel as a whole) in verses 1–2 and 6 but plural in verses 3–5 (indicating individual Israelites). *In that day you will say* in verses 1 and 4 divides this song into two equal parts.

The prophet urges Israel to praise Yahweh for having *comforted* them (v. 1), a term normally referring to return from exile (Isa 40:1; 49:13). *I will trust, and will not be afraid* (v. 2b) is a major teaching in Isaiah (Isa 7:2, 4, 9; 8:12–13). Verse 2c–d is almost identical to Exodus 15:2a–b. *You will draw water from the wells of salvation* (v. 3) is a metaphor meaning that Yahweh will sustain the restored people by being constantly present and delivering them (Ps 36:8–9).

When Yahweh delivers Israel from powerful oppressors by a mighty act, they cannot but *give thanks* (vv. 1, 4) and *make known among the nations what he has done* (vv. 4–5; Pss 66:1–12; 105:1–6). Those recently returned from exile and now living in *Zion* must *sing for joy* because Yahweh is in their midst (v. 6).

YAHWEH'S WORK AMONG THE NATIONS · 13:1–23:18

Isaiah 13–23 contains fourteen oracles proclaiming Yahweh's work among nations and individuals (compare Jer 46–51; Ezek 25–32; Amos 1–2): Babylon (13:1–14:23) and Egypt (19:1–20:6); Assyria (14:24–27) and Babylon (21:1–10); Philistia (14:28–32) and Edom (21:11–12); Moab (15:1–16:13); Arabia (21:13–17); Aram and Ephraim (17:1–11) and Judah (22:1–14); Assyria (17:12–14) and Shebna and Eliakim (22:15–25); and Ethiopia (18:1–7) and Phoenicia (23:1–18).

These oracles date from the late eighth (14:24–32; 17:1–11; 20; 22) to late sixth centuries BCE (13:1–14:23; 23). In the fifth century BCE book of Isaiah, they convey important theological messages. First, Yahweh governs all nations and uses them to accomplish holy purposes (13:2–5, 17; 19:1–4; 23:8–12). Second, Yahweh punishes Israel (17:1–11) and Judah (22:1–14), along with other nations (see Amos 3:1–2). The fate of Yahweh's people is bound up with the fate of the nations. Third, humanity's universal pervasive sin is pride, arrogance, self-sufficiency, hubris, ingratitude (13:11, 19; 14:12–15; 16:6; 17:4; 19:11–12; 22:15–19; 23:7–12), already affirmed of Judah (2:6–22) and Assyria (10:5–19). Fourth, Yahweh's "plan" alone prevails (14:24–27; 19:3, 11–12, 17; 23:8–9). Fifth, Yahweh has a *day* to punish or redeem nations (13:6, 9, 13; 17:4, 7, 9, 11; 19:18, 19, 21, 23, 24; 22:5, 8, 12, 20, 25).

13:1–14:23 The two-step sequence noting that Yahweh will restore his people and then overthrow his people's conqueror is common in Isaiah (see 11:10–12:6; 13:1–14:23; 30:18–26; 30:27–33).

Some have claimed that 13:2–14:27 was originally a unit denouncing Assyria for its arrogance in attacking Judah in 701 BCE, including an announcement that Assyria will destroy Babylon in 689 BCE (13:19–22; 14:22–23; see Erlandsson 109–27, 160–66). Similarly, some scholars believe that 13:2–14:23 contains prophetic fragments originating from Merodach-baladan II's rebellions against Assyria in the eighth to the fourth centuries BCE (Clements 129–38). It is more likely, however, that, as in 21:1–10, 47 and 48:14–20, a prophet in Babylon at the end of the exile (540 BCE) announces that Yahweh will incite the *Medes* (Medo-Persians under Cyrus, 41:25) to overthrow Babylon (13:17), slay her king, and return the Jews to Israel. This oracle contains four parts: Yahweh will use Medo-Persia to overthrow Babylon (13:1–22); Yahweh will restore Israel to Canaan (14:1–2); those restored will sing a taunt, mocking Babylon's defeated and dead king (14:3–21); and Yahweh reaffirms a promise to destroy Babylon (14:22–23).

> **Cyrus the Great**
> *Cyrus the Great (about 590–530 BCE) was founder of the Persian empire.*

The oracle announcing Babylon's defeat in 13:2–14:23 fits well with the message of *Isaiah son of Amoz* (v. 1). *The LORD of hosts* (v. 4 NRSV), *the Almighty* (Hebrew *shadday*), *raises a banner* (vv. 2; 5:26; 11:10, 12; 49:22; 62:10) to summon *warriors* (v. 3), an *army* (v. 4), *the Medes* (v. 17) *from a distant land* (v. 5 NRSV), to overthrow *Babylon* (v. 19). The terms *the whole earth* (v. 5 NRSV), *the earth* (v. 9 NRSV), and *the world* (v. 11) reflect Babylon's far-flung dominion in its prime.

The day of the Lord (vv. 6, 9), *the day of his fierce anger* (v. 13; vv. 3, 5, 9), *is near* to *punish* Babylon for its sins (vv. 9, 11) especially *pride* (vv. 11, 19). The day of Yahweh refers to Yahweh's intervention in history to punish or redeem a nation. Yahweh's coming impacts all creation in several ways: *the heavens tremble* and *the earth shakes* (v. 13; Joel 2:10; 3:16; Hag 2:6–7, 21); the *light* of the sun, moon, and stars becomes *dark* (v. 10; Zeph 1:15; Joel 2:1–2, 10, 31); *pain and anguish* seize the hearts of the Babylonians and their sympathizers *like a woman in labor* (vv. 7–8; Ps 48:6; Mic 4:9–10; Jer 4:31); and they flee in fear before their attackers (v. 14).

> **Cyrus' Conquest of Babylon**
> *Babylon gladly surrendered to Cyrus without resistance in 539 BCE (Pritchard 315–16), apparently owing to the unpopularity of the city's last king, Nabonidus. The city prospered until Seleucus I, Alexander the Great's successor, built Seleucia (end of fourth century BCE); then Babylon's citizens moved to Seleucia.*

The prophet announces that the Median devastation of Babylon and its allies will be cruel and thorough. They will make their victims *more rare* than *pure gold* (v. 12), looting houses, ravishing women (v. 16), slaughtering young men and children (vv. 16, 18), vacating cities and buildings so that wild animals may inhabit them (vv. 20–22), like *God overthrew* (NRSV) *Sodom and Gomorrah* (v. 19; Gen 19:24–28; Isa 1:9–10; 3:9).

14:1–2 Babylon's overthrow means freedom from captivity and return of the Jewish exiles to *the Lord's land*, Canaan, which Yahweh gave Israel after the wilderness wanderings (Josh 1:2–4, 11; 21:43–45). Yahweh rejected Israel for rebelling and sent Babylon to defeat and deport the nation (42:24–25; Jer 25:1–29). But now, in *compassion*, Yahweh will *choose* Israel again (Deut 7:6–8), execute "a second exodus," and *settle them in their own land. Aliens* (that is, non-Jews) will *unite with* them, aid them in their return (Ezra 1:1–4; 6:1–5), and become their slaves (45:13–17; 49:7, 22–23; 60:4–16; 61:5–7; Jer 30:16).

According to 14:3–21, after the Jewish exiles return home, they will take up a *taunt*, a mocking and satirical funeral lament, *against the king of Babylon*, Nabonidus, symbolizing all oppressive Babylonian rule. This taunt declares that: Yahweh has overthrown the king of Babylon (v. 5); the Babylonian king was cruel (vv. 6, 17, 20); nations subject to him rejoice in his death, because now they can be at peace (vv. 7–8); and rulers of other nations who preceded him in death come to meet him as he approaches Sheol, joyfully declaring that the world will remember them more favorably than Nabonidus, because of his ruthlessness (vv. 9–21).

A tyrant who oppresses people (v. 4) recklessly diminishes the ecological system. Forests suffer. When the tyrant dies, trees *exult* because they can rest from mistreatment (v. 8).

Death levels all humans, demonstrating that all are *weak* (v. 10) despite their *pomp* (v. 11). Verses 12–14 apply portions of a Canaanite myth about the god Baal to Babylon's deceased king. Like the *Day Star* (NRSV), the planet Venus (the Canaanite deity *Athtar*), which attempts to seize supremacy from Elyon (*the Most High*), Nabonidus (representing all Babylonian kings) tries to usurp Yahweh's place as presider over the gathering of the gods *on the mount of assembly* (*the heights of Zaphon*; NRSV), Syria's Mount Casius in the north where the gods assembled in Ugaritic mythology. Babylon's king's sin is pride, reflected in his self-assessment: *I will ascend* (twice), *I will raise, I will sit, I will make myself* (vv. 13–14). He assumes he is equal to or above God.

14:24–27 As in Isaiah 10:5–27b, here *the Lord of hosts* (NRSV) promises to execute a *plan* for Assyria. Having sent them to punish sinful Israel/Judah, Yahweh will next *stretch out his hand* to overthrow Assyria and expel them from the promised land, as when delivering Israel from Egypt (Exod 15:12;

The Death of Nabonidus

Nations usually give their rulers honorable funerals and burials. Babylon's king is an exception because he destroyed his land and killed his people (v. 20a–c). Maggots *and worms* swarm *over his body (v. 11c–d)* as it lies *on the ground for all passersby to humiliate (vv. 18–20c). In Isaiah 14, the Jewish remnant prays that this king will have no descendants to arise and repeat his brutalities (vv. 20d–21). Yahweh will redeem a "remnant"* (NRSV) *of Judah (vv. 1–2), will but sweep Babylon clean with the* broom of destruction.

Deut 4:34; 5:15; Isa 5:25), removing the *yoke* and *burden* confining his faithful remnant's mobility (Isa 9:4; 10:27).

14:28–32 This oracle dates from *the year King Ahaz died* (v. 28; probably 715 BCE). Isaiah addresses Philistine *envoys* who come to Jerusalem to encourage Ahaz's successor, Hezekiah, to join a rebellion against Assyria (v. 32). Shalmaneser V, the *rod* or *root of that snake* (v. 29), died in 722 BCE. A usurper, Sargon II (721–705 BCE), claimed the Assyrian throne, causing internal strife in Assyria. Philistia and other western states celebrated, hoping to throw off Assyrian domination. Isaiah tells the Philistine envoys that this rejoicing is premature. *A viper* (v. 29), Sargon II, will come with his army, pictured as *smoke . . . from the north* (v. 31), and subject the western states to Assyria again. Isaiah counsels Hezekiah to reject the proposal to join this rebellion and to trust in Yahweh to provide *refuge* for the *poor*, *needy*, and *afflicted* in *Zion* (vv. 30, 32), advice similar to that which he gave Ahaz when Rezin of Syria and Pekah of Israel threatened in 734 BCE (Isa 7:1–9). Apparently Hezekiah rejected this advice, as Sargon II says he invaded the western states and besieged Ashdod in Philistia because of an alliance between Philistia and Judah (711 BCE; Pritchard 287).

15:1–16:14 Isaiah 16:13–14 indicates that the description of Moab's devastation preserved in 15:1–16:12 was *in the past* (NRSV). The one who preserved this description (perhaps Isaiah or a later compiler) declares that *within three years* Moab will fall. At this point, a later prophet or author interjects earlier oral or written material in his work. There are striking similarities between Isaiah 15–16 and Jeremiah 48 (Isa 15:2c–7a parallels Jer 48:37a, 38, 34a, 31, 34b, 5, 34d, 36c; Isa 16:6–11 parallels Jer 48:29, 30b, 36a, 36b, 32c, 32b, 32a, 32d, 33, 36a, 36b), indicating borrowing from earlier statements concerning Moab. Isaiah 15–16 announces that Yahweh will overthrow Moab because of its pride (16:6), a major theme in Isaiah 13–23. Isaiah 15–16 contains four parts: the Moabites lament over their desperate condition (15:1–9); the Moabites seek help from Judah (16:1–5); Yahweh reluctantly rejects the Moabites' plea (16:6–12); Isaiah says the description of Moab's devastation in 15:1–16:12 will occur within three years (16:13–14).

Moab

The Transjordanian kingdom of Moab was organized by Mesha (see 2 Kgs 3) in the ninth century BCE. He revolted against his Israelite overlord to establish an independent entity that lasted until it became part of the Assyrian and subsequent empires.

Isaiah 15:1–9 describes how recently an enemy army has ravaged Moab *in a night* (v. 1), shedding much *blood* (v. 9), so that *her fugitives flee* (v. 5), carrying paltry possessions (v. 7); also, grievous drought devastated the land (v. 6; 16:8–10). Every Moabite city and village laments (vv. 5, 8; 16:7, 11), practicing customary mourning rites: weeping (vv. 2, 3, 5; 16:9), wailing (vv. 2, 3, 8; 16:7), crying out (vv. 4, 5, 8), shaving heads (v. 2; compare Job 1:20; Jer 16:6; Amos 8:10; Mic 1:16) and beards (v. 2; Jer 41:5), and wearing sackcloth (v. 3; Job 16:15; Amos 8:10). Yahweh himself is deeply touched by

Moab's plight and cries out over her (v. 5; *I* in v. 9 indicates that Yahweh is the speaker throughout vv. 1–9 as in 16:9, 11; Goldingay 109, 111). People rush to *temple* and *high places to weep* (v. 2) and pray (16:12). But Yahweh refuses to listen; he *will bring still more* punishment on *the fugitives*, or *the remnant* (NRSV), *of Moab* (v. 9; 16:12).

Moabite refugees temporarily stay in *Sela*, Edom's capital (vv. 1–5). Their leaders advise them to *send lambs as tribute* (2 Kgs 3:4) by envoys to Judah's *ruler* in *Zion* (v. 1). These envoys should describe Moab's desperate circumstances: their *women* are helpless and homeless *at the fords of the Arnon* river, the boundary between Moab and Judah (v. 2). They should beg Judah: *Grant justice* (NRSV); *let the Moabite fugitives stay with you*; give them protection and asylum from their assailants in your land (vv. 3–4b). The envoys should also reassure Judah that, when this crisis ends, a descendant of David *who in judging seeks justice and speeds the cause of righteousness* will reign over Judah (vv. 4c–5).

Judah's ruler and his advisors (*we*, v. 6) reject the pleas and assurances of Moab's envoys as self-centered and self-serving, and therefore *false*. Accordingly, Yahweh (*I*, v. 9; *my heart*, v. 11) decrees that Moab go on lamenting because its deplorable condition will continue (vv. 7, 9) in spite of its fervent prayers for relief (v. 12). Yahweh's heart goes out to these grieving people (vv. 9, 11), but their *overweening pride and conceit* (v. 6) demand continued suffering.

17:1–11 The setting of this oracle, like the one of chapter 7, is early in the Syro-Ephraimite war (734–732 BCE). Rezin of Aram (Syria) and Pekah of Ephraim (North Israel) allied to rebel against Tiglath-Pileser III of Assyria and invited Ahaz of Judah to join them, but he refused. They marched toward Jerusalem to replace Ahaz with the son of Tabeel (Isa 7:6). Ahaz and Judah thought the best political strategy was to ally with Assyria, but Isaiah urged them to trust in Yahweh alone (Isa 7:7–9). Apparently, Isaiah delivered the message of 17:1–11, as he had in 7:1–9, to Ahaz and Judah, assuring them Yahweh would overthrow Aram and Ephraim and urging them to trust in Yahweh alone for deliverance. *In that day* (vv. 4, 7, 9) divides this oracle into four parts.

Isaiah assures Judah that Assyria will reduce *Damascus*, Aram's capital, to *a heap of ruins* (on this expression, see Mic 1:6; 3:12), so that only animals will live there. As predicted, Tiglath-Pileser III later conquers Damascus and carries its inhabitants into captivity to Kir (732 BCE; 2 Kgs 16:9).

Further, Isaiah assures Judah that northern Israel (called *Ephraim* in v. 3 and *Jacob* in v. 4) will experience defeat, describing their destruction with several metaphors, such as physical deterioration of the sick (v. 4), *a reaper* collecting grain (v. 5), and harvesters *gleaning olives* (v. 6). Tiglath-Pileser III overthrew Israel's territory east of the Jordan (Gilead) and in the north, west of the Jordan (Galilee), carrying the survivors into captivity (732 BCE; 2 Kgs 15:29; Isa 9:1) and leaving only Samaria.

The destruction of Damascus and devastation of Galilee and Gilead will convince some northern Israelites to abandon their self-initiated, human-manufactured *Asherah poles* (symbols of the goddess Asherah, whom some ancient Israelites considered the consort of Yahweh) and *incense altars*, and return to *their Maker, the Holy One of Israel*.

Ephraim will desert its *strong cities* in the same way that *the Hivites* (Josh 9:1–2) *and the Amorites* (Gen 15:16, 21) (NRSV, following the Septuagint) deserted their fortified cities when the Israelites attacked them during the conquest of Canaan (v. 9). In verses 10–11, *you* is second feminine singular, thus referring to the nation of Ephraim or its capital, Samaria. The prophet denounces the northern Israelites for forgetting (forsaking) their *Rock*, God their protector (30:29; 44:8; Deut 32:4, 15; 1 Sam 2:2; Ps 18:2, 31) and engaging in foreign worship practices. Yahweh will bring such idolatrous practices to an end (Isa 2:8–9, 18–21).

17:12–14 The prophet pronounces a woe (Hebrew *hoy*) oracle (compare 5:8–23) against unnamed *nations* and *peoples* who are looting and plundering God's people (*us*). He compares the invaders with *the raging sea* and *the roaring of great* or *surging waters*, the simile Isaiah 8:7–8 uses to describe an attack of the Assyrians. In 17:12–14, the prophet declares that Yahweh will drive Assyria away *like chaff . . . before the wind* and like *whirling dust before the storm* (NRSV). Apparently the setting is Sennacherib's siege of Jerusalem (701 BCE), when Yahweh's angel killed 185,000 Assyrian soldiers *in the evening, before the morning*—that is, in one night (Isa 37:36). *Plunder* translates Hebrew *bazaz*, recalling the symbolic name of Isaiah's son *Maher-Shalal-Hash-Baz* (Isa 8:3; 10:2, 6).

> **Illicit Worship Practices**
> *Isaiah's audience practiced many religious rites that connected them to deities other than Yahweh. For example, they induced small plants to grow rapidly in pots or baskets in ritual gardens (Isa 1:29–31; 65:3), symbolizing the rising of the deity from the netherworld. This was a form of sympathetic magic guaranteeing bountiful crops and other blessings, a practice borrowed from Babylonian Tammuz worship (Ezek 8:14) and later incorporated into the Hellenistic Adonis cult.*

18:1–7 Ethiopia controlled Egypt during the Twenty-fifth (Nubian) Dynasty (715–663 BCE). Twice during this period, western states, including Egypt under the Ethiopian Shabaka and Judah under Hezekiah, plotted to rebel against Assyria. First, in 713–711 BCE, Philistia, Judah, Egypt, and other nations rebelled against Sargon II, but he suppressed their efforts by routing Ashdod (Isa 14:28–32; 20). Some scholars think this is the historical setting for Isaiah 18 (Clements 163–64). Second, in 705–701 BCE, Babylon, Judah, Egypt, and other nations rebelled against Sennacherib. Sennacherib brought his Assyrian army to the west, overthrew Judah's forty-six fortified cities, and besieged Jerusalem. This seems to be the setting for Isaiah 18 (Childs 138).

The prophet begins by declaring *woe* (Hebrew *hoy*) against Ethiopian authorities who sent *envoys* to Jerusalem *by sea in papyrus boats* (vv. 1–2b), apparently to negotiate an alliance with Judah (and perhaps other nations) to rebel against Assyria. He counsels these *messengers* to return home and abandon their mission (v. 2c-g). Then he summons *all . . . people of the world* to watch for Yahweh's *banner* and listen for his *trumpet* (v. 3) as signals to execute his plan to overthrow the Assyrians by his own power, which should convince all nations that Yahweh alone is God.

Until the time is right, Yahweh will calmly observe human activities from his heavenly abode, like one watches motionless wisps of *shimmering heat* and *a cloud of dew* hang over a valley or hill on a windless day (v. 4), suggesting that Hezekiah and Judah do likewise. At the right moment, Yahweh will *cut off, cut down and take away* the Assyrians as a tree surgeon severs *shoots* and *spreading branches* from overgrown, cumbersome foliage, leaving the bare plants exposed to *birds of prey* and *wild animals* (vv. 5–6). This prophecy was fulfilled when Yahweh's angel killed the Assyrian soldiers as they besieged Jerusalem (Isa 37:36). Yahweh's victory over the Assyrians will convince the Ethiopians that Yahweh alone is God, and they will bring *gifts . . . to Mount Zion*, showing homage, submission, and reverence to *the Lord of hosts* (NRSV) who rules over all the earth (v. 7; Isa 45:14, 23).

19:1–20:6   While it is impossible to determine the historical setting of the oracles in Isaiah 19, Isaiah 20:1 dates chapter 20 to the year the Assyrians under Sargon II conquered Ashdod (711 BCE). These chapters contain three oracles concerning Egypt: soon Yahweh will punish Egypt (19:1–15); afterwards, Yahweh will bless Egypt (19:16–25); and, finally, Isaiah urges Hezekiah and his advisors not to trust in Egypt and Ethiopia for help against Assyria (20:1–6).

In 19:1–15, the prophet portrays Yahweh as the one who *rides on a swift cloud* (Deut 33:26; 2 Sam 22:11; Ps 68:4, 33), a common description of and title for Baal in the Ugaritic texts. Yahweh strikes terror into the *idols of Egypt* and all *the Egyptians* (v. 1).

Yahweh's coming will have extensive consequences for Egypt. First, it will affect national stability. Yahweh will *stir up Egyptian against Egyptian*, causing civil war and political unrest (v. 2), *bring their plans to nothing* (vv. 3, 12), causing them to *consult* frantically *the idols, the spirits of the dead, the mediums,* and *the spiritists* to no avail (v. 3; 8:19), and then *hand* them over to . . . *a cruel master, a fierce king* (v. 4).

Second, Yahweh's coming will cause a drought (vv. 5–6), decimating four major industries in Egypt: farming (v. 7), fishing (v. 8), linen manufacturing (v. 9), and weaving (v. 10 NRSV).

Third, Yahweh's presence will expose the counterfeit wisdom of Egypt's political *officials, counselors, wise men,* and *leaders,* who are like *head or tail, palm branch or reed* (v. 15), also terms for Ephraim's leaders in Isaiah 9:14–15. They are *fools* (vv. 11, 13), *give*

Fine Linens

Egypt was a major grower of flax for the production of linen. Since the land of Israel also grew flax suitable for manufacturing everyday clothing, the book of Isaiah must have in mind the trade in luxury textiles, in which Egypt was a significant player.

senseless advice (v. 11), *are deceived, have led Egypt astray* (v. 13), and exhibit a *spirit of dizziness. They make Egypt stagger . . . as a drunkard staggers around in his vomit* (v. 14), also a simile for Judah's prophets and priests in Isaiah 28:7–8.

Verses 16–25 abruptly shift from announcing destruction of Egypt to announcing Yahweh's delivery of that nation. Isaiah 19:16–25 contains five promises, each beginning with the phrase *in that day* and each amplifying the previous promise.

The first promise (vv. 16–17) is that Yahweh's *uplifted hand* and *plan* (NRSV) and Judah's *land* will strike *fear* and *terror* into the hearts of the Egyptians. This sounds like the announcements of devastation in verses 1–15, but verse 22 may put it in a different light. As a surgeon must hurt a sick patient by operating in order to make the patient well, so Yahweh *strikes* in order to *heal*, not to destroy (compare 1:5–6; Jer 30:12–17).

The second promise (v. 18) states that *five cities in Egypt* will *swear allegiance* to *the Lord of hosts* (NRSV), Israel's God; and they will *speak the language of Canaan* (Hebrew). This reflects the exilic or postexilic period, when Jews lived in Egypt (Jer 42–44) and converted some of their Egyptian neighbors to the worship of Yahweh.

The third promise (vv. 19–22) declares that the Jews (perhaps along with their Egyptian proselytes to Yahweh) will set up an *altar* to Yahweh somewhere deep in Egypt and a *pillar* at some place on its border as a *sign and witness* that some in Egypt worship Yahweh. When enemies oppress Egypt, and the Egyptians cry out to Yahweh, Yahweh will send a *savior and defender* to *rescue* them, as he had rescued Israel from the Egyptians in the days of Moses (Exod 6:2–8; 14:21–31). Consequently, Egyptians will come to *know* Yahweh (NRSV). "The verb 'know' . . . does not mean to have information about; . . . [but] to acknowledge fully and embrace as sovereign" (Brueggemann, *Isaiah 1–39*, 163). This will lead these Egyptians to *worship* Yahweh *with sacrifices and grain offerings* and to *make vows* to Yahweh and *keep* them (Deut 23:21–23). Yahweh will *strike*, then *heal*, the Egyptians, as a surgeon operates on a patient in order to heal that patient. When the Egyptians repent, Yahweh will answer their prayers and heal them.

The fourth promise (v. 23) is that Yahweh will make a *highway from Egypt to Assyria* (Isa 11:16; 35:8; 40:3–4 also use the highway metaphor), and the Egyptians and Assyrians will *worship* Yahweh *together*.

The fifth promise (vv. 24–25) announces ecumenical fellowship between Yahweh's chosen people and *Egypt and Assyria*, symbolic of all nations. Yahweh

---

God's Blessing to the Nations

Yahweh's purpose in choosing a people was not to exalt them above the rest of humankind (exclusivism), but to use them as his instrument to convert the rest of the world to himself (inclusivism; Isa 2:2–4). He told Abraham: through your offspring all nations on earth will be blessed (Gen 22:18; 12:1–3; 26:3–5; 28:13–14; Ps 72:17; Jer 4:1–2). Isaiah 19:24–25 repeats that promise, using the term "bless" three times.

calls Egypt *my people*, Assyria *my handiwork*, and Israel *my inheritance*, making all humanity equal before God (Amos 9:7).

Chapter 20 relates a symbolic act of Isaiah. He appears in public *stripped and barefoot for three years*, in obedience to Yahweh, before Sargon II sends his army to crush the western states, including Philistia (*the people who live on this coast*, v. 6), *Egypt*, and *Ethiopia* (NRSV), for rebelling against Assyria (v. 1; 711 BCE). This act indicates that the Assyrians will defeat the Egyptians and Ethiopians and lead them into exile *with buttocks bared* (v. 4), bringing *shame* on Egypt and those who *trusted* in *Ethiopia* (NRSV) and *boasted in* or *relied on Egypt* (vv. 5–6), statements designed to dissuade Hezekiah and his advisors from allying with Egypt against Assyria.

21:1–10   This oracle's composer addresses God's people *crushed on the threshing floor* (v. 10), that is, oppressed in Babylonian exile, announcing that Babylon will soon fall (v. 9), ending the Israelites' captivity and actuating hope. Like 13:1–14:23, the setting is the end of the Babylonian exile (540 BCE). Yahweh or his spokesperson summons *Elam* and *Media* (equivalent to the Persian Empire under Cyrus the Great; Isa 13:17) to *attack* Babylon and *end all the groaning she caused* (v. 2; Isa 44:24–45:7). Arguments defending the setting of this oracle as Sennacherib's overthrow of Merodach-baladan II of Babylon in 700 BCE are unconvincing; some scholars suggest that the oracle originated in 700 BCE, and a later prophet reapplied it to the situation in 540 BCE (Childs 148–53).

Yahweh shows the prophet a *vision* (v. 2). *An invader*, Elam and Media (v. 2), approaches like *whirlwinds sweeping through the southland* (v. 1; Jer 4:11–13) to attack *Babylon* (v. 9). Thoughts of intense suffering by Babylon overwhelm the prophet, like Yahweh's anguished empathy for Moab's misery (Isa 15:5; 16:9, 11). *Pangs seize* him, *like those of a woman in labor* (vv. 3–4; Ps 48:6; Isa 13:8; Jer 4:31; 6:24). He sees Babylon's army and *officers* sharing a banquet, oblivious to imminent danger (v. 5; see Dan 5); then he sees a *lookout* observing approaching *chariots, horses, riders* invading Babylon. The lookout shouts dolefully: *Babylon has fallen!* (vv. 6–9). Isaiah concludes the oracle by assuring Jewish exiles in Babylon that he is repeating to them what he has *heard from the* LORD *of hosts, the God of Israel* (v. 10).

21:11–12   Edom (*Dumah* is a misspelling or wordplay), or *Seir* (Num 24:18; Judg 5:4; 2 Chron 25:14), allied with Babylon to plunder Jerusalem in 587 BCE (Obad 10–14; Ps 137). Now it suffers oppression by the Persians under Cyrus the Great, who recently captured Babylon (539 BCE). Edomites ask the prophet, *a watchman* (Ezek 3:16–21): *What is left of the night?* How long will Edom's suffering continue? The prophet replies that it will end soon, but return later.

21:13–17   The NIV and NRSV interpret this oracle differently. The NIV omits the word *for* (Hebrew *ki*) beginning verse 16, separating verses 13–15 from verses 16–17. In verses 13–15, according to the NIV, the prophet urges *Dedanites* and inhabitants of *Tema* to provide *water* and *food* for unnamed *fugitives*, which an unnamed army had recently defeated in battle. In verses 16–17, the prophet tells an unnamed audience that Yahweh informed him that *within one year, Kedar* will be decimated. However, the NRSV retains the word *for* at the beginning of verse 16. According to this translation, the prophet admonishes the *inhabitants . . . of Tema* to supply *water* and *bread* to the *Dedanites* who recently fled to *the scrub of the desert plain* after *Kedar's warriors* defeated them in battle; Yahweh declares that *within a year, all the glory of Kedar will come to an end*. The NRSV more correctly reflects the Masoretic text.

Dedan, Tema, & Kedar
Dedan is a city in Arabia about 300 miles southeast of the Dead Sea; Tema, a region in Arabia about 250 miles southeast of the Dead Sea (Job 6:19; Jer 49:7–8; Ezek 25:13); and Kedar, a region in northern Arabia (Isa 60:7; Jer 2:10; Ezek 27:21). It is impossible to know the dates and occasions of the battle and of Kedar's defeat mentioned here.

22:1–14 Like Amos 1–2, Isaiah 13–23 contains oracles concerning Ephraim (17:1–11) and Judah (22:1–14, 15–25) alongside oracles concerning other nations. God considers all nations sinful and yet objects of love and care (Pss 47; 67; Isa 2:1–5; 19:16–25; Amos 9:7).

Isaiah 22:1–14 relates an oracle Isaiah initially delivered when the Assyrian army lifted the siege around Jerusalem to join Sennacherib at Libnah to fight Tirhakah and the Egyptians approaching from the south (701 BCE; 2 Kgs 19:8–9; Isa 37:8–9). The author of the book of Isaiah preserved and repeated this oracle because its message spoke afresh to the people of Jerusalem when the Babylonian army under Nebuchadnezzar II lifted the siege around Jerusalem to fight Pharaoh Hophra and the Egyptians also approaching from the south (588 BCE; Jer 34:8–22; 37:5–10).

Yahweh sent the Assyrians to punish his people for their sins (vv. 5–8a; Isa 10:5–6), expecting them to repent, using customary mourning rites (v. 12; Isa 15:2–3, 5, 8; 16:7, 9–11). Instead of trusting in *the One who planned* the Assyrian invasion (Yahweh; v. 11c-d), Judah's *leaders* and soldiers *fled* before the invaders in fear (vv. 2c-3) or relied on their military strategies, including *weapons* stored in *the Palace of the Forest* (v. 8b-c; 1 Kgs 7:2–5; 10:17), diverting the water supply inside the city walls (vv. 9c-d, 11a-b; Isa 7:3; 36:2), and tearing down houses inside the city to *strengthen the wall* where the Assyrians had made *many breaches* (vv. 9a-b, 10; Jer 33:4). And when the Assyrians lifted the siege, instead of expressing deep remorse for their sins, the people of Jerusalem went up on the *housetops, full of shoutings* (NRSV), *tumult, revelry, joy*, festive *eating* and *drinking* (vv. 1–2b, 13), inappropriate responses to Yahweh's plan and actions (Ps 51:17; Joel 2:12–17). Contrariwise, the prophet weeps bitterly over Judah's spiritual bankruptcy (v. 4) and declares the reaction Yahweh revealed to him: *Till your dying day this sin will not be atoned for* (v. 14), since the people's behavior demonstrated they had apostatized so far from Yahweh they would never return (see Luke 13:34; Rom 1:24, 26, 28).

22:15–25 A comparison of Isaiah 22:15–25 with 36:3, 22 and 37:2 suggests that Isaiah delivered the message in 22:15–25 to Shebna shortly before Sennacherib's invasion of Judah in 701 BCE. At that time, Shebna was *steward* of the royal estate (v. 15); by the time the Assyrians besieged Jerusalem, Hezekiah replaced him with Eliakim and demoted him to *secretary* (Isa 36:3, 22; 37:2). Isaiah 22:15–25 appropriately follows another oracle initially delivered during the Assyrian siege of Jerusalem (22:1–14).

Shebna held the office of steward under Hezekiah shortly before Sennacherib's invasion. Isaiah rebukes Shebna for arrogance, which led him to abuse his office by misdirecting government funds to have a *grave* hewn out for himself in a wealthy section of Jerusalem (v. 16) and using *splendid chariots* for travel (v. 18). Isaiah says that Yahweh will *throw* him into *a large country* (perhaps have him carried into Assyria as a prisoner), where he will die as a *disgrace* to his master's (Hezekiah's) house (vv. 17–18), thus removing him from his *office* (v. 19).

> **The Royal Steward**
> *Solomon established the political office of* steward *as one* who is in charge of the palace (literally *"over the house"; verse 15), sometimes called* father *(v. 21; Gen 45:8; Isa 9:6) or he who wears* on his shoulder the key to the house of David (*v. 22), terms that describe one who governs the public and private possessions and functions of the king (Gen 41:41–45; 1 Kgs 4:6; 16:9; 2 Kgs 10:5; 2 Chron 19:11).*

Yahweh will *hand* Shebna's *authority over to Eliakim* (vv. 20–23). However, slowly but surely, Eliakim will commit nepotism, putting members of *his* own *family* in high governmental positions, which will ultimately lead to his own downfall (vv. 24–25).

23:1–18 The prophet announces that Yahweh (vv. 8–9, 11–12) will punish Phoenicia (that is, *Sidon* [vv. 2, 4, 12] and *Tyre* [vv. 5, 8, 13, 15, 17]), the *inhabitants of the coast* (vv. 2, 6 NRSV), for their arrogance (vv. 7, 9, 12). Yahweh will *bring low* and *humble* a region that is influential, powerful, and wealthy (vv. 8–9).

Scholars suggest several historical backgrounds for this oracle. Verse 13 indicates that the setting is the Babylonian siege of Tyre under Nebuchadnezzar II (585–573 BCE; see Jer 27:3–7; Ezek 26–28), who devastated the mainland portion of Tyre (Childs 165–67). Alexander the Great later destroyed its island portion (332 BCE).

> **Phoenicia**
> *The cities on the coast of what is now Lebanon were major ports connecting the Near East with the central and western Mediterranean. Tyre, in particular, served as the major point of commerce for the entire world of ancient Israel.*

Tyre's fall adversely affects Phoenicia's merchant trading with *Tarshish*, that is, Tartessos in southern Spain (vv. 1, 6, 10, 14), as well as with *Egypt* (vv. 3, 5, 10), *Cyprus* (vv. 1, 12), and other Mediterranean ports. But after *seventy years* (a normal human lifetime [Ps 90:10] but also the period of Babylonian captivity [Jer 25:11–12]), Yahweh will restore Tyre so that she will *ply her trade with all the kingdoms on the face of the earth as a prostitute* now aged and *forgotten* (vv. 15–17); however, now *her profit and her earnings* will help sustain Yahweh's people returned from exile (v. 18; Isa 18:7).

The meaning of Isaiah 24–27 is difficult. Hebrew *'erets* can mean "earth," "land," or "ground." The identity of the *city* (sometimes wicked; sometimes righteous) varies from passage to passage. Different voices speak to different audiences with different messages and purposes. The overall thrust of these chapters suggests their author was a Jew living in the last half of the fifth century BCE in Judah, addressing a small community of fellow believers who felt overwhelmed by their Persian overlords, to inspire them to trust in Yahweh as creator, sustainer, and controller of heaven and earth. A God who can control the universe can also deliver a struggling faith community. Isaiah 24–27 falls into six sections: Yahweh will punish the wicked of both heaven and earth (24:1–23); Yahweh will save earth's penitent (25:1–12); the faithful remnant prays that Yahweh will deliver his people (26:1–27:1); Yahweh will revive his vineyard (27:2–6); Yahweh will restore North Israel (27:7–11); and Yahweh will gather faithful exiles (27:12–13).

24:1–23 The prophet declares that Yahweh *is about to lay waste the earth* and all its inhabitants (vv. 1–3) because they have *broken the everlasting covenant* (vv. 5, 20c) Yahweh made with Noah and thus with the whole earth (Gen 9:1–17); even *the heavens languish* (v. 4 NRSV). Yahweh will remove all joy and pleasure from the earth (vv. 6–13), desolating *the ruined city* (vv. 10, 12), that is, all worldly cities: "every concentration of human power that functions effectively but is rooted in disobedience and defiance of Yahweh" (Brueggemann, *Isaiah 1–39*, 192). Voices rise *from the west,* and the prophet summons peoples *in the east* to join them in praising Yahweh for punishing the wicked (vv. 14–16b); but the prophet cannot join this chorus, because earth's sins and devastation disturb him too much (v. 16c–f). No one can escape Yahweh's punishment. God will gather the wicked of heaven and earth, *like prisoners bound in a dungeon* (Mic 4:11–13), and punish them *after many days* (vv. 17–23b). Then *the Lord of hosts* (NRSV) *will reign on Mount Zion,* and *before his elders . . . manifest his glory* (v. 23c–e NRSV) as they strive to lead the small community of returned exiles *in Jerusalem* in faithful service to Yahweh.

The Wicked in Heaven

The Bible often speaks of wicked forces "in heaven," that is, forces of larger than ordinary strength and scope. Examples of such forces can include the prince of Persia (Dan 10:13, 20), the prince of Greece (Dan 10:20), "the cosmic powers of this present darkness," "the spiritual forces of evil in the heavenly places" (compare Eph 6:12 NRSV), among others.

25:1–12 Yahweh punishes to remove corruption—to refine, not to annihilate. After punishing heaven's and earth's wicked (24:1–23), God will save earth's penitent. The faithful community or its representative (*I,* verse 1), including *all* *peoples* (vv. 3, 6–7), *praise* Yahweh for punishing *the fortified town* (v. 2; 24:10, 12)—that is, all self-centered cities. Yahweh *planned* (14:26–27; 19:12, 17; 22:11; 23:8–9) this *long ago* (v. 1). Such mighty deeds will lead people from all nations to *honor* and *revere* that God (v. 3) who has been *a refuge for the poor* and *needy* from *the ruthless* (vv. 4–5).

Yahweh will prepare a sumptuous banquet *on this mountain* (that is, Zion; verses 6–7) for *all peoples* (2:2–4; 19:23–25), and then will *destroy* the *shroud* or *sheet* of death and mourning which covers all peoples, *swallow up death forever*, and *wipe away the tears from all faces*. The remnant of the nations will praise Yahweh for saving those who *trusted in him* (vv. 6–10a).

Simultaneously, Yahweh will *trample down* Moab, "a figure for all detested powers that resist Yahweh and abuse Yahweh's people" (Brueggemann, *Isaiah 1–39*, 201), for its *pride* (16:6; 13:11, 19; 14:11–14; 23:9, 12), a fate from which it cannot escape, no matter how hard it tries (vv. 10b–12).

26:1–27:1   Orally uttered, *in that day* in 26:1, 27:1, 2, 12, 13 indicates to hearers that Isaiah 24–27 envisions the same future period. When Yahweh punishes heaven's and earth's wicked and restores earth's penitent (chapters 24–25), the restored (*we*: 26:1; *trust* in 26:4 is plural) will sing songs of praise (26:1–6), exalt and commit themselves to prayer (26:7–19), and wait for the punishment of the wicked (26:20–27:1).

According to 26:1–6, in their song, *the righteous nation . . . that keeps faith* (v. 2) or *trusts* (vv. 3–4) in Yahweh will declare that it has *a strong city* in *Judah*, Jerusalem (v. 1; 24:23; 25:6–7), which shall enjoy *peace* (v. 3) because Yahweh protects it. Conversely, Yahweh will *humble the lofty city* (vv. 5–6), *the city of chaos* (24:10, 12 NRSV), and *the fortified town* (25:2)—that is, all worldly cities.

In their prayer (26:7–19), the restored extol Yahweh for disciplining them because they had *not brought salvation to the earth* through example and teaching (vv. 16–18), vindicating *the righteous* (v. 7), that is, the penitent, and thereby expanding *the nation* (vv. 15, 19). They will applaud Yahweh for their accomplishments (v. 12) and for overthrowing their oppressors (v. 14), expressing *desire* to serve and honor Yahweh alone (vv. 8–9b, 13), and beseeching Yahweh to *consume* those who persist in wickedness (vv. 10–11).

Verses 9c–11 declare that *the people of the world learn righteousness* by observing Yahweh's *judgments* on the wicked (Ps 65:5–8; Amos 3:9–11). Yahweh's genuine servants never take credit for their accomplishments but recognize that their achievements are Yahweh's doing (v. 12). The metaphor of the pregnant woman experiencing labor (vv. 17–18) to denote penitence and grief occurs often in the Old Testament (13:8; Jer 4:31; 6:24). Verse 19 does not announce physical resurrection of individuals after death, but the re-enlivening, reviving, and restoring of penitent Jewish exiles to their homeland to resume faithful service to Yahweh (Ezek 37:1–14). Yahweh will rejuvenate his dejected people *like the dew* rejuvenates parched grass (Mic 5:7).

Accordingly, the prophet admonishes Yahweh's faithful remnant to wait for Yahweh to finish destroying evil persons and the power of evil itself, the mythological monster *Leviathan* (compare Ps 74:12–14).

The Leviathan

Leviathan, or the sea monster, functions primarily as a symbol of chaos and terror in the Bible. Yet this fearsome creature also falls under the control of Yahweh. Thus the reader need not fear it at all, but can express gratitude and awe before God, who defends the human race from its worst nightmares.

27:2–6 The prophet summons hearers (plural) to *sing* about Yahweh's vineyard (v. 2). Yahweh promises to reverse the punishment of the vineyard announced in 5:1–7. Previously Yahweh removed the hedge and broke down the wall around his vineyard, abandoning it to vagabonds (5:5), but now God will *watch over* and *guard it day and night* to prevent its harm (27:3). Reversing the previous command to the clouds not to rain on it (5:6), God will now *water it continually* (27:3). Previously angry with the vineyard (5:5–6), God now will *not* be *angry* (27:4). Previously he caused it to be overgrown with briers and thorns (5:6); now if his vineyard produces *briers and thorns*, he will go to battle against it, hoping it will seek protection and make peace (27:4–5 NRSV). Ultimately, the penitent remnant of *Jacob will take root, bud and blossom and fill all the world with fruit* (27:6), suggesting efforts by true Israelites to convert other nations to Yahweh (2:2–4; 19:23–25; 45:22–23).

27:7–11 The meaning of Isaiah 27:7–11 is uncertain. *Jacob* may mean northern Israel. *The fortified city* (v. 10) apparently refers to Samaria, which must destroy its *altar stones, Asherah poles*, and *incense altars* (typical elements of northern Israelite worship; see 2 Kgs 17:5–18) to *atone for* its *guilt* so that Yahweh can *remove* its *sin* (v. 9). Otherwise, Yahweh will have *no compassion on* them (v. 11). Yahweh punished northern Israel, but less severely than he did the Assyrians (vv. 7–8; compare 10:16–19; 14:24–27).

27:12–13 Yahweh will *thresh* the exiles (v. 8), separating wheat (true Israelites) from chaff (counterfeit Israelites); cause a *great trumpet* to *sound*, summoning the people to a great feast; and *gather* penitent, faithful exiles from *Assyria* and *Egypt to worship the Lord on the holy mountain in Jerusalem*.

YAHWEH PUNISHES & RESTORES THE PEOPLE THROUGH INVASION & EXILE · 28:1–39:8

In chapters 28–33, the prophet directs the first five *woes* (28; 29:1–14, 15–24; 30; 31–32) against Hezekiah and Judah for allying with Egypt against Assyria, and the last *woe* against Assyria (33). In each case, beyond the punishment, Yahweh promises redemption for the faithful remnant.

28:1–29 This chapter has three parts: Yahweh will punish *Ephraim*, or northern Israel, and save *the remnant* (vv. 1–6); Yahweh will punish Judah for allying with Egypt but deliver those who *trust* in him (vv. 7–22); and Yahweh punishes to restore, not to destroy (vv. 23–29).

The Structure of Isaiah

Three concepts hold together Isaiah 28–39: Yahweh punishes the people to purify them, not to destroy them; Yahweh works in parallel ways through Sennacherib's invasion and the Babylonian exile; the people must trust Yahweh, not in foreign allies and everything associated with them. These chapters fall into three parts: six "woe" sections (chapters 28–33); Yahweh will punish the nations, especially Edom, and restore Israel's faithful remnant (chapters 34–35); a narrative concerning Sennacherib's invasion and siege of Jerusalem and Yahweh's deliverance of the city (chapters 36–37); and Hezekiah's illness and recovery (chapters 38–39). The author combines materials from earlier times and circumstances and inserts some of his own, but "the crucial exegetical question remains . . . whether one can in the end discern any element of coherence in the rendering of the chapters in their final form" (Childs 200).

Probably speaking to Judean leaders in about 703 BCE, verses 1–6 repeat part of an oracle delivered originally to northern Israelite leaders about 724 BCE. Yahweh will punish *Ephraim* because of the *pride* of the *wreath* resting on its head, that is, its capital, Samaria (Isa 7:9). Punishment especially falls on Ephraim's self-indulgent leaders, who are *gluttons* (NRSV), *bloated with rich food*, and *drunkards* (vv. 1–4). Yahweh will send *one who is powerful and strong* (v. 2), namely, Assyria (Isa 8:7) under Shalmaneser V (2 Kgs 17:1–6), *like a storm* (v. 2) and like one eating *a first-ripe fig* (v. 4; Isa 17:4–6). Judean leaders would have approved of this message. The next two verses add that Yahweh will be *a beautiful wreath for the remnant of his people* (v. 5) and *a spirit of justice* to its rulers (v. 6).

Suddenly, in verses 7–22, Isaiah turns on Judean *priests and prophets*, accusing *these also* of being drunkards like their northern counterparts (vv. 7–8). A spokesman for these religious leaders angrily asks his associates: *Who is he* (that is, Isaiah) *trying to teach*? Does he think we are *children* recently *weaned* that he addresses us so? He acts like one trying to teach little children the alphabet.

Isaiah immediately throws his opponents' words in their teeth. Yahweh will indeed *speak to this people* (Judah), not in Hebrew, but *with foreign lips and strange tongues*, that is the Assyrian dialect of Akkadian. Since the Judeans have rejected *rest* based on trust in Yahweh (30:15), Yahweh will teach them the ABCs of his response to sin—that is, punishment by invaders who speak a foreign language (vv. 11–13).

Teaching Children the Alphabet

Verse 10 plays on two letters of the Hebrew alphabet, tsadhe and qoph, apparently mimicking the chants of schoolchildren (Clements 228; Brueggemann, Isaiah 1–39, 223; vv. 9–10).

Isaiah denounces those who *rule* Yahweh's people for making *a covenant with death* (alliance with Egypt; 30:1–7; 31:1–3) to protect themselves from Assyrian invaders, because Yahweh will send *an overwhelming scourge*, a storm with much *hail* and rain—that is, Assyria—to punish the rebellious people

(vv. 14–15, 17c–19; 8:7–8). Yahweh offers a safe haven from this storm, using the metaphor of a building. Its *foundation* is *a precious cornerstone*, bearing the inscription: *One who trusts will not panic* (NRSV; 7:9; 30:15; 31:1). The *measuring line* and *plumb line* for constructing its walls and roof are *justice* and *righteousness* (vv. 16–17b; 1:21, 27; 5:7, 16; 32:1, 16; 33:5; 59:9, 11, 14). Egypt gives no protection; it is like a *bed* that is *too short* and a *blanket* that is *too narrow* (v. 20). Yahweh, who defeated the Philistines before the Israelites led by David at *Mount Perazim* (2 Sam 5:17–25), and who defeated the king of Jerusalem and his Canaanite allies before the Israelites led by Joshua in the *Valley of Gibeon*, where the sun stood still (Josh 10:1–15), will do a *strange work* (contrast *strange tongues*, v. 11) by defeating the Judeans before the Assyrians. Nothing, including alliance with Egypt, can change the *destruction* Yahweh has *decreed against the whole land* (vv. 21–22).

In verses 23–29, the words *Listen, hear, pay attention* (plural) demonstrate that the composer of the book of Isaiah intended for professional performers or readers to present it orally to gathered worship audiences, and that verses 23–29 proclaim the core message of this composition. The speaker relates two similar parables in wisdom style. In the first, Yahweh is like a *farmer* who *plows soil* to prepare it for *planting* seed at strategic places to get maximum yield (vv. 24–26). In the second, Yahweh is like a skilled processor who prepares each foodstuff for consumption using the procedure suitable to that grain: beating *caraway with a rod* and *cummin with a stick*, and grinding *grain to make bread* (vv. 27–29). Yahweh's judgment is violent, like plowing and processing, but necessary to produce proper spiritual growth in people's hearts and lives, like a farmer produces good crops, or a processor, good consumer products. Accordingly, the fundamental message of the book of Isaiah is that Yahweh punishes sinners (including Israel), using means suitable to their nature and temperament, seeking not to destroy, but to refine for spiritual maturity, productivity, and divine blessing.

Agricultural Imagery

The Bible often uses agricultural imagery, which was familiar to ancient audiences of farmers. Since farming both destroys and creates, and involves both hard work and joyful productivity, it supplies numerous opportunities for spiritual and moral reflection.

29:1–14 The second woe contains two parts: Yahweh will send the Assyrians to besiege Jerusalem but will ultimately deliver the city (vv. 1–8); and the prophet denounces Jerusalem's prophets for being blind to Yahweh's ways and Jerusalem's citizens for counterfeit worship (vv. 9–14).

In verses 1–8, Yahweh announces a siege of *Ariel*, the altar hearth, which refers to the altar of burnt offering before the temple (Ezek 43:15–16) in Jerusalem. Jerusalem had previously been besieged by David when he captured it from the Jebusites (2 Sam 5:6–9). Now, a second seige will take place: Sennacherib's siege of Jerusalem (701 BCE). But just when the Assyrians think Jerusalem will fall, *as when a hungry man dreams that he is eating, but he awakens, and his hunger remains, suddenly, in an instant, the* LORD *of hosts* (NRSV) will deliver *Mount Zion* (37:36).

In the conclusion of this oracle (vv. 9–14), the prophet condemns Jerusalem's *prophets*, or *seers*, for their inability to understand the *vision* Yahweh revealed concerning Jerusalem, because they are spiritually *blind, drunk,* and asleep. The text also criticizes Jerusalem's inhabitants for "follow[ing] the rules and regulations of prescribed piety...lacking in...serious commitment of the heart" (Brueggemann, *Isaiah 1–39*, 235). At this point in Isaiah 28–32, this woe oracle may denounce Jerusalem's leaders and people for sending to Egypt for help rather than trusting in Yahweh.

29:15–24   The third woe oracle contains a short section of condemnation (vv. 15–16) and a long section of assurance (vv. 17–24).

In verses 15–16, Isaiah reproves Hezekiah and his counselors for allying with Egypt to protect Judah from Assyria (30:1–7; 31:1–3). They try to *hide* their *plan* from Yahweh by keeping their intentions from Isaiah. How naïve of *what is formed* (*the clay pot* represents human beings) to think that he *who formed it* (*the potter,* that is, Yahweh: 45:9; 64:8; Jer 18:1–6) is unaware of its activities!

In verses 17–24, Yahweh proclaims hope for the remnant of penitent believers *in a very short time* (v. 5): the *deaf, blind, humble,* and *needy,* whom Judah's *ruthless, mockers,* and *all who have an eye for evil* oppress by giving *false testimony* against them in court. Yahweh sent the Assyrians against Judah to punish it for its rampant injustice against the poor and afflicted (10:1–6). Soon, Assyria's work will end: Judean oppressors will fall, and innocent victims will enjoy vindication, leading them to *rejoice in, acknowledge the holiness of,* and *stand in awe of the Holy One of Israel* (or *Jacob*). Then those trying to serve Yahweh who are *wayward in spirit* and *complain* against Yahweh because Assyria invaded the land will *gain understanding,* or *accept instruction,* by observing how Yahweh works (28:23–29).

30:1–33   In this fourth woe oracle, the prophet denounces Hezekiah and his advisors for allying with Egypt against invading Assyrians under Sennacherib in 701 BCE (vv. 1–17). He then assures Yahweh's true followers that Judah will survive the Assyrians (vv. 18–33). Those who trust in Yahweh have no need for Egypt.

When Isaiah delivers this oracle, Hezekiah has already sent envoys to Egypt carrying tribute to persuade Pharaoh Shebitku to ally with Judah against Assyrian invaders (vv. 1–2); the envoys have traveled through dangerous terrain to avoid detection (v. 6); some negotiate *in Zoan,* while others *have arrived in Hanes* for consultations (v. 4). Such efforts contradict Yahweh's *plans* (v. 1). Egypt's powerlessness (vv. 5, 7) suggests the symbolic name: *Rahab the*

Israel & Egypt in Isaiah's Day
During Isaiah's time, Egypt fell under the rule of the Cushites, from northern Sudan. Their Twenty-fifth Dynasty competed with Assyria for domination of Palestine, as well. Judah, as a minor state between two superpowers, tried to negotiate its own survival. Isaiah criticized this political gamesmanship as both unwise and unfaithful to Yahweh.

Do-Nothing (v. 7). *Pharaoh's protection*, symbolized as *Egypt's shade*, will bring *only shame and disgrace* to Judah (vv. 3, 5).

Hezekiah and his advisors ignore Yahweh's message. Yahweh instructs Isaiah to *write it on a tablet for them* so that when Egypt fails and Yahweh delivers Judah's remnant, Isaiah's hearers cannot deny that Yahweh warned them, but they refused *to listen* (vv. 8–11). Because they *rejected this message* and *depended on* Egypt, they will *collapse like a high wall* and *break in pieces like pottery* (vv. 12–14). Yahweh offered them *salvation* and *strength* through *repentance, rest, quietness, and trust* in him, "the heart of Isaiah's message of trust in God through a quiet, unshakeable faith" (Childs 226), but they preferred to trust in *horses*, representing military might (Pss 20:7; 33:17; 147:10–11).

By sending Assyria to devastate Judah for its sins (10:5–6), Yahweh gave them *the bread of adversity and the water of affliction* (v. 20) and *inflicted* them with *bruises* and *wounds* (v. 26; 1:5–6; Jer 30:12–15), as a *Teacher* (v. 20; Job 35:10–11; 36:21–22) attempting to remove their sin (Isa 6:5–7) and humble them to repentance (v. 22). Yahweh's severe blows were meant *to be gracious* and *to show mercy* so his faithful ones would *wait for* (or hope) in him (vv. 18–19).

The future of God's people is bright. Yahweh will *send rain*, increase crops, multiply livestock, and heal the battered people (vv. 23–26). Further, Yahweh will come as *a consuming fire* and *a rushing torrent, with cloudburst, thunderstorm and hail* (vv. 28, 30) to *shatter* Assyria (v. 31) and overthrow her *king* (v. 33), Sennacherib, referring to the Lord's slaughter of 185,000 Assyrian soldiers in one night to end Jerusalem's siege (37:36), causing joyous celebration on *the mountain of the Lord* (vv. 29, 32). Jews returning from Babylonian exile in the last half of the fifth century BCE would have readily understood the relevance of Isaiah 30's message to their own situation.

The "Good Leader"

The Bible speaks often of the goals and character traits of good leaders. All biblical traditions agree that a leader's primary responsibility is the protection of the vulnerable, particularly of widows, orphans, the poor, and resident aliens. Leaders who use their power for self-aggrandizement or the building of military might come under divine judgment (see Deut 17:14–20; Ps 101; and many texts in the prophets).

31:1–32:20 The fifth woe oracle contains two parts: it is futile for Hezekiah and his advisors to seek Egypt's protection, because Yahweh will deliver the people from Assyria and establish a king and rulers to govern them with justice and righteousness (31:1–32:8); and Yahweh will devastate Jerusalem, with its complacent women, until the divine spirit instills justice and righteousness in the people (32:9–20).

In 31:1–32:8, Isaiah denounces Hezekiah and his associates because they *go down to Egypt for help*, *rely on horses*, and *trust in . . . chariots* rather than relying on Yahweh (31:1–3; 30:1–7). Yahweh will protect Jerusalem from Assyria *as a lion* protects his slaughtered prey from shepherds, and *like birds hovering overhead* protect their young on the nest

(Luke 13:34); accordingly, Isaiah urges Yahweh's people to return (31:4–7). Further, Yahweh will overthrow the Assyrians: *a sword, not of mortals, will devour them* (31:8–9; 30:31–33; 37:36).

Then Yahweh will establish a new government in Judah, a *king* (Hezekiah after he repented for relying on Egypt and sought Yahweh's help [37:8–20]) and *rulers* who will maintain *righteousness* and *justice* (5:7, 16; 9:7; 28:17; 59:9, 14), providing protection and relief to the oppressed (vv. 1–2). The wise leader of Yahweh's people will *see, hear, know, understand, be fluent and clear,* and *make noble plans* with regard to Yahweh and his fellow human beings (vv. 3–5, 8), shaming *the fool* whose *mind is busy with evil* to afflict the defenseless, depriving *the hungry* of food and *the thirsty* of *water*, and destroying *the poor* and *needy with lies* in court (vv. 6–7; 1:16–17, 23; 10:1–4).

In 32:9–20, the prophet announces affliction on the rich, powerful, *complacent* Judean women *who feel secure*, who receive and maintain their enviable position in society at the expense of the oppressed and mistreated, along with the securities on which they depend: good *harvest* (vv. 10, 12–13b), *houses of merriment* (v. 13c), *fortress, citadel and watchtower* (v. 14; 3:16–4:1; Amos 4:1–3).

This affliction will continue *until a spirit* (or *power*, Luke 1:17) *from on high is poured out* (NRSV) on Yahweh's (*my*) people (v. 18), transforming *the desert* into *a fertile field* (v. 15), producing abundant crops and bountiful grazing for *oxen and donkeys* (v. 20), nullifying *the forest* and *the city* as exponents of wealth and power and corruption (v. 19), and promoting *justice* and *righteousness* between people as harbingers of *peace, quietness,* and *trust* (vv. 16–18 NRSV).

33:1–24   The sixth woe oracle is a liturgy designed for oral presentation by six trained speakers, or singers, before a worshiping community. The first orator (v. 1) notifies Assyria (*destroyer*) that when Yahweh finishes using it to punish his people, he will *destroy* it (10:5–19). The second spokesperson (vv. 2–6), representing the faith community (*we, us, our*), prays that Yahweh will give the people strength and protection daily (v. 2), and be *the stability of your* (the community's) *times* (NRSV), *a rich store of salvation and wisdom and knowledge* (v. 6a–b), as formerly (vv. 3–5 refer to Yahweh's mighty acts in the past [NRSV], not the future [contrary to NIV]), filling *Zion with justice and righteousness* (v. 5b; 5:16; 9:7; 32:1, 16). *The fear of the Lord* means genuine reverence for Yahweh (as opposed to false reverence [see 29:13]) and connects Yahweh's people with this *treasure* (v. 6c).

The third speaker (vv. 7–9) describes an extensive drought in northern Israel—*Lebanon, Sharon, Bashan, Carmel* (or "the whole land")—as Yahweh's punishment of Judean aristocrats for rejecting *envoys of peace* and breaking a *treaty* (that is, not honoring business agreements) and for defrauding the poor (5:22–23; 10:1–4; 32:6–7).

The fourth voice (vv. 10–12) is Yahweh's through the prophet (*says the Lord*), reacting to the previous speaker's description of Judah's dismal situation. Yahweh will *arise, be exalted, be lifted up* (2:11, 17, 19, 21; 31:2). Judah's leaders' corruption indicates they have no spiritual substance but *conceive chaff* and *give birth to straw, so that their own breath is a fire that consumes* them, as well as *the peoples* (5:24; 30:27–30).

The fifth orator (vv. 13–16) is also Yahweh, now addressing worshipers seeking entrance into the Jerusalem temple. These verses contain an "entrance liturgy," or "Torah liturgy," similar to Psalms 15 and 24. First, Yahweh summons those who are *far away* and those who are *near* spiritually (29:13) to *hear* of Yahweh's deeds and acknowledge them, as worship leaders proclaim them before the assembly (Pss 66:5–20; 105:1–6). Then *sinners* and the *godless* who have come with penitent hearts ask how they can survive Yahweh's *devouring fire* (vv. 11–12).

Yahweh's Requirements for the Righteous
Yahweh enumerates six qualities one must possess to survive. One must: walk righteously; speak what is right (Ps 15:2); reject gain from extortion (Exod 22:25; Lev 25:35–37); decline to accept bribes (1:23; 5:23; compare Deut 16:19; Ps 15:5; Prov 15:27); refuse to participate in plots of murder or in schemes to kill or oppress others (Prov 1:10–19); and avoid contemplating evil (Mic 2:1–2). Such people will enjoy Yahweh's security and provisions.

The sixth spokesperson (vv. 17–24) announces that Yahweh will revive and restore the destitute people. God will enthrone a righteous *king* (v. 17; 32:1), perhaps the penitent Hezekiah (37:1–7, 14–32), Josiah (2 Kgs 22–23), or an ideal descendant of David (Jer 33:14–26). Yahweh will also remove the Assyrian invaders (vv. 18–19; 28:11; 30:31–33; 31:8–9), make Jerusalem a *peaceful* and secure *abode* (vv. 20–21), be the people's *judge* (or deliverer; Judg 3:9–10, 15; 11:27), *ruler* (NRSV) and *king* (v. 22; 6:1, 5). God will give the remnant the enemies' *spoils* (Hebrew *shalal*) and *plunder* (Hebrew *bazezu*) (Isaiah here again makes wordplay on the name *Maher-Shalal-Hash-Baz* [see also 8:1, 3; 10:2, 6]) in spite of the remnant's weakness (v. 23), and *forgive those who dwell* in *Zion* of their *sins* (v. 24). *Our* (vv. 20, 21, 22) and *us* (v. 22) refer to the prophet and his comrades. *Your* (vv. 17, 18, 20, 23), *you* (vv. 19), and *look* (v. 20; masculine singular) are the whole assembly addressed as one individual.

34:1–35:10 The setting of Isaiah 34–35 is near the end of the Babylonian exile (540–536 BCE) or later; this is first evident because 34:5–17 announces the destruction of Edom, who helped Babylon overthrow Jerusalem in 587 BCE, using language like Obadiah 1–16; Jeremiah 49:7–22; Ezekiel 25:12–14; Psalm 137:7; and second, because 35:3–4 and 8–10 proclaim that Judean exiles in Babylon will return to Zion, which occurred under Zerubbabel and Joshua in 536 BCE (Ezra 1:1–2:2), Ezra in 458 BCE (Ezra 7:1–10), and Nehemiah in 445 and 433 BCE (Neh 2:1–16; 13:4–9). Such Scriptures use the highway metaphor, which is characteristic of passages comparing the return from Babylon (the "second exodus") with the exodus from Egypt (Isa 11:15–16; 40:3–5; 43:14–21). Blenkinsopp (*Isaiah 1–39*, 450, 456) details striking contrasts between Isaiah 34 and 35, demonstrating the coherence of these chapters. Isaiah 34–35 announces that Yahweh will punish the wicked of both heaven and earth (especially Edom [34:1–17]) and restore Zion's faithful remnant (35:1–10).

In 34:1–4, the prophet declares that Yahweh is *angry with all nations, peoples, earth, world,* and *all the host of heaven* (that is, rebellious angels) (vv. 4–5; 24:21–23; Dan 10:13, 20–21; Matt 25:41; Eph 6:12; Rev 12:7–9) and *will give them over to slaughter.*

Specifically, Yahweh will destroy *Edom* (vv. 5, 6, 9, 11; 63:1–6) as a priest slaughters a lamb for *sacrifice* (vv. 6–7; Zeph 1:7–8; Jer 46:10). Yahweh has a *day of vengeance* and *retribution* (v. 8; 61:2; 63:4; Jer 46:10) against Edom, bringing complete *desolation* so that only *thorns, nettles, brambles* (v. 13a–b; 7:23–25; 9:18; 10:17), wild animals, and birds can live there (vv. 9–15). Human beings can inhabit it no longer, but will give it the symbolic name *No Kingdom There* (v. 12 NRSV). For confirmation, hearers may consult *the book of the* LORD (NRSV), where Yahweh decreed that these creatures would inhabit Edom (vv. 16–17).

In bold contrast to Isaiah 34's description of the desolation Yahweh will bring on Edom, chapter 35 announces Yahweh's redemption for Zion's faithful remnant. This redemption is presented in an alternating pattern which describes Yahweh as transforming the wilderness (A) and Yahweh as restoring the weak, exiled, faithful devotees of Zion into a fertile land (B):

A   verses 1–2
B   verses 3–6b
A' verses 6c-7
B' verses 8–10

According to 35:1–2, Yahweh will change the *desert, parched land,* or *wilderness* into the *glory* or *splendor* of Yahweh manifested in *Lebanon, Carmel and Sharon* (33:9), producing great joy. In verses 3–6b, the prophet encourages despondent Judean exiles in Babylon (plural imperatives): *strengthen* your *feeble hands, steady* your *knees that give way* (Heb 12:12–13), and *say to* the *fearful, Be strong, do not fear; your God will come . . . to save you;* he further promises that Yahweh will give sight to *the blind,* hearing to *the deaf,* agility to *the lame,* and speech to *the dumb.*

According to verses 6c–7, Yahweh will cause abundant *water* to *gush forth* in the *wilderness,* or *desert,* just as the Israelites received water from the rock (Exod 17:1–7; Num 20:1–13), and magnificent plants will grow there (41:17–20).

Verses 8–10 depict Yahweh preparing a *highway* in the wilderness, *the Way of Holiness,* not for *the unclean* (6:5; 52:1, 11) or *wicked fools,* but *only the redeemed, the ransomed of the Lord,* Judean exiles who have genuinely repented and turned to Yahweh (1:27–28; 57:14–15). They will return to *Zion* with great *joy,* free from threatening dangers on the road (11:11–16; 40:3–5; 51:11; 65:17–25).

36:1–39:8   Isaiah 36–39 parallel 2 Kings 18–20 and 2 Chronicles 32, omitting some sections (notably 2 Kgs 18:14–16), adding others (significantly, Isa 38:9–20), and changing the order of others (Isa 38:21–22 appears after verse 20,

Critical Issues in Isaiah 36–39

Space allows only brief discussion of the critical issues posed by Isaiah 36–39. First, how are 2 Kings 18–20 and Isaiah 36–39 related? Since both accounts are theologically relevant in their present positions in these two books, the authors probably adapted a common tradition, either oral or written, to their own respective compositions (Childs 260–62).

Second, how many sources lie behind the account of Sennacherib's invasion in 2 Kings 18–19 and Isaiah 36–37? John Bright thinks these chapters present one account of two invasions: one in 701 BCE and one in 688 BCE (Bright 298–309). Most scholars believe these chapters combine three accounts: A (2 Kgs 18:14–16), B1 (2 Kgs 18:17–19:9a = Isa 36:1–37:9a), and B2 (2 Kgs 19:9b–35 = Isa 37:9b–36). Another possibility is that Isaiah 36–37 reports one Assyrian siege of Jerusalem, which the Assyrians lifted briefly to fight against the Egyptians.

Third, why are Isaiah chapters 36–39 in their present position in the book? Most scholars agree they function as the bridge from the Assyrian to the Babylonian periods (chapters 40–55) in the book of Isaiah.

but belongs after verse 6, as 2 Kings 20 and common sense demonstrate). Isaiah 36–39 breaks down as follows: Assyria overthrows Judah's fortified cities and besieges Jerusalem (36:1–37:7); the Assyrians withdraw to Libnah to encounter the Egyptians (37:8–9a); the Assyrians resume the siege of Jerusalem; Yahweh's angel kills 185,000 Assyrian soldiers (37:9b–38); Yahweh heals Hezekiah (38); and Judah and Babylon ally against Assyria (39).

36:1–37:7 According to 36:1, in 701 BCE *Sennacherib king of Assyria* devastated the forty-six *fortified cities of Judah* (Pritchard 287–88). According to verses 2–21, Sennacherib sent his *field commander with a large army from Lachish* near the Mediterranean to Jerusalem to negotiate with Hezekiah's officials: *Eliakim the palace administrator, Shebna the secretary, and Joah the recorder.* The Assyrian field commander chides Hezekiah and Judah for having *confidence* in *strategy and military strength* (such as *chariots and horsemen*, *Egypt*, and *Yahweh*, who, according to the field commander, are no match for Assyria). In fact, he asserts, *The Lord himself told me to march against this country and destroy it*, which Isaiah 10:6 confirms (Pharaoh Neco of Egypt made a similar claim to Josiah, 2 Chron 35:21). Hezekiah's officials request that the field commander speak in *Aramaic*, fearing he is tearing down the morale of Judean soldiers on Jerusalem's walls by speaking in Hebrew (vv. 2–11).

The field commander, however, responds loudly in Hebrew, admonishing the Judean soldiers not to *trust in* Hezekiah or Yahweh, boasting that no *god of any nation* had successfully resisted *the king of Assyria*, including *Samaria* (which allegedly served

The Punishment of the Gods
Ancient Near Eastern nations believed the gods of a city or nation gave that city or nation to invading armies to punish their followers for disloyalty or sin. Thus Babylon's priests gave Babylon to Cyrus without a battle.

Yahweh), concluding: *how then can the Lord deliver Jerusalem from my hand*? The soldiers remain silent in obedience to Hezekiah's instruction (vv. 12–21).

Hezekiah's officials report the field commander's words. Hezekiah laments, tearing his clothes (Jer 36:24; Ezra 9:3) and wearing *sackcloth* (2 Sam 3:31; 1 Kgs 21:27), as do his officials. Hezekiah sends his officials to *Isaiah*, asking him to *pray for the remnant that still survives so* that Yahweh will deliver them from the Assyrians. Isaiah encourages Hezekiah with the words: *do not be afraid* (7:4; 8:12–13), because Sennacherib *will return to his own country* and die there by *the sword* (v. 38; 31:8).

Another report occurs in 37:8–38: while the Assyrian field commander and his army besiege Jerusalem, the Egyptians under *Tirhakah* move north to fight against the Assyrians. Sennacherib learns of this and withdraws from *Lachish* north to *Libnah*. The Assyrian field commander lifts the siege of Jerusalem so his soldiers may join Sennacherib at Libnah to fight against the Egyptians (22:1–14).

When Sennacherib learns that Tirhakah and the Egyptians are advancing from the south to fight against his forces, he sends a *letter* (v. 14) to Hezekiah, threatening to destroy the Judeans if they do not surrender. He alleges that Yahweh and his king Hezekiah have no more chance to resist *the king of Assyria* than *the gods of* other *nations* and their kings whom the Assyrians overthrew earlier.

Hezekiah takes the letter to the Jerusalem temple and asks Yahweh to deliver Jerusalem, *so that all kingdoms on earth may know* the truth of Israel's faith. The primary reason Yahweh works mightily for the people is to convince the nations that he alone is God. Hezekiah extols Yahweh as Lord of hosts, king, creator (v. 16), the only God (vv. 16, 20), *the living God* (v. 17). He acknowledges that Assyria's kings overthrew other nations and their gods but affirms that the gods they overthrew are *not gods*, since they are *fashioned by human hands* (2:8, 20; 44:9–20).

Sennacherib's Invasion
The story of Sennacherib's invasion closes with three events that validate Isaiah's message: the angel of the Lord puts to death 185,000 Assyrian soldiers besieging Jerusalem (29:6; 31:8); the Assyrians return to Nineveh and do not invade Judah again; twenty years later (681 BCE), two of Sennacherib's sons murder him, and Esarhaddon his son becomes king of Assyria (Ezra 4:2).

According to verses 21–35, *Isaiah* sends Yahweh's *word against Sennacherib* to *Hezekiah*, responding to Sennacherib's letter. The response includes several elements: *Zion, or Jerusalem, despises and mocks* Sennacherib (v. 22); Sennacherib has boasted *in pride* and *insolence* (vv. 23, 29) of his victories over *foreign lands*, but the real reason for his triumphs is that Yahweh, *the Holy One of Israel, brought to pass* events *planned long ago* (vv. 23–27); and, finally, because of Sennacherib's arrogance, Yahweh will *make* him *return by the way* he *came* (vv. 28–29), leading him home like captors lead prisoners into exile (Amos 4:2–3; Blenkinsopp, *Isaiah 1–39*, 477) or "the way a hunter treats a wild ox on the way to putting it in the royal zoo" (Goldingay 212; see Ezek 19:1–4).

Yahweh's *sign* to Hezekiah that this will occur (7:14–16; 8:4, 18) is that, three years hence, Judean agriculture will return to normal, and *out of Jerusalem will come a remnant* (7:3; 10:20–22), due to *the zeal of the LORD of hosts* (vv. 30–32 NRSV). Yahweh assures Hezekiah and the Judeans that Sennacherib *will not enter this city* (Jerusalem), but *by the way that he came he will return*. Yahweh will *defend* and *save* Jerusalem (30:31–33; 31:5) for his sake and *for the sake of David* (vv. 33–35; 29:1–8; see 1 Kgs 11:13; 15:4; 2 Kgs 8:19; Ps 78:68–72).

Following 2 Kings 20:1–11, it seems best to rearrange Isaiah 38 as verses 1–6, 21–22, 7–20. This chapter reports Hezekiah's illness, Yahweh's cure, and Hezekiah's thanksgiving. These events occurred before Sennacherib's siege of Jerusalem in 701 BCE (chapters 36–37), which verse 6 anticipates, probably during 705–703 BCE.

In verse 1, Yahweh smites Hezekiah with a fatal boil (v. 21) as punishment for his pride (v. 17; 2 Chron 32:24–26); Isaiah declares that the king will die. When Isaiah leaves, Hezekiah prays that Yahweh will spare him, weeping bitterly. Yahweh sends Isaiah back to Hezekiah (2 Kgs 20:4 says that Yahweh apprehended the prophet *before Isaiah had left the middle court* of the palace) with Yahweh's message: *I have heard your prayer and seen your tears; I will add fifteen years to your life* (Hezekiah died in 687 BCE), and *I will deliver you and this city from . . . the king of Assyria* (vv. 2–6).

Isaiah tells those attending Hezekiah to apply *a poultice of figs* to the boil to promote recovery. Hezekiah asks what *sign* Yahweh will give that he will recover (7:14–16; 37:30–32). Isaiah says Yahweh *will make the shadow cast by the sun go back the ten steps it has gone down on the stairway of Ahaz*. By lengthening the day, Yahweh symbolically assures Hezekiah that he will lengthen his life (vv. 21–22, 7–8). The text also emphasizes the contrast between Hezekiah's faithfulness in seeking a sign and his father Ahaz's stubborn refusal to do so (see 7:10–17).

Hezekiah's prayer song (vv. 9–20), thanking Yahweh for healing, falls into two parts. First, Hezekiah describes his despondent feelings when he was near death. He lamented that he would die *in the prime of . . . life* (v. 10). No more would he commune with *the Lord* or *mankind* (v. 11). His illness arrested his life so abruptly that he could hardly believe or bear it (v. 12). But Yahweh was the one afflicting him to humble him, causing great pain which he could hardly endure. In his distress, he cried out: *O Lord, come to my aid!* (vv. 13–15). Second, Hezekiah thanks Yahweh for answering his prayer: *Oh, restore me to health and make me live!* (v. 16 NRSV). He acknowledges that he *suffered such anguish* for his own good. But Yahweh forgave him and spared his life (v. 17). Therefore, he will tell the next generation as well as his fellow believers *in the temple of the Lord* what Yahweh did for him (vv. 18–20).

In 39:1–8, Merodach-baladan II (Marduk-apla-Iddina II) learns of Hezekiah's *illness and recovery*, and sends *envoys with letters and a gift*, "ostensibly to inquire about his health, but probably to encourage his rebellion against Assyria" (Tucker 304). Hezekiah haughtily shows them all *his treasures* (vv. 1–2). Isaiah questions

Hezekiah concerning the identity of his visitors and transactions between them; Hezekiah responds (vv. 3–4).

Isaiah rebukes Hezekiah for allying with Babylon, declaring that all Judah's treasures *will be carried off to Babylon*, and some of Hezekiah's direct descendants *will be taken away, and . . . will become eunuchs in the palace of the king of Babylon*, portending the carrying off of Jehoiachin, ten thousand citizens of Jerusalem, and Judah's treasures to Babylon by Nebuchadnezzar II in 597 BCE (2 Kgs 24:8–17; Jer 29:1–2; Ezek 19:5–8). Hezekiah accepts Isaiah's message, selfishly comforting himself that its realization will not affect him, since he will die in peace.

YAHWEH'S PROMISE TO RETURN JUDAH'S REMNANT TO JERUSALEM · 40:1–55:13

Approximately 160 years separate the setting of Isaiah 1–39 (742–701 BCE) from that of Isaiah 40–55 (about 540 BCE), during which time disciples of Isaiah and/or advocates of his messages preserved, deleted, modified, rearranged, and expanded them in chapters 1–39 orally for application in new situations; later, the composer/s of chapters 40–55 attached their oracles to chapters 1–39. Many earlier and some contemporary scholars see great incoherence between these two sections (Blenkinsopp, *Isaiah 40–55*, 41–55), while several contemporary scholars find coherence throughout the book (Seitz, "Isaiah 40–66," 309–21, 327–30). This commentary follows the latter approach.

> **Parallels in Isaiah**
> *The book of Isaiah teems with parallels. As Yahweh delivered Judah from Assyrian siege (30:31–33; 31:4–5, 8; 37:36–38), so will Judah escape Babylonian exile (40:1–11; 48:20–21; 52:7–12). Yahweh sent Assyria (10:5–6) and Babylon (40:2) to punish Judah for its sins. Assyria destroyed Judah's fortified cities (36:1); Babylon destroyed the cities of Judah, Jerusalem, and the temple (44:26–28). As Babylon rose up against Assyria (39:1–8), Cyrus and Medo-Persia will rise up against Babylon (41:2–4, 25–27; 44:28–45:3; 45:13). Isaiah's author(s) theologically connect chapters 1–39 and 40–55 (or 40–66).*

40:1–11   Four voices are evident in verses 1–11, consistent with the notion that "in antiquity all writing was meant to be heard, to be read out loud, and therefore writers would be drawn to use phenomena characteristic of oral delivery" (Blenkinsopp, *Isaiah 40–55*, 64). The sixth-century BCE exilic prophet (first voice) proclaims Yahweh's word (*says your God*) to his associates (*comfort, your, speak, proclaim* are masculine plural): *Comfort my people* addresses *Jerusalem*, assuring them they have stayed long enough in exile to pay for *all* their *sins*, which led Yahweh to send them into exile (Lam 1:2–5, 8, 12–14, 17–18, 22). *Jerusalem* may mean exiles from Jerusalem in Babylon, or it may refer to the uninhabited city itself.

In verses 3–5, an angelic member of the heavenly council (second *voice*) encourages his fellow angels (in the masculine plural) to *prepare in the desert a highway for our God*, as forerunners prepare a road for a victorious king's journey home, for Yahweh will bring the redeemed, transformed people back to Jerusalem from Babylon (35:8–10) as he led the people to the promised land from Egypt (Deut 4:37–38; Ps 78:51–55). This mighty defeat of Babylon and restoration of the exiles will make clear Yahweh's *glory* to *all mankind*, convincing them that Yahweh alone is God.

In verses 6–8, another angel (third *voice*) instructs the prophet (referred to as *I*): *Cry out* (singular) that *all men* (the arrogant Babylonians; Whybray 51) *are like grass* that thrives briefly, then *withers*. In bold contrast, *the word of our God* (Yahweh's assurance that he will restore his redeemed exiles to Jerusalem) *stands forever*.

In verses 9–11, the sixth-century BCE spokesperson of Isaiah 40–55 (fourth voice) summons *Zion*, calling *Jerusalem* to be Yahweh's *herald of good tidings* (NRSV) to *the towns of Judah*, announcing that Yahweh is coming from Babylon to Jerusalem as a victorious king, bringing *his reward*, or *recompense* (spoils; redeemed exiles), with him; *like a shepherd* ("shepherd" symbolizes king; see, for example, 2 Sam 5:2; Ps 78:70–72), he *tends, carries, leads* his flock on safe paths to good pasture.

40:12–31 Hoping to convince Judean exiles in Babylon around 540 BCE to trust in Yahweh, the prophet emphasizes Yahweh's incomparability to all creation, using rhetorical questions (vv. 12–14, 18–19, 21, 25–28) like *To whom . . . will you liken God?* (vv. 18, 25), expecting the reply "no one."

In verses 12–14, Yahweh constructs *waters, heavens, earth, mountains, hills* (in other words, the universe) according to predetermined dimensions (compare Job 38:4–7); no one, including Babylonian gods, *directed* (NRSV), *instructed, enlightene*d, *taught*, or *showed* him.

According to verses 15–20, *the nations*, including Babylon, *are like a drop from* (NRSV) *a bucket, dust on the scales, nothing, worthless, less than nothing* compared with Yahweh. One cannot *compare* Yahweh with persons or things, so one cannot symbolize Yahweh with an *image* or *idol* (Deut 4:15–20), which people must nail to a solid surface so it *will not topple*, and carry from place to place (Jer 10:3–5).

According to verses 20–26, one cannot *compare* Yahweh with persons or things, because Yahweh *created* everything and constantly sustains *the earth, its people, the heavens*, and *the starry host* by *his great power and mighty strength* (Neh 9:6; Ps 104:1–4, 10–30; Job 36:26–37:24; compare Heb 1:2–3). He *sits enthroned* as king above the earth, bringing its *princes to naught* and its *rulers to nothing*; before him, *its people are like grasshoppers*.

"There Is No God but Yahweh"
Isaiah 40 engages in interreligious polemic. Against Babylonian claims that Marduk created the world and thus sustains the power structure of their empire, Israel's prophet speaks of Yahweh as creator and the nations as insignificant and temporary. He then describes the foreign gods as mere fetishes, objects without power, feeling, or meaning. This chapter is thus the first in the Bible to deny the very existence of gods other than Yahweh, and it illustrates a major turning point in biblical religion.

At last, in verses 27–31 the spokesperson or persons of verses 12–26 addresses his audience specifically: *Jacob* (that is, *Israel*) in Babylonian exile (v. 27), the *faint, weary* (vv. 28–31), and despondent, and the heartless (Ezek 37:11). His message is that Yahweh has not *disregarded* the people; *the everlasting God, the Creator of the ends of the earth*, who never becomes *tired or weary, will renew* the *strength* of *those who hope* in him, empowering them to *walk, run*, and *soar*.

41:1–42:17   In this speech, Yahweh (*I, my, me* throughout) addresses the nations and their gods (41:1–7, 21–29; 42:10–17) and Judean exiles in Babylon (41:8–20; 42:1–9). On the one hand, Yahweh challenges the nations and their gods to themselves be able to identify events they predicted and caused to happen (41:4, 21–29; 42:14–17); on the other hand, the prophet assures Judean exiles of Yahweh's presence in their oppression and impending deliverance from their bondage (41:8–20; 42:1–9, 16).

In 41:1–7, summoning *the nations* to *come forward and speak*, Yahweh asks rhetorically: *Who has stirred up one from the east* (Cyrus) and subdued *nations* and *kings*? It is Yahweh. This strikes *fear* in the hearts of all who see it; they hire a *craftsman* to make an *idol* to protect them; they *nail* it to a solid surface *so it will not topple* (40:20).

Verses 8–20 portray Yahweh encouraging *Israel*, or *Jacob*, the *servant*, whom he *chose* by delivering it from Egyptian bondage: *do not fear* (vv. 10, 13, 14), *for I am with you* to *strengthen* and *help* you. Israel's opponents are *as nothing* (40:17). By Yahweh's power, Israel will *thresh* and *crush* them. Yahweh will supply abundant resources to *the poor and needy* to make their journey to Jerusalem enjoyable.

In verses 21–29, Yahweh challenges the nations' gods to announce *what is going to happen, what the future holds* and cause it to occur, as proof they are gods. They cannot do this, because they are *less than nothing* (37:18–20; 40:17). In contrast, Yahweh has *stirred up one from the north* (Cyrus; v. 2), who *treads on rulers* of many nations, performing what he announced earlier (v. 27). One should conclude that gods other than Yahweh *are all false*.

In 42:1–9, Yahweh turns back to present (vv. 1–4) and addresses (vv. 5–9) his *servant*, Israel (not Cyrus, contrary to the claims of Blenkinsopp, *Isaiah 40–55*, 210–12; 41:8–9). Yahweh has *chosen* Israel to *bring justice to the nations, on earth*, faithfully, gently, quietly, and unobtrusively (vv. 1–4), "the reordering of social life and social power so that the weak (widows and orphans) may live a life of dignity, security, and well-being" (Brueggemann, *Isaiah 40–66*, 42).

He who created the heavens and *spread out the earth* and sustains people who live on it, who announces events before they occur and makes them happen, assures Israel he will protect it and *make* it *a light to the Gentiles* to *open blind eyes* and to *free* prisoners (vv. 5–9; 2:2–4; 49:8–12).

Verses 10–17 summon *the ends of the earth* to *sing* to Yahweh *a new song* (Pss 96:1; 98:1), to *give glory to* him, to *proclaim his praise*, because he will *march out like a warrior* (Exod 15:3) and *triumph over his enemies* (such as Babylon) (vv. 10–13).

Yahweh has *kept silent for a long time*, but now he will come, devastate Babylon as one drains *pools*, and *lead the blind* (the Judean exiles) (vv. 18–19; 43:8) *by ways they have not known*, home to Jerusalem, turning *darkness into light before them*; at the same time, he will reject *those who trust in idols* (vv. 14–17).

42:18–44:8   As Yahweh's messenger, the sixth-century BCE prophet among Judean exiles in Babylon (43:14) rebukes his comrades for not understanding (42:25) the message Yahweh tried to communicate to his people by sending them into exile: Yahweh was punishing them for sin (42:24) to bring them to repentance. He compares their spiritual obtuseness with being *deaf* and *blind* (42:18–19). This message falls into six units: the prophet chides Judean exiles for not understanding Yahweh's message taught by the exile (42:18–25); Yahweh admonishes penitent exiles to *fear not*, because Yahweh will restore his people safely to Judah (43:1–7); Yahweh summons the nations and Judean exiles to testify that their respective gods are true (43:8–13); the prophet declares that Yahweh will overthrow Babylon and prepare a way for penitent Judeans to return to Jerusalem (43:14–21); Yahweh resolves to destroy Judean exiles for persistent sins (43:22–28); and, finally, Yahweh admonishes penitent exiles, *do not be afraid*, because God will multiply their offspring to unite all the nations in worship (44:1–8).

> **The Decree of Cyrus**
>
> *Cyrus of Persia decreed that deported populations within the former Babylonian Empire could return to their homelands. The so-called "Cyrus Cylinder," a barrel-shaped clay text written in cuneiform, gives one version of his decree. Ezra 1:2–5 gives another.*

In 42:18–25, Yahweh accuses his *servant/messenger* Israel (41:8–9) of being spiritually *deaf* and *blind* (vv. 18–20), although Yahweh *handed Jacob (Israel) over* to Babylonian *plunderers* (Hebrew *bozezim*, recalling Isaiah's son's name, *Maher-Shalal-Hash-Baz*, 8:3) to bring them to their senses (vv. 22, 24–25) because they *sinned* by failing to *obey his law* (vv. 21, 22, 24). Although the Babylonians *consumed* them, *they did not understand* (v. 25).

> **Yehud**
>
> *Under the Persian Empire, some Israelites returned to Judah, now called Yehud. There they took on the name Yehudim, or "Jews." (And after this period, we speak of Jews, whereas before the Exile, the proper title was Israelites.) However, some remained in Babylonia and elsewhere. The Jewish community in Iraq lasted until 1949, when it emigrated en masse to the new state of Israel.*

In 43:1–7, the prophet announces Yahweh's message to the people Yahweh *created* and *formed* (vv. 1, 7) at the exodus, penitent exiles who understood the message of the exile: *fear not, for I am with you* (vv. 1–2, 5). They may *pass through waters, rivers, fire*, but Yahweh will protect them. The exiles' deliverance is costly, necessitating Yahweh giving a *ransom* of *Egypt, Ethiopia* (NRSV), and *Seba in exchange for them* (v. 3), since he considers them *precious and honored* and loves them (v. 4). Yahweh will reassemble Israelites throughout Babylon, and return them to Judah (vv. 5–6).

In 43:8–13, while generally the Judean exiles are spiritually *blind* and *deaf*, Yahweh's exiling his people opened the eyes and ears of a few (the remnant). Yahweh summons them and *all the nations* to appear for a court trial or international debate concerning the identity of the true God. The summons says, *Bring forth the people who are blind, yet have eyes, who are deaf, yet have ears"* (NRSV). The nations are *witnesses* to their gods (v. 9), and penitent Judean exiles are *witnesses* (v. 10) to Yahweh (vv. 10, 12). A god is true if he or she *declared* or *foretold* events and caused them to happen (vv. 9, 12; 41:21–24). Only Yahweh can satisfy such a condition, and therefore only Yahweh is God (vv. 10–13).

In 43:14–21, the sixth-century BCE exilic prophet announces that Yahweh, *the Holy One of Israel*, will *send* Cyrus and the Medo-Persians to overthrow *Babylon*, preparing a *way* (v. 19; 11:15–16; 35:8–10; 40:3–5; 42:16) for penitent Judean exiles to return to their homeland from Babylon to Jerusalem. Their migration will relive the key events of Israel's history, such as the deliverance from the Egyptians at the Sea of Reeds (vv. 16–17) and the provision of *water in the desert* (v. 20). Yahweh will once again supply traveling Israelites with water from a rock, just as at Meribah and Massah (Exod 17:1–7; Num 20:1–13; Ps 78:15–16). Yahweh urges penitent Judean exiles *not* to *dwell on the past* (the exodus) but to observe the *new thing* Yahweh is doing by returning exiles to Jerusalem and to *praise* him for it (vv. 18–21).

Although Yahweh had not *burdened* or *wearied* the people with *demands* for sacrifices, they *burdened* and *wearied* him with their *sins* (1:14; 7:13), like their *first father*, Jacob (43:22–28; 58:14; Deut 26:5). Yahweh repeatedly forgave their sins, but they persisted in rebelling against him, so he *delivered Jacob to utter destruction* (v. 28b NRSV) through the Babylonian exile.

Isaiah 44:1–8 proclaims Yahweh *Israel's King, Redeemer, the Lord of hosts* (v. 6 NRSV), *the first and . . . the last* (v. 6), the only *Rock* (v. 8), who alone is *God* (vv. 6, 8), as demonstrated by predicting events and making them happen (vv. 7–8; 41:22–23, 26–27). The prophet again admonishes penitent Judean exiles: *do not be afraid* (vv. 2, 8; 41:10, 14; 43:1). The fact that Yahweh created (v. 2) and *chose* (vv. 1–2) *Jacob* (*Israel* or *Jeshurun*) (compare Deut 32:15; 33:5, 26) to be a *servant* (vv. 1–2; 41:8–9; 42:19) and *witness* (v. 8; 43:10, 12) proves to the world that Yahweh alone is God. Thus the main example of executing a publicly declared plan is the creation and redemption of Israel, both originally and in a new time.

Yahweh next promises faithful Judean exiles to *pour out* his *spirit* (NRSV; principle of life), or *blessing*, on their *offspring*, causing them to grow and flourish (vv. 3–4; Ezek 37:1–14), like *water* causes plants to spring up and thrive on *thirsty land*. The cycle of promise and fulfillment will continue in the future, and this reality will lead people from other nations to devote themselves to Yahweh (v. 5; 45:14, 20–23; Whybray 95; Baltzer 187).

44:9–20 The prophet contrasts the only God (vv. 6, 8) with idols. Yahweh created and sustains *all who make idols* (vv. 9, 10, 15, 17, 19), such as *craftsmen*

(v. 11), *the blacksmith* (v. 12), and the *carpenter* (v. 13), who get hungry and thirsty (vv. 12, 16, 19). They *shape, cast, and forge* iron (vv. 10, 12, 13) and *wood* (vv. 14–17, 19) into an idol *in the form of man* (v. 13) and cover it with gold and silver (40:18–20; 41:6–7). Artisans can do only so much with wood: burn it for warmth or cooking (vv. 15–16, 19) and *fashion a god* out of it (vv. 15, 17, 19), *which can profit* them *nothing* (v. 10). The maker is superior to what he/she makes. Thus one who makes an idol, then *bows down* and *worships* it (vv. 15, 17, 19) and *prays* to it to *save* him/her (v. 17), is *blind* (vv. 9, 18), *ignorant* (v. 9), *deluded* (v. 20), and *knows* and *understands nothing* (vv. 18–19).

44:21–45:25 Resuming the declaration that Yahweh alone is God *and there is no other* (45:5, 6, 14, 18, 21, 22) from 44:6, 8, the prophet announces in 44:21–45:25 that Yahweh will send Cyrus, king of Medo-Persia, to overthrow Babylon (44:28; 45:1–3) and deliver the Judean exiles (45:13), convincing the nations that he alone is God and converting them (45:20–23).

Through the prophet, Yahweh, creator of everything (v. 24) and confounder of *false prophets, diviners,* and *the wise* (v. 25), addresses *Jacob,* or *Israel,* his *servant* (vv. 21, 26 NRSV), namely, the Judean exiles, whom he *formed* (v. 21 NRSV; v. 24) and *redeemed* (vv. 22, 23, 24). God assures those who *return* of forgiveness for their sins (v. 22) and proclaims that he will *fulfill the predictions* of the prophets that *Jerusalem* and Judah's fortified *towns* will be *rebuilt,* the *foundations* of the *temple* laid, and *Cyrus,* Yahweh's *shepherd*/king (2 Sam 5:2; 7:7; Ps 78:70–72), *will accomplish all that* Yahweh wants (vv. 26–28), including Babylon's overthrow, using the metaphor of evaporating the sea (v. 27; 42:15; 50:2; Koole, *Isaiah 40–48,* 424). The prophet thus summons the basic features of the universe to rejoice over Yahweh's mighty deeds (v. 23).

Generally, Judean exiles opposed the prophet's declaration that Yahweh chose a foreign king to deliver Israel. In 45:1–13, the prophet counters this reluctance to accept foreign domination. He declares that *Cyrus* is Yahweh's *anointed* (Hebrew *meshiach,* "messiah"), whom Yahweh selected *to subdue nations* (notably, Babylon). Yahweh will precede Cyrus to prepare the way for him to do Yahweh's bidding so Cyrus

Idol Making

In the ancient Near East, the manufacture of statues of deities was a high art. After the artists finished their work, priests would wash out the statue's mouth, offer numerous prayers and incantations—often in a garden—and then move the statue to its proper place in a temple. The whole process could require an extended time, and was regarded as a highly spiritual occurrence. The book of Isaiah points out, however, that no created thing can possibly symbolize the sovereign Lord of the universe, and therefore to worship the creation instead of the creator makes little sense.

Cyrus

Isaiah 44–45 recognizes that Cyrus was a Zoroastrian and not technically a follower of Yahweh. Yet Cyrus himself, in his inscriptions, honors various local deities. The book of Isaiah makes a theological claim (that Yahweh is ruler of the political order), not a historical one (that Cyrus believes in Yahweh).

will not misunderstand Yahweh's uniqueness (vv. 5, 7), even though Cyrus does *not acknowledge* Israel's God (vv. 4, 5). This is *for the sake of* Yahweh's *servant, Jacob/ Israel* (v. 4). One proof that Yahweh can do this is that he is creator: of *light* and *darkness, prosperity* and *disaster* (v. 7; literally: "good and evil," evil referring to "punishment," not "sin"; see, for example, Jer 1:14; 6:1). Yahweh summons the *heavens*, or *clouds*, to *rain down* Yahweh's *righteousness* and *salvation* (deliverance of Judean exiles) on *earth*, indicating that Yahweh is the source and support of Cyrus' work for a renewed Israel (Seitz, "Isaiah 40–66," 395).

Yahweh, creator of *earth* and *heavens* (v. 12), is *the potter*, Israel's *Maker*, and Judean exiles in Babylon are *the clay*; Yahweh is the Judean exiles' *father* and *mother*, and they his *children* (vv. 9–10). Thus, it is inappropriate for them to *question* or instruct him (v. 11) about appointing *Cyrus* to *rebuild* Jerusalem and liberate the *exiles* (v. 13).

In 45:14–25, Yahweh promises through the prophet that Yahweh's faithful people will receive goods from prisoners coming from *Egypt* and *Ethiopia* (NRSV), and the *Sabeans* as subjects, who will acknowledge that Yahweh is God and *there is no other god* (v. 14). The prophet addresses Yahweh, *who hides himself* while working invisibly in history to carry the people into exile and release them without any visible idol to represent him (Deut 4:15–20). Yahweh will put *makers of idols to shame* but will *save* Israel, who *will never be put to shame* (vv. 15–17).

Yahweh, creator of everything, has *not spoken in secret* (vv. 18–19), but rather summons idol worshipers to testify that their *gods* announced future events and caused them to happen. Idols cannot respond, demonstrating that Yahweh alone is God. Thus Yahweh invites: *turn to me and be saved, all you ends of the earth*; declaring that *every knee will bow* and *every tongue swear* (compare Rom 14:11; Phil 2:9–10), and proclaiming *in the Lord alone are righteousness and strength*. Yahweh will *put to shame* all opponents, and bestow righteousness on *all Israel's descendants* (vv. 20–25).

46:1–48:22   Yahweh's message in Isaiah 46–48 is that he will send Cyrus to defeat Babylon and its gods and deliver penitent, faithful Judean exiles from exile. These chapters fall into three parts: Yahweh promises to summon Cyrus to overthrow Babylon and restore a faithful remnant to Zion (46:1–13); Yahweh informs Babylon and its enchanters of their impending defeat (47:1–15); and Yahweh charges penitent Judean exiles to leave Babylon to return home (48:1–22).

Isaiah 46:1–13 addresses *all the remnant* (NRSV; 7:3; 10:20–22; 11:11, 16; 28:5; 37:31–32) of the *house of Jacob/Israel* (v. 3), whom he *carried since birth* and *will carry to old age* (vv. 3–4), assuring them that the Babylonian gods *Bel* and *Nebo*, which are so helpless

> **The Parade of Deities**
>
> *In the ancient Near East, deities periodically went on parade during major festivals. Worshipers would move their statues around a pre-appointed circuit and offer sacrifices at each stop. The book of Isaiah uses this practice as evidence that the "gods" were helpless, since humans had to move them.*

that *beasts* must *carry* them, will themselves *go into captivity* (vv. 1–2). The sharp contrast between Yahweh carrying his people and the nations carrying their gods on *their shoulders* (v. 7) or on animals' backs (v. 1) demonstrates Yahweh's incomparability (v. 5). How foolish to *worship* a *god* a *goldsmith* fashions. Humans must decide its location, from which it can do nothing for worshipers (vv. 6–7; 40:18–20; 41:7; 44:9–20).

Yahweh addresses the remnant a second time, as *rebels* (v. 8) because they refuse to accept what he *planned* (14:24–27; 22:11; 30:1; 37:26): to *summon a bird of prey from the east*, namely, Cyrus, to overthrow Babylon and deliver his people (v. 11; 44:24–45:7; 45:13). He charges them to *remember the former things*, when he proved to be the only God by announcing events and making them happen (vv. 9–10; 41:21–29; 45:20–21).

Yahweh addresses the remnant a third time, as *stubborn-hearted*, *far from righteousness*, resisting Yahweh's *righteousness*, or *salvation*, through Cyrus (v. 11), who is returning faithful Judean exiles to *Zion* to begin again Yahweh's work through his people (Goldingay 269).

In 47:1–15, Yahweh turns to address *Babylon*, or *Chaldea* (vv. 1, 5 NRSV), announcing that he will *take vengeance* on her (v. 3) because: the city claims to be God, using the language of Yahweh's exclusiveness, *I am, and there is none besides me* (vv. 8, 10; 45:5, 6, 14, 18, 21, 22; 46:9); it believes itself invincible, declaring, *I will continue forever—the eternal queen* (v. 7), *lounging in . . . security* (v. 8); it *showed no mercy* to Judeans whom Yahweh gave into its hands to punish for their sins (54:7–8), but *laid a very heavy yoke* upon them (v. 6); and it is confident that its sorcerers (vv. 9, 12), conjurers (v. 11), magicians (v. 12), astrologers, and stargazers (v. 13) can stave off Yahweh's wrath (vv. 13–15). Like Judah (2:6–22) and other nations (16:6; 23:9), Yahweh overthrows Babylon for its pride (13:11, 19; 14:4, 11–14). Yahweh will demote Babylon from *mistress* (vv. 5, 7 NRSV) to slave (vv. 1–2, 5), remove its *throne*, or exalted position, among the nations (vv. 1, 5), expose the city's *nakedness* and *shame* (vv. 2–3; compare Jer 13:26), and defeat *her* (vv. 3, 11, 14) so *she* will suffer *loss of children and widowhood* (vv. 8–9).

Cities & Nations as Female
The prophets often use sexual imagery to describe cities and nations. Since place names in Hebrew are feminine, such a metaphorical use of gender must have seemed an easy shift to make for the ancient writers. The extremely graphic images of debasement in texts like this caught the attention of an audience.

Again, verses 48:1–22 address the citizens of *Jacob* (Israel/Judah) in Babylonian exile (vv. 1, 12; 46:3), some of whom pretend to *rely on the God of Israel but not in truth or righteousness* (vv. 1–2), are *citizens of the holy city* (Jerusalem) in name only (v. 2), are *stubborn* (v. 4), *treacherous*, rebellious (v. 8), and ignore Yahweh's *commands* (v. 18). Some, however, are faithful to Yahweh and have genuinely repented after being *refined* or *tested in the furnace of affliction*, that is, the Babylonian exile (v. 10; 30:20, 26).

Yahweh, not the *idols* that Judah tended to serve (vv. 5, 14; Judg 2:17, 19; 3:6), *foretold former things long ago* (possibly Judah's fall and exile, Jer 1:13–19; 6:26; 25:8–11); later, he *acted, and they came to pass* (vv. 3, 18–19). Now, Yahweh announces *new things* (vv. 6–7): a *delay* in executing *wrath* on an apostate people and a refusal to *cut* them *off* (v. 9). Rather, the creator and sustainer of *earth* and *heavens* (v. 13) will send Cyrus to *carry out his purpose against Babylon* (vv. 14–15).

Against Judean exiles who reject Yahweh's decision to use Cyrus to overthrow Babylon and deliver a penitent people, the prophet (v. 16d; some say Yahweh's servant) declares Yahweh's promise to *teach* the people *what is best for* them and to *direct* them *in the way* they *should go* (v. 17), as they should have learned from their ancestors' disobedience (vv. 18–19). The prophet proclaims, *the Lord has redeemed his servant Jacob* (v. 20; verse 17; 41:14; 43:1; 44:23; 50:2; 52:9) from Babylonian captivity. Thus, Yahweh summons the exiles to *leave*, or *flee from*, *Babylon* (v. 20; 52:11–12; compare Jer 50:8), just as the Israelites left Egypt (Exod 12:41; 13:3–4; Deut 9:7; 16:3). On the way home, Yahweh will supply *water from the rock*, as he did for Israel in *the deserts* (v. 21; Exod 17:1–7; Num 20:1–13; Neh 9:15; Pss 78:15–16, 20; 105:41; 114:8). Not all Judean exiles will heed Yahweh's call: they are *the wicked*, for whom *there is no peace* (v. 22; compare vv. 18; 57:21).

49:1–53:12 Yahweh's purpose to use his servant, faithful Israel, to bring back the majority of Israel and the nations is the fundamental declaration of Isaiah 49–53. Speakers and addressees vary from passage to passage. These chapters fall into seven units: Yahweh's servant tells the nations his God-given mission (49:1–6); Yahweh encourages the servant to lead Judean exiles to Canaan (49:7–13); Yahweh promises to restore deserted Jerusalem (49:14–50:3); Yahweh's servant declares his steadfast trust in Yahweh and summons the faithful to do likewise (50:4–11); Yahweh promises faithful exiles to deliver them from captivity (51:1–8); Yahweh's servant beseeches Yahweh to deliver the faithful exiles from Babylon (51:9–11); and, finally, Yahweh calls faithful exiles to leave Babylon and return to Judah (51:12–52:12).

49:1–6 Yahweh's *servant* (vv. 3, 5–6), *Israel* (v. 3; 41:8; 44:1–2, 21; 48:20), tells the *islands* and *nations* (v. 1) the mission Yahweh gave him: *to bring Jacob (Israel) back to him* (v. 5), *to restore the survivors of Israel/Jacob* (v. 6), and to be *a light to the nations that* Yahweh's *salvation may reach to the end of the earth* (v. 6; 42:1–4; 45:20–25). Despite the servant's feeling that he failed in executing this mission (v. 4), Yahweh offers him *strength* to persist

> **The "Servant" Israel**
>
> *The identity of the servant in these chapters is difficult to discern. As Childs (387) puts it, "The extension of the servant's role in chapter 49 is not an attempt to replace an earlier corporate understanding of the servant Israel with that of an individual prophetic figure. Rather, the servant always remains Israel, but Israel is now understood within the dynamic movement of the prophetic history as embodied in a suffering, individual figure who has been divinely commissioned to the selfsame task of the deliverance of the chosen people and the nations at large."*

(vv. 5–6). Baltzer (295–317, 393–429) argues the *servant* is Moses, and Koole (*Isaiah 49–55*, 1–25) calls him "the great Saviour of the future." But verses 3, 5–6 state he is (the faithful remnant of) *Israel, formed* to bring unfaithful Israel and the nations to Yahweh.

In chapter 49, through the prophet (see the formula *This is what the Lord says*, vv. 7, 8), Yahweh promises the faithful *servant* (v. 7) (that is, *his people* or *his afflicted ones* [v. 13]), whom *the nations* (v. 7 NRSV) *despised and abhorred* when Jerusalem fell and the Jews went into exile (60:14; Jer 33:24; Lam 1:7–8; 2:15–16), that God will *help* him and *make* him *a covenant for the people* (v. 8). Yahweh charges the servant to embolden Judean *captives* to *come out* of Babylonian exile and *be free* (v. 9a-b; 42:6–7), offering to provide food, water, protection, guidance, and roads conducive to travel (40:3–4; 42:16) for the journey home (vv. 9c–12), just as when Israel in the wilderness followed God like a flock does its shepherd (40:11; Pss 78:52–53; 80:1). Then, through the servant, Yahweh will *restore the land* of Canaan and *reassign its inheritances* to a faithful people (v. 8; Josh 13–21). The prophet summons *heavens, earth* and *mountains* to *rejoice* because Yahweh *comforts* oppressed *people* in this way (v. 13).

49:14–51:11   In this section, personified, uninhabited *Zion* (Jerusalem) (40:9; 41:27; 52:1–2, 7–8) protests, *the Lord has forsaken me* (v. 14). Yahweh replies through the prophet (*This is what the Lord says*, 49:22, 25; 50:1): *a mother* may *forget* her *baby*, but *I will not forget you* (v. 15). Several biblical texts present God as mother (Num 11:12; Isa 42:14; 66:13; Matt 22:37; Luke 13:34). Yahweh *engraved*, inscribed, or tattooed a blueprint (outline) of Jerusalem bounded by *walls on the palms of his hands* as he eagerly contemplates her rebuilding (v. 16; 44:26, 28), paralleling "the outline of the Sumerian city of Lagash in the lap of the statue of its ruler, King Gudea" (around 2000 BCE; Blenkinsopp, *Isaiah 40–55*, 311; Whybray 144; Koole, *Isaiah 49–55*, 56–57). Jerusalem's *sons* (vv. 17, 18, 22), her *people* (v. 19), and *children* (vv. 20, 25), will *hasten back* (v. 17) to Zion in such numbers the city cannot accommodate them, to its amazement (vv. 19–21). Jerusalem will *wear them as ornaments like a bride* (v. 18), giving the city new splendor.

As "the great King over all the earth" (Ps 47:2, 7) or "the nations" (compare Jer 10:7; Ps 47:8), Yahweh will do the impossible: overthrow Judah's captors and *oppressors* (Babylon) and subject them to his people (vv. 23c-26b), raising a *banner* as a signal (5:26; 11:10, 12; 13:2; 18:3; 30:17; 62:10) to the nations to do Yahweh's bidding. As *foster fathers* and *nursing mothers*, the nations will *bring* (*carry*, 40:11; 46:3–4, or escort) God's *sons* and *daughters* (namely, the Judean exiles in Babylon) safely to Judah (vv. 22–23b).

To Zion's children (49:17–18, 20, 25), Yahweh denies being arbitrary in allowing Judah to be deported, since he gave her a *certificate of divorce* (compare Deut 24:1–4; Hos 2:2; Jer 3:1–11)—that is, he *sold* her as a slave into Babylonian exile *because of* her *sins* (v. 1). Recently Yahweh *came* and *called* the exiles to leave Babylon and return to Judah in order to *ransom* and *rescue* them, but they did not respond (see 65:1–5; 66:4). Consequently, Yahweh will bring drought and *darkness* upon them (vv. 2–3).

Abruptly, Yahweh's servant (Israel's faithful remnant in exile) speaks again (50:1–11; compare 49:1–6) to fellow exiles (*you* and *your* in verses 10–11 are plural), affirming three things: Yahweh *sustains the weary* (40:29–31) with the *word* the prophet had been *taught* (vv. 4–5); the prophet tolerated persecution, mockery, and false accusations that opponents brought against him, confident that since Yahweh *helps* him (vv. 7, 9), he will *not be disgraced* (vv. 6–9); and he admonishes the larger group of exiles to *fear*, *obey*, *trust*, and *rely on* Yahweh through the servant's *word*, warning those who *walk in the light of* their own *fires* that they will *lie down in torment* (vv. 10–11).

Suddenly in 51:1–8, Yahweh speaks again through the prophet (*Listen to me*: verses 1, 4, 7; 49:7–50:3) to Judean exiles *who pursue righteousness* by *seek[ing] the Lord*. He says that, just as Yahweh transformed Judah's ancestor, *Abraham, one man*, into *many*, so will he *comfort Zion* (v. 19; 40:1; 61:2–3; 66:13), transforming her *ruins* (*deserts* and *wastelands*) into *the garden of Eden* (35:1–2, 6–7; 41:17–20), producing *joy, gladness, thanksgiving*, and *singing*. Yahweh's *justice, righteousness*, and *salvation draws near speedily* and, unlike *the heavens* and *the earth* (v. 6) and those who *reproach* or *insult* Yahweh's true followers (vv. 7c–8b), *will last forever* (vv. 5, 6, 8). God will restore a faithful people, *who know what is right* and *have* Yahweh's *law in their hearts* (v. 7), from exile to Jerusalem (v. 3) and to be *a light to the nations* (vv. 4, 5; 42:6; 49:6).

In 51:9, the speaker again changes abruptly, this time to Yahweh's servant (referring to the faithful exiles), who implores Yahweh's strong *arm* to *awake* (three times) *as in days of old* (Exod 6:6; 15:16; Deut 4:34; 5:15; 7:19), that is, at creation, when God defeated the mythological monster *Rahab*, or *the dragon, the sea* and *the waters of the great deep*, or chaos (Gen 1:2; Job 26:12–13; Pss 74:12–15; 89:9–10); and at the Sea of Reeds, when God parted the waters so Israel could escape from Egypt on dry land (43:16; 50:2; Exod 14:21–22; Ps 77:16–20). Then *the ransomed of the Lord will return* to Zion with *singing, everlasting joy*, and *gladness* (v. 3; 35:10; 44:23–28; 55:12).

51:12–52:12   Yahweh responds to the servant's pleas. He urges faithful exiles not to *fear mortal men* (that is, their Babylonian oppressors), for they cannot stand before Yahweh, Israel's *Maker* (45:9, 11; 54:5), creator of *the heavens and the earth* (51:12–13, 15–16; 40:21–22, 26; 42:5; 45:18; 48:13). Yahweh *will soon set* Judah's *prisoners* in Babylon *free* (51:14; 52:2) and *put* his *words in* the *mouth* of the servant (here again equaling the faithful exiles) and *cover* him *with the shadow of* his *hand* (51:16a–b; 49:2). Yahweh assures *Zion* (51:16–17; 52:1–2), which is in *ruins* (51:19; 52:9) as a result of the Babylonian destruction of the city (2 Kgs 25:1–12; Jer 39:1–10; 52:3–16), having *drunk* deep of *the cup of* Yahweh's *wrath* (51:17, 20–22; Jer 25:15–29), that he is *her God* (51:20) and *she is his people* (51:16, 22; 52:5, 6, 9). Yahweh will *comfort* (51:12, 19; 52:9), *defend* (51:22), *redeem* (52:3, 9), and, in short, save Jerusalem (52:7, 10). The prophet cries out to Zion, *Awake, awake!* (51:17; 52:1). Yahweh will fill the city with Judeans returning from exile and *put the cup of* Yahweh's *wrath into the hands of* Zion's *tormentors* (51:22–23). Yahweh will deliver the people from Babylon in a way reminiscent of their earlier deliverance from *Egypt* and *Assyria* (52:4–6). A *messenger* (NRSV) *brings good tidings* to the uninhabited, devastated *ruins of Jerusalem* (compare Nah 1:15), announcing, *your God reigns* and *returns to Zion*, leading the exiles home. Jerusalem's *watchmen* will spot evidence of God's intervention when it first appears on the horizon and will *shout* the wonderful news for all to hear.

The prophet says that there will be two responses to Yahweh's salvation of the Jewish people. First, *all the nations* and *all the ends of the earth will see* Yahweh's *salvation* (52:7–10). Second, the prophet urges the exiles to *depart, depart* from Babylon with *the vessels of the Lord* (Ezra 1:7; 6:5). *Haste* and *flight* are unnecessary, unlike Israel's departure from Egypt (Exod 12:11; Deut 16:3), because *the Lord will go before you, the God of Israel will be your rear guard* (52:11–12), just as the angel and pillar of cloud protected Israel from the Egyptians (Exod 14:19–20; 13:21–22; 23:20; 33:2; Deut 1:30–33).

52:13–53:12   The theme of this section is the humiliation and exaltation of Yahweh's servant. This poem contains three parts: in the first and last, Yahweh will exalt his servant (52:13–15 and 53:11–12); in the middle unit, Jewish exiles whom Yahweh's servant restored extol his vicarious suffering for them (53:1–10). Probably "a double chorus was used in the dramatic performance" of this passage (Baltzer 404). Secondary literature and diverse interpretations of this passage are vast and humbling. No one can claim definitive understanding of its meaning. Provisional suggestions follow.

The Audience of Isaiah

As throughout the book of Isaiah, and indeed much of the rest of the Bible, here Yahweh's saving actions have two audiences, the nations of the earth and Israel itself, both of whom should respond with awe and thanksgiving.

The section opens in 52:13–15. Here Yahweh speaks concerning *my servant*, probably the remnant of Jewish exiles whom Yahweh restored through the exile (49:1–6; 50:4–11), declaring *he will be highly exalted*. Formerly, *many nations were appalled at him*, because he was *so disfigured*, but now he will awe *kings* because, through him, Yahweh will empower them to *see* and *understand what they were not told* and *have not heard*—that is, Yahweh's servant will be a light to the nations (42:6; 49:6).

The larger body of Judean exiles in Babylon (*we, us, our, my people*) proclaim that the remnant suffered vicariously because of its *transgressions* and *iniquities* and stubborn impenitence. Yahweh's servant *grew up before* Yahweh with *no beauty or majesty to attract* his fellows to him; they *despised and rejected* him (vv. 1–3).

Initially, the larger exile group considered Yahweh's servant *stricken, smitten, and afflicted by God*, but now they realize that *he was pierced* and *crushed* because of their *transgressions*, and *by his wounds* they *are healed*. They *have gone astray,* and Yahweh *has laid on* his servant (namely, the faithful remnant) the *iniquity* of the larger group (vv. 4–6; 50:6).

Yahweh's servant voluntarily went *like a lamb to the slaughter* to be *stricken* because of *the transgression of* Yahweh's *people*, the larger exiled body. Reflecting his sacrificial attitude, *he did not open his mouth*. Though he was innocent, he suffered the indignity of burial in *a grave with the wicked* and *rich* for the sake of his comrades. In this way, *the Lord's will will prosper in his hand* (vv. 7–10).

In verses 11–12, Yahweh speaks again concerning his servant (*my righteous servant*). Not only will Yahweh's servant, the faithful Judean exiles, restore some of their fellows, but he will also *bear the sin of* and thereby *justify many* nations (52:15; 49:5–6), or in other words, make *intercession for the transgressors*. "The individual servant's suffering and death are Israel's, on behalf of the nations" (Seitz, "Isaiah 40–66," 462).

54:1–55:13 Yahweh admonishes personified, abandoned Jerusalem not to be afraid (54:4, 14), for he will take her back because of his unfailing love for her (54:10) and will populate her with numerous people (54:1–17), as a husband takes back a wife he divorced (54:5–6). Yahweh summons faithful, penitent Judean exiles in Babylon to forsake their evil ways, receive his forgiveness (55:6–7), enter an everlasting covenant with him (55:4), and leave Babylon for Jerusalem (55:12) to attract the nations to Yahweh (55:1–13, especially 5).

54:1–17 Yahweh, through the prophet, addresses Jerusalem, the *afflicted city* (54:11), using the metaphor of a *barren woman who never bore a child*, and declares she will have many children (vv. 1–3).

Isaiah 53 in Early Christian Interpretation

In the time of Jesus, Jews interpreted the Suffering Servant of Isaiah 53 to be Israel as a whole. This is notably true of the Targum of Isaiah, a work finished in about 200 CE but including older interpretations of the biblical book (see Hayes 550). Early Christians read the story of the Servant typologically. Since Jesus took on many aspects of Israel (see Matt 1–4 especially), it was fitting that his career as the Suffering Servant par excellence should be interpreted in light of the beautiful images of Isaiah 53. Whatever the original intent of the chapter, it became an ideal portrayal of the one who died so that all might live.

He admonishes her *not* to *be afraid*, for Yahweh her *Maker* is her *husband* and will *call* or *bring* her *back* into a *covenant of peace* (v. 10; Mal 2:14), that is, their marriage relationship. Yahweh's actions come out of *deep compassion* (vv. 7–8, 10), *everlasting kindness* (v. 8), and *unfailing love* for her (v. 10), although he formerly *rejected, abandoned, hid* his *face from*, and divorced her (vv. 4–6; 50:1; Hos 2:2–15) out of anger (vv. 8–9). God's punishment of the people in the Babylonian exile is like the destruction of humankind by the flood in *the days of Noah*. Yet, just as God *swore* never to destroy humanity again by flood (Gen 8:21–22), so now God vows never to punish Israel again by exile.

Yahweh promises to *build* abandoned Jerusalem, including its *foundations*, *battlements*, *gates*, and *walls*. Yahweh will teach its residents, establishing the city *in righteousness* (1:26), liberating it from *fear*, and defeating all enemies. Accordingly, *the heritage of* Yahweh's *faithful servants* (namely the core group who urged their fellow exiles to return to Yahweh), is a bright future because of Yahweh's *vindication* (vv. 11–17).

In chapter 55, Yahweh offers the exiles free, *good, rich* drink and food that can *satisfy* their deepest longings, in contrast to Babylon's expensive, insipid, nonnutritious fare that *does not satisfy*. Yahweh desires to enter into *an everlasting covenant* with them, thus demonstrating the *unfailing kindnesses* (54:8, 10) *promised to David* (2 Sam 7:11–16; Ps 89:19–37). Like David, they will be *a witness to the peoples*, and *nations* that *do not know* them *will hasten to* them, or to be concrete, will depend upon them economically and will bring tribute to build up Jerusalem and provide her protection (Ps 18:43), *because* Yahweh *has endowed* them *with splendor* (vv. 1–5).

> **The Land & the People Will Be Healed**
>
> *Isaiah 55 says that, just as war and deportation led to ecological degradation, so now the recovering land itself will symbolize the return of God's people to their promised state of wholeness under God, who created nature as well as them.*

Yahweh admonishes the exiles to *seek, call on,* and *turn to* him, promising that *his ways* and *thoughts* will prevail. As *rain and snow* nourish plants to produce grain for *bread*, Yahweh's *word* that he will deliver Judean exiles and restore them to their land *will accomplish what* Yahweh *desires* (vv. 6–11). *The wicked* (v. 7) are Judean exiles "who are so settled in Babylon and so accommodated to imperial ways that they have no intention of making a positive response to Yahweh's invitation to homecoming" (Brueggemann, *Isaiah 40–66*, 160).

The prophet concludes by promising faithful Judean exiles that they will exit Babylon *in joy* (52:11–12), as Israel *went out* from Egypt (Exod 12:41; 13:3; Deut 9:7; 11:10). In short, they will experience a new exodus. All creation, and in particular, the *mountains, hills,* and *trees*, will rejoice in Yahweh's magnificent salvation of his people.

OBJECTIVES & CONTROVERSIES IN YAHWEH'S POSTEXILIC
COMMUNITY · 56:1–66:24

According to Isaiah 56–66, both penitent and unreceptive Judean exiles have now heard Yahweh's announcements in chapters 40–55 of deliverance from Babylon and return to Judah. Passages in chapters 56–66 date originally from the period of rebuilding the Jerusalem temple (536–516 BCE) to rebuilding its walls (about 445–432 BCE). But despite the fact that they postdate the events of Isaiah, they are nevertheless an integral part of the book as they continue, combine, reinterpret, reapply, and emphasize with greater clarity major teachings of chapters 1–55. Chapters 56–66 fall into seven sections (56:1–8; 56:9–57:21; 58:1–59:21; 60:1–62:12; 63:1–6; 63:7–64:12; 65:1–66:24).

56:1–8　Some Judean exiles now inhabiting Jerusalem wish to exclude *eunuchs* and *foreigners* from Yahweh's people. The fifth-century BCE prophetic composer of Isaiah 56–66 denounces this practice. Yahweh declares through the prophet (*This is what the Lord says* [vv. 1, 4]) that *salvation* and *righteousness* (46:13; 51:5–6, 8) are very near (v. 1). Therefore, the prophet charges his followers to *maintain justice and do what is right* (v. 1; 1:16–17; 5:7, 16; 10:1–2), which in this context means especially to *keep the Sabbath* (vv. 2, 4, 6; Exod 20:8–11; Jer 17:19–27) and to *keep* one's *hand from doing any evil* (v. 2) by *hold[ing] fast to* Yahweh's *covenant* (vv. 2, 4, 6).

Yahweh will *bless* anyone *who does this*: the chosen *people* (v. 3), *foreigners* (vv. 3, 6), *eunuchs* (vv. 3–4), and *all nations* (v. 7; 2:2–4; 25:6–8; 45:20–23; 51:4–5; 66:18–19; Zech 2:11; Ruth 2:10–12). He will *exclude* none *joined to the Lord* (v. 3), *who bind themselves to serve, love, and worship the name of the Lord* (v. 6). Although eunuchs cannot have *sons and daughters* to preserve their memory (Job 18:16–17), Yahweh will *give them* something better: incessant fellowship with him (vv. 3–5). He will *give* foreigners *joy in* his *house* and *accept their sacrifices* (v. 7). Yahweh has already *gathered* some *exiles of Israel*, but he *will gather others* (v. 8). Judean exiles returned from Babylon in several waves.

56:9–57:21　Division arose among different exiled groups who returned to Judah. The prophet uses several introductory formulas (*This is what the high and lofty One says* [57:15]; *says the Lord* [57:19]; *says my God* [57:21]) to show that Yahweh speaks directly to denounce sinners and announce punishment upon wicked leaders (56:9–12; 57:3–13b, 20–21). At the same time, God commends and promises to bless *the righteous* (57:1–2, 13c–19).

In 56:9–12, Yahweh summons *all beasts* to *devour Israel's blind watchmen* (*shepherds*) (Jer 12:9–13; Ezek 34:1–10), namely the wicked leaders of the small Jerusalem community, here false prophets (Jer 6:17; Ezek 3:16–21; Koole, *Isaiah 56–66*, 34–35). They *lack knowledge* and *understanding*; they should warn the community of spiritual dangers, but they are *mute dogs*. They should be alert to protect the people, but they *lie around* and *love to sleep*. Their primary care should be the flock, but their only concern is to satisfy their own appetites and acquire their *own gain* (compare Jas 4:1–4).

Chapter 57 opens with the wicked killing *the righteous*; but this is a blessing, because in death Yahweh spares the righteous from further ill treatment by their oppressors; he gives them *peace* and *rest* from additional affliction *in death* (see Job 3:11–19).

According to 57:3–13b, the exile did not cure God's people of idolatry. Jeremiah condemned fellow Jews who went to Egypt after Jerusalem's fall for worshiping idols (Jer 44). In Isaiah 57:3–13b, Yahweh condemns certain groups of exiles returned to Judah for worshiping Baal and Molech, labeling them *sons of a sorceress, offspring of adulterers and prostitutes* (v. 3), *brood of rebels, offspring of liars* (v. 4). By turning to idols, God's people *mock, sneer at, stick out* their *tongue at*

(v. 4), *forsake* (v. 8), are *false to*, do not *remember*, and *do not fear* Yahweh (v. 11). *Among the oaks, under every spreading tree* (v. 5), *on a high and lofty hill* (v. 7; Deut 12:2–3; 1 Kgs 14:22–24; 2 Kgs 17:9–11; Jer 2:20; Ezek 20:27–29; Hos 4:11–13), they practice cult prostitution as an act of worship to the fertility god Baal (vv. 5, 7–8); and *in the ravines, under the overhanging crags* (v. 5), they *sacrifice* their *children to* the Ammonite deity *Molech*, or Milcom (Deut 12:31; 1 Kgs 11:7; 2 Kgs 16:3; 17:31; 21:6; 23:10; Jer 19:4–5; Ezek 16:20–22; Mic 6:6–7; Zeph 1:4–6). They offer *drink offerings* and *grain offerings* to foreign deities (v. 6). All these religious activities *weary* the participants, but they find *strength* to proceed (v. 10). Thus, Yahweh resolves to be *silent* no longer, but to *expose* the wicked exiles' *righteousness* and *works* (vv. 11–12). When they petition for *help*, Yahweh will summon their gods to rescue them. Their gods can do nothing, so *the wind carries them off* (v. 13a–b).

> **False Gods in Israel after the Exile**
>
> *After reading the gorgeous promises of Isaiah 40–55, it is disturbing to find in chapters 56–66 that Judah returned to some of its old ways. However, the book of Isaiah offers hope even under such difficult circumstances, since Yahweh continues to work to redeem the people and to win them to worship of the one true God.*

In 57:13c–19, there are some returned exiles who *make* Yahweh *the high and lofty One, who lives forever, whose name is holy*, who *lives in a high and holy place* (v. 15), their *refuge* (v. 13c) and are *contrite and lowly* (v. 15); these Yahweh will maintain in Judah (v. 13c), *revive* (v. 15), *heal* (vv. 18–19), *guide and restore comfort to* (v. 18), *creating praise* from mourners (v. 19) and *peace* for those who trust in Yahweh. At one time, Yahweh was *angry* and *enraged by* the people's *sinful greed* and *punished* them, but in vain (vv. 16–17). Yet, to keep them from tiring or losing all hope, the prophet now summons his forerunners to *prepare the road* for additional exiles to return from Babylon (v. 14; 40:3–5). God has resolved to save the people, even though their *ways* are *willful* (v. 17). By contrast (vv. 20–21), *the wicked* among the restored Judean exiles have *no peace* but are continually miserable and restless (48:22).

58:1–59:21 Isaiah 58–59 reflects the situation shortly before Nehemiah rebuilt the walls of Jerusalem (445 BCE, 58:12). Yahweh's people are oppressing one another, and Yahweh is punishing them; they hold a great fast and strictly observe the Sabbath to persuade God to stop the punishment. The prophet declares that Yahweh desires justice and righteousness, that is, right treatment of one's fellow human beings, not mere external fasting and observing the Sabbath (58:1–14). Yahweh yearns to save the people but cannot do so as long as they treat each other with violence, oppression, and injustice (59:1–21).

In 58:1–14, Yahweh charges the fifth-century BCE prophet to *declare to* his *people their sins* (v. 1) of pride, arrogance, and self-centeredness. In a line reminiscent of charges in the book of Judges, the prophet notes that they *do as* they *please* (vv. 3, 13). Outwardly, *they seem eager* to have a close relationship with

Yahweh *as if* they kept Yahweh's *commands* (v. 2). They meticulously *fast* and keep the *Sabbath*, but Yahweh *has not noticed* (vv. 3a–b, 4c–5), because in daily life they *exploit all* their *workers* (v. 3c), *quarrel, strive, strike each other with wicked fists* (v. 4a–b), and utter *malicious talk* against their fellows (v. 9). *The kind of fasting* Yahweh desires is to *loose the chains of injustice* from the mistreated, *set the oppressed free* (vv. 6, 9, 10), *share food with the hungry* (vv. 7, 10), *provide the poor wanderer with shelter, clothe the naked*, and care for needy relatives (vv. 6–7; Matt 25:31–46).

If they do this, Yahweh will transform their *darkness* into *light* (vv. 8, 10), *heal* them, protect them, *answer* their *cries for help* (vv. 8–9b), *guide* them, *satisfy* their *needs, strengthen* them, be their spiritual foun-
tain (v. 11; Jer 2:13), and empower them to rebuild Jerusalem, bearing the symbolic names *Repairer of Broken Walls, Restorer of Streets with Dwellings* (v. 12). They will now *find* their *joy in the Lord* and prosper in the promised *land* (v. 14).

The prophet declares that Yahweh is ready and able to *save* the people (v. 1), but their *iniquities* drown out their cries for deliverance (vv. 1–2). Their fundamental sin is *injustice, unrighteousness* in deal-

> **Dialogue with the Prophet**
> *In chapter 59, the themes of Isaiah 58 continue. However, the speaker is no longer Yahweh. Chapter 59 is a dialogue between the fifth-century* BCE *prophet (vv. 1–8, 15c–21) and the sinful people (vv. 9–15b).*

ing with other human beings (vv. 4, 8). Their hearts devise wicked plans to hurt others: they *conceive trouble* (v. 4), and *their thoughts are evil* (v. 7). These erupt in sinful speech: their *lips* and *tongues* make *empty arguments* and *speak lies* in court cases (v. 4) and daily speech (v. 3). They *mutter wicked things* (v. 3) and engage in sinful actions, especially violence against the vulnerable. Thus the prophet charges that their *hands are stained with blood* of *innocent*, unsuspecting victims they killed or mistreated in *evil deeds* and *acts of violence* (vv. 3, 6, 7; Prov 1:10–19). In addition, *their feet rush into sin* (v. 7), destroying the *peace* that should prevail among God's people (v. 8).

Some of the prophet's hearers respond (*we, us, our*), confessing guilt for sins of which he accused them. The prophet uses a series of synonyms to illustrate how odious is the behavior of the people of God: *offenses, sins, iniquities, rebellion, treachery, turning* their *backs on God, oppression, revolt, uttering lies* their *hearts conceived*, absence of *truth* or *honesty* (vv. 12–15). The people acknowledge that this is why Yahweh's *justice, righteousness, light, and deliverance do not reach* them, and they *feel* their *way like the blind, stumble at midday*, having become *like the dead* (vv. 9c–11b).

The prophet responds to the penitent. He declares that Yahweh *was displeased* that *no one* in Judah's restored community arose to promote *justice* among God's people. So Yahweh donned a warrior's uniform: the *breastplate* of *righteousness, helmet of salvation, garments of vengeance*, and *cloak* of *zeal* (vv. 15b–17; compare 1 Thess 5:8; Eph 6:10–17) and marched forth *like a pent-up flood* (see 8:7–8) to punish his *enemies*, namely, the Judeans in the community who oppressed and mistreated their fellow Jews (vv. 18–19). Yahweh acted to motivate foreign peoples to *fear* the divine *name* and *revere his glory* (v. 19), and to redeem *those in Jacob who repent of their sins* (v. 20; 1:27–28). Yahweh assures those who faithfully keep his *covenant* that his *spirit* (NRSV), or power or energy, and *words* (or law) will be with their descendants *forever* (v. 21).

60:1–62:12 Zion is the central focus of Isaiah 60–62. Zerubbabel and his companions finished the temple in 516 BCE (60:7; Ezra 6:13–18), but Nehemiah's rebuilding of Jerusalem's walls (445 BCE; Neh 6:15–7:4) is yet to come (60:10, 18). The population of Jerusalem is small (Neh 7:4); religious division plagues the returned exiles. The fifth-century BCE prophet persuaded some to repent (59:20). In Isaiah 60–62, he announces that Yahweh will restore other penitent exiles to Zion, who will convert foreigners to Yahweh.

In chapter 60, the fifth-century BCE prophet informs Zion through second-person imperatives (*arise, shine, lift up*, etc.) and feminine singular pronouns (*you, your*) that Yahweh's *light* (*glory* and *deliverance*) (58:8, 10) *has come*, while *the peoples* are in *darkness* (vv. 1–2, 19–20). The prophet announces that *nations will come to* this *light* (v. 3; 2:2–4; 42:6; 49:6). They will *serve* God's people (vv. 10, 12, 14), escort Zion's *sons* and *daughters* home (vv. 4, 8–9, 22; 49:22–23), provide their *riches* to help faithful Judeans recuperate (vv. 5–6, 11, 16–17), *rebuild* the *walls* of Jerusalem with *gates* (vv. 10–11, 18; 54:12), and join Yahweh's people in *praise* and *honor of the Lord* (vv. 6, 10), including making *offerings* to Yahweh at the Jerusalem *temple* (vv. 6–7).

Yahweh will replace Zion's *violence, ruin, destruction*, and *sorrow* (vv. 18, 20; 58:3–4, 6, 9–10; 59:6–7) with *peace* and *righteousness* (v. 17). Zion will become *radiant* (v. 5) and full of *splendor* (vv. 9, 21), and God will *adorn* and *glorify the place of* the *sanctuary* (v. 13) and multiply their numbers (v. 22). By sending the Babylonians to devastate Judah (587 BCE; Jer 25:8–10), *in anger* Yahweh *struck* that nation (v. 10; 54:7; 57:16–17) so that it was *forsaken and hated* (v. 15; 49:14; 54:6; 62:4). However, God will now restore

---

The Message of Isaiah 60–62
The prophet's message has several elements. First, he declares that Yahweh will use the nations to increase Jerusalem's population by restoring more exiles to it, and Yahweh's people will bring foreigners into their religious community (60:1–22). Second, the penitent Judean remnant declares that Yahweh sent the prophet to encourage returning exiles to be faithful to Yahweh (61:1–11). Third, the prophet and his associates beseech Yahweh to restore Zion. Graciously, Yahweh consents (62:1–12).

Symbolic City Names
In the ancient Near East, parts of cities or their fortifications often bore symbolic names. The most famous case was in Babylon, which bore several dozen poetic names for the city itself and many more for various temples, shrines, and other locales within it. The book of Isaiah thus uses a common practice in naming parts of Jerusalem's walls, but does so for highly spiritual reasons.

the nation (v. 10; 49:15; 54:7–10). Zion will receive symbolic names such as *The City of the Lord* and *Zion of the Holy One of Israel* (v. 14). This will be true even of the city walls (v. 18).

In chapter 61, it is impossible to identify the speaker in verses 1–7, 10–11: possibly the fifth-century BCE prophet; more likely, the penitent, faithful remnant of restored exiles distinguished from the larger body of Jews (42:1–7; 57–59). Yahweh speaks in verses 8–9. The faithful remnant recognizes that Yahweh's *spirit* (NRSV) is upon it, because Yahweh *anointed* (designated) and *sent* it on a mission to announce to the people that they will soon exchange their great problems for great blessings. Like their capital city, these new converts will receive a symbolic name, *Oaks of Righteousness, a Planting of the Lord*, and thus will become Exhibit A *for the display of* Yahweh's *splendor* (vv. 1–3; 60:9, 21).

The new converts will *rebuild, restore,* and *renew* neglected *ruins* in Judah and Jerusalem. *Aliens* and *foreigners* will join them to care for Judah's *flocks, fields, vineyards,* or, in other words, the primary elements of the nation's economic life (49:22–23; 60:10). The converts receive another symbolic name, *priests,* or *ministers of the Lord,* selected by Yahweh to bring to reality the original purpose for all Israel to bring the nations to God (Exod 19:4–6). Yahweh's faithful *people will rejoice* in receiving their *inheritance in their land,* which Yahweh intended for the people all along (vv. 4–7; see Gen 13:14–18; 15:7–21).

Yahweh responds to the cries of the chosen people, promising to *reward* and *make an everlasting covenant with* the faithful remnant who practices *justice* (1:27–28; 58:1–12; 59:15c–19), declaring that *all the nations who see them* as they faithfully serve Yahweh *will acknowledge they are a people the Lord has blessed* (vv. 8–9; 19:24–25; 44:3).

Judah's faithful remnant responds to Yahweh's assurances with joy, because Yahweh *clothed* them *with garments of salvation, a robe of righteousness,* and deliverance like an adorned *bridegroom* and *bride.* Moreover, Yahweh offers to bring all the nations into a state of well-being and justice like *soil causes seeds to grow* (45:8; 55:10–11). As Whybray (246) says, "The nations will be observers and witnesses of the salvation conferred upon God's people" (compare Isa 52:10).

> **Yahweh's Promise**
>
> *Isaiah 62 relates a dialogue between the prophet (vv. 1–7, 10, 12) and Yahweh as reported by the prophet (vv. 8–9, 11).* Notice the clauses, the Lord has sworn (*v.* 8) *and* the Lord has made proclamation (*v.* 11).

In chapter 62, just as Amos interceded for Israel (Amos 7:2, 5), the prophet (v. 1) and his associates (*watchmen,* v. 6) resolve *not* to *keep silent* but to "nag" Yahweh incessantly, *till* Jerusalem's *righteousness* (*vindication* [NRSV] or *salvation*) occurs—that is, until Yahweh elevates Jerusalem to a position of international prominence so it can bear witness to the glory of its God (vv. 2, 6–7). Yahweh will change Jerusalem's symbolic name from *forsaken* (Hebrew '*azuvah;* 49:14; 54:6–8) and *Desolate* (Hebrew *shemamah*) to *My Delight Is In Her* (Hebrew *cheftsivah*) and *Married* (Hebrew *be'ulah = Beulah;* NRSV), indicating *the Lord will take delight in* the city (vv. 4–5). Restored Jerusalem *will be a crown of splendor* and *a royal diadem* that Yahweh holds so all may admire it (v. 3; compare vv. 1–7). The possibly embarrassing idea of Jerusalem's *sons* marrying their own mother city (v. 5a–b) has provoked numerous textual emendations and interpretations, none of which is satisfactory (Koole, *Isaiah 56–66*, 310–11). One aspect of the solution must be that "the prophet proceeds from such a close relationship between Zion and her land that he identifies both here" (Koole, *Isaiah 56–66*, 311).

Yahweh swears *never again* to give the *grain* and *new wine for which* the faithful returned exiles *have toiled* to *enemies* and *foreigners* (65:21–22; Deut 28:30; Amos 5:11). Instead, the returned people will benefit from their own labor and enjoy its use (compare Amos 9:14), and so they will *praise the Lord* (vv. 8–9).

The fifth-century BCE prophet responds by summoning Judeans already returned to Jerusalem to *prepare the way* (40:3–5; 57:14) for others still in foreign lands to return. "Apparently the majority of this people is in the Diaspora, and the people present in Jerusalem are responsible for their return. . . . Given the salvation . . . they themselves have experienced, Zion's inhabitants can make the way of salvation attractive to those who are absent" (Koole, *Isaiah 56–66*, 321–22). Then the prophet summons these Judeans to *raise a banner* (5:26; 11:12; 13:2; 18:3; 49:22) *for the nations* to abandon their gods in order to worship and serve Yahweh (v. 10; 2:2–4; 19:23–25; 42:1–7; 45:20–23; 49:1–7).

Yahweh instructs *the ends of the earth* to tell *Zion* that its *salvation* (NRSV) *comes.* By fighting for Jerusalem, Yahweh has earned the *reward,* or *recompense,* of *salvation* for Zion (v. 11; 40:10).

To emphasize Yahweh's restoration of Jerusalem, the prophet declares additional *new names* (vv. 2, 4) that Yahweh gives its inhabitants: *the Holy People* (6:13; 63:18), *the Redeemed of the Lord* (1:27–28; 35:8–10), *Sought After* (Jer 30:14, 17), *the City No Longer Deserted* (v. 4; 54:7–8). As before, these symbolic names reinforce the hearers' sense of God's care for them.

Israel & Edom

Edom's historical relationship with Israel was a complex one. The two nations thought of themselves as kin, as the stories of Jacob and Esau, their ancestors, show. During the Persian and Hellenistic eras, the Edomites moved west into the land of Israel proper and converted to Judaism.

63:1–6 Edom joined Babylon to overthrow Judah when it concluded that Babylon would prevail (Ps 137:7–8; Obad 10–14). Like chapter 34, this section announces Yahweh's *day of vengeance* against *Edom* (v. 4; 34:8; 61:2) for oppressing Judah. A watchman (21:11–12; 62:6–7) asks two questions (vv. 1a–d, 2), each of which Yahweh answers (vv. 1e–f, 3–6). The first is: *Who is this coming from Edom?* (Hebrew *'edom*). The question is much like our "Who goes there?" Yahweh replies to the question, *It is I,* announcing vindication (NRSV), *mighty to save;* that is, God comes to punish Israel's oppressors and captors and to deliver them from them (v. 1).

The second question is: *Why are your garments red*? (Hebrew *'adom*), a word-play on *Edom* (Gen 25:30). Yahweh answers this question by saying, *In my anger* (see vv. 3, 5, 6), *I have trodden the winepress* (that is, Edom) *alone* (vv. 3, 6; 59:16; compare Lam 1:15; Joel 3:13; Rev 14:19–20; 19:15) without using other nations. The prophet quotes God as saying that the Edomites' *blood spattered my garments* on my *day of vengeance* (vv. 3–4; Isa 61:2). Red wine suggests *blood* (vv. 1–3, 6).

63:7–64:12 Here the sixth-century BCE prophet speaks on behalf of Yahweh's faithful people (*we, us, our*: 63:7, 15, 16, 17, 18; 64:3, 5, 6, 7, 8, 9, 11, 12; compare the labels in 63:17, 18; 64:4, 5, 9). He rehearses Yahweh's past mighty deeds on behalf of the people (63:7–14), then beseeches Yahweh to redeem them yet again (63:15–64:12). The text uses the form of communal laments seen in Psalms 44, 85, 89, and so on. This oracle originally dates between 587 BCE and 536 BCE, since the *sacred cities* of Judah lie in ruins; *Zion*, or *Jerusalem*, is uninhabited; and the Jerusalem *temple has been burned with fire* (64:10–11). In the flow of the final form of Isaiah, concern for the restoration of Yahweh's faithful exiles (63:7–64:12) naturally follows a description of Yahweh's destruction of Edom and its allies, especially Babylon, who demolished Judah and Jerusalem (63:1–6).

In 63:7–14, as in Psalms 44:1–8, 85:1–3, and 89:1–37, the prophet, as spokesperson for Yahweh's faithful servants, rehearses Yahweh's former mighty *deeds for the house of Israel* (v. 7), especially in *the days of Moses* (vv. 11–12). He enumerates the key events of the crossing of the Reed Sea (vv. 11–13; Exod 14:21–15:18) and the wilderness wanderings (Ps 78:51–55). To emphasize Yahweh's immediate presence with the people, the prophet also mentions *the angel of his presence* (v. 9; Exod 23:20–23; 32:34; 33:2; Num 20:16; Judg 2:1–5; following the NIV contra the NRSV; Blenkinsopp, *Isaiah 56–66*, 260–61) and *God's holy spirit* (NRSV), or presence (Pss 51:11; 139:7), whom *he set among them* (v. 11), and by whom he gave them *rest* (v. 14; Westermann 389). These deeds reveal Yahweh's *mercy* and *steadfast love* (vv. 7, 9; NRSV), which accrue *everlasting renown* and *a glorious name* in the eyes of Israel and the rest of the nations (vv. 12, 14). The prophet notes that Yahweh assumed the redeemed people would be faithful (v. 8), but they *grieved his holy spirit* (v. 10 NRSV; compare Gen 6:6; Ps 78:40) so he *became their enemy* (v. 10; Isa 1:24; see Lam 2:5).

The appeals to God follow several lines. First, the prophet says that with the Judeans in exile, there is no evidence of Yahweh's *zeal, might, tenderness and compassion* toward the people. In other words,

> **The Prophet Appeals to God**
> In Isaiah 63:7–64:12, just as in Psalms 44:9–26, 85:4–13, and 89:38–51, as the faithful exiles' spokesman, the prophet uses several incentives to persuade Yahweh to help the oppressed people (63:15; compare 57:15; Pss 14:2; 33:13–15; 80:14). The prophet asks God to return (63:17) and to rend the heavens and come down as at Mount Sinai when the mountains trembled, fire burned hot as in a kiln, and people quaked (64:1–3; Exod 19:16–20). That is, the prophet appeals to divine honor and the precedents of the past in order to shape a present reality.

God's basic characteristics seem obscured (63:15). Second, God's people depend on Yahweh, not on *Abraham* or *Israel* (*Jacob*) as their *Father* to protect and nurture them. Therefore, his absence can seem a way of making the people *wander from his ways* and *harden* their *hearts* (Exod 4:21; 7:3; 9:12; 14:4, 8, 17; Josh 11:20) *so they do not revere* him (63:16–17). Third, Yahweh's temple has fallen to hostile pagans, making Yahweh's people *like those whom* Yahweh does *not rule, like those not called by Yahweh's name* (63:18–19; NRSV, contra NIV). The loss of the temple seems to nullify Yahweh's role as the people's *Redeemer* (63:16). Fourth, Yahweh's people are in an unsolvable dilemma: their incomparable God delivers obedient, faithful people, but their sins have made them like an *unclean* menstrual cloth. The prophet uses a series of disgusting images to illustrate their disgusting behavior (compare Rom 1:22–32). *How then can* they *be saved?* (64:4–7). They wonder whether Yahweh would consider delivering them in spite of their stubbornness. Fifth, Yahweh is Israel's *Father* (63:16) and *potter* (29:16; 45:9–10), while they are Yahweh's *people* (63:8, 18) and the *clay* Yahweh *formed* (43:1, 21; 44:2, 21). Therefore, they beseech Yahweh not to keep punishing them for their *sins forever*, but, considering this intimate relationship, to forgive and restore them (64:8–9; Ps 103:8–14). Sixth, the prophet notes that the *sacred cities* of Judah, *Zion* (that is, *Jerusalem*), and the *temple* have all experienced destruction at the hand of the Babylonians (2 Kgs 24:1–4; 25:1–12). He then asks whether God can remain aloof from the sufferings of the chosen people (64:10–12; compare 42:14; 57:11). These appeals to God cumulatively paint a picture of a penitent people who have lost everything and seek to regain the one thing that matters—their relationship with the redeeming God who repeatedly rescued them and who will, they hope, do so again.

65:1–66:24 Responding to Israel's complaint that Yahweh did not answer them when they called to him for help (63:15, 17; 64:1, 7, 9, 12), Yahweh declares that he repeatedly *called* to them, but most of them *did not answer*; he *spoke* to them, but they *did not listen* (65:1, 12, 24; 66:4); instead, they were *obstinate*, pursued *their own imaginations* (65:2), and *did evil in* Yahweh's *sight* (65:12; 66:4). But a small remnant returned to him; ultimately, he will restore them (65:8–10, 17–25; 66:2, 10–16), and they will bring peoples from *all the nations* to Yahweh (66:18–23). Yahweh distinguishes between his true *servants* and those who pretend to be his people (65:8–16; 66:5). Isaiah 65–66 falls into three sections: Yahweh will destroy his people who rebelled against him but restore a remnant (65:1–16); Yahweh will bless his true servants (65:17–25); Yahweh promises his true servants in Zion (Jerusalem) a bright future but decrees harsh punishment for his people who worship idols (66:1–24).

65:1–16 Yahweh denounces Judean exiles as a whole for rejecting the call, *Here am I, here am I.* They refused to *ask for* or *call on his name* (55:6–7; 58:2; 64:7), practicing illicit *sacrifices*, sitting *among graves*, keeping secret vigil at night, eating pork and other *unclean meat*, maintaining they were holier than others (65:1–5b,

7b–c; 1:29–31; 57:4–10; 66:3). Consequently, they are *smoke in* his nostrils, *a fire that keeps burning all day* and provokes him to anger (Deut 32:22; Pss 18:8; 74:1; Jer 15:14; 17:4). Accordingly, Yahweh will punish them (65:5c–7b, 7e–f).

The text uses several agricultural images to indicate that, conversely, Yahweh will rescue those from *Jacob* (that is, northern Israel) and *Judah*. First, just as viticulturists save a *cluster of grapes* still containing *juice*, so will God preserve them. Second, they will graze their *flocks* and *herds* in choice *pasture* and *resting place*[s] in their land, *Sharon* (35:2) and *the Valley of Achor* (Hos 2:15). In other words, their territory will extend well beyond the tiny limits of the Persian province of Yehud into the original territory of the kingdom of Judah.

On the other hand, God will destroy with the *sword* the majority of Israel. The prophet defends this destruction by noting that the majority *forsake the Lord*, do *not answer* when he calls, and do *evil in* his *sight*, including practicing idolatry by spreading *a table for* the god *Fortune* (Hebrew *Gad*) and filling *bowls of mixed wine for* the deity *Destiny* (Hebrew *Meni*) as means of communing with them (65:8–12).

Summarizing, Yahweh's true *servants will eat, drink, rejoice, sing*, receive *another name* (56:5; 62:2–4, 12), *invoke a blessing*, and *swear by the God of truth* (compare Deut 10:20) *in the land*, forgetting their *past troubles*. On the other hand, apostate worshipers will experience physical, mental, and spiritual deprivation, and ultimately they will die ignominiously (65:13–16).

For his small band of true servants in Judah, Yahweh will remove *the former things*—that is, their past troubles (65:16) and *the sound of weeping and crying*, and he will *create new heavens and a new earth* so *Jerusalem can be a delight and its people a joy* (65:17–19). There are three dimensions to this new creation. First, Yahweh's true servants will not die in infancy but will live to a very old age (65:20, 23). Ancient peoples considered long life a great blessing, particularly since their childhood mortality rate was so high. Second, Yahweh's true servants *will long enjoy the works of their hands* and realize the benefits and blessings of their labors (65:21–22; 62:8–9; Deut 6:10–11; 8:12; but see Deut 28:30, 38–44). Another great blessing was meaningful work. Third, Yahweh will *answer* the prayers of his true servants *before they call*; he will be eager to provide for their needs, and he will promote peace between hostile groups and individuals in society (65:24–25; compare 11:6–9).

In chapter 66, the fifth-century BCE prophet proclaims Yahweh's message, using standard formulas for introducing divine speech (*this is what the Lord says;*

> **Gad & Meni**
> *The identities of the deities Gad and Meni are obscure. The names may be epithets of otherwise known ancient gods (much as one calls George Herman Ruth "Babe" or "The Sultan of Swat"). Or they may have been minor deities that Israelites worshiped to forestall bad things happening to them. Whatever their identity, worshiping them illustrated a lack of confidence in Yahweh's management of the future. Hence the prophet's strong condemnation.*

hear the word of the Lord; declares the Lord; says the Lord [see 66:1, 5, 12, 17, 21, 22, 23]). He speaks to the small Judean community in Jerusalem, consisting of both counterfeit and true servants of Yahweh.

On the one hand, Yahweh announces *harsh treatment* on the people who worship other gods and treat their fellow human beings unjustly; all others will despise them (66:3–4, 17, 24). Yahweh rejects the sacrifices and other forms of worship of this group because: *they have chosen their own ways* rather than Yahweh's (55:8–9); *their souls delight in their abominations* (idols) (vv. 3, 17; compare 44:19; 65:2–4; Ezek 5:9, 11); they did not *answer* when Yahweh *called* (65:1–2, 12); and *they did evil in* Yahweh's *sight* (65:12) by oppressing the poor and defenseless (58:1–12; 59:3–8). All these indictments repeat themes of 1:10–17.

On the other hand, Yahweh, who *made all things* and rules the universe from the *heavenly throne, esteems* people who are *humble and contrite in spirit and* [who] *tremble at* the divine *word* (vv. 1–2; 57:15). Their wicked opponents in the faith community *hate* and want to *exclude* them, but Yahweh promises to make things right. God will come as a mighty warrior to bless the true followers and *execute judgment upon* counterfeit worshipers with *fury, fire, chariots, anger and sword* (vv. 5–6, 14–16; 65:6–7). Yahweh will empower *Zion* (*Jerusalem*) to *give birth* to numerous *children* (that is, to grow rapidly in population), and *will extend prosperity* (NRSV) *to her like a river* and *the wealth of nations like a flooding stream* (60:5–14; 61:5), so that Yahweh's true servants who live there, those who now *love her* and *mourn over her*, will *drink deeply* and *delight in her overflowing abundance* (vv. 7–12). *As a mother comforts her child,* Yahweh will *comfort* his new faith community in Jerusalem (v. 13; 49:14–15).

The book concludes with a vision of Yahweh assembling all *nations and tongues* to *see his glory*. The righteous remnant will also *proclaim* God's *glory among the nations* and will reassemble the chosen people from their various locations throughout the Near Eastern world. All Jews will return to *the temple of the Lord in Jerusalem as an offering to the Lord.* Yahweh will *select some* of the foreigners from other nations to be his *priests and Levites.* Jerusalem's *name and descendants will endure* throughout the generations, and *all mankind will come and bow down before* Yahweh there (vv. 17–23; 45:20–25; 56:6–8). "This is . . . a great inclusive, universal reach of Yahweh to claim sovereignty over all peoples and to include all nations in the protected, blessed, covenanted community" (Brueggemann, *Isaiah 40–66*, 258).

Universalism in Isaiah

The final vision of the book of Isaiah, like so much of the rest of the book, offers a picture of universal human well-being under the rule of God. Israel does not exist for its own sake alone, but for the sake of all humanity. The universalizing vision of the book draws deeply from the biblical tradition and leads to both Judaism's views of itself as a chosen people bearing witness to God and to Christianity's desire to heal all the nations (see Rev 22:2).

THEOLOGICAL REFLECTIONS

The authors of the book of Isaiah in its present form were addressing a small Jewish community in and near Jerusalem in the mid- to late fifth century BCE, consisting of both faithful servants of Yahweh and counterfeit worshipers. The authors reapplied Yahweh's former activities to this new situation, emphasizing the characteristics of Yahweh that these activities demonstrated as denunciations of the wicked and encouragements to the righteous.

Yahweh *created, formed, made, stretched or spread out* the universe and all that is in it, including humankind (29:16; 37:16; 40:26, 28; 42:5; 45:12, 18; 48:13; 51:13, 16; 54:16; 66:1–2); God created different physical conditions on earth (41:17–20); he made Jacob (Israel) (43:1, 7, 15; 44:2, 21–24; 45:9, 11; 49:5 [the remnant]; 54:5); God is the author of righteousness, punishment, and blessing (45:7, 8), and of new and hidden things previously unknown (48:6–7); he will create a new heaven and a new earth, with Jerusalem as a joy (65:17–18). All creatures belong to God, demonstrating God's power, wisdom, love, and care.

Yahweh acts in human history to accomplish eternal purposes, controlling kings, nations, and events. After destroying human life on earth with the flood, Yahweh promised never to do so again (54:9). He redeemed Abraham from Ur of the Chaldees (29:22) and promised to multiply his descendants greatly (51:1–2). He delivered the Israelites from Egyptian bondage (10:24–26; 11:11, 15–16; 43:12, 16–17; 63:7–9), supplied their needs during the wilderness wanderings (48:20–21), and gave them the promised land as a precursor to delivering their descendants from Assyria (11:15–16; 30:15; 37:20, 35) and Babylon (35:8–10; 40:3–4; 43:14–17; 52:3–6) to prosper in the promised land again (60:21; 61:7; 62:4). Yahweh established David and his dynasty, empowering David to capture Zion/Jerusalem and make it Yahweh's dwelling place (1:27–28; 2:2–4; 4:2–6; 8:18; 12:6; 14:32; 18:7; 24:23; 29:1–8; 31:4–5; 33:20; 35:10; 51:3, 11; 52:1–8; 55:3; 60:14; 62:11–12); God raised up penitent Hezekiah of the Davidic lineage to restore justice and righteousness in Judah (8:21–9:7; 32:1–8). Yahweh used Tiglath-Pileser III of Assyria to overthrow Syria and North Israel and to punish Ahaz and Judah (7:17, 20; 8:7–8); Sennacherib to destroy the cities of Judah and besiege Jerusalem as punishment for the sins of Hezekiah and Judah (1:2–9; 10:5–19; 36–37); Nebuchadnezzar to devastate Jerusalem and carry many Judeans into exile (47:6–7; 54:6–8); and Cyrus to *redeem* (1:27–28; 41:14; 43:1, 14; 44:6, 22–24; 47:4; 48:17, 20; 49:7, 26; 52:9; 54:5, 8; 59:20; 60:16; 63:16) or *save* (35:4; 43:3, 11; 45:15, 17, 21; 49:25–26; 60:16) Yahweh's faithful servants from captivity and return them to their land (13:17–19; 14:1–2; 41:2–3, 25; 44:24–45:7; 45:13; 46:8–11).

Yahweh is *the Lord, and there is no other; besides him there is no god* (44:6; 45:5, 14; 46:9). Other gods are false because they are the work of human hands and can do nothing (2:8, 18–21; 21:9; 40:19–20; 44:9–20; 46:1–2), whereas Yahweh is *the living God* (37:4, 17) who intervenes in nature and history to accomplish holy purposes. Yahweh is incomparable (40:18, 25; 46:5, 9). To emphasize God's transcendent majesty, Isaiah affirms that God is *holy* (5:16; 6:3; 52:10; 57:15), calls him *the Holy One* (*of Israel, or Jacob*) (twenty-nine times; for example, 1:4; 5:19, 24; 29:19, 23; 54:5; 55:5), and extols his *glory* (3:8; 6:3; 10:16; 35:2; 40:5; 42:8; 48:11; 58:8; 59:19; 60:1–2; 62:2; 66:18–19). Yahweh is *king* of the individual (6:1, 5), of Israel (33:22; 41:21; 43:15; 44:6; 52:7), of the nations (24:21), and of all creation, including the angelic hosts (24:21–23).

Yahweh has an intimate, daily, personal relationship with the chosen people Israel, which Isaiah compares with the relationship of king to people (6:1–5; 33:22; 40:1–11; 52:7–12), husband to wife (50:1; 54:1–8; 62:1–5), parent (father and mother) to child (1:2–4; 45:9–11; 49:14–15; 63:16; 64:8; 66:13), shepherd to sheep (40:11), vinedresser to vineyard (5:1–7; 27:2–6), doctor to patient (1:5–6), potter to clay (29:15–16; 45:9; 64:8), and teacher to student (28:5–13; 30:19–26; 48:17–19).

This relationship experienced certain vicissitudes, which essentially form the backbone of Isaiah's message. First, Yahweh chose Israel as a people in the exodus, wilderness wanderings, giving of the law at Sinai and settlement of the land (14:1; 41:8–10; 44:1–2; 51:10), like a husband marrying *the wife of his youth* (54:5–8). God chose Israel to be his *servant* (41:8–10; 43:10; 44:1–2, 21, 26; 45:4; 48:20; 49:3, 5–7; 50:10; 52:12; 53:11) and *witnesses* (43:10, 12; 44:8), *messenger*(*s*) (42:19; 44:26), and a *light* (42:6; 49:6) to the nations to open their blind eyes and deaf ears (42:7; 52:13) so they will serve Israel's God. As Yahweh's *servant*, Israel's "great task is to bear testimony that Yahweh alone is God, that there is no savior beside him" (Muilenburg 405), and by doing this attempt to bring the nations to Yahweh.

Second, Israel *forsook* Yahweh (1:4, 28; 65:11) like a wife forsakes her husband for other lovers (50:1). Pride, arrogance, self-centeredness, and ingratitude ruled Israel's heart (2:11–17; 5:15, 21), motivating them to abandon Yahweh for other gods (2:8, 18–21; 10:10–11; 31:6–7; 44:9–20; 57:5–10; 65:2–5), trust in military strength and foreign nations rather than Yahweh (7:1–17; 8:3–10; 30:1–7; 31:1–3), practice external religious rituals although the worshipers' hearts were far from Yahweh (29:13–14), and oppress the defenseless and poor (1:10–17, 21–26; 3:13–15; 5:1–17, 22–23; 10:1–4; 58:1–14). Israel, whom Yahweh appointed to help the nations *see* and *hear* was itself *blind* and *deaf* (6:9–10; 42:18–20; 43:8).

Third, Yahweh punished Israel like a husband *forsakes*, *abandons*, and *divorces* his wife as a last resort for her infidelity (50:1; 54:5–8). On *the day of Yahweh* (2:12–17; 7:18–25; 22:5–14), God *sent* Assyria (7:16–20; 8:7–8; 10:5–19; 28:1–4) and angrily gave *Israel into Babylon's hand* (39:1–6; 47:6).

Fourth, however, Yahweh still loves Israel (54:5–8; 62:4–5) and yearns for her to return to him (65:1, 12, 24; 66:4).

Fifth, Yahweh will woo and marry the penitent in Israel, the remnant (46:3), once more (54:5–8; 62:4–5). The authors of Isaiah have placed 28:23–29 strategically to summarize how Yahweh works with his rebellious, then penitent, people. Sweeney comments that the farmer "plows, harrows, and overturns the earth, but it is of limited duration. Because his purpose is to provide food, he plants seeds and orders his land so that cummin and the various grains will grow. Likewise, when he harvests his crops, his actions are essentially destructive, but again they are not thoroughly destructive in that they lead to a positive result. In this manner, the actions of the farmer are compared to those of the coming invader. There will be destruction and hardship, but the result will be the reestablishment of Yahweh's glory and justice once the incompetent leadership is removed" (Sweeney 366; compare Beuken, *Isaiah Chapters 28–39*, 59–68).

Yahweh's comprehensive plan is to use his faithful elect to *save* the nations. Though world powers, the nations *are like a drop from a bucket, as dust on the scales* (40:15), *as less than nothing* (40:17), *like grasshoppers* (40:22) before Yahweh. He uses the nations to punish his people (5:26–30; 10:5–19; 44:24–45:7) and to return them from captivity (49:22–23; 60:10–16). Like Israel (2:6–22), the nations are full of pride, arrogance, self-centeredness, and ingratitude (13:11, 19; 14:11–15; 16:6; 23:7–12; 47:8–11). Therefore, like Israel, on *the day of Yahweh*, Yahweh punishes them (13:6–13; 19:1–15; 23:1–18; 47:1–15). But Yahweh's ultimate purpose is to draw in the nations to *save* them (2:2–4; 19:23–25; 45:20–25; 49:1–6; 52:13–53:12).

Jesus, born and raised a Jew, took up this Isaianic vision and gathered around himself a *little flock* (Luke 12:32) of twelve Jewish disciples, first commissioning them to *go nowhere among the Gentiles, and enter no town of the Samaritans, but go rather to the lost sheep of the house of Israel* (Matt 10:5–6). But after his resurrection, he commissioned them to *go and make disciples of all nations* (Matt 28:19). Everywhere Paul, *a Hebrew born of Hebrews* (Phil 3:5), traveled proclaiming God's message of salvation, he went first to the Jews, then to the Gentiles (Rom 1:16; Acts 13:44–48). He designated those who came to God through Christ the *true Israel of God* (Rom 9:6–8; Gal 6:11–16). Like Isaiah, the New Testament distinguishes between faithful, penitent servants of God and those who pretend to serve him (Titus 1:16; 1 John 2:19; Heb 10:32–39).

The Remnant

"Remnant" in Isaiah refers to different groups in different contexts: physical survivors of northern Israel after Tiglath-Pileser III's invasion (7:3–9; 17:6; 28:5); Judah after Sennacherib's invasion (1:9; 4:3; 37:4, 31–32); Babylon (14:22), Philistia (14:30), Moab (15:9; 16:14), and Aram (Syria) (17:3); spiritual survivors of northern Israel after Tiglath-Pileser III's invasion (10:20–23; 11:11, 15–16); and Judah after Babylon destroyed Jerusalem (46:3). Isaiah's author addresses the book to the remnant of Judah in Jerusalem and its environs in the mid- to late fifth century BCE. This remnant consists of faithful "servants" of Yahweh, as well as counterfeits (54:11–17; 63:15–19; 65:8–16; 66:14–16); Yahweh's future lies with the faithful.

FOR FURTHER STUDY

Blenkinsopp, Joseph. *Opening the Sealed Book: Interpretations of the Book of Isaiah in Late Antiquity*. Grand Rapids: Eerdmans, 2006.

Childs, Brevard S. *The Struggle to Understand Isaiah as Christian Scripture*. Grand Rapids: Eerdmans, 2004.

Couey, J. Blake. *Reading the Poetry of First Isaiah: The Most Perfect Model of the Prophetic Poetry*. Oxford: Oxford University Press, 2015.

WORKS CITED

Baltzer, Klaus. *Deutero-Isaiah: A Commentary on Isaiah 40–55*. Minneapolis: Fortress, 2001.

Beuken, Willem A. M. *Isaiah Part II*. Volume 2: *Isaiah Chapters 28–39*. Leuven: Peeters, 2000.

Blenkinsopp, Joseph. *Isaiah 1–39*. New York: Doubleday, 2000.

———. *Isaiah 40–55*. New York: Doubleday, 2002.

———. *Isaiah 56–66*. New York: Doubleday, 2003.

Bright, John. *A History of Israel*. 3rd ed. Philadelphia: Westminster, 1981.

Brueggemann, Walter. *Isaiah 1–39*. Louisville: Westminster John Knox, 1998.

———. *Isaiah 40–66*. Louisville: Westminster John Knox, 1998.

Childs, Brevard S. *Isaiah*. Louisville: Westminster John Knox, 2001.

Clements, Ronald E. *Isaiah 1–39*. Grand Rapids: Eerdmans, 1980.

Erlandsson, Seth. *The Burden of Babylon: A Study of Isaiah 13:2–14:23*. Lund: Gleerup, 1970.

Goldingay, John. *Isaiah*. Peabody, MA: Hendrickson, 2001.

Hayes, John H. "Isaiah, Book of." In *Dictionary of Biblical Interpretation*, 1:549–56. Nashville: Abingdon, 1999.

Hayes, John H., and Stuart A. Irvine. *Isaiah the Eighth-Century Prophet: His Times & His Preaching*. Nashville: Abingdon, 1987.

Koole, Jan L. *Isaiah III*. Volume 1: *Isaiah 40–48*. Kampen: Kok, 1997.

———. *Isaiah III*. Volume 2: *Isaiah 49–55*. Kampen: Kok, 1998.

———. *Isaiah III*. Volume 3: *Isaiah 56–66*. Kampen: Kok, 2001.

Motyer, J. Alec. *The Prophecy of Isaiah: An Introduction and Commentary*. Downers Grove, IL: InterVarsity Press, 1993.

Muilenburg, James. "The Book of Isaiah Chapters 40–66: Introduction and Exegesis." In *The Interpreter's Bible*, edited by George Buttrick et al., 5:381–773. Nashville: Abingdon, 1956.

Oswalt, John N. *The Book of Isaiah Chapters 1–39*. Grand Rapids: Eerdmans, 1986.

Pritchard, James, ed. *Ancient Near Eastern Texts*. 3rd ed. Princeton: Princeton University Press, 1969.

Seitz, Christopher R. *Isaiah 1–39*. Louisville: John Knox, 1993.

———. "The Book of Isaiah 40–66: Introduction, Commentary, and Reflections." In *The New Interpreter's Bible*, edited by Leander Keck, 6:307–552. Nashville: Abingdon, 2001.

Sweeney, Marvin A. *Isaiah 1–39 with an Introduction to Prophetic Literature*. Volume 16 of *The Forms of the Old Testament Literature*. Grand Rapids: Eerdmans, 1996.

Tucker, Gene M. "The Book of Isaiah 1–39: Introduction, Commentary, and Reflections." In *The New Interpreter's Bible*, edited by Leander Keck, 6:25–305. Nashville: Abingdon, 2001.

Watts, John D. W. *Isaiah 1–33*. Waco, TX: Word, 1985.

Westermann, Claus. *Isaiah 40–66: A Commentary*. Philadelphia: Westminster, 1969.

Whybray, Roger N. *Isaiah 40–66*. London: Oliphants, 1975.

Wildberger, Hans. *Isaiah 1–12*. Minneapolis: Fortress, 1991.

Jeremiah

Keith N. Schoville

CHAPTER CONTENTS

MAPS, TABLES, & FEATURES

The Book of Jeremiah is a collection of oracles revealed to the inspired prophet. These are primarily poetic in form, as is true of other prophets. The main feature of Hebrew poetry is parallelism, that is, a line that repeats or supplements the thought in a previous line. For example, in Jeremiah 1:5–6 we read:

> Before I formed you in the womb I knew you,
> before you were born I set you apart;
> I appointed you as a prophet to the nations.

In addition to poetic oracles, however, prose elements may appear within or between oracles (as in 9:12–16), including biographical information. Most contemporary English translations identify these elements and set them off appropriately, so it is relatively easy to identify poetry from prose. Being aware of poetic expression helps us appreciate the cooperative creativity of the Lord and the prophet. Jeremiah's words combine the inspirational activity of God with the verbal activity of the prophet, making the combined effect memorable.

CONTEXTS

Jeremiah lived and fulfilled his ministry in a crucial period in the history of God's people. As the historical prologue (1:1–3) indicates, Josiah was in his thirteenth year as king of Judah when Jeremiah heard the Lord's call to prophesy (627 BCE). Josiah was eight years old when he became king (640 BCE), so he was twenty-one when Jeremiah answered the Lord's call. We do not know Jeremiah's age at the time; perhaps he was about the same age as the king. Five years later, workers found the scroll of the Law in the temple as they refurbished the building (2 Kgs 22). The young king was horrified at the sorry state of the religion of his people when compared to the covenant stipulations in the scroll (probably Deuteronomy or part of it). After the reign of Hezekiah in the days of the prophet Isaiah, Manasseh and his son Amon, grandfather and father of Josiah, led the nation astray. In the aftermath of the discovery of the scroll, Josiah instituted the reforms for which he is famous (2 Kgs 24:25). This involved cleansing the temple of all its unorthodox elements, eliminating worship at places other than Jerusalem, purifying the priesthood, and reestablishing the religious practices of the Law of Moses.

Thirteen years later (609 BCE), Josiah met his death when he and his kingdom became involved in the international politics of the day. Three major power centers—Egypt, Assyria, and Babylonia (Chaldea)—struggled for dominance over the region between the Euphrates River and the Sinai Peninsula. Assyria, which had dominated the region for over a century and carried the northern kingdom Israel into exile in 722 BCE, declined in power after the fall of Nineveh in 612 BCE. Egypt was allied to Assyria at the time, and Pharaoh Neco moved north through Palestine to thwart the growing power of Nabopolassar of Babylon. King Josiah attempted to stop the Egyptians in a battle at Megiddo but died in battle. Pharaoh Neco then replaced Josiah's immediate successor, Jehoahaz (Shallum; Jer 22:11), with his brother, Eliakim, and gave him the throne name Jehoiakim. Neco also required an excessive tribute from the Judeans.

In order to maintain their dominance in the region, the Egyptians had to confront the growing power of Babylon. The decisive battle was at Carchemish, a ford over the Euphrates River, in 605 BCE. The new king of the Babylonians was Nebuchadnezzar, who succeeded his father upon Nabopolassar's death. King Jehoiakim of Judah then became a vassal of Babylon for three years, but rebelled against Nebuchadnezzar when the latter fought Egypt in 601 BCE. Ultimately, Nebuchadnezzar put down the rebellion by besieging Jerusalem and capturing it in 597 BCE. No details survive about Jehoiakim's death in 598 BCE, but Jeremiah had predicted that he would not receive a king's burial (Jer 22:19; 36:30). Jehoiakim's son Jehoiachin, who assumed the throne as Jeconiah, or Coniah, surrendered to the Babylonians after a three-month reign. Nebuchadnezzar then placed Jehoiachin's uncle, Mattaniah, on the throne of Judah and gave him the throne name Zedekiah. Zedekiah was caught between pro-Egyptian and pro-Babylonian political groups in Judah. Despite the warning of Jeremiah that Nebuchadnezzar was the Lord's instrument to punish his rebellious people, Zedekiah entertained an anti-Babylonian conference of leaders of neighboring peoples in 594 BCE (Jer 27:3). Finally, in 589 BCE the Judeans revolted, expecting support from Egypt.

The Babylonians rampaged across the country, and by early 588 BCE the siege of Jerusalem had begun. Jeremiah remained in Jerusalem throughout the siege. Zedekiah sought and received the prophet's counsel—that the only way to save himself and the city was to surrender (21:1–14). Zedekiah, however, did not follow that advice in the face of the strong pro-Egyptian element in his advisory court. The Egyptian army did move into the region, causing the Babylonians to lift the siege briefly to shift their forces against the Egyptians (Jer 37:5), but soon the Egyptians withdrew, and the siege of Jerusalem resumed. The Babylonians breached the walls and stormed the city, probably in July 587/6 BCE (the exact year remains uncertain). Nebuchadnezzar deported a large number of people, particularly leaders of the Judeans, and appointed a governor, Gedaliah, to administer the region. Insurgents murdered the governor within months and forced a considerable number, including Jeremiah and Baruch the scribe, to seek refuge in Egypt, apparently fearing Babylonian reprisals. This brought a third and final round of deportation to Babylon (Jer 52:28–30). The Babylonians continued to control the region until Cyrus the Great wrested control of the empire from them in 539 BCE, ushering in a new era allowing those in exile to return to their homelands.

Other commentators may and often do perceive the structure of the book somewhat differently.

Chapters 1–25:14 form the core of the book, which, except for the words of a compiler(s) or editor(s), Baruch wrote on a scroll at the prophet's dictation (Jer 36:4). This material was expanded after King Jehoiakim burned the original scroll (36:23; 32). Many scholars believe that Baruch was the major compiler or editor of the book, but we

The Masoretic Text

All English translations of Jeremiah are based on the Masoretic Text. This Hebrew text had a history of development, and it reached its final form after about 250 BCE. At that time, the Greek translation of Hebrew Scriptures (the Septuagint, or LXX) began, and the Greek version of Jeremiah came to be sometime after that date. The Sepuagint is shorter than the Masoretic Text, and the arrangement of the materials of the book differ. This indicates some fluidity in the transmission of the text.

may assume that at least the final verses (52:31–34) were written some time after the death of both Jeremiah and Baruch in approximately 560 BCE. Other editorial additions appear in the text.

Initially intended for the Jerusalem audience of his contemporaries, Jeremiah gave his prophecies orally. Later they were written down, making them available to other audiences, in particular those in exile in Babylon.

There are similarities in vocabulary and ideas between Jeremiah and Deuteronomy. Critical scholarship has related the composition of Deuteronomy to the time of Josiah, based on the discovery of the "book of the law" (2 Kgs 22:8). The scholarly perception also identifies Deuteronomy as the beginning of a Deuteronomistic History that ends with 2 Kings. The German scholar Martin Noth, the primary formulator of the theory in a 1943 publication, attributed the authorship of the history to "a single exilic author/compiler." Whether or not a single individual or a group of Deuteronomists compiled the prophecies, many scholars suspect that individual or group largely formed the book of Jeremiah. Such scholars search for and highlight evidences within the book to support their views of its composition.

> **The Compilation of Jeremiah** *According to Timothy Willis:*
> The author/compiler (probably Baruch) is inspired by God to present particular prophecies in a particular arrangement for the purpose of giving a written message from God to readers living long after these events had transpired. Some prophecies that were spoken originally at separate times and under separate circumstances are now placed side by side. Such placement has an intended (and inspired) effect on later readers (*Willis* 21).

The details of the composition of the book elude us, and space does not allow an extended discussion of the matter. But the observations of at least one scholar who deals with the subject evenhandedly are useful:

> Jeremiah *himself* may have been a Deuteronomist of sorts in that he grew up in a Levitical community north of Jerusalem in which this tradition was rooted. . . .
> If then, when dictating his messages for reading at the temple, he did so in a Deuteronomic style, it would not be surprising. That was the style he grew up with. . . . (Miller 154)

COMMENTARY

HISTORICAL PROLOGUE · 1:1–3

The opening words of the book of Jeremiah place the prophet in his historical time and place. These words were not written by the prophet himself, but by the final person(s) involved in the collecting, editing, and arranging of the materials in the book. However, readers learn more about Jeremiah than any other prophet.

He was from a priestly family from Anathoth in Benjamin, about three miles northeast of Jerusalem.

The dates in this superscription range from 627/6 BCE, *the thirteenth year of the reign of Josiah*, through 609–598 BCE, *the reign of Jehoiakim*, to 586 BCE, *down to the fifth month of the eleventh year of Zedekiah*. The text mentions neither the three-month reign of Jehoahaz, nor that of Jehoiachin (598–597 BCE), who was also known as Jeconiah or Coniah. (See 2 Kgs 23–24 for Jehoahaz and Jehoiachin.)

PROPHECIES OF DESERVED DISASTER · 1:4–29:27

1:4–19 *The word of the Lord came to me* marks the beginning of a communication from Yahweh to Jeremiah, but we do not know by what means the prophet received that word. It may have come through a vision, a dream, audibly, or through some kind of mental awareness. Whatever the mode of transmission, the message was personal and specific. The call came in 627/6 BCE, but we do not know Jeremiah's age at the time of the call. He was but a *child* (Hebrew *na'ar*), or better, a *youth* (RSV).

The Lord rejected Jeremiah's sense of inadequacy and reluctance and countered with: *you must go . . . and say whatever I command you.* The Lord's words, *Do not be afraid . . . I . . . will rescue you*, and action, *reached out his hand and touched my mouth*, reassure and empower, similarly to Isaiah's experience (Isa 6:8–10).

The Lord's agenda for Jeremiah lays out in general terms the career of the new spokesperson. He is to speak the Lord's words, which have extraordinary power to bring destruction and reconstruction, not just to Judah (Israel) but also to other nations and kingdoms. The collected materials from the prophet's work, that is, the rest of the book of Jeremiah, illustrate his faithfulness to the divine call.

Two visions follow. The first in Hebrew has a play on words: *almond branch* (Hebrew *shaqed*) and *for I am watching* (Hebrew *shoqed*). This literary nicety cannot be translated into English, but it reveals the book's linguistic creativity. In the second vision Jeremiah sees a *boiling pot, tilting away from the north* toward the south. It symbolizes the disaster that will reach Jerusalem from the north in the person of unnamed invaders. Historically, Babylonian armies under Nebuchadnezzar invaded Judah. The plural *kings* refers to the great king of Babylon and his vassal kings. The boiling pot will spill over Judah as Yahweh's judgment on their paganized religious practices, a refrain that echoes throughout Jeremiah (for example, 2:26–28; 7:9; 10:3–5). Similar expressions of God's righteous judgment on his people appear in 2 Kings (21:10–15; 22:14–17).

> **"The People of the Land"**
> *The prophet learns again of God's presence and power to protect him as he faithfully confronts the entrenched political and priestly powers and* the people of the land. *The latter group are not the poor, common people but the "landed gentry"* (Bright 6).

2:1–3:5 The prophetic call is immediately followed by a series of pronouncements in which Jeremiah confronts the Judean powers with the charges the Lord brings against them.

The Septuagint in verses 1–2a says only *And he said, Thus saith the Lord.* The city is personified in the expression: *in the hearing of Jerusalem.*

In verses 2b–3, with imagery harking back to Hosea 1–3, the Lord reminds Judah of their mutual love and expresses care for, and protection of, them in the wilderness wanderings. What their forefathers had experienced, Jeremiah's generation shared in potential as descendants of that first generation. *Israel was holy to the Lord*, sanctified, set apart for special purposes. The generation to which Jeremiah spoke should also have been holy to the Lord. The imagery of the Lord's people as bride continues in the New Testament with the church as the bride of Christ (2 Cor 11:2; Eph 5:23–27).

The expression *declares the Lord* is a recurring divider between independent prophetic sayings. *House of Jacob* and *clans of the house of Israel* exhibit the characteristic parallelism of Hebrew poetry; they are equivalent. Though the northern kingdom, Israel, ended with the Assyrian conquest in 721 BCE, the Judean contingent of God's people is also a remnant of Israel—that is, Jacob's descendants.

Verse 5's rhetorical question begins this word of the Lord. The implicit answer to the question is that your ancestors did not find a fault in me, yet they strayed far from me! According to verses 6–9, memory of Yahweh's past care should have played a vital role in Israel's religious understanding, but the priests had failed as teachers and transmitters of the Torah (Lev 10:11; Deut 24:8). They had lost an intimate awareness of the Lord; they *did not know me*. *Kittim* (Crete) and to the east *Kedar* (Arabia) indicate the extremities of east and west. An individual may change deities, but never had an entire nation done so, except for Judah. *Their Glory* refers to God, who had blessed them with a land flowing with milk and honey. The *lions* are a metaphor for foreign rulers from both Egypt and Mesopotamia (the latter referring to Assyria and Babylonia). Israel fears foreign powers because they *have no awe* before God.

> **Yahweh as Water**
> *In contrast to* worthless idols, *Yahweh is* the fountain of living waters, *like a spring, an ever-flowing source of pure, life-sustaining liquid. In ancient Israel, the only other source of precious water was rain caught in plastered cisterns. In contrast, the* worthless idols *are* broken cisterns.

The charges God brings through the prophet speak both of *long ago* and of *this generation.* Theirs was a persistent practice. The prophet depicts their rebellion in terms of prostitution and of a choice vineyard whose stock has reverted to wild, bitter fruit. Their pursuit of other *Baals* (lords) is as persistent as eager males pursuing a she-ass in estrus. God's people have been caught red-handed, serving gods of their craftsmanship—until a crisis strikes. Then they cry out to the Lord. The entire nation is guilty, but the text mentions the leaders—kings and their advisors, priests, and prophets—specifically. They bear the greater responsibility. The Lord's punishment serves for the ultimate good of his people, but they *did not respond to correction*. Again and again, Scripture describes them as a stiff-necked people (Exod 32:9).

The Lord now focuses on Jeremiah's generation. The rhetorical question pairs *desert* with *land of great darkness*. Desert and darkness bear negative connotations. Deserts largely lack the necessities of life; deep darkness restricts movement. The truth to be understood is exactly the opposite. The Lord brought them into a fertile land, a land where one is *free to roam* and live. But they used their freedom to forget and forsake Yahweh. The *lifeblood of the innocent poor* offers clear testimony against them. Protesting innocence will not save the guilty from the Lord's judgment. Rather than trusting in the Lord, they trusted in Egypt. But just as the Assyrians had carried away the Lord's people with their hands bound above their heads, so Judeans in Jeremiah's time will be captives.

Jeremiah 3:1–5 emphasizes the sacredness of the marriage bond. Once sundered by divorce and remarriage, it is an abomination to the Lord for the first husband to take his former wife back (Deut 24:1–4). God's people had played the harlot with pagan gods, though they had been like a bride to him (v. 2). God had sought to get their attention to correct them. He withheld the precious rains, resulting in drought. Yet they *refuse to blush with shame* while they blame God, asking, *Will your wrath continue forever?* Their deeds speak louder than their talk, even though their words are couched in the endearing, *My Father*. They had forsaken the Lord while deluding themselves, saying, *I am innocent; he is not angry with me*. Self-delusion is the most pernicious kind.

3:6–4:4 *During the reign of King Josiah* is the book's first historical reference since the superscription. What is written is a reminder to the prophet of the history of *faithless* Israel, again using metaphors of marriage, adultery, and divorce. Israel's intimate relationship with the Lord was sullied and sundered. Because of northern Israel's idolatry and pernicious practices, God sent them into exile over a century before Jeremiah heard this word from the Lord. *On every high hill and under every spreading tree* denotes pagan worship at high places where there were sacred oaks. A related expression, *committed adultery with stone and wood*, refers to the materials for making images. Despite the example Israel set for Judah, the southern kingdom only pretends to return to the Lord. Their *pretense* of repentance is an abomination to the Lord.

In verses 11–13, God tells Jeremiah to focus his message *toward the north*, in the direction of the land Israel once occupied and even beyond, toward Assyria, the land of their captivity. God's long-suffering exceeds human comprehension. Even in their deserved captivity, God asks only for the acknowledgment of guilt, an action associated with repentance, so that he could show them his mercy.

According to verses 14–18, God is faithful and will save a remnant (see Isa 10:22; 28:5), *one . . . from every town and two from every clan* of those who will turn from faithlessness. He will bring the remnant back, not to Samaria,

The Ark of the Covenant

Bezalel, chief craftsman, constructed the ark (Exod 37:1–9) as a container for the Ten Commandments (Deut 10:2–5), a pot of manna (Exod 16:33–34), and Aaron's rod (Num 17:8–10). The dimensions of the ark were "two and a half cubits long, a cubit and a half wide, and a cubit and a half high" (50 × 30 × 30 inches). Made of acacia wood, and covered with gold foil, the ark resided in the inner sanctum, the most holy place, of the tabernacle and later the Jerusalem temple. The ark signified God's presence in those holy places and in the midst of his people. While the Bible does not document the disappearance of the ark from the temple, it occurred either prior to or during the Babylonian conquest and destruction of Jerusalem. It is very doubtful that a substitute ark was ever in the Second Temple, for the Roman general Pompey found its inner sanctum empty in the first century BCE *(See Josephus,* Antiquities, 14:71–72; Jewish War, 1:152–53).

but to Zion. He will provide *shepherds*, leaders wise in the ways of the Lord and dedicated to the welfare of the people, unlike their former leaders (2 Kgs 17:21–23). In that time, *the ark of the covenant of the Lord* will fade from memory, replaced by the city of Jerusalem, *The throne of the Lord*, and so recognized by *all nations*. The remnant will represent a reunification of Israel and Judah. This section looks to the distant future and is a hopeful word injected into the preceding condemnation of the faithlessness of God's people, both in Israel's past and in Jeremiah's own time.

After the word of hope for restoration, 3:19–4:4 continues with themes we have heard before. The contrast between the Lord's kindly intention and the faithless people's rejection is clear. The *cry* of those who *have forgotten the Lord their God* draws a response urging them to return. Whether the dialogue between the Lord and the people is real or an expression of what the Lord desires is not clear. Verses 22b–25 indicate what God wants to hear: faithlessness turned to faith (*you are the Lord our God*), and a confession of guilt, the preliminary of repentance. Words alone are not sufficient; appropriate actions must follow (4:1–2).

The prophetic instruction and hope contained in 3:14–4:2 appear to have come from a later time than Josiah's reign. These words address those in exile, assisting them to understand God's intent for a future restoration. Jeremiah 4:2–4 returns to the Lord's effort to call *the men of Judah and people of Jerusalem* to repent.

4:5–31 History proves that Judah ignored the Lord's call for repentance. Jeremiah must now announce the coming disaster, the Lord's *wrath* that *will . . . burn like fire . . . with no one to quench it*. Jeremiah must announce the coming invasion and the necessity to prepare for it. The unnamed *lion* can be none other than Nebuchadnezzar, *a destroyer of nations*. All that happens will be an expression of *the fierce anger of the Lord*. All the leaders, to whom the people might have looked for hope, will themselves be hopeless *in that day*.

In verse 10, the prophet's identification with his audience is evident in this aside remark to the *Sovereign Lord*, particularly as he notes that the sword of the invader is at *our* throats. In verse 11, the desert wind from the east (sirocco) is a metaphor for destruction. The prophet enlarges the image in the following poetic lines, then interrupts with the urgent plea of verse 14. The warning of the invader's approach comes from the north, *from Dan . . . from . . . Ephraim.*

The Lord's words are followed by the heartrending verses 18–21, expressing the prophet's (or God's) deep anguish. He must not only speak the word of the Lord; he must also witness and experience as *disaster follows disaster.* The Lord's own assessment of the tragedy (v. 22) unfolding before the prophet's eyes provides a pause before Jeremiah continues to describe the ultimate outcome of the conflict.

God's Emotions
The Bible often portrays God with human emotions (anger, love, joy, dismay, though not fear or uncertainty). Yahweh relates to human beings at their most basic level of understanding.

In a prophetic vision, Jeremiah in verses 23–26 paints a picture of the chaotic results of the invasion on the environment and the people, the result of the Lord's *fierce anger.*

The word of the Lord continues in verses 27–31 with a description of inevitable results. This is what war was like for Judah in the face of overwhelmingly superior Babylonian forces. The image of the harlot expresses again the implacable nature of Judean idolatry. And so Jerusalem, *the Daughter of Zion,* is in her final travail, like a woman in the throes of birthing just before she dies. The Lord would not turn back from that decision (v. 28).

5:1–31 The Lord urges the prophet to search for one honest, truth-seeking individual in Jerusalem. The people of Jerusalem were guilty of swearing falsely because they had rejected the living God for gods of "stone and wood" (3:9; 4:1b–2).

The word of the Lord (vv. 7–11) against Judah again pours forth from the lips of the prophet. The God of all grace rejects forgiveness for his people who swear by *gods that are not gods* in place of truly believing and swearing, *As surely as the Lord lives* (v. 2). Jeremiah depicts their sins of sexual obsession and immorality with the metaphor of *lusty stallions.* The metaphor of a stripped vineyard depicts the land stripped of its inhabitants, but even here the grace of God is visible when God declares *do not destroy them completely.*

Rich & Poor in Jeremiah
In conversation with the Lord, Jeremiah responds in verses 3–6. The poor are set in their unrepentant ways because they do not know the way of the Lord. But the leaders, who have leisure time to learn, have cast off all restraints. Like cattle on the loose, prey for predators, both the leaders and their followers will suffer for their rebellion and backslidings.

In verses 12–13, Jeremiah here injects his own observations on the self-delusion of the people. In self-denial they scoff at the idea that Yahweh would allow *harm to come to us.* The same twisted mentality appears in 7:4. The relationship of verse 12 to verse 13 is enigmatic. Those who *lied about the Lord* and denied that he would bring any harm may have been false prophets. In that case, verse 13 is "Jeremiah's indignant rejoinder" (Bright 40). Or these may be words of disdain aimed at Jeremiah and other true prophets, ". . . so they treated his prophets as false, and said that the punishment would fall on them" (Cawley and Millard 658). The Septuagint supports the latter view, with the people saying, *Our prophets became wind, and the word of the Lord was not in them.*

Jeremiah responds in verse 15 to what the people have said with a word from the *Lord God Almighty.* He emphasizes the awesome supremacy of Yahweh, whom he serves. The people may disdain his words, but the Lord has made them a consuming fire that the people will experience.

In verses 15–17, Jeremiah brings the word of the Lord to this people whose faces are harder than stone. In poetic form it is a graphic description of the coming invasion and destruction. In verses 18–19, God gives a passionate word of hope for the future for Jeremiah to deliver to the puzzled people.

Echoing Isaiah 6:9–10, verses 20–25 remind Jeremiah's hearers that Yahweh deserves respect, for almighty power is manifested in the barrier between land and sea. But they, spiritually deaf and blind, fail to recognize, respect and fear the God who sustains life through the cycles of the seasons.

In private conversation with Jeremiah, which he will make public, the Lord explains (vv. 26–29) why he is justified in bringing calamity to his people. Many are guilty of exploiting the most vulnerable among their people, the widows and orphans, rather than assisting and defending them.

Before the division of Jeremiah into chapters and verses, verses 30–31 would have been a prelude to 6:1–3 (Willis 85). They highlight the moral morass that (false) prophets and priests create and in which the people wallow. Generally, the morality of the populace will rise no higher than that of their religious leaders.

6:1–30   In answer to the question, *But what will you do in the end?*, the Lord describes the *end* that is coming (vv. 1–3), advising the people to *flee*. Benjamin, just north of Jerusalem, remained with Judah after the northern kingdom went into exile. *Tekoa,* (hometown of Amos) to the south of Jerusalem, and *Beth Hakkerem* to the west signify the coming encirclement of Jerusalem. The *shepherds* are the military leaders; *their flocks* are their warriors.

According to verses 4–5, God is privy to the battle plans of the invaders, and Jeremiah reveals those plans to his audience.

The Lord Almighty (literally "Lord of hosts," commander of the heavenly army) urges on the attackers in verses 6–9 because the city deserves punishment. He then uses his message as a last-ditch effort to urge them to change. But the coming devastation will be complete. Invaders will strip the land clean like a gleaned vineyard.

In verses 10–11a, Jeremiah bemoans his lack of an attentive audience. Those to whom he speaks will not listen; *the word of the Lord is offensive to them.* Yet he cannot refrain from speaking. He is the container of the burning wrath of the Lord and must empty himself of it.

The Lord responds in verses 11b–12 to Jeremiah, *Pour it out*. The prophet must proclaim the Lord's wrath to every segment of society, for all *who live in the land* will share the loss.

Following the instructions to Jeremiah, verses 13–15 describe the social and moral ills to which their lives testify. Rank materialism permeates their society. Though they speak peace, "there is no peace for the wicked" (Isa 48:22; 57:21). So calloused are they, they have no shame. They have even lost the ability to blush! God will punish them.

In verses 16–21, God offers the opportunity to return to *the ancient paths . . . the good way*, the way taught by Moses, but they refuse to go that way. The *watchmen* warn a city of approaching dangers. These were God's true prophets (Ezek 3:17), but the Lord's people would not listen to the prophetic warnings. Two witnesses, the nations and the earth, must thus witness the rightness of God's judgment. Though the Judeans act religiously, offering sacrifices, the odor is a stench to God, who desires that his people "act justly and . . . love mercy and . . . walk humbly" with their God (Mic 6:8). Therefore, the Lord will trip them up, and they *will perish*.

Verses 22–26 report a conversation. First the Lord, through Jeremiah, alerts the *Daughter of Zion* (Jerusalem) with a graphic description of the approaching army. Their fearful reply follows. Jeremiah appears to be speaking in verse 26; the use of *us* indicates his identification with his people. Jeremiah is not a disinterested bystander.

In verses 27–30, the Lord speaks directly to Jeremiah. The metaphor of metallurgy indicates that the people are as hard as bronze and iron, and Jeremiah must test them. But testing and refining is fruitless; they cannot be purified *with fire*, so the Lord rejects them.

7:1–29 The "Temple Sermon" appears both here and in 26:1–6. Harrison calls this a "celebrated attack upon popular confidence in the Temple as an absolute guarantee of Jerusalem's inviolability" (Harrison 84). Jeremiah 26:1 places it *early in the reign of Jehoiakim*, thus in 609/608 BCE, likely at the time of one of the pilgrimage religious festivals (Deut 16:16–18; Lev 23:4–44; Exod 23:14–19). Recent translations, including NIV, indicate a change here from poetry to prose through 8:4.

The Prophet as Mediator

In ancient Israel, the prophet spoke to God for the people and to the people for God.

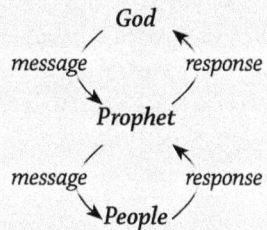

Den of Robbers

Jesus, six hundred years later, would recall Jeremiah's words about the temple as a den of robbers (Matt 21:13; Mark 11:17; Luke 19:46), though Jeremiah was not criticizing the temple establishment per se, as Jesus was.

In 7:1–15, Jeremiah must proclaim the word *at the gate of the Lord's house*, the entrance to a courtyard within the temple (26:2). Josiah's reforms focused the religion on the Jerusalem temple (2 Kgs 23:4–23). The Lord, through Jeremiah, rejects the inviolability of the temple and calls instead for moral and ethical change. The people's security is to be based on right actions rather than in impressive buildings. Shiloh (Arabic *Seilun*), eighteen miles north of Jerusalem, where the tabernacle and the ark were initially located, was apparently destroyed by the Philistines (1 Sam 4:10–11). *The people of Ephraim* are the people of Israel, the northern kingdom.

Kiriath-Jearim

Kiriath-Jearim is modern Abu Ghosh, approximately eight miles northwest of Jerusalem. Here the ark rested for twenty years after its recovery from the Philistines before King David brought it into Jerusalem with great fanfare (2 Sam 6).

Yahweh addresses the remarks in verses 16–20 directly to Jeremiah. The prophet has a soft heart toward his people, so the Lord commands him to refrain from pleading for them. *The Queen of Heaven*, mentioned elsewhere in the Old Testament only in Jeremiah 44:17–25, is likely Ishtar (Assyrian-Babylonian religion), also identified with the Canaanite god Astarte (King 102–7). The righteous wrath of God will wreak havoc on both people and land.

In verses 21–26, Yahweh sarcastically instructs Jeremiah with an additional word for his audience. From the beginnings of Israel, the Lord has put obedience above the sacrificial system (1 Sam 15:22). The Lord's prophets repeatedly emphasize obedience.

The sober instruction in verses 27–29 concerns the prophet himself. Some commentators correctly connect verse 29 with the following section. The command, *Cut off your hair*, has a feminine pronoun in Hebrew; thus it refers not to the prophet but to the city or the nation.

7:30–8:3 Cutting off the hair and lamenting (vv. 29–34) express profound sorrow. Such sorrow is appropriate; the Lord has *rejected and abandoned* Judah for practicing idolatry in the very temple of Yahweh. Further, they offered child sacrifices *in the Valley of Ben Hinnom* (on the western and southern bounds of Jerusalem). This occurred in the reign of Manasseh (2 Kgs 21:5). In the place in which paganized Judeans sacrificed children, the bodies of those slain in the coming conflict would become carrion or be buried in mass graves. For a body to remain unburied was a terrible fate for an Israelite (Deut 28:26). A devastated and depopulated land would no longer witness the joys of weddings, the promise of a future for its people.

The litany of horror continues in 8:1–3. The attackers will ransack the rock-cut tombs of the elite, which are likely to contain valuable grave goods. In the process, they will cast out the bones, exposing them to the heavens, the astral deities they had honored. And the few survivors will wish they were dead.

Here the text returns to the poetic form that continues through chapter 10. The speaker(s) and audience vary. It is probable that the person(s) who assembled these prophetic statements, which may have come to and from the prophet over a long period of time, placed them here to supplement the Temple Sermon.

In verses 4–7, to return to the Lord is to repent. The Judeans do not follow normal human patterns, unlike migrating birds; they *do not know* what they should have known. Their teachers failed to instruct them in *the requirements of the Lord*.

According to verses 8–13, the scribes who copy the *law of the Lord* should know it better than anyone else; they were also teachers. But they *handled it falsely* and will pay the price for their folly. Verses 10–12 repeat 6:13–15. No doubt the prophet repeated himself over the years, particularly as he attempted to move his audiences to repentance and change. For a people who *all are greedy for gain*, the drought conditions promised will hit them where it hurts. In verses 14–16, the people respond with abject fear, but they put the blame on *the Lord our God*. Yet the invaders (in v. 17) cannot be dissuaded. They are like *vipers who cannot be charmed*.

A despairing cry comes from Jeremiah. The note with verse 18 identifies a textual problem, and *Comforter* indicates a title for God. The larger context suggests "Grief has overcome me" (Bright 62). A better reading for *from a land far away* is "from the length and breadth of the land," similar to Isaiah 33:17, where the same expression occurs (Hyatt 887). The question in verse 19b is a terse response to Jeremiah from the Lord, and in verse 20, the people cry out in dire circumstances.

Knowing God
Jeremiah often emphasizes the importance of knowing God, which he equates with living a highly ethical life and trusting and reverencing God.

Jeremiah's lament continues in 8:21–9:2. There is no healing salve nor anyone to apply it. The prophet's tear ducts cannot produce the flow of tears

Child Sacrifice
Little material evidence for child sacrifice in ancient Israel exists, but biblical and other written sources testify to the practice among both Israelites and neighboring Moabites and Arameans. The descendants of the ancient Canaanites, the Phoenicians, practiced child sacrifice, and the predominant evidence for tophets *has come to light at Phoenician (Punic) sites in North Africa, at Carthage and el Hofra (Albright 237).* Topheth *denotes a "hearth" or "roaster." A Punic* tophet *was the cultic installation where the sacrifices occurred and an adjacent burial ground for burned bones. The underlying motivation for all sacrifice is to obtain the favor of the unseen powers, for good or ill, that humans cannot control. Apparently, to the pagan mind, the ultimate sacrifice of one's own offspring was sometimes necessary, but it was an abomination to Yahweh (see Mic 6:6–7).*

he longs to pour out for the fate of these people who have brought it upon themselves. Another alternative is his desire to withdraw far away from them and their sinfulness.

In verse 3, Yahweh supplements Jeremiah's complaint that the people are adulterers and unfaithful. They are also liars whose fundamental error is that they do not *acknowledge* (literally, "know") *me*.

The Lord warns the prophet (vv. 4–6) not to trust anyone in his society. The masculine singular pronoun, *you*, confirms that Jeremiah is the audience.

In verses 7–9, the Lord again addresses Jeremiah with these poignant words, and God grieves (see 4:19–22) that there is no alternative to the punishment because of *the sin of my people*. Yet, he still calls them *my people*; God holds out hope for their redemption.

In verse 10, Jeremiah sorrows for the desolation of the countryside, and in verse 11, God responds that city and villages will also be desolate.

In the prose of verse 12, Jeremiah asks why *the land has been ruined and laid waste*. Some commentators consider this to be an insertion by an editor in the exilic period. But even Jeremiah in distress could ask it. The response of the Lord in verses 13–16 answers the question—his are a disobedient and stubborn people *who have followed the Baals*. Baal means "lord." They have chosen to submit to the false lords rather than to the Lord Almighty. The *bitter food* and *poisoned water* are metaphors for exile, slavery, and *the sword*.

With a word from the Lord (9:17–22), Jeremiah advises the people to summon the professional mourners. The funeral laments are for ruined Zion, all who dwell therein, and for all who die within it, "without respect to age or sex" (Harrison 91).

The word in verses 23–24 reveals the mind of the Lord and is timeless in its relevance. Neither wisdom, power, nor wealth is significant. To know God intimately is to reflect God's character of *kindness, justice, and righteousness*.

Verses 25–26 contrast the preferred circumcision of the heart with the less important circumcision of the foreskin. Circumcision for *the whole house of Israel* was supposed to signify a covenant relationship with Yahweh, but in reality they were no different from the neighboring nations.

THE PEOPLE, THE COVENANT & JEREMIAH'S PROPHECY · 10:15–29:32

10:1–5 In poetic speech, Jeremiah admonishes the *house of Israel* about the folly of the religious ideas and practices of other nations. He merely repeats *what the Lord says*. Verse 5 describes the well-attested Ancient Near Eastern practice of carrying statues of gods in parades during festivals.

Contemplating the Lord in contrast to pagan deities, Jeremiah praises Yahweh (vv. 6–10). Even when made of silver imported from *Tarshish* (either in Spain or Sardinia) and gold from *Uphaz* (possibly identical with Ophir in the Arabian Peninsula [but see Baker 6:765]), the idols are nothing. Yahweh is *the true God*.

Only in verse 11 do we find a verse in Jeremiah written in Aramaic (see NIV note). It may be original with the prophet, used for rhetorical effect. Or it may have been a marginal scribal note that later merged into the text.

According to verses 12–16, in contrast to pagan gods, the creator controls his creation. Verse 13 echoes Psalm 29. *Portion of Jacob* (that is, Israel) is another biblical title for Yahweh, found elsewhere only in Jeremiah 51:19.

10:17–22   Direct from the Lord, Judah receives marching orders from Jeremiah (10:17–18). This warning sparks in Jeremiah, the bearer of the bad tidings, an outpouring of grief at the coming destruction described in the following verses.

Verses 19–22 offer the voice of Jerusalem personified as a woman in despair (note *my sons*) at the mortal wound she has suffered. Again, the destroyer comes from the north.

10:23–25   Jeremiah notes first the Lord's sovereignty over him; the prophet had not chosen his path in life. It was the path of obedience to the divine director. He trusts the Lord to discipline him justly and to deal appropriately with *the peoples who do not call on your name*. Compare Psalm 79:6–7, which Jeremiah is apparently quoting.

Personified Places
The Old Testament often personifies places. Since most place names in Hebrew are feminine nouns, the places are often portrayed as women in various roles. Jerusalem as mother and wife also figures prominently in Lamentations.

11:1–17   Most commentators distinguish a change here from the preceding materials, with the initial focus on the broken covenant. The close of the new section may occur at 12:17, 15:21, 20:18, or 24:1. Such disparity of views illustrates the difficulty of identifying the relationships of the materials in the book of Jeremiah.

According to verses 1–8, the covenant to be heeded is that given at Sinai, given *when I brought them out of Egypt*. The Ten Commandments contain both religious and ethical requirements. Obedience brings blessings; disobedience brings curses (Deut 28). The text compares slavery in Egypt to an iron-smelting furnace (as in Deut 4:20; 1 Kgs 8:51). Verses 6–8 repeat and emphasize the message the prophet is to proclaim.

The reforms of Josiah seem to have been short-lived. The people have fallen back into their old ways (vv. 9–11). They have broken the first commandment (Deut 5:6–7). Let them cry out to Baal and the other gods to whom they burn incense; these false gods *will not help them*. This passage is similar to 2:27–28.

As in 7:16, verses 14–17 command Jeremiah not to pray for *this people*; their moral and religious corruption is beyond the intercession of a righteous person. The Hebrew text of verses 15–16 "is exceedingly corrupt, and any reconstruction conjectural" (Bright 82). The translation of the NIV is a satisfactory guess. It emphasizes that sacrifices cannot replace covenantal obedience, and that which the Lord has deemed lovely may still be worthy of destruction by fire, the same element used in *burning incense to Baal*.

11:18–23 This incident may have occurred during the reign of Jehoiakim (reigned 609–598 BCE; Huey 136). The Lord had promised Jeremiah that he would be with him as he faced opposition (1:17–19). The plotters were his kindred, *the men of Anathoth*, Anathoth recalled the words of Jesus, *Only in his home town and in his own house is a prophet without honor* (Matt 13:57). Jeremiah asks Yahweh to bring divine *vengeance upon them*, a request that reflects the human character of the prophet. Yahweh promises to discipline Jeremiah's opponents.

> **Jeremiah's Linen Belt**
> *The* linen belt *described in 13:1–7 was more like a kilt worn under the outer garments. Commentators have struggled to identify the location where Jeremiah first buried, then later retrieved, the garment. The* NIV *identifies it as* Perath, *with a footnote giving the alternative location, the (River) Euphrates, as translated in many versions of the Bible. If the latter, Jeremiah had to make two round trips of approximately 700 miles each. Perath (*Khirbet el Fara*), however, is some six miles northeast of Jerusalem. Nothing in the text indicates that this symbolic act was public; it appears to have been instructive to Jeremiah alone.*

12:1–4 Of all the prophets, only in Jeremiah do we find laments and confessions such as this. Similar material occurs in chapters 15, 17, 18, and 20. Here the prophet's concern is the timeless question, *Why does the way of the wicked prosper?* The question arises out of his reaction to being "like a gentle lamb led to the slaughter" (11:19).

12:5–17 The response in verses 5–6 evades the question. Instead, the Lord urges Jeremiah to stiffen his backbone for even more difficult situations. The text uses the metaphor of a runner racing against a swifter competitor in more difficult terrain.

Jeremiah's complaint pales in comparison with the lament of the Lord (vv. 7–13). While loving the people (*inheritance*), God will deliver both land and people into the destructive power of their foes. This saying of the Lord answers Jeremiah's question. Prosperity is not God's ultimate treatment of the wicked; in the end, they will encounter divine punishment.

In verses 14–17, the prophet emphasizes God's sovereignty over all nations. Although these neighbors—Edom, Moab, Ammon, etc.—are unwitting instruments of judgment against Judah, they also are subject to the Lord's judgment. Yet grace is also available to them under the conditions given here.

13:1–11 This is the first of several symbolic acts in the ministry of Jeremiah. Each is a stark, visual statement that underscores the related prophetic word.

The Lord interprets the action for Jeremiah. God chose Israel to be as near to him as the linen garment was to the prophet. But they had become *ruined and completely useless*, as had the linen belt.

13:12–14 Wineskins do not smash; the Hebrew word *nevel* signifies a ceramic jar, holding about ten gallons of liquid. Every Judean, from king to commoner, like wine jars, will be stupefied by what they hold within them—confusion and panic in the face of the attackers. Jars shatter, and so will Judah.

13:15–17   The mode of expression in verses 15–27 returns to poetry. Jeremiah again urges his audience to honor *the Lord your God* to prevent the threatened catastrophe. Jeremiah takes no pleasure in the dark scene he describes for them. His sorrow will bring bitter tears to his eyes.

> **The Queen Mother**
>
> *The mention of the queen mother indicates the significant role of that position in the Judean monarchy (see 1 Kgs 2:19).*

Verses 18–19 command Jeremiah to inform the king (Jehoiachin) and his mother (Nehusta) of their coming humiliation. Enemies will besiege cities in the southland (*Negev*), and no one can save them. *All Judah*, that is, the bulk of the people, even a few who remained after the exile, including Jeremiah, will be deported.

The subject of verse 20 is Jerusalem (LXX and v. 27). The leaders (*shepherds*) will have no followers, and former allies will dominate the city. With euphemisms, verse 22 describes the rape of the city. The remainder of the section explains the national destruction as the result of idolatry.

14:1–15:21   In relaying a message about the drought, Jeremiah gives both the land and cities human characteristics, depicting them as mourning and crying out. In a land with few springs, people collected rainwater during the two rainy seasons (the "former" and "latter" rains, in the late fall and spring) in cisterns cut into the limestone bedrock and sealed with plaster. Wild animals acting in such uncharacteristic ways are evidence of the severity of the drought.

Verses 7–9 are likely the words of the people rather than a prayer of Jeremiah on their behalf (see 3:22b–25). Their plea for help includes a confession of sins which appears to be hypocritical, in light of their past practices. They also urge Yahweh to act on their behalf *for the sake of your name*, that is, to protect God's honor and reputation.

In verses 10–12, Jeremiah quotes the Lord directly in this response to their plea. Their treacherous past has caught up with them. Again the Lord tells Jeremiah not to petition on behalf of his people. Even when they do religious things, it will be to no avail. Their destruction is certain through war, starvation, and disease.

In verses 13–16, Jeremiah shows his compassion for his people because false prophets have led them into complacency. Yet following false prophets is no excuse. Both prophets and their followers will suffer exactly what the prophets say will never befall them—sword and famine. The prophet speaks a brief lament in verses 17–18 to the people on behalf of the Lord. The land and Jerusalem are in the midst of the Babylonian invasion. In verses 19–22, the people plead again for the Lord to save them, confessing their *wickedness and the guilt of our fathers*. In what appears to be sincere repentance, they confess that their only hope is in Yahweh their God. Yet according to 15:1–4, God has sealed their destiny. Even if the two great men of God from their past—Moses and Samuel—were to plead for this people, God would not relent. So awful is their end that the dead, from whatever cause, will lie unburied, carrion for vultures and dogs. Manasseh epitomized the guilty leader (compare 2 Kgs 21.3–16.)

The Lord had said that he would *make them abhorrent to all the kingdoms of the earth*. In verses 5–9, the prophet paints the sickening scene. Overwhelmed by the destruction to come, Jeremiah cries out in despair (vv. 10–11). The Lord reassures him; those who curse him now will seek him in their disaster and distress (see 21:1–6; 37:3).

Yahweh speaks to the people through the prophet in 15:12–14. *Iron from the north* is the superior military technology the invader brings. Armed resistance will prove futile because of the anger of the Lord.

Again, Jeremiah laments to the Lord in verses 15–18. He pleads his loyalty and explains his devotion, even the joy he has known, in his prophetic duty. But now he experiences the resulting suffering. He asks, Can there be no end to it? Will Yahweh fail him? Thus he offers his own lament as counter-point to Judah's.

The Lord Rebukes Jeremiah
When Jeremiah is at his lowest ebb, the Lord responds (vv. 19–21). Jeremiah must turn from self-pity and not speak worthless words if he is to continue to be God's spokesman. The Lord again reassures the prophet of divine power to strengthen him in every situation and to rescue him from all peril (compare 1:17–19).

16:1–17:18 This section contains instructions to Jeremiah from Yahweh. They deal with his personal situation (16:1–13), with prophetic messages he is to deliver to the people (16:14–18), and with warnings and exhortations in poetic form (16:19–17:18). The latter begin with 16:19.

According to verses 1–4, Jeremiah's bachelorhood is a visual testimony to the truth of his warnings to the people. Thereby, the Lord also saves him from the personal loss and grief the coming disaster will bring upon others. Verses 5–10 forbid Jeremiah to participate in funerals or weddings. Such bizarre behavior sets the prophet apart from his society and adds to the burden of his service to the Lord. Jeremiah must tell his audience that he cannot participate in such normal human activities (vv. 10–13) because of their disobedience to the Lord.

Prophetic Sign Acts
Prophets often behaved strangely in order both to internalize in full their message and to symbolize its effect on their audience. They might walk around naked (Isaiah), play with model cities (Ezekiel), or bury a loincloth (Jeremiah).

Verses 14–15 contain a word of hope similar to 23:7–8 (see also Isa 28:5–6; 29:5–8; Joel 3:18–21). The restoration *out of all the countries where [the Lord] banished them* will be more striking than was the exodus from Egypt. Restoration is in the future (vv. 16–18); the present brings disaster. *Fishermen* and *hunters*—the invaders—will see to it that there will be no escapees from the *double* jeopardy the Lord intends, due to the people's wicked ways. In poetic form, Jeremiah praises Yahweh as his shelter (vv. 19–21), and he anticipates the time when the Gentile nations will acknowledge Yahweh as the only true God. Jeremiah will teach them to recognize God's almighty nature.

The Septuagint omits 17:1–4. In the meantime in Judah, the people's corrupt natures are so immersed in sin that their sin is permanently inscribed on their hardened hearts and *on the horns of their altars* (stone altars with upward projecting corners). Expiation for sin came when the priest anointed the horns of the altar with the blood of the sacrifice (Lev 16:18), but Judah's sin, now engraved in stone, cannot be cleansed. The *Asherah poles* were symbols of the Canaanite goddess, Asherah. Archaeological evidence suggests the widespread mixture of Canaanite elements in Israelite folk religion, interrupted by the reforms first of Hezekiah and later of Josiah, but never completely eradicated until the Babylonian exile. The Temple Mount (*My mountain*) in the holy city contrasts with the high places (*bamot*) in the countryside; however, God will destroy both kinds of sanctuary.

Verses 5–8 are verses of wisdom, similar to Psalm 1, which distinguish the two ways open to individuals. Trusting God opens the way to a fruitful life. Wisdom continues in verses 9–13. The state of the unredeemed *heart* exceeds human comprehension, but God knows and deals justly with everyone. If a person's conduct resembles the proverbial partridge's, that person will ultimately be a loser. Those who forsake the *Lord, the hope of Israel*, forsake the sustenance of a life-giving water source. In the present context, the *glorious throne* that is *the place of our sanctuary* is not the temple itself but God who occupies the throne and makes it glorious. Inserted in verses 14–18 is Jeremiah's appeal for Yahweh's support in the face of those who doubt the prophet's word. He testifies that he has been faithful as the Lord's shepherd, and he prays for the continuing support of the Lord.

The Potter & the Clay

In 1902, Adelaide Pollard wanted to serve as a missionary in Africa. Discouraged by her failure to raise funds, she overheard an old woman pray, "Lord, it doesn't matter what you bring into our lives – just have your way with us." That night she meditated on Jeremiah 18:1–6 and the old woman's prayer. Jeremiah's image of the potter and the clay inspired Pollard to pen the lines of one of America's best known hymns:

> *Have Thine own way, Lord!*
> *Have Thine own way!*
> *Thou art the potter; I am the clay.*
> *Mold me and make me after Thy will,*
> *While I am waiting, yielded and still.*

Years later, Pollard went to Africa. During her lifetime, she wrote more than eighty other hymns. Pollard died in 1934 at the age of seventy-two.

17:19–27 The Sabbath is an integral part of God's covenant with his people (Exod 20:8–11). Jeremiah instructs both king and people, on the authority of Yahweh, and he does this in the gates of Jerusalem through which many passed, assuring a wide distribution of this vital word. Keeping the Sabbath was crucial to the continuation of the Davidic dynasty and to the survival of the city. The Lord threatens to destroy Jerusalem's defenses unless the people uphold the sanctity of the Sabbath. The people's fate and that of their city ultimately lay in their own hands through obedience or disobedience.

18:1–19:15 18:1–12 lays the foundation for the poetic word that follows. At the potter's house, Jeremiah observes the potter at work. That work becomes a paradigm for the sovereignty of Yahweh over the destiny of nations, including the *house of Israel*. The Lord warns all that remains of that house—*the people of Judah*—that *I am preparing a disaster for you*. Repentance and reformation can change the final form that will result, but the Lord anticipates that the people will reject Jeremiah's warning to them.

> **Mount Hermon**
> *"Sirion" is the Phoenician name for the heights of Mount Hermon (Deut 3:8). At 9,100 feet above sea level, the peak is often covered with snow. Melting snows feed perennial springs. The constancy of nature is starkly contrast to the fickle ways of the Lord's people. Disaster will result, viewed in astonishment by all who pass by.*

The oracle in verses 13–17 supplements the previous proverb of the potter's house by the editorial *Therefore*. *Virgin Israel* (see 14:17) experiences the original state of the people's relationship to Yahweh (2:2–3). The Lord asks two rhetorical questions; both questions expect "No!" as a response. *The snow of Lebanon* translates the Hebrew *siryon*.

Verse 18 sets the stage for the following poetic section. Jeremiah continually warns the people of coming disaster, but they retort that things will remain the way they have been, with priests, sages, and prophets going about their business. They attack Jeremiah by spreading the word to ignore him.

In utter disgust, Jeremiah calls on the Lord in verses 19–23 to bring the disaster he had faithfully prophesied on his opponents. Some scholars cannot accept such demands as being worthy of a true prophet of God. But the prophet's humanity surfaces in this outburst of righteous indignation at the plots posed against him.

Instructed by the Lord, Jeremiah in 19:1–15 executes another symbolic action that illustrates what he will tell both leaders and people. *Some of the elders of the people and of the priests* come along as witnesses. Jeremiah carries the jar he had purchased to the valley on the southern boundary of Jerusalem. It is the valley for the refuse dump, where people sacrifice infants to Molech (see 7:29–34). There the prophet smashes the clay jar. In like manner, God will smash Judah and Jerusalem. So horrible will be the siege that the living will practice cannibalism in a desperate effort to stop their hunger (see Deut 28:53–57; Lam 4:10).

After delivering his message to the witnessing elders of the people and priests, Jeremiah returns to the *court of the Lord's temple* and renews his warning to *all the people* on the authority of God.

20:1–6   We must distinguish between this Pashhur and Pashhur son of Malkijah (21:1). This *son of Immer* is the priest in charge of temple security. He considers Jeremiah a threat to temple order. Apparently the threat was short-lived, and he releases Jeremiah the following day. None of this escapes the all-seeing eye of the Lord. Jeremiah clearly describes the terror this man and his associates will experience and their ultimate end in Babylon. To prophesy is to speak out, and Pashhur has spouted lies. *Magor-missabib* means "terror all around," a favorite phrase of Jeremiah's (Jer 6:25; 20:10; 46:6; 49:29; compare Ps 31:14).

20:7–8   In poetic form, Jeremiah voices his inner struggles to Yahweh. He charges the Lord with deceiving him (vv. 7–10). The NIV note, *persuaded*, is too weak. The Hebrew word translated here means to "seduce" (a virgin) in Exodus 22:16, and to "lure" in 1 Kings 22:20. Jeremiah must be a perpetual prophet of doom; none react positively to his messages. But he cannot withhold the Lord's announcement of punishment, even when he tries to do so.

His ultimate hope for validation is in the presence of the Lord (vv. 11–13). Jeremiah is confident that he has been true to his calling and that the Lord will vindicate him by bringing vengeance on his persecutors. The thought sparks a psalm of praise: a "brief note of hope and joy pervades the gloom of the section as a whole" (Harrison 114).

Sentiments similar to Job 3 in verses 14–18 reflect Jeremiah's deep depression, "the result of his impossible task" (Overholt 628). *The towns the Lord overthrew without pity* apparently refers to Sodom and Gomorrah (Gen 19:24–28).

21:1–14   Unlike the difficulty of dating much of the previous material, the mention of King Zedekiah (597–586 BCE) clearly dates this section. Apparently, this incident occurred relatively late in his reign, just before the city fell to Nebuchadnezzar. In extreme duress, the king and his associates finally seek a word from the Lord from the very prophet they have rejected so often (see also 37:3–10).

The Last Kings of Judah	
Josiah	640–609 BCE
Jehoahaz/ Shalum	609 BCE
Jehoiakim	609–598 BCE
Jehoiachin	598–597 BCE
Zedekiah	597–587/6 BCE

Despite Jeremiah's devastating reply to his visitors, he communicated an alternative the Lord offered to those who would surrender to the Babylonians— life rather than death by *plague, sword and famine*. The contrast between life and death is reminiscent of Deuteronomy 30:15–16. But to the royal house, who should have, but failed to administer, daily justice to the oppressed, the Lord threatens punishment.

22:1–30   Chapter 22 opens after the preceding poetic judgment above with a similar condemnation in narrative form. Here the identity of the *king of Judah* is not certain, but the righteous requirements for every ruler remain the same. The Lord demands social justice. If this demand goes unmet, destruction will follow.

Verses 6–8 promise to destroy the king's grand palace and the entire city. The ruins will become a conversation piece for foreigners passing by. And the explanation for the destruction will be covenant breaking and idolatry on the part of the former inhabitants.

Verse 10 instructs survivors for whom to mourn. Weep for the exiled, who shall never return; but do not grieve for dead kings. Jehoiakim was guilty of oppressing his people and exhibiting presumptuous pride (vv. 13–14). This was in contrast to Josiah (vv. 15b–16). Verses 18–19 poetically describe the nation's demise. The NIV uses *Babylonians* and footnotes *Chaldeans*, the actual word in the Masoretic Text. Nebuchadnezzar was from the Chaldean tribe. Jehoiakim spent three years under Babylonian control, then rebelled in concert with neighboring allies. *Bashan* is to the north; *Abarim* is a mountainous region in Moab. The *Lebanon* of verse 23 is "the house of the forest of Lebanon" (1 Kgs 7:2–5; Isa 22:8), the palace of the kings in Jerusalem.

Jehoiachin the Captive
Jehoiachin *is also called Coniah (37:1) and Jeconiah (24:1). The condemnation of Jehoiachin in verses 24–30 proclaims the judgment of Yahweh delivered by Jeremiah to the king before he was taken as a hostage to Babylon, from which he never returned. Archaeologists discovered ration tablets allocating provisions to Ya'u-kin, dating to around 570 BCE in the excavations of Babylon (Pritchard 308). He will be known as Jehoichin the captive, and none of his heirs (1 Chron 3:17) will inherit his throne.*

23:1–8 This *Woe* in narrative form (vv. 1–4) provides the backdrop for the future-oriented pronouncement (vv. 5–6) in poetic form. The figure of irresponsible undershepherds explains the scattering of the flock in exile. Yahweh, the Good Shepherd, will *gather the remnant*, restoring them from exile to *their pasture*. He will also appoint responsible leaders to care for them.

Verses 5–6 promise the restoration of *a righteous Branch* sometime in the future. This king from the line of David will do all that previous Davidic kings failed to do.

The Branch is a messianic designation (see 33:15; Isa 9:2–7; 11:1–9; Mic 5:1–5; Zech 3:8; 6:12). In the New Testament, the name *The Lord Our Righteousness* is applied to Jesus by Paul (1 Cor 1:30), though Zechariah 3 and 6 apparently connect the image to Zerrubbabel. Verses 7–8 repeat 16:14–15.

23:9–32 The preceding oracles dealt with political leaders; this section focuses on religious leaders. In verses 9–10, Jeremiah speaks out of personal anguish when he contrasts *the Lord and his holy words* with the evil of the prophets. Yahweh agrees and adds that evil fills the holiest place in the land (2 Kgs 21:5; Ezek 8:6–18). The Lord will punish them with disaster. As disgusting as were the prophets of Samaria, *the prophets of Jerusalem* are far worse. Their lying, immoral lives encourage others toward wickedness, recalling the degraded inhabitants of Sodom and Gomorrah. Ungodliness is poisonous and bitter in its results. The prophets who exhibit and encourage ungodliness will suffer poetic justice—*bitter food . . . and . . . poisoned water* (figures of speech for bitter judgment).

According to verses 16–22, the false prophets con the people with exactly the opposite of Jeremiah's warnings. They have never *stood in the council of the Lord*. Other references to the heavenly council are in 1 Kings 22:19–22; Job 1–2; 15:8; and Psalms 82:1; 89:6–7. Jeremiah warns his audience of the coming *storm of the Lord*, the anger of the Lord pouring forth on people and prophets alike.

The two questions in verses 23–24 focus attention on the transcendence (*far away*) and immanence (*nearby*) of Yahweh, the God of the universe. God sees everything (see also Ps 139:7–16; Isa 66:1; Amos 9:2–4).

Verses 25–32 compare the practices of false prophets with those of a genuine prophet. (Dreams are one means by which the Lord reveals his will. Two others are by *Urim* and by prophets [1 Sam 28:6].) But dreams can also be delusional. The true prophet will not *lead my people astray*. The word of the Lord will burn away dross; it is a hammer that "shatters all pretension and self-confidence" (see also Heb 4:12; Huey 218). Beware false prophets; they lead people astray in every age.

23:33–40 The Hebrew word *massa'* connotes both "burden" and "oracle." Thus, an oracle is the burden of the word of God the prophet delivers to an audience (Nah 1:1; Hab 1:1). The Lord, through Jeremiah, informs the false prophets who seek a message from God that they are the *burden*. The following verses expand on this theme and end with the condemnation of the false prophets.

24:1:1–10 This vision is datable to mid-summer, when figs begin to ripen, in the year 597 BCE. The vision has immediate and distant connotations. In the near future, the bad figs (Zedekiah and others) would end disastrously. In the distant future, the good figs (descendants of the deportees listed in 24:1) would lead in the restoration of the Lord's people *in this land*. All this is the work of *the Lord, the God of Israel* who sends away and restores.

Distinguishing True from False Prophets

The outward appearance of Jeremiah did not differ much from that of the false prophets, and both claimed to be speaking what God had revealed to them. The uncritical listener could not tell the difference, and uncritical individuals prefer that which they want to hear: there is no necessity to turn from their wickedness (23:14), they should trust in false hopes that they will have peace (23:17), and adultery is permissible because the false prophets do it and, therefore, so can the people (23:14). False prophets ignore the revealed will of God, the moral and ethical teachings of the Mosaic covenant.

The more discerning listener could recognize the moral and ethical integrity of the prophet from Anatoth. "Absolute loyalty and obedience to the revealed will and word of the Lord was the ultimate criterion for distinguishing between true and false prophets" (Harrison 123). Jeremiah is the epitome of the faithful and true spokesman for Yahweh.

25:1–14 This word of the Lord to Jeremiah actually precedes that of the two baskets of figs, an illustration that the scribes did not arrange the book of Jeremiah chronologically. Because events recorded in 36:2–4 occurred at about the same time as those in 25:1, some scholars believe 25:1–7 is the introduction to the scroll dictated by Jeremiah to Baruch.

In verses 1–17, for the first time since the historical prologue (1:2), we can firmly date part of Jeremiah's prophecies. His ministry began in 627 BCE, when Josiah was twenty-one years old and had been on the throne thirteen years. Five years later (622 BCE), "the Book of the Law was found in the temple of the Lord" (2 Kgs 22:8). It is interesting to note that it was the prophetess Huldah whom the king's advisors consulted about the implications of this discovery. As one would expect from a true prophetess, her response was very similar to the content of Jeremiah's prophecies (2 Kgs 22:15–17). By the time of the events in chapter 25, Jeremiah had been faithfully fulfilling his calling for twenty-three years—with little evidence of success. The majority of the people, and particularly the religious and political leaders, had not responded positively to his call for repentance in order to escape the coming calamity. The very survival of his oracles, however, indicates that a remnant of his audience believed his prophecies and saved them. Yahweh showed graciousness toward Judah *again and again* with offers of clemency and encouragement toward reconciliation, but to no avail. They continued to provoke Yahweh *with what [their] hands have made*, namely, representations of deities in ceramics, wood, and metal, as well as cakes for the Queen of Heaven. They ignored the invisible Yahweh, God of hosts.

Nebuchadnezzar, upon the death of his father, Nabopolassar, in 605 BCE, became ruler of the Babylonian Empire. In securing his dominance over the region from the Euphrates to Egypt, he became the Lord's *servant*. (The Septuagint omits *my servant*.) The Babylonians did not realize that they were instruments of Yahweh to *completely destroy* Judah. The same Hebrew word describes the total destruction of the Canaanites by Israel during the conquest (see Deut 20:17; Josh 6:21, 10:28; 1 Sam 15:3). Theirs was to be *an everlasting ruin*. The Hebrew word rendered "everlasting" can mean "forever," but it can also be translated "a long, long time." In fact, the destruction layer left by the Babylonians in Jerusalem and in other Judean sites still remains, hidden beneath subsequent layers of occupation. With the physical destruction and slaughter or deportation of much of the population, the usual cultural sounds will cease. This devastation would not only occur with Judah, but also with any other peoples who opposed the Babylonians.

The Babylonian empire lasted just over seventy years, from 612–539 BCE, counting from the fall of Nineveh, the Assyrian capital, to the capture of Babylon by Cyrus, king of the Medes and Persians. But from the destruction of Jerusalem in August 586 BCE until the fall of Babylon in 539 is less than seventy years. Scholars have struggled to determine whether the seventy years in this prophecy is literal or symbolic. If the seventy-year period is literal, then the difficulty is in deciding when to begin the count. If the number is symbolic, it could signify whatever the appropriate time of punishment might be. The number seven and its multiples occur symbolically throughout the Bible (for example, Gen 4:24; Matt 18:22). Second Chronicles 36:21, in the postexilic period (about 400 BCE), notes that *the land enjoyed its Sabbath rests; all the time of its desolation it rested, until the seventy years were completed in fulfillment of the word of the Lord spoken by Jeremiah*. Since the Sabbath is the seventh day, and seventy is a multiple of seven, symbolism may underlie the seventy years. Another way to compute the time, however, is to count back seventy years from the fall of the Babylonian Empire in 539 BCE, that is, 609 BCE. The latter date was the seventeenth year of the reign of Nabopolassar, the father of Nebuchadnezzar, and the Babylonians were not yet in control of Judea and Jerusalem. So the puzzle remains unsolved.

The phrase *written in this book* probably refers not to the book of Jeremiah as we presently have it, since at that time it was not yet completed, but to the earlier book (or scroll) destroyed by King Jehoiakim (36:23). The book likely consisted of most if not all of the materials we have in chapters 1–25 (Bright 163).

Verse 13 in the Septuagint does not include the last part of the verse, *and prophesied by Jeremiah against all the nations*. In the Greek version of Jeremiah, immediately following *written in this book*, are the oracles against the nations (chapters 46–51), beginning with Elam. The order of the nations does not exactly follow the Hebrew text, which begins with Egypt (46:2). The Septuagint picks up 25:15 at the beginning of its chapter 32.

25:15–29   Here the NIV follows the order of the Hebrew Masoretic Text rather than that of the Septuagint. Scribes likely inserted the section on God's judgment against the nations here to expand on the coming destruction of Babylon prophesied in verses 12–14. Perhaps, too, 25:15–38 stands as a fit conclusion to the initial section of Jeremiah (Masoretic Text), acting as a closing envelope (called an *inclusio*) to the beginning: *I appointed you as a prophet to the nations* (1:4) and *See, today I appoint you over nations and kingdoms to uproot and tear down, to destroy and overthrow, to build and to plant* (1:10). This section consists of two parts—verses 15–29 are prose while verses 30–38 are poetic.

Inclusio
The practice of beginning and ending a literary section with identical or very similar material.

To understand verses 15–29 literally is to assume that Jeremiah visited all the places indicated in verses 17–26. This seems to be a physical impossibility, since he would have to have traveled to *all the kingdoms on the face of the earth* (v. 26). And it would have been virtually impossible for him to have access to the throne rooms of the Pharaoh of Egypt or that of Nebuchadnezzar or the other kings; powerful monarchs limited access to their persons as a precaution against possible assassination. An alternative is to interpret the passage symbolically. This alternative assumes that each of the nations named had representatives present in Jerusalem. Jeremiah would have offered these representatives the "cup." Chapter 27:3 mentions envoys in Jerusalem from several nations, which may support this approach. However, another more reasonable approach is to understand this passage as a visionary experience (see for example Gen 15:1; Rev 9:17). With this interpretation, Jeremiah told his audience in Jerusalem all that the Lord revealed. Jeremiah also remembered and wrote down these prophecies for the further instruction of those in exile in Babylon, as well as for succeeding generations, including our own.

The *cup filled with the wine of my wrath* is a graphic image of the reality of Almighty God's righteous disgust and anger with not only Jerusalem and Judah but also all the kingdoms of this earth. The rebellious nature of all humanity leads to a form of madness as nation rises against nation in cycles of seemingly endless wars and conflicts. This is *the sword I will send among them*. The cup of God's wrath is a symbol of his judgment found elsewhere in Scripture (for example, Ps 11:6; Isa 51:17; Jer 8:14). Above all else, this prophetic unit speaks clearly of the sovereignty of God over all nations and peoples. His righteous judgment begins with his chosen people but extends to all nations.

Harrison (126) notes that "All the peoples mentioned in chapters 46–51 are included here except for Damascus." Egypt, Philistia, Edom, Moab, Ammon, Tyre, Sidon, and Arabia are generally well-known and identifiable on maps of the biblical period. *Uz*, associated with Job (1:1), was a country in northwest Arabia. *Dedan* was "an important commercial settlement located at one of the major oases in northwest Arabia" (Gen 10:7; 25:3; Graf). *Tema* is identified with Tayma, a caravan city on an oasis in northern Arabia (Knauf), and *Buz* also was in northern Arabia—likely a tribal region rather than a particular place. Buz was Elihu's country (Job 32:2). The phrase, *all who are in distant places* (v. 23) is more accurate in the NIV footnote and appears again in 49:32 in connection with Kedar. These were Bedouin tribes of north Arabia and related to the Ishmaelites of Genesis 25:13. *Zimri* as a place name is otherwise unknown, although it is possibly associated with *Elam* (Bright 161), in the highlands of modern Iran known as Khuzistan (Vallat). *Media* was in northwestern Iran.

There is no possibility of escaping or refusing to experience the wrath of the Lord Almighty. As Jesus stated, *for all who draw the sword will die by the sword* (Matt 26:52).

In verses 30–31's arresting imagery of the deafening roar of a lion and the loud noise of those trampling grapes in the wine press, this poetic prophetic saying emphasizes again the awful and

Athbash

The last kingdom to drink of the cup of the Lord's wrath is the king of Sheshach, *apparently a cryptogram (also found in 51:41) for Babylon formed by exchanging the order of the Hebrew alphabet from first to last. Thus* BBL, *consisting of the second* (beth) *and twelfth* (lamedh) *consonants, is written* SHSHKH, *consisting of the next to the last* (shin) *and the eleventh letter counting backward from the end of the (Hebrew) alphabet. This system of reverse writing is called* athbash.

inevitable judgment of the Lord *against the nations . . . on all mankind*. While the preceding prophecy speaks of the coming judgment, verse 32 describes the immediacy and expansion of the rising storm of disaster.

Verses 33–38 depict the catastrophic scope of the spreading disaster in terms of *those slain by the Lord*. There will be either no survivors or an insufficient number to mourn and bury the dead, and the worst fears of those dying will be realized—they will remain unburied, scattered across the landscape. The leaders of the people, the shepherds, will die also. All this will be the result of *the fierce anger of the Lord*, realized by means of *the sword of the oppressor*—unknowing instruments in the hand of the Lord. The NIV footnote alerts us to the possibility that the original word here was *anger* rather than *sword*. The expression "sword of the oppressor" does occur in the indicated verses. It is possible here, however, that the "anger of the oppressor" balances and equates to *the Lord's fierce anger*. The imagery of Yahweh as a lion in verses 30 and 38 acts as an envelope for the poetry within, another *inclusio*.

26:1–24   Chapters 26–29 focus on conflicts Jeremiah faced as he faithfully presented the word of the Lord to the Judeans, particularly in the time of the kings Jehoiakim and Zedekiah. Other prophets, priests, and certain political leaders opposed Jeremiah. The opposition was so intense that they threatened Jeremiah's very life. Nevertheless, he remained true to his calling and mission, which included not only warnings and exhortations to his contemporaries in Jerusalem but also encouragement and instructions to those already in exile in Babylon. All this material from Jeremiah has been called "Baruch's Book" because of the scribe's role revealed within the section. The first incident relates to the "Temple Sermon," the same incident as Jeremiah 7:1–15.

Baruch

It is likely that the scribe Baruch was instrumental in preserving Jeremiah's prophecies, which devout people in Babylon during the exile then assembled and enhanced with explanatory comments.

Early in the reign of Jehoiakim places this event in 609 BCE (but see 28:1). Again, the chronological order of events was a secondary concern to the compilers of Jeremiah, since 25:1 is set in *the fourth year of Jehoiakim*. The *courtyard of the Lord's house* lay within the gate(s) of the temple compound. Priests alone had access to the temple structure proper. The particular pilgrim feast when most of the men of Judah came to Jerusalem is not identified; it could have been Passover, Pentecost, or Tabernacles. The latter occurs in the fall, while the first two are spring festivals (Lev 23).

Jeremiah reveals in these verses the general instructions Yahweh is giving to him. The verses that follow give the exact message he is to communicate to his audience. The Lord's intent is to bring the people to repentance, that they might turn from their evil ways and escape the coming disaster. God offers grace, but it is conditional.

Verses 7–9 are not a first-person account; rather, they are a report. For the content of Jeremiah's message, see 7:1–15. The religious assembly (priests, prophets, and people), who trusted in religious ritual but ignored the moral requirements of the covenant relationship with God, found Jeremiah's ultimatum unbearable. They were all ready to silence him forever. The intensity of the situation is clear. They were prepared to commit murder *in the house of the Lord*. (The Septuagint identifies the prophets as *pseudoprophets* in verses 7, 8, 11, and 16. The expression "false prophet" does not occur in the Masoretic Text.)

The sound of the commotion in verses 10–16 drew the attention of *the officials of Judah*, who must have feared a riot. The royal palace was adjacent to but south of the Temple Mount. The location of the *New Gate* is uncertain, but it was likely in the southern wall of the temple facing the palace compound. (The current southern wall of the Temple Mount enclosure is farther south than that of the Solomonic complex, since Herod the Great enlarged the Temple Mount.) It may be a reference to the gate constructed by Jotham (2 Kgs 15:35; Harrison 127).

The officials *took their places*, that is, they sat in the places of authority within the city gate to hear and judge matters of dispute. This was a common practice (see Deut 21:19; 22:15; Josh 20:4). Jeremiah's defense in court repeats what the Lord had instructed him to say, and what he had said to the priests, prophets, and people. His life was in their hands to do with him as they wished, but if they put him to death, they would be guilty of shedding *innocent blood*. Jeremiah insists he is innocent because Yahweh truly sent him to deliver the message they had heard. Written words on a page cannot capture the tone of voice, posture of body, and intensity of Jeremiah's compelling response. Jeremiah won supporters, who demanded that *the priests and the prophets* release him. The phrase *all the people* is a general expression. Clearly, many of them were open to persuasion by those who held positions of authority. The judgment of the officials became their opinion as well.

Further strengthening that judgment, the elders recall the case of *Micah of Moresheth* in verses 17–19. The quotation of Micah 3:12 makes the point that the great king of former days, Hezekiah, took Micah's message seriously, rather than threatening him with death. And the result was that the Lord relented and did not bring the threatened disaster. If the Judeans reject Jeremiah's message, the disaster he predicted could happen to them. As it happened, Jehoiakim, though a descendant of Hezekiah, did not seek God's favor.

Note that verses 20–23 form a parenthetic remark. The final editors of the book, or more likely Baruch himself, could have inserted the incident. We know nothing more of the prophet Uriah. His

Micah

Micah's name is a shortened form of Micaiah, "Who is like Yah(weh)?" His hometown, Moresheth-Gath, was a small village near the larger Philistine city of Gath, now tentatively identified with the site Tell el-Judeideh in the foothills some twenty-five miles southwest of Jerusalem.

name means, "Yah[weh] is my light." Scribes included the account of Uriah's activities and subsequent death at the hands of King Jehoiakim here to emphasize the danger Jeremiah confronted in his resolute stance as a true prophet of Yahweh. The fact that the king had Uriah buried with *the common people*, rather than returning him to his family burial place, underscores the king's disdain for him. The common people were buried in the Kidron Valley rather than in rock-cut family tombs which the upper classes possessed.

Apparently the support of *Ahikam son of Shaphan* (v. 25) was significant in saving Jeremiah from dying at the hands of his accusers. This man and his father were both important in Josiah's reign (2 Kgs 22:3–14), and he clearly was still a powerful and respected person in Jerusalem at this time.

27:1–22 Chapters 27–28 are a unit involving a symbolic act. A yoke, first worn by Jeremiah, is removed from his neck by Hananiah (a false prophet). Hananiah then breaks the yoke as a symbolic act to illustrate the supremacy of his own prophecy, which contradicted that of Jeremiah.

As the NIV footnote to verse 19 states, most Septuagint manuscripts do not have this verse, which provides the historical setting for the yoke incident. Another note indicates that the name of the king, either Zedekiah or Jehoiakim, varies in Hebrew manuscripts. The context that follows supports the identification as Zedekiah. The date for the incident is likely 594 BCE. It is worth noting that the Septuagint varies considerably from the Masoretic Text in this chapter. It is shorter, indicating that the Hebrew original behind the Septuagint translation was shorter. These textual differences, however, do not alter the basic message of this section.

The yoke which Jeremiah fashioned and wore symbolized the yoke worn by a work ox. A yoked animal obeys its master's commands. Jeremiah is to speak directly to the envoys of the surrounding nations who had come to Jerusalem, apparently to plan with Zedekiah rebellion against the Babylonians (2 Kgs 25:1). Even though Zedekiah's predecessor was in exile in Babylon because he had rebelled against Nebuchadnezzar, Zedekiah did not shrink from following the same course. The message to *Edom, Moab, Ammon, Tyre and Sidon* was from an authority superior even to the Babylonian king—*the Lord Almighty* (the word "Almighty" here translates *tseva'ot,* "hosts/armies [of heaven]"). Yahweh controls all the powers of heaven and earth and can determine whatever shall occur. At the present, God wills that these minor kingdoms

Ancient Divination
Diviners sought to determine the future by looking for "signs," such as observing the pattern of drops of oil in a cup of water (lecanomancy) or examining the entrails of a sacrificed animal (extispicy). Mediums consult with ghosts or spirits; a necromancer is a medium who inquires of the dead (Kuemmerlin-McLean 469). Sorcerers are magicians and practitioners of witchcraft. Jeremiah, speaking verbatim for the Lord Almighty, warned the rulers of these nations not to listen to the advice of such counselors. To heed their advice would lead to exile.

shall wear the yoke of the Babylonian monarch and serve him. To rebel against Nebuchadnezzar is to rebel against God, and the punishment for rebellion is *sword, famine, and plague.*

The counselors of kings included *prophets, diviners. . .interpreters of dreams . . . mediums . . .* [and] *sorcerers.* It should come as no surprise that other kingdoms than Judah had prophets (Huffmon). The confrontation of Elijah with the religion of Baal involved prophets of Baal (1 Kgs 18:19). To wear the yoke of Nebuchadnezzar was to survive as his servant in one's own land.

In verses 12–15, Jeremiah gave the same message to Zedekiah and offered the same alternatives: the possibility of survival as a servant of Nebuchadnezzar or disaster and death for both Zedekiah and those who were *prophesying lies* to him in the name of Yahweh.

In verses 16–22, Jeremiah's message from the Lord to the political leaders of Judah and the surrounding kingdoms was to submit to the rule of Babylon and survive. To the priests and people of Judah, however, his message was in opposition to the false prophets.

True prophets, Jeremiah emphasizes, would be praying for the lesser treasures of the temple that yet remained, not those already plundered. These were larger items made of bronze. By the word of the Lord, Jeremiah prophesied that they, too, would be carried away to Babylon *until the day I come for them.* Even in a message of doom and destruction, the Lord provides a word of hope and a glimpse into a future restoration.

The Temple Vessels

The Jerusalem prophets falsely anticipate the imminent end of the exile and the return of the holy vessels that Nebuchadnezzar had taken to Babylon in 597 BCE, when he first conquered Jerusalem and Judah (2 Kgs 24:13). Daniel 5:2 also mentions Nebuchadnezzar blasphemously drinking wine from the holy vessels and praising false gods; later Jews who returned from exile under Cyrus, the Persian king, after he conquered Babylon in 539 BCE, restored the holy vessels.

28:1–17 The incidents in this chapter grow directly out of the previous account regarding false prophets. Here the false prophet *Hananiah son of Azzur* personifies the opposition to Jeremiah and to his message from Yahweh. We know nothing more about this prophet than is given here—his name, his father's name, and his hometown, Gibeon (modern Tell el-Jib, located five miles north of Jerusalem). Gibeon was a town assigned to priests (Josh 21:17), so he may have been a priest, as was Jeremiah. Different manuscript traditions have different kings in verse 1.

In a very public place before *the priests and all the people,* Hananiah flatly contradicted the message of Jeremiah, using the exact introductory words that Jeremiah had used (27:4). Rather than accepting the yoke of Babylonian domination, Hananiah insists that Yahweh will act the opposite of what Jeremiah had predicted. *Within two years* the Lord would remove Babylonian rule and restore all the holy vessels to Jerusalem. The restoration would include the captive King Jehoiachin and the other exiles. Jeremiah had earlier prophesied that Jehoiachin would never return (22:26–27).

The *Amen!* of Jeremiah's response (v. 5) has been translated variously: *I hope so* (JB), *So be it* (NJB), *May it be so* (NEB), and *Amen* in the NIV, KJV, NRSV, NAB, and NJPS (Huey 248 n. 17). We cannot recover the tone, but it may have been tinged with sarcasm.

The only way to prove the validity of Hananiah's prophecy was to see if it came true. As events unfold, Jeremiah did not believe that Hananiah's hope for the future was true and from the Lord.

Verses 10–11 offer a report of what followed, written in the third person, perhaps by Baruch, who could have been an eyewitness to these events. Hananiah took the yoke from Jeremiah's neck and broke it before the audience in his own symbolic act, giving the meaning of his actions by the repetition of his prophecy. God would break Nebuchadnezzar's rule over Judah and the surrounding nations within two years. Having faithfully carried out the Lord's mandate, Jeremiah departed. The people who heard the two prophets were left to decide which to believe. Human nature would tend to embrace the message of Hananiah, encouraging those who were conspiring to revolt against Nebuchadnezzar. Those in captivity in Babylon who heard Hananiah's words would oppose settling down in their place of exile (29:5–6).

Jeremiah accuses Hananiah of lying. The lies were twofold: Hananiah had lied about receiving a word from the Lord, and by persuading the nation that it would be free of Nebuchadnezzar's rule within two years. The nation would not have to wait two years to see whether or not Hananiah's words were true. Jeremiah warned Hananiah that he would die within the year; two months later, he died. His death authenticated the validity of Jeremiah's prophetic ministry, though many continued to oppose him.

29:1–23 Those responsible for assembling the materials in the book of Jeremiah placed this letter immediately following the account of Jeremiah's confrontation with Hananiah. This

Jeremiah versus Hananiah
No word of the Lord had come to Jeremiah in the midst of his confrontation with Hananiah, and so he had departed, but in verses 12–17 the word of the Lord came to Jeremiah. Jeremiah does not give an exact indication of the time that had elapsed. He quotes Yahweh directly to Hananiah. The nations will serve Nebuchadnezzar as surely as it is impossible to break a yoke of iron. Even animals will submit to him, perhaps a reference to the hunting prowess of Mesopotamian monarchs illustrated in the reliefs of Assyrian palaces.

Gemariah Son of Hilkiah
Gemariah son of Hilkiah is unknown other than in this text. Although both he and Jeremiah are called son of Hilkiah, they were probably not brothers, since Hilkiah was a common name. Clearly Gemariah and Elasah were aides of Zedekiah, and Jeremiah trusted them to carry the letter to Babylon. Communications between Judah and Babylon were a normal feature of life under Nebuchadnezzar's rule.

arrangement is appropriate, since the letter deals with unwarranted assumptions by some Judeans in exile that they would soon return home to Jerusalem and their native land.

Verses 1–3 enable readers to understand details about the letter not revealed in the text of the letter itself. Someone other than Jeremiah authored them. The letter includes the intended recipients. *Surviving elders* would include those not slain by the Babylonians who survived the long journey into exile. They and the others named were leaders of Judean society in Babylon, including political and religious officials as well as artisans, officers, and fighting men. According to 2 Kings 24:14, "a total of ten thousand" were carried away in the initial exile in 597 BCE.

Jeremiah gave the letter to *Elasah son of Shaphan and to Gemariah son of Hilkiah* to deliver to the exiles. Elasah may have been the brother of Ahikam son of Shaphan (26:24) and of Gemariah son of Shaphan (36:10).

The letter consists of four prophetic sayings that Jeremiah passes along to the exiles. Verses 4–9 comprise the first message. It is noteworthy that the people in exile learn that the Lord was the cause of their transfer from Jerusalem to Babylon; Nebuchadnezzar was simply an instrument in God's hands. Immediately, the letter informs the recipients that they will live there a long time. They should, therefore, establish a normal pattern of life, seeking *the peace and prosperity* of their new home rather than dreaming of the old homeland. They must *pray to the Lord* for the welfare of their new home. That Judeans could worship the Lord in a foreign land was a new idea. They had thought that the temple of the Lord in Jerusalem was inviolable (7:4) and shared the widespread idea that national deities were territorial (1 Sam 26:17–20; 1 Kgs 20:28).

The prophets and diviners were clearly stirring up the people and urging them on with ideas about an imminent return to Jerusalem. This was exactly the activity of the false prophets in Jerusalem, with whom Jeremiah contended. In both instances, the Lord insists, *I have not sent them.*

The second word from the Lord (vv. 10–14) offers hope. The seventy years are an approximate figure (see 25:12–14 above). "From the fall of Nineveh (612) to the fall of Babylon (539) was seventy-three years; from Nebuchadnezzar's accession (605) to the fall of Babylon was sixty-six years" (Bright 209). Yahweh promises to come to those in exile to fulfill his *gracious promise* to restore them, because of positive plans for them. For every generation these words are precious: *You will seek me and find me when you seek me with all your heart.*

The third word from the Lord (vv. 15–19) concerns those remaining in Jerusalem, and it contrasts starkly with the word of hope for those in exile in Babylon. They shall experience *the sword, famine and plague.* Implicit in this word is that a quick return from exile would put returnees back into the terrible disaster that was coming upon Jerusalem. The coming disaster was due to their failure to listen to *my servants the prophets.* But Jeremiah asserts the same charge of failure to heed the word of the Lord against the recipients of this letter. They have escaped the coming disaster in Judah by grace.

Except for one manuscript, the Septuagint does not contain verses 16–20, suggesting they are a secondary addition. There is a natural flow of the text from the end of verse 15 to the beginning of verse 21. Nevertheless, the contrast between the bad figs in Jerusalem and the good figs in Babylon (see 24:1–10) offers a motivation for those in exile to squelch further thoughts about an early return to Jerusalem.

The two doomed prophets, Ahab and Zedekiah, are under God's judgment for *prophesying lies.* Further, they are morally corrupt. It is likely that Nebuchadnezzar executed them for stirring anti-Babylonian aspirations among the community in exile.

Punishment by Fire
The Babylonian practice of punishment by fire appears also in Daniel 3:20. The Persians who conquered the Babylonian Empire used other forms of punishment (Dan 6:16), for fire was sacred to them (Harrison 132).

29:24–32 Although incorporated in chapter 29, these events occurred some time after Jeremiah's letter had reached Babylon. Apparently, that letter had so angered the false prophets in Babylon that Shemaiah had sent a letter of complaint back to the religious authorities in Jerusalem.

We do not know anything else about *Shemaiah. Nehelamite* is likely a reference to his place of origin, but *Nehel* is unknown. Shemaiah sent his letter to all the priests, but in particular to *Zephaniah son of Maaseiah.* His name appears also in 21:1 and 37:3. Zephaniah was second in rank to Seraiah, the high priest (52:24; 2 Kgs 25:18). He may have been a brother of the false prophet Zedekiah *son of Maaseiah* mentioned in verse 21.

Note that the Lord charged him with sending letters *in your own name.* That is in contrast to Jeremiah, who consistently attributed what he wrote to the Lord. Shemaiah testifies that Zedekiah's appointment came from the Lord, but then urges the priest to reprimand Jeremiah. Shemaiah was clearly aligned with the other Babylonian false prophets who were pushing the exiles to believe in an early return.

Rather than reprimand Jeremiah, Zephaniah reads the letter from Shemaiah to the prophet (vv. 29–32). The Lord instructed Jeremiah to send his second letter to the community in exile rather than to Shemaiah alone. Yahweh was informing the entire community that Shemaiah spoke lies; he had never received his message from the Lord. The entire community would witness in due time the punishment of Shemaiah indicated in the letter. Neither he nor any of his descendants would live to see the development of a flourishing life in the exilic community nor to share in the promised return.

Jeremiah & Zephaniah
As both a prophet and a priest, Jeremiah may have been on friendly terms with the priest Zephaniah. The word from the Lord apparently came to Jeremiah immediately as he stood before Zephaniah.

Following Jeremiah's correspondence with those in exile encouraging them to adjust patiently to life in their new location, the compilers of the book inserted a series of prophetic sayings expressing hope for the future. These are undated prophecies, for the most part consisting of poetic expressions. Each begins with the introductory refrain, *This is what the Lord says*, with the added occasional insertion *declares the Lord*. Some of the prophecies anticipate events long after the Babylonian and Persian periods. Because of the content, scholars call this section "The Book of Consolation" or "The Book of Comfort."

30:1–24 Verses 1–3 are a prose introduction to the collection. As a faithful prophet, Jeremiah is to *write in a book* (scroll), but behind the writing are the words of Yahweh. Jeremiah probably called upon the writing skills of Baruch the scribe and dictated the words to him. It is useful to remember that the Old Testament prophets often had a circle of supporters and assistants, often unnamed (see Isa 8:16).

Verse 4's *the Lord* (Yahweh), in verse 2 appears as "the God of Israel." Israel represents the ideal and totality of God's people, but here the two groups—Israel and Judah—are recognized. The prophet expresses interest in the entire nation, not just Judah.

Verses 5–7 depict the agony of days of disaster here with a striking word picture. *Every strong man* looks like a pregnant woman at the time of delivery, as he suffers fear and terror *in a time of trouble for Jacob*. Jacob is Israel, God's people. It is impossible to know whether the time of trouble refers to the fall of Jerusalem, the fall of Babylon, or some other unspecified calamity. The important truth is that *he will be saved out of it*.

In that day (v. 7) is equivalent to "the day of the Lord," usually destructive, as in Amos 5:18–20, Isaiah 2:12–21 and Zephaniah 1:14–18. Here, however, *that day* will mean freedom from serving foreigners and freedom to serve Yahweh *their God and David their king*. The promise is not to resurrect the dead David, but to raise up a worthy successor of David (see also 23:5–6; Ezek 34:23–24; Hos 3:5).

Verse 10 picks up from verse 7 with references to "Jacob" and "save." This allows for the possibility that verses 8–9 intrude between verses 7 and 10. However, the reference to *that day* in both verses 7 and 8 weakens that interpretation. Scholars note a similarity in expression between verse 10 and Isaiah 41:8–10, 13–14; 43:1, 5; and 44:1–2 (Hyatt 1024).

These verses speak particularly of the trouble out of which God will save Israel. Rather than fear and terror, *Jacob will again have peace and security*. Even in a distant place of exile, the Lord is present and in the future will save. Yahweh will bring all nations and peoples to just judgment, as he has in the past. However, God may obliterate other nations but *not completely destroy you*.

The Septuagint omits verses 10–11, but they do appear in that version in 26:27–28. With minor variations, the Masoretic Text repeats them in 46:27–28.

The initial focus of verses 12–17 is on the sorry state of Judah, described in terms of a person suffering deadly injuries for whom no healing or healer is available. *All your allies* may be the surrounding peoples mentioned in 27:3: Edom, Moab, Ammon, Tyre, and Sidon. Yahweh caused this incurable situation, which is fully deserved. Although this declaration from the Lord is distinct from the preceding prophecy, it contains a similar promise that God will punish the oppressors of Yahweh's people and heal the people. What no human being can do, the Lord is fully capable of accomplishing, and God will care for the place *for whom no one cares*, Zion.

The reference to Zion in verses 18–22 may have been the cause for placing this prophecy immediately following the preceding sayings. Here the promise is for the restoration of Jerusalem and her inhabitants, identified as *Jacob*. The expression *Jacob's tents* recalls the former days when Israel followed Yahweh through the desert (2:2) and dwelt in tents (Num 24:5–6). Jerusalem *will be rebuilt on her ruins*, literally, "on her tell." Verse 19 is a reversal of the disaster described by Jeremiah in 5:14–17. The *songs of thanksgiving* could refer to joy at the harvest and *the sound of rejoicing* to wedding festivities, although both may also refer to worship in a restored city and sanctuary. The Lord promises peace and security after punishing *all who oppress them*. One of their own will rule them rather than a foreigner, fulfilling the promise of Moses (Deut 17:15). Since the leader will *arise from among them*, which suggests a lowly beginning like that of David, this hints that it will be a fulfillment of verse 9. To draw near to God unbidden or unauthorized is to risk death (Exod 28:34–35), so that even priests must follow the correct protocols. But this ruler in the future will have close fellowship with God, who will himself *bring him near*.

> **Archeological Tells**
> A "tell" is an archaeological term for a mound of debris built up by successive periods of occupation and destruction.

Verses 23–24 occur with slight variation in 23:19–20. The final compiler may have wanted to emphasize that the restoration would come only on the Lord's timetable. The promises lay in the future as he wrote, but in the future they would come to understand divine providence.

Recalling that chapter divisions were not in the original book, some scholars associate 31:1 with these verses (Hyatt 1027). *In days to come* (v. 24), in this interpretation, refers to *At that time* (v. 24). All these promises will come to pass in the future, after *the storm of the Lord* has passed. When the renewed relationship between God and the people becomes a reality, understanding will come.

> **Messianic Prophecy**
> Though there are interpreters who deny the messianic tones of this passage, the messianic interpretation is the stronger one. Verse 22 foresees the reestablishment of a close relationship between the Lord and Israel, and its basis will be a new covenant (31:33–34; verse 22 is lacking in the Septuagint).

31:1–40 God's interest is not in the exiles of Judah alone. As in the wilderness of Sinai and until the division of Israel and Judah, Yahweh was *God of all the clans of Israel*. God intends the reuniting of all the people, including a remnant of the exiled northerners who will be reestablished in Samaria. Watchmen, usually stationed atop city walls to warn of an approaching enemy, now in time of peace stand atop the fruitful hills, "watching for the first appearance of the new moon or for the arrival of other pilgrims" (Huey 270). They now summon their people to worship *the Lord our God* in Jerusalem. There is no longer any hint of pagan deities or places of worship. All of this is due to the activity of God, who exhibits *everlasting love* and *loving-kindness*.

Verses 7–9 call for exuberant, joyful singing. The words to the song pray to Yahweh to *save your people*; the Lord will gather the remnant that remains *in the north* and from every place on the earth. Even those who might have lost hope will return—*the blind . . . the lame . . .* the pregnant and even those in labor, probably referring to those who would give birth along the way. As they travel, they will be weeping (tears of joy) and praying (thanksgivings). As a father sees to the needs of his family, so God will meet the needs of the travelers. This return will be like a second exodus, with *streams of water* in a dry and thirsty land, recalling the rock which Moses smote to satisfy the thirst of the Israelites in the wilderness (Exod 17:1–7).

What Yahweh does for Israel is a story to tell to the nations (vv. 10–14). First Jeremiah calls them to attention—*Hear the word of the Lord*. Then the story begins. Yahweh has scattered the people, but *like a good shepherd* has never lost sight of them. God will *ransom*, buy back, and *redeem* them. To redeem is to deliver from a hopeless situation, such as slavery (Mic 6:4). The redeemed will express unrestrained joy in the city of the Lord and in *the bounty of the Lord*. They will return to a land of milk and honey (Exod 3:8) where they will know *comfort and joy instead of sorrow*. The fields, flocks, and herds will be bountiful, providing abundant sacrifices in which the priests share, and feasting rather than famine for the Lord's people.

Verse 15 introduces a new prophecy (vv. 15–22). Long before the time of Jeremiah, Rachel died giving birth to Benjamin at Ramah (Gen 35:16–21). She was buried nearby at Zelzah, according to 1 Samuel 10:2. Located five miles north of Jerusalem, Ramah is the modern er-Ram, the place from which the Judeans taken into exile departed for Babylon (40:1). In poetic imagery, the long-deceased Rachel weeps at the loss of her children being taken into exile. Due to a scribal explanatory note (gloss) in Genesis 35:19, Israelites came to associate Rachel's burial place with Bethlehem. This association may have come about by the confusion of Ephrath with Ephrathah (see also Ruth 4:11 and Mic 5:2). The tra-

Typology

Early Christians and their Jewish contemporaries often read biblical texts as referring to persons or events in their own times by way of analogy. The pattern of ancient biblical realities repeated themselves in a new situation.

dition that Rachel was buried near Bethlehem, however, was already well-established by about 250 BCE, for it appears in the Septuagint of Genesis 35:19. This reading provided Matthew (2:18) with grounds for a typological reading of Jeremiah 31:15.

But the word of the Lord consoles the weeping matriarch and those in exile. *Your work* (v. 16) apparently refers to Rachel's grief and tears. The consolation is that *They will return . . . there is hope for your future*.

Those in exile have responded to the harsh discipline that Yahweh rightly imposed on them. *An unruly calf* fights against rope and halter, refusing to follow its master, an apt figure of God's rebellious people. Now disciplined, they pray for restoration. They now submit to the lordship of God.

The heart of the Lord is touched by their confession. Verse 20 is a timeless portrait of the love, longing, and compassion of God for Israel. God encourages them with instructions for the way back *to your towns*. They are to mark the way into exile so they can find their way back home again. His address to them, *O Virgin Israel*, signifies that Yahweh has cleansed them and restored them to a virginal condition. With God, nothing is impossible. All of this lies in the future for those in exile. Until that time, the question in verse 22 remains.

The final sentence of the verse is so puzzling that the original intent escapes us. The saying may have been proverbial, understandable to Jeremiah's audience but not to us. It is clear, however, that the *new thing on earth* is a creation of the Lord. A woman encompassing a man is a reversal of the normal order, so traditional readers have assumed a messianic message within the saying, that is, that the new thing was God in Christ reconciling the world to himself. This meaning would not have been apparent to those in exile.

The revelation in verses 23–30 came to Jeremiah while he was sleeping. The previous section refers to Ephraim. Here the Lord explicitly names Judah. The Lord will act to restore them, and they will acknowledge their redemption by blessing the (rebuilt) temple on the holy mountain in a rebuilt Jerusalem.

Farmers in ancient Israel lived in villages and went to and from their outlying fields, vineyards, and olive orchards. Herdsmen pastured their flocks on untillable areas and, after the harvest, benefited by letting their sheep and goats feed in the harvested fields. Refreshment and sustenance for the weary came from the produce of the land to which the Lord had restored Judah. Jeremiah's vision of harmony and prosperity was sweet, for he had observed the desolation of conflict and famine (v. 28).

The Lord assures him (and those who would hear or read his words) that he will protect those restored *in those days*. The sour grapes proverb, also found in Ezekiel 18:2, contrasts the present point of view among the exiles of collective, communal, and intergenerational guilt and responsibility (Lam 5:7) with the view that will hold *in those days*, in the future. Set as it is just before the prophecy of the new covenant, the new sour grapes saying points to the time when individual responsibility will be normal.

The promise of a new covenant with *the house of Israel* (and) *Judah* was an important word of hope for those in exile (vv. 31–34). They, as well as *their forefathers*, had broken the covenant even though Yahweh *was a husband to them*. This expression, appearing also in 3:14 and in Hosea 2:16, reflects the close relationship Yahweh desired with Israel within the Sinai covenant. Their rebellious ways generation after generation resulted in the estrangement of the exile. The new covenant Yahweh will establish at an undetermined *after that time* will realize in full an intimate relationship with the people. Those who *know the Lord* will mean complete forgiveness of their sins. Sin will not be eliminated, but forgiven and forgotten by the Lord.

Two brief sayings from the Lord (vv. 35–37) emphasize Yahweh's sovereign power over the universe. God's limitless power guarantees that he will never completely forsake his people Israel. (The Septuagint has reversed the order of these two prophecies.)

> **"Know the Lord . . ."**
>
> *Jeremiah calls Israel to "know the Lord" (9:24; 22:16), that is to imitate God's treatment of the oppressed. Jeremiah understands the Torah to concern the people's relationship to each other, as well as to God.*

Verses 38–40, a final word of hope for the future, must have come to Jeremiah as Jerusalem lay in ruins after the Babylonian assault. Just as the Lord promised to bring people back from exile to the land, he promises that Jerusalem *will be rebuilt for me* (literally, "for Yahweh"). Although some of the places can no longer be identified with certainty, the description moves from the north wall (Neh 3:1; 12:39; Zech 14:10) along the western side of the city down the Valley of Gehenna (*where dead bodies and ashes are thrown*) to the south and east (*the Kidron Valley*). God would forever reverse the defilement caused by Judah's sins (2:7, 23; 7:30–34; 19:13; 32:34–35; Huey 288). Once again, Jerusalem would become the Holy City.

32:1–44 Verses 1–2 sketch the environment and time frame in which Jeremiah purchased the field. Written in the third person, they are clearly the work of an editor/compiler. Nebuchadnezzar had placed Zedekiah on the Davidic throne after he had captured the city. Zedekiah replaced his nephew, Jehoiachin, whom the Babylonians deported. But Zedekiah had revolted (2 Kgs 25; Jer 39:1), bringing the Babylonian siege of the city. *The courtyard of the guard* must have included related rooms in which Jeremiah was detained.

Possibly written by the same hand as verses 1–2, verses 3–5 explain why Jeremiah was incarcerated. Restricting his freedom also restricted his morale-destroying prophecy from spreading through the besieged population. *Until I deal with (visit) him* does not appear in the Septuagint. Nebuchanezzar did deal with Zedekiah face to face (2 Kgs 25:4–7). Zedekiah was blinded and taken to prison in Babylon, where he died.

The purchase of the field was not Jeremiah's idea but was initiated by the Lord (vv. 6–8). It was another symbolic act with implications for *this people* (vv. 15, 42–44). Leviticus 25:25–28 contains rules for redeeming property. The war may have impoverished Hanamel. It was Jeremiah's right to purchase the field, but it was also his *duty*. By all means possible, it was to remain within the (extended) family. Family land was a sacred inheritance (see 1 Kgs 21:1–16). Because of Jeremiah's imprisonment, the transaction of necessity took place in *the courtyard of the guard*.

Hyatt notes that verses 9–12 represent "the only occurrence in the O.T. where such details [of a land purchase] are given" (1044). *Seventeen shekels of silver* refers to weight (see NIV footnote), not to coins; the use of coinage did not develop until the sixth century BCE. We have no information on the source of Jeremiah's income. Although not stated, *Baruch son of Neriah* must have been the scribe who drafted the documents. This is the first mention of Jeremiah's secretary and associate.

Archaeological evidence indicates that such deeds of sale (vv. 13–15) were trifolded, tied with a string with a small lump of clay spread over the knot, which a scribe then impressed with a signet ring. This guaranteed that the unopened document was the original and unaltered. The clay jar provided a virtually moisture-free environment for long-term storage of the documents. The discovery of the Dead Sea Scrolls in jars in 1947 proves the effectiveness of this method.

Some scholars are skeptical that the entire prayer in verses 16–25 comes from Jeremiah, claiming only verses 16, 17a, and 24–25 are from the prophet (Bright 298). However, their skepticism is due to their presuppositions; there is nothing in the prayer foreign to Jeremiah's thought.

The first section of the prayer (vv. 17–19) acknowledges the greatness of God. The second part of the prayer (vv. 20–23) illustrates the power of God. Jeremiah recalls how Yahweh redeemed Israel from Egyptian bondage and gave them the promised land. But as he prayed, Jeremiah noted the present siege and the reason for it: disobedience to Yahweh's law. The third section of the prayer (vv. 24–25) reminds the Lord of the siege and the end of it now revealed to the prophet. Expressing surprise at God's instructions to buy a field, ". . . Jeremiah could scarcely believe that a reliable and consistent deity would instruct him to acquire property when the end of organized life in Judah was at hand" (Harrison 42).

Following Jeremiah's prayer, the Lord responds to his confusion (vv. 26–440). Jeremiah had prayed, *Nothing is too hard for you*, and Yahweh reaffirms that truth,

Baruch's Ring

The impression of a signet ring bearing an inscription relating to Baruch surfaced on the antiquities market of Jerusalem and is now on display in the Israel Museum. Although not recovered in an excavation, few doubt its authenticity. Published by Israeli scholar Nahman Avigad, the inscription reads "Belonging to Berekyahu (Baruch) son of Neriyahu (Neriah) the scribe."

with the self-description *the God of all mankind*, literally, *all flesh* (KJV, RSV). Yes, the city is destined for destruction at the hands of the Babylonians. Its inhabitants had turned from rather than to the Lord. They had refused the Lord's teaching and discipline. They had polluted the temple that bore Yahweh's *Name*, just as they had polluted their homes with idols. And they had served their master, Baal, by offering their children to Molech in the Valley of the Sons of Hinnom.

Jeremiah had prophesied *sword, famine and plague* for Jerusalem (14:12; 21:7; 24:10; 27:8; 29:18). These were words he had heard from the Lord, and they were valid. However, *the Lord, the God of Israel* now had an additional word for both prophet and people. God would restore them to *this place*, Jerusalem and Judah, a safe place for them in the future. Verses 38–41 are an expansion of 31:33.

With limitless power, the Lord will ultimately turn calamity into prosperity for *this people*. Many would perish before their descendants would participate in the fulfillment of these promises, yet the promises will become reality. Family properties will be restored in the place Jeremiah calls *a desolate waste*. Thus a modest land transaction had exploded into a magnificent hope because nothing is too hard for the Lord.

33:1–26 This chapter continues the theme of restoration that began in chapter 30. Three aspects of restoration come into focus here: of the people to the land (vv. 1–8), of the land to prosperity (vv. 9–13), and of a Davidic king (vv. 14–26).

The expression *a second time* ties verses 1–9 to 32:2. Yahweh as creator echoes 32:17. The Lord invites Jeremiah to pray for new and added insights or revelations.

The NIV translation of verses 4–5 veils a difficult and obscure Hebrew text. Some words appear to have dropped out of the original. As rendered, the translation points to a military strategy in which city leaders remove buildings adjacent to the besieged walls at strategic points along them to improve the defenses of the city.

Yahweh has ordained the destruction of Jerusalem, but aims at *health . . . healing . . . peace* and *security* for the future. Verse 8 echoes and expands on 31:34b, "For I will forgive their wickedness and will remember their sins no more." Because people will recognize the future prosperity of Jerusalem as coming from Yahweh, they will offer praise and honor *before all nations*. Isaiah 62:2, 7 express similar thoughts.

Another brief saying from the Lord (vv. 10–11) continues the theme of restoration. Jeremiah speaks of what he sees—total desolation—describing the aftermath of the siege of the Babylonians. What Yahweh sees for the future is the return of inhabitants to *towns of Judah* and *Jerusalem*, with the restoration of normal social and religious activities. These are marked by joyful events such as weddings. The people rightly recognize *the Lord* as the *Almighty*, who has brought this about and is worthy of praise and thanksgiving. The praise comes from Psalm 136:1, and the editor of Jeremiah probably intends it as a reminder of the entire psalm.

In verses 12–13, another promise for the future looks to the restoration of flocks grazing over an area from the north of Jerusalem (Benjamin) to the south (*Negev*). Similar territorial descriptions occur in 17:26 and 32:44. Shepherds will keep tabs on their flocks, counting them as they come into the fold to see that none is missing.

Verses 14–26 are lacking in the Septuagint, but textual variations do not negate the importance of the passage. The focus of restoration now turns to the promise of the continuation of the Davidic kingship and the Levitical priesthood. Verses 15–16 reflect the announcement in 23:5–6, which is in the Septuagint. In contrast to the string of wicked and unjust kings of Judah in the past, the coming monarch *will do what is just and right*. His character will be so dominant that the city will wear the name *The Lord, our Righteousness*, the name of the coming king in 23:6.

The Coming King
Like other prophetic texts, Jeremiah 33 expects a future monarch to restore Israel's fortunes. Jeremiah does not specify his identity. Here and in chapter 31, he expects this king to rule alongside a renewed priesthood in answer to charges that God has reneged on his promises (v. 24). Later Jewish and Christian interpreters connected these and similar passages to the coming messiah.

Historically, the Davidic monarchy ended in Babylon with the death of Jehoiachin (unrecorded in the Bible), the last mentioned king of Judah (2 Kgs 25:27). Although some argue that Zedekiah was the last king of Judah, he too died in exile in Babylon. Zerubbabel, a prince of the Davidic line, was a leader in the return to Jerusalem (Ezra 2:2), but neither he nor anyone else became king. He is called "governor" in Haggai 1:1, 14; 2:2, 21.

Verse 18 foresees the restoration of the Levitical priesthood in a functioning temple. The second temple was rebuilt and dedicated in 516 BCE (Ezra 6:14–15). The priestly leader in the first return of the Jews from Babylon was Jeshua (Joshua) son of Jehozadak, of the line of Aaron. The priesthood in the Second Temple period undergoes transitions and a loss of prestige due to political changes. The Hasmonean priest-kings replaced the Zadokite priestly line in the second century BCE. Controversy over the legitimacy of the high priest resulted in the establishment of the community responsible for the Dead Sea Scrolls. Beginning with the Roman period, the civil rulers appointed the high priests. With the destruction of the temple by the Romans in CE 70, the high priesthood ended, although priestly family connections (the Jewish family name Cohen and its variations) continue to the present.

THE LAST DAYS OF JUDAH · 34:1–38:13

Turning from the Book of Consolation (30:1–33:36), the compilers of the book of Jeremiah present next a series of events (34:1–38:28) in which Jeremiah interacts with the Judean rulers prior to the final fall of Jerusalem to Nebuchadnezzar's army. These events are of varied dates and not necessarily sequential.

34:1–7 Verses 1–7 give the timing of this prophetic warning and promise to Zedekiah. The Babylonian ruler had engaged Jerusalem; however, his main focus lay on destroying all the fortified cities of Judah outside the capital. His forces included *all the kingdoms and peoples in the empire*. As vassals of the mighty king, they provided whatever support he required. Only Lachish (Tell ed-Duweir, about thirty-five miles southwest of Jerusalem) and Azekah (about 10 miles north of Lachish) remained unconquered before the entire Babylonian force turned against Jerusalem. Both sites are in the Shephelah, the foothills between the Philistine Plain and the Central Highlands.

The Lord told Jeremiah to warn Zedekiah that Yahweh is about to hand over Jerusalem to the Babylonians. Zedekiah will not escape. He will appear before King Nebuchadnezzar, who will deport him to Babylon. All this happened according to the word of the prophet. However, after having looked into the eyes of Nebuchanezzar, Zedekiah fell blind or became blind. He was captive in Babylon, but he never saw the place (39:7; 52:10–11). The prophet also transmits a promise of Yahweh to Zedekiah. He will not die in battle. The *funeral fire* is not a reference to cremation. It will be a fire to honor him, as was the custom (2 Chron 16:14; 21:19).

34:8–22 King Zedekiah apparently initiated the emancipation of slaves some time after the siege of the city began, early in 588 BCE. It seems to have been an effort to placate the Lord. The slaveholders entered into a solemn agreement before Yahweh (v. 15) to free all *Hebrew slaves*. The text does not mention slaves who were not Hebrews. Then they reneged on their promise and reenslaved those freed. This covenant-breaking *profaned* the Lord's name. The law forbade lifelong enslavement of Hebrews by Hebrews unless willingly entered into (Exod 21:5–6). Otherwise, the slave must be freed after six years of servitude (Exod 21:2; Lev 25:39–46; Deut 15:1, 12–18). The prophetic word reminded the slaveholders of the Lord's will, which they and their forefathers had disdained.

In an ironic statement, the Lord gave the slaveholders their *freedom*—to suffer the consequences of their rebellious ways. The *calf they cut in two* refers to the ancient practice of sacrificing an animal when making a solemn covenant (see Gen 15:9–17). The Hebrew expression for making a covenant is "to cut" a covenant.

The timing of this event is related to the lifting of the siege by the Babylonians (v. 21). Jeremiah 37:5–8 indicates that the withdrawal of the Babylonians was due to the approach of an Egyptian army coming to the aid of the Judeans; however, according to Ezekiel 17:15–17, the Egyptian effort failed, and when they returned to Egypt, the Babylonians took Jerusalem.

The Lord takes covenants very seriously (Num 30:2; Deut 21–23; Josh 9:15–18; Eccl 5:4–5; Matt 21:28–32).

35:1–9 Verses 1–5 occur *during the reign of Jehoiakim*, probably dating to 598 BCE. The incident is related to the raiding parties of *Babylonian and Aramean armies* (v. 11). Second Kings 24:2 provides the setting for the invaders' activities.

Both chapters 35 and 36 relate to the reign of Jehoiakim and appear between the preceding and following chapters associated with King Zedekiah. There is no apparent explanation for why the compilers made this arrangement.

The invitation to the Recabites came *from the Lord* via Jeremiah. What Yahweh commands, the prophet faithfully does. The *side rooms* were built adjacent to the sanctuary proper and served as storerooms, meeting rooms, and as temporary living quarters for the priests on duty. *Jaazaniah son of Jeremiah* points to the popularity of the name Jeremiah, and was not the prophet's son. The people mentioned are otherwise unknown, except for *Maaseiah son of Shallum*, probably the father of the priest Zephaniah (21:1; 29:25; 37:3). Door keeping at the temple was an important priestly function, preventing the entry of ritually unclean persons. The doorkeepers were also in charge of funds set aside for the repair of the temple (2 Kgs 12:9–10). The name *Igdaliah* occurs only here. The Septuagint has Gedaliah, so the longer form is simply an alternative spelling of the name.

As with other symbolic acts of the book, Jeremiah publicly offered wine to the Recabites, knowing they would refuse to drink it, to make a point. Even in the temple of the Lord at the invitation of the prophet of the Lord, they refused to break the covenant of the clan. That they were dwelling in Jerusalem was a temporary interlude in their normal life away from settled places. For their safety and survival, they had entered the city to escape the rampaging *Babylonian and Aramean armies*.

Instruction to Jeremiah from Yahweh was immediate (vv. 12–17). The people of Judah and Jerusalem saw an example of obedience to a family covenant by the Recabites. Would they be moved by that example to observe the covenant relation with Yahweh that he had established? Past performance gave little hope that they would. Disaster awaits those who *did not listen* and *did not answer*.

The Lord promised condemnation to Judah (vv. 18–19) but gave commendation to the Recabites. Because of their faithfulness, the Recabites would survive to serve Yahweh "while the earth remains" (Septuagint).

36:1–32 This second event during Jehoiakim's reign occurred in 605 BCE, the year in which Nebuchadnezzar defeated Egypt at Carchemish, a ford across

> **The Recabites**
>
> *The Recabites were a clan begun by Jonadab (Jehonadab), a supporter of the revolt of Jehu against the house of Ahab (2 Kgs 10:23). He apparently became disillusioned by the subsequent actions of Jehu, who "was not careful to keep the law of the Lord" and "did not turn away from the sins of Jeroboam" (2 Kgs 10:31). So he withdrew from the urban and agrarian culture of Israel to a nomadic way of life. The Recabites were related to the Kenites (1 Chron 2:55), who may have been metalworkers, also itinerant traders. The event in Jeremiah 35 provides the bulk of biblical information about the group—they dwelt in tents, neither drank wine nor owned vineyards, and never built houses nor practiced agriculture. Noteworthy is the fact that they had been carrying on this lifestyle for two and a half centuries by Jeremiah's time.*

the Euphrates River. After this victory, the Babylonians began to extend their control over the rest of the ancient Near East. Jeremiah was then in his twenty-third year of ministry.

What Jeremiah had spoken over the years for the Lord was now to be written down (vv. 1–3). Some who had heard the prophecies had died. What Jeremiah presented orally in the past now would take on a more permanent form, so that the current generation would know the warning. The reason for writing is that they might repent and escape from the disaster to come.

Although Jeremiah mentions Baruch in 32:12, verses 4–7 mark his earliest appearance in the events of Jeremiah's ministry. Why Jeremiah was *restricted* (prevented from entering the temple) is unclear. He may have been ceremonially unclean, or he may have been barred from entry by temple officials who considered him a troublemaker (see chapters 7, 26). He does not seem to have been under arrest, because he is free to move about in verses 19 and 26. Baruch is to read the scroll in public on a fast day when the people are likely to pray (*bring their petition*). The Old Testament does not establish any set fast days (but see Zech 7:5), but with the threat of foreign invaders, priests had announced a special fast day. This fast was apparently related to Nebuchadnezzar's sack of Ashkelon in the nearby Philistine plain.

According to verses 8–10, The scroll contained *the words of the Lord*, although dictated by Jeremiah. Baruch faithfully carried out Jeremiah's instructions, reading to those assembled from the *room of Gemariah*. This was likely a portico, opening on the *upper courtyard* in which those entering the New Gate could congregate. Shaphan, father of Gemariah, was high official under Josiah (2 Kgs 22:3, 8). Gemariah's brother, Ahikam, stood by Jeremiah when he was threatened (26:24), so Baruch was in a friendly environment as he read Jeremiah's words to the people. Gemariah, however, was not present (v. 12).

Micaiah reported the gist of what Baruch had read to his father and the others in conference (vv. 11–19). The officials were meeting in the office of *Elishama*, another official. He is likely the same individual mentioned in 41:1 and 2 Kings 25:25, and was related to the royal family. All these men were high-ranking members of the king's court. The Bible does not mention *Jehudi son of Nethaniah* elsewhere, but noting his ancestors to the third generation suggests that he was an important individual; normally only the father is named. While commanding Baruch to bring the scroll to them, these officials treated him respectfully, inviting him to be seated. The words of Jeremiah struck fear in the hearts of

Gemaraiah

Archaeologist Yigael Shiloh found evidence for "Gemaryahu son of Shaphan" in the city of David excavations in the form of a bulla, a piece of clay that authenticated a sealed papyrus document which had been impressed by Gemaryahu's seal. (Gemaryahu is a longer form of Gemariah.) Fire destroyed the papyrus document but hardened the clay so it survived until its recent discovery (King 94).

the listeners, as the officials heard Baruch read them. As the king's advisors, they determined that the king should hear the message in the scroll. After learning that Jeremiah dictated the message that Baruch read, and anticipating a negative reaction on the part of Jehoiakim that would endanger both Baruch and Jeremiah, they ordered both men to hide for their personal safety. (Much later unconfirmed tradition identifies their hiding place north of the Damascus Gate in what is now called the Grotto of Jeremiah.)

The reaction of Jehoiakim to the prophetic word testifies to his unbelief and disdain (vv. 20–26). In midwinter, he was keeping warm with heat from a *firepot* (brazier), probably burning charcoal. Despite the suggestion that the scroll was made of parchment (Harrison 150), it was more likely a papyrus scroll.

Burning leather would have given off a terrible stench; furthermore, parchment was not invented until the second century BCE. Unlike the fear felt by the group of court officials who heard Baruch read the scroll, the king and his circle of closest advisors treated the prophetic words skeptically. They rejected the wise counsel of *Elnathan, Delaiah and Gemeriah*. As *Jehudi* read column after column of the scroll, the king cut off a few columns, adding it to the fuel in the brazier. His actions contrast sharply with those of his father, Josiah, when the scroll was discovered in the temple during his reign (2 Kgs 22:8–13). *Son of the king* was a title that indicated a close but not necessarily a blood relationship to the monarch. The king did not discover Baruch and Jeremiah.

Jeremiah's Second Scroll
To the second copy, Jeremiah added many similar *prophecies. This second scroll was likely the beginning stage of our Book of Jeremiah. Just as Yahweh provided the second set of tablets for Moses (Exod 32:19; 34:1), so he provided for the survival of the word Jehoiakim destroyed* (Huey 326).

The anger of Jehoiakim against Jeremiah and Baruch subsided in due time, and the Lord instructed Jeremiah to dictate again to Baruch the contents of the destroyed scroll (vv. 27–32).

The Lord also gave a personal word to Jehoiakim through Jeremiah. He would fall to the very force he denied—*the king of Babylon*. He would die and have no proper burial, nor would a son succeed him. His son and successor, Jehoiachin, ruled but three months (2 Kgs 24:8).

37:1–21 The text now returns to events in the reign of Zedekiah (see 2 Kgs 24:17–25:7). From 37:1 through 44:30, the book of Jeremiah focuses on events just prior to the fall of Jerusalem, the fall itself, and its aftermath. The section is almost entirely written as a narrative, probably by Baruch.

Verse 1 is a succinct version of 2 Kings 24:17–20, which states that Zedekiah *did evil in the eyes of the Lord*. He ignored the prophetic warnings of Jeremiah, and *the people of the land* followed the example of their leader. *Jehucal son of Shelemiah* was no friend of the prophet. In 38:1, 4, he, among others, urges Jeremiah's execution. *Zephaniah*, the next in rank after the high priest, treated Jeremiah with respect in 24:24–29. Zedekiah will not accept the word of the Lord from the prophet, but he recognizes Jeremiah's intimate relationship with Yahweh and asks him to pray to Yahweh *our God*. The Babylonians had temporarily halted their siege of Jerusalem, due to the threat from the Egyptian forces of Pharaoh Hophra, identified by name in 44:30 (589–570 BCE). Zedekiah perhaps hoped prayer would make the withdrawal permanent, as verse 7 indicates. This event occurred before the prophet was imprisoned (32:2).

The king had requested that Jeremiah pray (vv. 6–10). There is no indication that Jeremiah did as requested. However, the revelation he received from the Lord is clear. The Lord denies the desire of Zechariah. Egypt will withdraw, and the Babylonians will return to destroy Jerusalem. The city's doom is inevitable, even in the unlikely but extreme circumstances depicted in verse 10.

> **The Benjamin Gate**
> *The* Benjamin Gate *was in the north of the city wall (compare 38:7; Zech 14:10); gates bore the name of the places toward which traffic was headed, as with the modern Jaffa Gate.*

The arrest of Jeremiah also occurred during the period in which the Babylonian forces had withdrawn from besieging the city (vv. 11–16). The prophet had personal business to attend to outside Jerusalem in the territory of the tribe of Benjamin. The property involved is apparently not that which he purchased as a symbolic act (chapter 32). *Irijeh* is otherwise unknown in the Bible, but he was not related to the false prophet Hananiah (28:1, 10).

The captain of the guard arrested Jeremiah and charged him with *deserting to the Babylonians*. He was likely under suspicion because he had urged people to surrender to the enemy (21:9; 38:2), and some had done so (38:19). The *officials* are here unnamed, but they were probably those listed in 38:1. These were not the officials of 36:12, 19, who had been sympathetic to Jeremiah. A decade had passed and an earlier group had accompanied Jehoiachin into exile.

Although he was imprisoned in a *house*, his was not a benign house arrest. He endured beating and isolation in *a vaulted cell in a dungeon*. The dungeon was in the basement of the house; vaulting supported the the floor above.

King Zedekiah's secret desire for a (good) *word from Yahweh* finally brought Jeremiah out of his prison and into the palace (vv. 17–21). Apparently, the king feared what his officials, who were pro-Egyptian, might do to him, if he asked Jeremiah the question publicly (Huey 331). A man of courage and integrity, despite the possible consequences, Jeremiah gave the word of doom from the Lord.

Taking advantage of the opportunity to speak directly with the king, Jeremiah pled his case. The reality of current events had proven the false prophets were false. Jeremiah's prophecies had proven true. To his credit, Zedekiah removed Jeremiah (still under arrest) to better surroundings and rations.

38:1–13 There are similarities between this and the previous incident: in both, officials charged the prophet with treason and threw him in prison; both have private interviews with the king; and in both Jeremiah ends up in *the* *courtyard of the guard*. But there are differences as well. The setting for the arrests differ. Jeremiah stays in two different prison environments, and the king deals with each incident differently. Either this chapter is an alternative version of chapter 37 or, more likely, a separate incident.

Gedaliah son of Pashhur may be the son of the Pashhur who had mistreated Jeremiah (20:1–6). *Jehucal*, mentioned in 37:3, has a shortened name, *Jucal*, here. *Pashhur son of Malkijah* appears in 21:1. Jeremiah had frequently spoken the same or similar prophetic words given in verse 2 (21:9; 34:2, 22; 37:8). The charge is not that of encouraging people to escape the doomed city, but the effect of Jeremiah's prophecies on the morale of the defenders.

The king's response to his officials reminds one of Pilate handing Jesus over to the mob. By referring to himself in the third person, (*The king can do nothing to oppose you*), Zedekiah distances himself from his actions. Surprisingly, the officials who had deemed Jeremiah worthy of death, rather than executing him immediately, put him in a cistern. Perhaps they intended that he die there slowly, by starvation. The cistern was much worse than the dungeon in Jonathan's house.

But Jeremiah had a friend in the royal court— *Ebed-Melech*, a Cushite. When he heard what officials had done with Jeremiah, he went directly to the king. Zedekiah was at the same gate where Jeremiah had been arrested in the previous incident, probably seeing to the defenses. Invaders had always approached Jerusalem from that direction due to the strategic value of the heights of Mount Scopus. While the king had earlier put the fate of Jeremiah in the hands of his angry officials, he acted forthrightly here, even assigning a considerable contingent of men to assist Ebed-Melech, perhaps to prevent any interference from the officials mentioned in 38:1. (On the other hand, one Hebrew manuscript has three rather than thirty men; and RSV follows this translation.) We see the thoughtfulness of Ebed-Melech for the condition of Jeremiah in the cushioning he provided from the pressure of the ropes on his malnourished body. He would receive his reward from the Lord (39:16–18).

Cisterns

Cisterns were cut into bedrock and plastered to hold water in many ancient cities. That only mud remained in the cistern puts the event late in the summer dry season, likely in July or August, shortly before the Babylonians breached the wall in 587 BCE (52:5–7).

ZEDEKIAH QUESTIONS JEREMIAH AGAIN · 38:14–28

Rather than questioning Jeremiah "in the palace" as previously (37:17), the king is in *the third entrance to the temple of the Lord*. The location of this gate in the Solomonic temple is unkown; it may have been an entrance adjacent to the king's palace (Hyatt 1076).

Cush

Modern northern Sudan. In Jeremiah's time, the Cushites were heavily Egyptianized. Earlier they ruled Egypt as the Twenty-Fifth Dynasty (eighth through the seventh centuries BCE).

Verses 15–16 reflect Jeremiah's previous experience with the king; however, the king's oath convinced the prophet to respond to Zedekiah's request. Yahweh offers the king two dismal outcomes (vv. 17–18). Surrender offered a better result than capture, but fear of mistreatment at the hands of Judeans who had already surrendered to the Babylonians dominated the king's mind (v. 19). Jeremiah first urges Zedekiah to surrender for his own personal good. Then the prophet paints a stark picture of what will happen to the king's *women* (his harem of concubines and wives) and children. Four lines of poetry that will be uttered by his wives will utterly shame and humiliate the king if he refuses to surrender. These words possibly point to the pro-Egyptian officials of Zedekiah's court, his advisors (v. 1). These men had earlier desired to slay Jeremiah, as the king knows, so he commanded Jeremiah not to reveal the content of their discussion to the *officials*, should they inquire of him. Jeremiah obeyed the king. He did not reveal the heart of his conversation with the king, but he did tell them what the king wanted them to hear.

39:1–18 What Jeremiah had prophesied happened (vv. 1–7). The Babylonians had sacked Jerusalem. For reasons we cannot discern, the compiler(s) of our book repeat the fall of the city in 52:4–16, which itself comes almost verbatim from 2 Kings 25:1–12. The shortened version of the Septuagint does not include verses 4–13. The siege "began in January 588 and lasted until July 587 (with a brief interlude, probably in the summer of 588)" (Bright 242). The approach of Egyptian forces noted earlier caused the interlude. The breach of the walls occurred on *the ninth day of the fourth month*, still observed by Jews as the Ninth of Av.

The leaders of the Babylonian forces held an immediate conference in the *Middle Gate*. That location is uncertain. The manuscript tradition has garbled some of the names of the officers. *Nergal-sharezer*, though mentioned twice (v. 3), may be the same individual as in verse 13. The Babylonians, upon entering the city, would have moved cautiously and methodically into unfamiliar streets with armed defenders still within the walls. Zedekiah and his soldiers fled the city under cover of darkness through *the gate between the two walls* (a narrow postern gate). They entered the Kidron Valley on the east side of the city and fled toward the Jordan Valley. Pursued and captured, they appeared before Nebuchadnezzar at his headquarters in central Syria, *Riblah in the land of Hamath*. There the mighty ruler took his vengeance on the petty king who had caused him so much grief. As excessive as the Babylonian treatment of prisoners seems, it was normal in the warfare of the ancient Near East.

Verses 8–10 offer an account of the destruction of the rebellious city. The account telescopes events. *Nebuzaradan* arrived in the city a month after its capitulation rather than the day the walls fell (52:12). The destruction of the city was complete, making it virtually uninhabitable. The phrase *and the rest of the people* at the end of verse 9 is a scribal error. The correct reading should follow 52:15, "the rest of the craftsmen." Those whom Nebuzaradan left behind and to whom he gave *vineyards and fields* could be an asset to the meager provincial government formed by the captors and to the "Babylonian soldiers" who served with Gedaliah (41:3).

Verses 11–14 give the first of two slightly differing accounts of the release of Jeremiah. The second follows in 40:1–6. Jeremiah's release from his imprisonment in the *courtyard of the guard* came at the hand of the Babylonians, not by action of Zedekiah's officers. This apparently occurred on the day the city fell to the Babylonians. Nebuzaradan, however, was not in the city that day and did not arrive for another thirty days. The key to understanding Jeremiah's initial release is the word *sent* (v. 14). Apparently, the leading officers were at their field headquarters in "Ramah" (40:1) and sent the orders for Jeremiah's release. The succinct text does not give many particulars. Jeremiah may have been brought to Ramah (modern er-Ram), some five miles north of Jerusalem. They also placed him in the custody of *Gedaliah*. As governor, he stayed in Mizpah (40:5), three miles north of Ramah.

Verses 15–18 logically connect with 38:28. Scribes placed this section here because it relates to Jeremiah's confinement in the *courtyard of the guard*. Acting out of a compassionate heart, *Ebed-Melech the Cushite* had rescued Jeremiah from a deadly situation in the cistern. Now the Lord had compassion on him because of his faith in Yahweh. The Hebrew is more emphatic than *I will save you*. The grammatical construction (infinitive absolute + imperfect) means, "I will surely save you" (compare NRSV).

Nebuchadnezzar & Jeremiah

Skeptics might insist that Nebuchadnezzar would not have known about Jeremiah nor have given orders for his welfare. Yet Zedekiah had feared the Jews who have gone over to the Babylonians (38:19). *Surely they informed their Babylonian interrogators about the prophet who had encouraged them to surrender and foretold the conquest of the city by Nebuchadnezzar's forces. Although the Babylonian king knew about Jeremiah, it is doubtful that they ever met face to face.*

JEREMIAH'S WITNESS AFTER JERUSALEM'S FALL · 40:1–45:5

40:1–6 *The word came to Jeremiah from the Lord* should introduce a prophetic oracle, but none follows. The next mention of a word from the Lord to the prophet occurs in 42:7. The text has a history we do not know. Clearly it has suffered damage here. On the other hand, Willis (319) thinks that Nebuzaradan's words to Jeremiah comprise the oracle.

Lacking details, we cannot know how Jeremiah ended up in chains in Ramah, where he was again

Gedaliah's Seal

A stamp seal found at Lachish in 1935 bearing the inscription, "[Belonging to] Gedalyahu, the one over the house," may be related to Gedaliah. If so, he was serving Zedekiah as the royal steward (manager of the palace staff) until the city fell (King 98). Nebuchadnezzar would thus have appointed an experienced administrator to be governor.

freed. Another possibility is that the account in 39:11–14 has compressed within it the events in this section. In other words, Jeremiah went from the courtyard of the guard in chains to Ramah to see Nebuzaradan, who released him there. Yet Nebuzaradan's advice to Jeremiah to *Go back to Gedaliah* indicates that Jeremiah had been with Gedaliah before ending up in Ramah. Whatever the actual sequence of circumstances, Jeremiah chose to remain in the land. *Gedaliah son of Ahikam* was the grandson of Shaphan (39:14). Shaphan, in the service of Josiah, had a role in the discovery of the scroll of the law (2 Kgs 22:3–20). Ahikam was a supporter of Jeremiah (26:24).

40:7–41:16 The text does not mention Jeremiah or Yahweh again until 42:2. We learn much about Jeremiah in this book, but it is not a biography of the prophet. According to verses 7–10, the *army officers and all their men* had apparently escaped the conquerors, finding temporary refuge *in the open country*. Harrison (160) suggests that they were guerrilla fighters. Variants of the names of the officers occur in the Septuagint and some Hebrew manuscripts. *Ishmael*, of the house of David, perhaps had an attitude of superiority over Gedaliah. A clay bulla reading "Belonging to Ishmael the son of the king" exists, and may refer to this person; however, it came from the antiquities market and may be a forgery (King 98–99).

Gedaliah was intent on pacifying the countryside. He attempted to reassure the officers and their men by oath (presumably taken before Yahweh) and by his political authority. Gedaliah was rightly concerned about the harvest of vintage grapes, summer fruits, and olives. The survival of the remnant that remained in the land depended upon an adequate food supply. Harvest times for these crops occurred in August/September.

Besides the remnant of the Judean army, refugees in Transjordan and elsewhere returned (vv. 11–12). Combined with *the people who were left behind in the land* (v. 6), the military group and the refugees were able to enjoy an abundant harvest.

Johanan son of Kareah led a deputation to warn Gedaliah of the plot against his life (vv. 13–14). The Ammonite king, Baalis, orchestrated the plot in concert with Ishmael son of Nethaniah. Baalis probably hoped to control the Judahite territory with Gedaliah out of the way. Gedaliah could not believe such a thing could be true, and he rejected Johanan's offer to preemptively assassinate Ishmael.

The Bulla of Baalis
Archaeologists discovered a bulla of Baalis in excavations at Tell el-Umeiri south of Amman, Jordan in 1984.

In the seventh month was less than three months after Gedaliah became governor (41:1–3). The assassination of the governor may have occurred one or more years later than the year in which Jerusalem fell, however. The text does not specify the year, and three months seems insufficient time for the return of the refugees and the harvest.

Ishmael and his men were guests at the table of Gedaliah. They broke the key custom of hospitality in the ancient Near East by slaying their host. So awful was the deed that the Jews observed a fast day in October in the Second Temple period as a memorial (Zech 7:5; 8:19). The others killed—a small contingent of Babylonian soldiers and *all the Jews who were with Gedaliah*—probably refers to others at the meal, not to all the inhabitants of Mizpah (see v. 10).

The murder of all present at the dinner apparently left no one to escape and spread the alarm (vv. 4–15). The men arriving from *Shechem, Shiloh and Samaria* were coming from the north, apparently on a religious pilgrimage to the ruined holy place in Jerusalem. While Leviticus 19:28, 21:5, and Deuteronomy 14:1 forbid the religious act of cutting oneself some people apparently practiced it. Ishmael went out to meet them, falsely showing evidence of a similar grief, and drew them into his deadly ambush. Only ten survived; the others were thrown into a mass burial in an empty cistern, *along with Gedaliah*, and we can assume the rest of those murdered at the meal. The text includes a historical note, associating the construction of the cistern with the defenses built by *King Asa* (1 Kgs 15:22).

Besides *the king's daughters*, Jeremiah was apparently among the captives (42:2 mentions him among those rescued). Ishmael, his men and his captives, headed eastward toward Ammonite territory across the Jordan.

Johanan and his associates rescued the captives *near the great pool in Gibeon*. Perhaps Ishmael was aware of pursuers and was attempting to circumvent them. In the melee, Ishmael and eight of his men escaped to the Ammonites.

41:16–43:13 Johanan and his men realized the assassination of Gedaliah represented rebellion against Nebuchadnezzar and Babylon (vv. 16–18). Rather than return to Mizpah, they and those whom they had rescued headed south past ruined Jerusalem. Fearing Babylonian reprisals, they headed toward Egypt for refuge. They stopped to assess their situation at *Geruth Kimham near Bethlehem*. We cannot now identify the location. It may have been a piece of property given by King David to Kimham in recognition of his support (2 Sam 19:38), and the name of which continued through the centuries.

Gibeon

Gibeon (Tell el-Jib) is actually southwest of the site identified as Mizpah (Tell en-Nasbeh) rather than east.

According to 42:1–6, the entire group was uncertain what they should do, but they all acted in one accord to approach Jeremiah to pray to Yahweh (*your God*) on their behalf. In a crisis, this irreligious group turned to the one person who had a relationship with Yahweh. They do not seek spiritual guidance, simply physical safety.

Jeremiah agrees to pray to "Yahweh *your God*," perhaps using the occasion as a teachable moment. They swear a modest form of oath to obey whatever the Lord *your* God requires; however, they finally acknowledge Yahweh as *our* God. It should be noted, however, that the Septuagint reads *our God* in verses 4–5.

The duration *ten days later* presents a test of their faith and patience (vv. 7–12). Jeremiah presents the reply in the Lord's words. The ultimate decision is in their hands. Yahweh's word comes in "if/then" clauses, urging them to stay and benefit from what God promises to do for them. The Lord has compassion on them because of their suffering. And as sovereign of all nations, God will see to it that Nebuchadnezzar will treat them compassionately. The Lord promises his sustaining presence with them.

In verses 13–18, Jeremiah injects his own preliminary warning to the group about what will happen to them if they refuse to stay in the land, thus disobeying the Lord. From the practical point of view, Egypt looked like a haven from the horrors of their recent experiences, but asylum in Egypt was not God's will for them. *The word of the Lord* substantiates the word of his prophet. In Egypt, they would suffer the very things they seek to escape. All of this would come upon them, despite the compassion of the Lord, if they chose to rebel.

Jeremiah completes his presentation in verses 19–22 by emphasizing in his own words what the oracle from the Lord had stated. He sensed they had *made a fatal mistake* by asking him to seek the Lord's direction for them because they had already determined that they were going to go on to Egypt. They had not made their petition in good faith. They sought only Yahweh's confirmation of their plans. Apparently, Jeremiah could tell by the body language of his audience that they *still have not obeyed the Lord* [their] *God in all he sent* [Jeremiah] *to tell* [them].

In 43:1–3, the *arrogant* men flatly rejected the prophet's reply, accusing him of lying. For the first time, we learn that *Baruch* is also among the group rescued at Gibeon. Likely he conferred with Jeremiah during the ten days' wait for the word of the Lord. The arrogance of the men comes through in their accusations against Jeremiah and Baruch. Baruch himself no doubt penned the narrative that connects the flow of the dialogue.

The arrogance of these men is also evident in their breaking of the solemn pledge that they would all obey whatever the Lord revealed to Jeremiah concerning their future (42:5–6). The text emphasizes their rebellion by the repeated words *disobeyed* (v. 4) and *disobedience* (v. 7). *Tahpanhes* (meaning "the Fortress of Penhase") is the modern Tell ed-Defenna/ Dafna, a site in the eastern Delta bordering Sinai.

The remnant who sought safety in Egypt receive a further word from the Lord (vv. 8–13) by means of another symbolic act by Jeremiah in view of the assembled group. Basically, the action and the word of the Lord assure the group that has sought safety from Nebuchadnezzar in Egypt that they will not escape.

Jeremiah in Egypt

Jeremiah and Baruch entered Egypt too. Some commentators think they went of their own free will, to assist the remnant of Judah. *Others think the group forced them to go along, which seems the more likely alternative. Huey (362–63) speculates, "The question remains unanswered why they would want Jeremiah to accompany them, since they repudiated him as God's spokesman."*

Jeremiah lays the foundation stones on which the Babylonian monarch will place his throne. He will bring *death . . . captivity . . . the sword*. These are the very horrors the remnant from Judah sought to escape. And it will be the Lord's doing. The *temple of the sun* may refer to a temple in Heliopolis (also known as On), "the city of the sun," located about ten miles northeast of Cairo.

A fragmentary inscription, now in the British Museum, provides evidence that Nebuchadnezzar made a brief invasion of Egypt in his thirty-seventh year (568–567 BCE). He did not, however, conquer the country or depose the ruling pharaoh, Amasis (570–526 BCE). Some commentators, however, do not believe the subjugation of Egypt by Nebuchadnezzar, as depicted here, ever took place. Rather, Jeremiah uses the symbolic action and related oracle to assure the disobedient Jews that what had happened to Jerusalem would also reach them (Willis 377).

44:1–30 This chapter consists of a dialogue between Jeremiah and the people from Judah who had come to Egypt. It naturally divides into three parts: Jeremiah first presents the Lord's charges against them of idolatrous worship and the consequences (vv. 1–14); the people responded (vv. 15–19); and the Lord described their fate followed by the promise of an historic event that would be a sign assuring their punishment.

The message from Yahweh concerns *all the Jews living in Egypt*, not just the recent refugees at Tahpanhes (vv. 1–14). Some of these people had migrated to Egypt at least since the fall of Samaria in 722 BCE. The location of *Migdol* is uncertain, but it was in Egypt's northeastern sector. *Memphis* (Noph), the capital of Lower Egypt, is at the head of the delta, just south of modern Cairo. *Upper Egypt* (Pathros) is southern Egypt, from Cairo to Aswan. A colony of Jews were living on the island of Elephantine (Yeb) near Aswan, perhaps before the destruction of Jerusalem.

Destroyed Jerusalem and the towns of Judah are examples of what Yahweh has done when *provoked . . . to anger* by idolatrous worship. The anger in part also stemmed from their treatment of his *servants the prophets*. The "why?" questions caused the audience to consider the tragic results of failing to *humble themselves, show reverence*, and obey the *law* of *the Lord God Almighty*. Thus the same end will befall those who sought refuge in Egypt as happened to Jerusalem and Judah—*sword, famine and plague*, except for a very few fugitives.

> **The Elephantine Papyri**
>
> *The Jewish mercenary colony on Elephantine Island, near Egypt's southern border near the First Cataract, left behind numerous letters, contracts, and even one literary text, all dating from about 500 to 400 BCE. The letters in particular give important evidence for Jewish life in the Diaspora just after Jeremiah's time.*

In verses 15–19, the people reply, rejecting the appeals voiced by Jeremiah. From their point of view, when they turned from idolatrous worship to serve Yahweh, likely referring to the religious reforms of Josiah, they lost everything, often including their lives. This is in contrast to the prosperous former times when they had burned incense to the *Queen of Heaven*. (As noted earlier, this deity is a version of the Mesopotamian goddess Ishtar or the Canaanite Astarte [King 102–7].) This is probably a reference to the time of Manasseh, prior to the Josianic reforms. The wives and husbands had acted in concert and would continue to do so in pagan worship; the women may have led the way (Willis 341).

Jeremiah responds in verses 20–28 with an oracle of the Lord. To paraphrase, "Do what you have vowed to do—and suffer the consequences." Yahweh swears by his *great name*. No more emphatic word could be offered. Since they had chosen the Queen of Heaven, never more would they be able to validate any statement by the name Yahweh. Verse 28 reiterates the end of verse 14. Time will validate the truth of the word of the Lord. In contrast to all other ancient religions, the prophet's understanding of Israel's faith demanded exclusive worship of only one god.

Verses 29–30 promise a validating sign for the near future, a historical event. Behind the circumstances that will bring *Pharaoh Hophra* down is the sovereign Lord, the same Yahweh who ended Zedekiah's reign. In 566 BCE, Hophra was put to death by his rival and successor, Amasis. Whether Jeremiah lived to see that day is unknown. These are the last recorded words of Jeremiah.

45:1–5 The date of this oracle to Baruch is 605 BCE, *the fourth year of Jehoiakim*. It is associated with the scroll incident in chapter 36. Bright moves the passage to place it in conjunction with that chapter (184–86). The compiler of the book of Jeremiah, however, who may have been Baruch himself, may have placed it here to contrast with the texts that immediately precede it (Willis 345). It may also have been placed here because the first readers, those in exile in Babylon, had, like Baruch, also escaped with their lives.

Baruch's woe, whether expressed verbally or only in his mind, reached the Lord. Scholars have likened his groanings to the confessions of Jeremiah, who also struggled with the horrendous weight of his prophetic ministry (15:10–21; 20:7–18). Jeremiah brought to his faithful scribe and associate the response of the Lord, similar to the Lord's words to Ananias concerning Saul, "I will show him how much he must suffer for my name" (Acts 9:16). In a world experiencing *disaster*, Baruch can expect nothing for himself, but he learns that he will *escape with [his] life*. (God gave the same promise to Ebed-Melech, 39:18.)

The biblical record leaves both Jeremiah and Baruch in Egypt. One can speculate, however, that Baruch either ended up in Babylon or saw to it that those in exile received the oracles of Jeremiah. The Lord chose those in exile in Babylon to initiate the restoration, and that community cherished and preserved the words of Jeremiah that Baruch faithfully recorded.

PROPHECIES AGAINST FOREIGN PEOPLES · 46:1–51:64

46:1–28 The Lord appointed Jeremiah "a prophet to the nations." His oracles to the nations comprise chapters 46–51. Originally they may have followed immediately after 25:13a, which is where they appear in the Septuagint. The order of the nations differs in the Septuagint, as well. We find similar oracles against foreign nations in a number of other prophets (Isa 13–23, Ezek 25–32, and Amos 1–2). Jeremiah 46:1 introduces prophecies concerning surrounding peoples. The verse is lacking in the Septuagint. The oracles are in poetic style with an occasional line or two of narrative prose interspersed between poems.

The initial oracle in verses 2–12 concerning Egypt dates to 605 BCE, *the fourth year of Jehoiakim*. Four years earlier, *Pharaoh Neco* had been responsible for the death of King Josiah, as the Judean king, allied with the Babylonians, moved to prevent the Egyptians from assisting the Assyrians, who were their allies (2 Kgs 23:29–30).

Carchemish
The Egyptian defeat in 605 BCE at Carchemish, a ford of the Euphrates River, was decisive in opening Syria and Palestine to the advancing Babylonian forces.

Those preparing for battle are infantrymen, charioteers, and calvarymen. The Egyptians are *terrified* and flee in disorder. The swelling Egyptian forces rise up like the Nile when the annual flood surges down the valley from the highlands of Ethiopia and Central Africa. Neco's Egyptian forces also included men from regions south of Egypt—Ethiopians, Somalis, and Luds (not Lydians; compare Gen 10:13).

Despite the urging of the leaders, the day belongs to Yahweh, *the Lord Almighty*. The day of *vengeance* will avenge the death of good king Josiah. The slain Egyptians will be a *sacrifice* that the Lord will offer by means of the Babylonian sword. The Lord urges wounded Egypt to obtain the legendary balm of Gilead (compare 8:22), but to no avail. Its defeat is certain and *the nations* will witness the debacle.

The second word concerning Egypt (vv. 13–24) relates to the invasion of Egypt by Nebuchadnezzar. Although the Babylonians were on the Philistine plain in 604 BCE, threatening Egypt, Nebuchadnezzar's invasion of Egypt did not occur until 568 BCE. That event probably occurred after Jeremiah's death, "but the prophet seems years earlier to have regarded such an invasion as certain" (Bright 308). The Babylonians, however, were never able totally to conquer and devastate Egypt. It seems more likely that the Babylonians, when they withdrew early in the siege against Jerusalem, posed a serious threat to the Egyptians (37:6–8). This oracle, then, describes the psychological impact of the Babylonians upon Pharaoh Hophra's army. No matter the efforts of the Egyptian warriors, *the Lord will push them down*.

As a result, people everywhere will scorn *the king of Egypt*. The *one who will come* refers to Nebuchadnezzar. His prominence as a military leader is as visible as are the two mountains, Tabor, near Nazareth, and Carmel, rising from the sea at modern Haifa.

Using bovine, reptilian, forest, and insect imagery, the text depicts the demise of the Egyptian forces. Egypt had no actual forests, depending on Lebanon for timber.

Almighty God will punish Amon, the chief deity of Egypt, who was worshiped in a temple in Thebes (vv. 25–280). Despite the calamity to befall Egypt, there is a word of hope: the land will be *inhabited as in times past*.

Appended to this last oracle to Egypt is a word of hope for Yahweh's chosen people. The text here basically repeats 30:10–11. Whether or not Egyptians ever heard these oracles, they were instructive for the Lord's people in exile. Thus the word of hope for Egypt provides a setting to recall the word of hope for *Israel*.

47:1–7 Verse 1, an editor's remark, establishes the time when the oracle came to Jeremiah. The phrase *before Pharaoh attacked Gaza* is missing in the Septuagint. The exact date for the oracle is not clear—perhaps before Josiah's death at Megiddo (609 BCE); perhaps after the battle at Carchemish (604 BCE). Gaza was a major Philistine city. The figure of *waters . . . rising in the north*, however, points to the Babylonian attack. After his victory at Carchemish, Nebuchadnezzar overran Philistia.

Whether Egyptian or Babylonian, the overwhelming horde of armed men struck terror in the hearts of the Philistine people. Even parents abandoned their children in a desperate effort to escape. *Tyre and Sidon* were Phoenician coastal cities to the north of Philistia; apparently they had some sort of mutual defense arrangement. In poetic parallelism, Jeremiah associates *Philistines* with *Caphtor* (that is, Crete, a stop in their migration eastward to Canaan). *Ashkelon* was the next Philistine city on the coast north of Gaza. The *remnant on the plain* likely refers to the two inland Philistine cities, Ekron and Gath. Ultimately, the oracle testifies to the sovereignty of Yahweh. Though foreign armies destroy Philistia, they are but the outward manifestation of *the sword of the Lord*.

48:1–47 Moab occupied a part of the Transjordanian plateau between the deep, east-west valleys of the Arnon to the north and the Zered to the south. The boundaries of the Moabites, however, fluctuated over time. According to Genesis 19:37, the Moabites were descended from Lot.

This long poem has two main segments divided by *This is what the Lord . . . says* (48:1, 40). It is rich in place names, not all of which are identifiable. Some of them occur on the famous Moabite Stone (about 840 BCE), discovered at Dibon in 1868. Although we find no date, the oracle clearly relates to the time of Jeremiah and to the conquests of Nebuchadnezzar.

Nebo here refers to a Moabite city rather than the mountain. The plotters in *Heshbon* are likely that city's conquerors as they prepare to continue their conquests. *Madmen* is the transliteration of a Hebrew place name. *Chemosh* is the chief deity of Moab. His image and those who believe in him will go into exile. They are powerless against the God of Israel, who orchestrates the destruction of Moab.

The Mesha Inscription
The best evidence for Moabite history comes from an inscription of the ninth century Moabite king, Mesha (also mentioned in 2 Kgs 3). The so-called Moabite Stone, or Mesha Stele, reports his defeat of Israel, his building projects, and his trust in his patron god, Chemosh.

Like well-aged wine, Moab has survived undisturbed, but that will change by the will and word of the Lord (vv. 11–17). *Bethel* is in poetic parallelism with Chemosh and refers to the name of a deity rather than a place (Hyatt 1113). The fall of Moab is at the word of *the King. . .the Lord Almighty*. The broken scepter and staff are symbols of "the end of its power and glory" (Huey 391).

The description of the calamity to befall Moab continues in verses 18–25. The long list of place names emphasizes the totality of the conquest. The *horn* is a symbol of power (see Ps 18:2).

Moab is to drink the cup of God's wrath (vv. 26–28; compare 25:15–16, 27–29) to the point of drunkenness, that is, utter devastation. With poetic justice, the nation that had ridiculed Israel will now face ridicule.

Many similarities exist between verses 29–39 and other biblical texts: verse 29 to Isaiah 16:6; 31–35 to Isaiah 16:7–10; 34 to Isaiah 15:4–6; 36 to Isaiah 15:7 and 16:11; and 37–38 to Isaiah 15:2–3 (Hyatt 1115–16). This lament over Moab points not only to God's sovereignty over all nations but also to divine sorrow at the price they must pay for their sins.

The *eagle* likely is a figure of speech referring to Nebuchadnezzar and his army (vv. 40–47). The destruction of Moab *as a nation* began with the Babylonian conquest. Then came the incursion of the Nabateans, an Arab tribe, into which the remnant of the Moabites assimilated by the time of Christ. Verses 43–44 echoes ideas similar to Amos 5:18–19.

Verses 45–47 are missing in the Septuagint. Yet the restoration of Moab *in days to come* is a word of hope, perhaps to encourage Israel (Huey 397). In light of the subsequent history of the Moabites, it may ultimately be messianic in intent (Harrison 178).

> **"In later days . . ."**
> *The Hebrew phrase "in later days" (Jer 48:47) usually refers to an unspecified future, not the eschatological turning point of New Testament texts. For Jeremiah, God is ultimately a restorer of nations, not their destroyer.*

49:1–6 The Ammonites also derived from Lot (Gen 19:38). They occupied a region to the north of the Moabites in Transjordan. *Molech* (also known as Milcom) was the chief deity of the Ammonites. Gad, an Israelite tribe living east of the Jordan River, went into exile with the Assyrian conquest (721 BCE). *Rabbah* was the Ammonite citadel atop one of the seven hills in what is today Amman, Jordan. As with Moab, the Ammonites succumbed to Babylon. As a result, Arabs encroached on their territory and ultimately absorbed them into their tribes. Similar to the oracles against Egypt and Moab, this one ends with a word of hope.

49:7–22 The Edomites descended from Esau (Gen 36:1). Edom occupied the territory south of Moab from the Dead Sea to the Gulf of Aqabah. The territory extended eastward into the Arabian desert.

There is no word of hope in the oracle about Edom (vv. 7–11). The rhetorical question about the departure of *wisdom* expects a "yes" response. Traditionally, Edom was a seat of oriental wisdom (Obad 8), and one of Job's wise visitors was Eliphaz from Teman (in Edom). Dedan was an oasis in the Arabian desert southeast of Edom. Because they are neighbors, Jeremiah warned them of the coming disaster. The imagery indicates total devastation, but the compassion of the Lord for the most vulnerable among the Edomites is instructive. Widows and orphans cannot trust in humans, but they can trust in the Lord.

A prose insertion in verses 12–13 recalls the metaphor of the cup of wrath in 25:15–29. The solemn oath of the Lord certifies the destruction of Edomite Bozrah.

Verses 14–16 have close parallels to Obadiah 1–4. The early Edomite center was a mesa-like stronghold alluded to in verse 16. The Asiatic lion inhabited the jungle-like growth along the River Jordan; only a few survive today in reserves in India. Verse 18 also occurs in 50:40, and verses 19–21 appear in 50:44–46, referring to Babylon. The clause *Who is the chosen one I will appoint for this?* is an effort to translate a problem passage in the Masoretic Text. The NRSV renders it *and I will appoint over it whomever I choose.* The text does not name anyone; however, it is God who will appoint the destroyer of Edom, most likely Nebuchadnezzar.

Idumeans

The Edomites who moved into former Israelite territory converted to Judaism beginning in the second century BCE. Herod the Great was the most famous Idumean.

The disdain against Edom expressed in the Bible is to a large degree surely due to their failure to aid Judah during the Babylonian conquest. Rather, Edom took advantage of the opportunity to migrate into the depopulated area of southern Judah. Eventually, they occupied the region as far north as Hebron, and their descendants were the Idumeans. At the same time, the Nabatean Arabs moved into the former Edomite territory.

49:23–27 Damascus was the power center of Aram (a kingdom in Syria), located north of Israel. Hamath and Arpad were small Aramean city states to the north of Damascus. An occasional ally of Israel and often an enemy, Aram fell first to the Assyrians, then to the Babylonians (2 Kgs 16:9). They formed a part of the Babylonian forces attacking Judah (2 Kgs 24:2). Verse 26 is also found in 50:30, and verse 27 is a quotation from Amos 1:4. *Ben-Hadad* was both a personal and a dynastic name. All that befalls Damascus is due to the sovereign will of *the Lord Almighty.*

49:28–33 Kedar and Hazor denote tribes and tribal areas in the Syrian desert east of Palestine (Harrison 182). Rather than *kingdoms*, these were desert chiefdoms. Babylonian records confirm Nebuchadnezzar's attack on Kedar in 599 BCE (Huey 405). Why attack Bedouins? "Perhaps the purpose for including these relatively insignificant peoples was to show that no one, however unimportant by our standards, would escape God's judgment" (Huey 405).

49:34–39 Elam was a significant kingdom east of Babylon in what is now southwestern Iran. The oracle dates to 597 BCE, *early in the reign of Zedekiah.* The Elamites were famed archers (Isa 22:6). The text mentions Elam among the nations that must drink the cup of the Lord's wrath (25:25) but gives no theological reason. Yet Yahweh is sovereign over all nations and peoples, even those far distant from Judah and Jerusalem. After they have tasted *disaster*, the Lord promises restoration *in days to come* (better with NRSV *in the latter days*).

50:1–51:55 The oracles against Babylon form an appendix. We can assume scribes assembled them during the exile. There is practically no internal evidence for dating these writings, except that they do not mention Persia, Babylon's conqueror in 539 BCE, so they must predate that event. We can date only 51:59–64 to year four of Zedekiah's reign. It is difficult to distinguish one oracle from another, but one theme unites them all: the downfall of Babylon and the restoration of the Jews to their homeland. For convenience, we will follow the divisions of the material employed by Timothy Willis.

In the oracle consisting of 50:1–32, Jeremiah predicts a reversal of Israel's catastrophe. In the Septuagint, verse 1 is shorter, reading "The word of Yahweh, which he spoke concerning Babylon" (Bright 339).

Bel ("lord") is the Akkadian equivalent of the Northwest Semitic "Baal," with an identical meaning. Bel signifies the chief deity of Babylon, Marduk (Hebrew *Merodach*).

Just as Babylon, the nation from the north, had threatened Judah, so *a nation from the north* will attack Babylon. In fact, it will be *an alliance of great nations*. At that time, the people of Yahweh will turn their faces toward their homeland. Despite the fact that the Lord employed first Assyria then Babylon as instruments to chasten Israel, Babylon *has sinned against the Lord* and faces punishment (vv. 11–17). Like a shepherd leading his flock, Israel shall *graze on Carmel and Bashan*, referring to the highland extending westward from Megiddo to modern Haifa and to today's Golan Heights south of Mount Hermon. By his grace the Lord *will forgive the remnant*.

God's anger against Babylon will occur because *she has defied the Lord* (v. 29) and because she is *the arrogant one* (vv. 31–32). *I will kindle a fire in her towns* recalls similar actions by the Lord in the oracles against the nations in Amos 1–2.

Despite the oppression of the exile, *the Lord Almighty* will redeem the people of Israel. They will know *rest*; Babylon will experience *unrest* (vv. 33–46). Once a thriving city, Babylon will be uninhabited. The ruins of Babylon have lain vacant for centuries. In spite of excavations and reconstruction for tourism in the last century, the city remains uninhabited.

The army from the north included those who *ride on their horses*, probably Scythian horsemen allied with the Medes and Persians and renowned for their horsemanship. Verses 44–46 are practically identical to 49:19–21, where they refer to Edom.

Though a shepherd to Israel, Yahweh will be as a hungry lion decimating the flock Babylon.

Turning to 51:1–32, the people of *Leb Kamai* are the Chaldeans. This is another instance of *athbash*—that is, as the NIV notes, "a cryptogram for Chaldea." The Hebrew *Leb Kamai* actually means "the heart of those who rise against me."

The *gold cup in the Lord's hand* occurs as a figure elsewhere (13:12f; 49:12). The *vengeance* of the Lord (v. 6) means vindication for Israel (v. 10). God takes vengeance *for his temple*. Those who return are to tell the good news *in Zion*. Cyrus the Great of Persia will conquer the *Medes*, whom the Lord has stirred up (550 BCE).

Jeremiah praises the power of Yahweh and contrasts it with the impotent idols created by *every goldsmith*. Jeremiah 51:15–19 repeats 10:12–16, where we examined the *Portion of Jacob*. The text does not identify the *war club* that shatters, but it probably symbolizes a reversal of Babylon's role. "The description [is] applied to Babylon (see 50:23) as well as to her conqueror, both instruments in God's hands" (Cawley and Millard 657). *Ararat, Minni and Ashkenaz* were peoples north of the Medes. Ararat (ancient Urartu) was north of Lake Van in modern east Turkey. Minni (ancient Mannai) was south of Lake Urmia. Ashkenaz were the Scythians, horse nomads to the east of Lake Urmia. Those who attack Babylonia will burn the marshes, preventing escapees from hiding in them. Because of what Babylon had done to Jerusalem and its people, those in exile from Zion pronounce a curse on Babylon (51:33–35).

Yahweh will fulfill the curse against Babylon (vv. 36–57) by preparing a drunken *feast for them*. As they slumber in a stupor, they will never awaken. The *Sheshach athbash* occurred in 25:26. As the Lord destroys *Bel in Babylon*, he calls for his people to be prepared to flee for their lives. The Lord's vengeance is certain. It is a case of poetic justice. Just as Babylon slew *the slain in all the earth*, so Babylon must fall. God's people in exile must be mindful of the Lord and not forget Jerusalem. As they well know, *the Lord is a God of retribution*. Just as God had repaid them in full for their sins and follies, so will Babylon receive full punishment. God is not a respecter of persons.

Nebuchadnezzar built *Babylon's thick wall* and it was wide enough to drive chariots on it (v. 58). The *peoples* whose work is in vain are probably those carried into exile whom the Babylonians put to work in constructing the revamped city under Nebuchadnezzar.

The note at the end of verse 64 marks the end of the oracles of Jeremiah. It closes the book that begins in verse 1 with "The words of Jeremiah." This provides a verbal envelope called an *inclusio*—a fitting end to the great prophet's work (Huey 430).

Seraiah Son of Neriah

Seraiah son of Neriah (*vv. 59–64*) *was very likely the brother of Baruch. Archaeologists have discovered a bulla of Seraiah. The scroll he carried to Babylon when Zedekiah was king must have included the material in chapters 50–51. In this symbolic action, after having read the prophecy against Babylon, he was to cast the weighted scroll into the Euphrates, demonstrating that the great city would sink into oblivion.*

52:1–30   There is little variance between this appendix and 2 Kings 24:18–25:30. Scribes probably added it to Jeremiah's oracles to show their fulfillment in the fall of Jerusalem and the exile of most of its people. There are two major differences between the accounts. The events relating to Gedaliah are missing here but are in the account in 2 Kings. However, Jeremiah 40–41 gives the details concerning Gedaliah. The second difference is the list of three deportations in verses 28–30, absent in 2 Kings 25. This listing does not occur in the Septuagint. The third group, taken *in his twenty-third year*, probably experienced deportation after the murder of Gedaliah. The total taken into exile does not agree with 2 Kings 24–25, where the text records ten thousand taken in the first exile. Discrepencies could occur if the criteria for counting varied—for example counting only the men.

52:31–34   It is not likely that Jeremiah was alive when Jehoiachin was released from prison; he would have been about ninety years old by then. Also, the text makes no mention of Zedekiah, who must have died in prison prior to this event.

No doubt the final compiler(s) of the book of Jeremiah ended with the release of Jehoiachin from prison because it was a hopeful note for those in exile. He was of the Davidic line. With God nothing is impossible.

THEOLOGICAL REFLECTIONS

What can we discern about the nature of God and humans and their interrelationships from this book? Every author dwells and writes within a particular environment, as did Jeremiah. Deuteronomy fueled the reforms of Josiah and undergirded Jeremiah's understanding of himself and the developing history of his people.

As Willis observes, "Deuteronomy sets the stage for Israel's entrance into the Promised Land. Jeremiah sets the stage for Israel's expulsion from the Promised Land" (Willis 13).

Jeremiah lived through the demise of his city and country at the hands of foreigners.

In the midst of crisis, Jeremiah provides both teaching and example to the person called of God to live to the praise of his glory. While he sometimes struggled to understand and survive the Lord's tests, he remained faithful to the end. We can say the same of Yahweh. God fulfilled promises to Jeremiah at his call, including his abiding presence and strength. Jeremiah's opponents could not overcome him because the Lord was with him and enabled him (1:19).

While at times Jeremiah seemed to suffer alone at the hands of those in political and religious power, he drew supporters, especially Baruch. The Lord sustained him. This was because he understood that Yahweh, the Lord God Almighty, is both creator and sustainer.

Against paganized people, false prophets, compromised priests, and unprincipled politicians, Jeremiah stood in his determination to fulfill faithfully his mission as a spokesperson for God. The religious and political institutions of Judah, temple and palace, had undermined the covenantal relationship with God established through Moses at Sinai. This brought the destruction and exile about which Jeremiah warned. God is holy and righteous and will punish the unrepentant. But the Lord is willing and will save a remnant. So there is a word of hope at the very time that seems hopeless.

God is gracious. Not only is there a promise of restoration, there is the promise of a new level of relationship between the faithful and the Lord. For Jeremiah, "the . . . future was not focused on temple or king but on a new covenant by which God would establish a new individualized relationship with his people (31:31–34)" (Huey 34). Jeremiah spoke and wrote to his people and their times, but by God's grace, he has spoken to generation after generation, including our own.

FOR FURTHER STUDY

Brueggemann, Walter. *To Pluck Up, To Tear Down: A Commentary on the Book of Jeremiah*. Grand Rapids: Eerdmans, 1988.

Davis, Ellen F. *Biblical Prophecy: Perspectives for Christian Theology, Discipleship, and Ministry*. Louisville: Westminster John Knox, 2014.

Holladay, William L. *Jeremiah I: A Commentary on the Book of the Prophet Jeremiah*. 2 vols. Minneapolis: Fortress, 1986–89.

Lundbom, Jack R. *Jeremiah*. 3 vols. New Haven: Yale University Press, 1999–2004.

McKane, William. *A Critical and Exegetical Commentary on Jeremiah*. 2 vols. Edinburgh: T & T Clark, 1986–96.

Pixley, Jorge. *Jeremiah*. St. Louis: Chalice, 2004.

WORKS CITED

Albright, William F. *Yahweh and the Gods of Canaan*. Winona Lake, IN: Eisenbrauns, 1968.

Baker, David W. "Uphaz." In *The Anchor Bible Dictionary*, 6:765. New Haven: Yale University Press, 1992.

Bright, John. *Jeremiah*. Garden City, NY: Doubleday, 1965.

Cawley, F., and A. R. Millard. "Jeremiah." *The Eerdmans Bible Commentary*, edited by D. Guthrie, J. A. Motyer, A. M. Stibbs, and D. J. Wiseman, 5:626–58. Grand Rapids: Eerdmans 1970.

Graf, David. "Dedan." In *The Anchor Bible Dictionary*, 2:121–23. New Haven: Yale University Press, 1992.

Harrison, R. K. *Jeremiah & Lamentations*. Downers Grove, IL: InterVarsity Press, 1973.

Huey, F. B., Jr. *Jeremiah/Lamentations*. Nashville: Broadman, 1993.

Huffmon, H. B. "Ancient Near Eastern Prophecy." In *The Anchor Bible Dictionary*, 5:477–82. New Haven: Yale University Press, 1992.

Hyatt, James P. "The Book of Jeremiah." In *The Interpreter's Bible*, edited by George A. Buttrick, 5:775–1,142. Nashville: Abingdon, 1956.

Jones, Richard, and Zbigniew Fiema. "Tahpanhes." In *The Anchor Bible Dictionary*, 6:308–9. New Haven: Yale University Press, 1992.

Josephus. *Works*, edited by H. St. John Thackeray. 10 vols. Cambridge, MA: Harvard University Press, 1926–65.

King, Philip J. *Jeremiah: An Archaeogical Companion*. Louisville: Westminster/ John Knox, 1993.

Knauf, Ernst Axel. "Tema." In *The Anchor Bible Dictionary*, 6:346–47. New Haven: Yale University Press, 1992.

Kuemmerlin-McLean, Joanne. "Magic (OT)." In *The Anchor Bible Dictionary*, 4:468–71. New Haven: Yale University Press, 1992.

Miller, John W. *Meet the Prophets*. New York: Paulist Press, 1987.

Overholt, T. W. *The Threat of Falsehood: A Study in the Theology of the Book of Jeremiah*. Napierville, IL: Allenson, 1970.

Pritchard, J. B., ed. *Ancient Near Eastern Texts Relating to the Old Testament*. 3rd ed. Princeton: Princeton University Press, 1969.

Thomas, D. W., ed. *Documents from Old Testament Times*. London: Nelson, 1958.

Willis, Timothy M. *Jeremiah–Lamentations*. Joplin, MO: College Press, 2002.

Lamentations

Mark W. Hamilton, Nathaniel D. Lollar, & David I. Shaw

CHAPTER CONTENTS

FEATURE

L amentations consists of five discrete poems mourning the Babylonian destruction of Jerusalem in 586 BCE. The first four poems are acrostics, with each verse or cluster of verses beginning with a successive letter of the Hebrew alphabet. Even the last poem, though not an acrostic, contains 22 lines, the number of letters in the Hebrew alphabet. The use of acrostics allows singers not only to memorize the songs but also to make interconnections among the poems (Renkema 50). The poems gorgeously express Israel's dismay at their fate, their questioning of God, and their timid hope for restoration.

CONTEXTS

Multiple voices appear in each chapter. Probably inhabitants of Jerusalem, especially surviving priests, sang them in their communal worship settings during the Babylonian exile. Perhaps women

City Laments

A few texts survive from the ancient Near East that mourn the fall of a city. From about 2000 BCE comes the Sumerian "Lamentation over the Destruction of Sumer and Ur," whose 436 lines mourn the fall of the Ur III empire. Its opening and closing lines are reminiscent of Lamentations: "He has abandoned his stable . . . the lord of all lands has abandoned it. . . . Enlil has abandoned the shrine of Nippur," and "O Nanna in your city again restored, may your praise be sung!" The Israelites may not have known that already ancient song, but they were familiar with the literary conventions for lamenting the tragic fall of a city.

composed these songs, since they were primarily responsible for mourning in ancient Israel. Someone later wrote down these orally performed texts to preserve them for a postexilic community. Lament of the present reminded the future of the precariousness of life and everyone's dependence on God.

Jewish tradition attributed Lamentations to Jeremiah, but no evidence for this exists in the book itself or elsewhere in the Bible. The laments of Jeremiah mentioned in 2 Chronicles 36:25 cannot refer to this book, since they concern Josiah's death twenty years earlier. Like many biblical books, this one is anonymous.

COMMENTARY

THE DESERTED CITY · 1:1–22

Like most Hebrew dirges, the poetry of chapter 1 uses the *qinah* meter, in which the first half of the line is roughly 50 percent longer than the second half, though with frequent exceptions. *Qinah* poetry has a musical association and is sung as a lament over the dead (see 2 Sam 1:17–27; 2 Chron 35:25; Garr 60). The speaker's point of view changes from third person ("he"; 1:1–11) to first person ("I"; 1:12–16) to third again (1:17), and back to first (1:18–22)

1:1–11   In verse 2, the word for *comfort* (here and in verse 16) has the connotation of a gift that shows respect or pays homage to the receiver, or it can show an alliance between kings (2 Kgs 20:12; Isa 39:1). The clause *no one shows me/her mercy* creates a refrain here and in 1:9, 17, 21. In verse 5, *children* really means "infant" or "toddler," evoking the even more poignant image of babies as captives of war. In verses 8–10, the poet uses the intensive form of the verb ("she sinned, O how she sinned!") twice to convey the magnitude of Jerusalem's sin (House 354). *Unclean* in verse 8 refers to a woman's menstrual discharge (Lev 12:2, 5; 15:19; House 354), as does *filthiness* on her skirts. This kind of exposure and public nudity in the Israelite mind was a source of insufferable shame. Verse 10's *treasures* refers at one level to the temple treasures, but it is also a euphemism

---

The Suffering Female in Lamentations & the Prophets

The Old Testament often uses female imagery for Israel or the cities in it.

Two controlling metaphors lead to the elaborate set of female images that appear in these texts. First, place names in Hebrew are feminine, and second the idea of a "male" God having a wife was common in the ancient world. Since Yahweh was not really male and did not have a goddess as a wife, Israel became that spouse.

Starting from the metaphoric equation Yahweh is to Israel as a husband is to a wife, the texts can spin out images of marriage and fertility (as in Isa 62:4, an answer to Lamentations), but also of rape, adultery, and so on. However problematic we may find this imagery, and however shocking the prophets and lamenters themselves meant it to be, it powerfully captures a sense of the estrangement between God and God's people.

for the private parts of the personified woman Jerusalem. Thus the looting of the temple is metaphorically a rape of Yahweh's wife, Jerusalem.

1:12–22 In verse 13, the fire burns inside the city, and the net spreads around and prevents the inhabitants from escaping. As a result the poet is weak and overcome, unable to escape (House 358). The *winepress* imagery moves in two directions: the red color of wine suggests the gush of warriors' blood, and the fragility of the grape compares to Judah's inability to stop its enemy from crushing it.

THE ANGER OF GOD · 2:1–22

The second chapter begins like the first, with *How*. This new dirge, like chapter 1, follows an acrostic pattern and *qinah* (3:2) meter. Chapter 2 divides into two sections, each with a different speaker. The chapter also links verses with catchwords: for example, verses 1 and 22 both speak of *the day*, and 2 and 21 mention God's lack of *pity*.

> **The Hebrew Alphabet**
> *The stanzas beginning with the Hebrew letters* ayin *and* pe (NIV *verses 2:16, 17; 3:46–48, 49–51; 4:16, 17) are reversed (thus* pe, ayin) *in chapters 2, 3, and 4, indicating that when the poems were written the Hebrew alphabet may not have been rigidly set.*

2:1–10 Verses 1–10 speak of Yahweh in the third person ("he") and the divine destruction of the physical structures in Israel and particularly Jerusalem. Focusing on the physical destruction of the nation, the poet uses the acrostic pattern to take a tour through the city and especially the temple precincts. We should imagine the poet walking in a line of captives past the structures he or she describes. The Lord burned every house (v. 2) with fire (vv. 3–4). The royal palaces lie in ruins (v. 5), along with the city's fortifications (v. 5). Then the Lord destroys the temple, where key festivals (NIV *meetings*) occur (v. 6), and the poet sees the sanctuary and the altar (v. 7).

Princes in verse 2 is the masculine form of the word translated *queen* in 1:1 (see 2:9). In 2:4 and 5, *like an enemy* is one Hebrew word and occurs in both of these verses as the third word of the first line, giving the verses assonance and rhythm. Verses 9 and 10 give a beautiful transition from the destruction of the landscape to the devastation of the people. The destruction of Jerusalem's gates (v. 9) symbolizes God's refusal to interact with the people through the traditional mediators—the priesthood, prophecy, and kingship. Verse 10 has a very potent connection that links verses 1–9 with 11–22. Verses 10a and 10c deal with the people—the honored and respected elders and the lowly but cherished young women. These groups represent both ends of the social spectrum, but they both sit in the ground, recalling verse 1's declaration that the Lord has cast Israel from heaven to earth (*ground* in verse 10 is the same word for *earth* in verse 1). Verse 10b fully captures the connection between the physical destruction and the destroyed people, when the people cover themselves with dirt (a different word that connotes dust or filth rather than the word translated *ground* in 10a and c). The chosen people are social rubble.

2:11–22 Verses 11–22 change to the point of view of a single lamenter speaking in the first person. The poet is now one exile among many on the road outside the city. Verses 15–17 recount the horror that has befallen the population. The poet does not mention the city anymore in this poem, save in an outburst to the city wall in verse 18; the deportees see the wall last and speak to it as their failed protector. In verse 12, *wounded* is literally "pierced," so the corresponding *wound* in verse 13 is deep as the sea. In verses 15–16, clapping of hands here is a mocking, derisive act. *Clap* may mean slapping one's thigh (Jer 31:19; Ezek 21:17); striking hands out of anger (Num 24:10); slapping a person (Job 34:26); striking or splashing (Jer 48:26); or mocking (Job 27:23). The image accompanies similar mocking acts and may have elements of physical hostility associated with it, as well (House 389). *Scoff* in verses 15 and 16 is literally "hiss," another hostile and insulting act (compare 1 Kgs 9:8; Job 27:23; Isa 5:26; 7:18; Jer 19:8; 49:17; 50:13; Ezek 27:36; Zeph 2:15; Zech 10:8). *Hissing* and *clapping* hands occur together also in Job 27:23. In Zechariah 10:8, the Lord hisses to signal Israel to gather together again.

In 2:20, the poet puns *treated* (Hebrew *'olalta*) and *children* (Hebrew *'olaley*), and the latter word ties verse 20 back to verse 19. In 2:22, the Hebrew literally says, "You summon as a day of feasting," implying that the Lord's proclamation goes out as though it were an invitation to a celebration, but with a disappointing result.

ONE WHO HAS SEEN AFFLICTION · 3:1–66

Chapter 3 abandons the third person perspective, and a man speaks out as the personified city. The text falls into three sections (vv. 1–25; verses 42–51; vv. 52–58) with several expansions between them (vv. 26–41; verses 59–63), and with a small conclusion at the end (vv. 64–66). Unlike the rest of the book, chapter 3 contains hopeful verses as well as direct address toward God.

3:1–25 The poem maintains the traditional Jewish lament pattern except for the address to God at the beginning. However, 2:22 sets up the divine addressee as the antagonist through the first portion of chapter 3. The vivid imagery of God's actions against the warrior persona of Zion takes on the language of military engagement. Yahweh has *surrounded* and *built up walls* and *targeted [Zion] with His bow*, creating an image of siege tactics employed to take a city. Yet the speaker suddenly counters images of broken teeth (v. 16), humiliation (v. 14), and debasement (v. 15) with a declaration of hope. While laments in the Psalms usually express some kind of hope or praise for God (for example, Ps 22; 129; 140), this hopeful refrain in Lamentations 3 does not perform the customary role of ending the song. Perhaps the narrator falls back into lament because the magnitude of his suffering is too great, or perhaps the text wants to contemplate further possible transgressions against God (vv. 31–42; Dobbs-Allsop 120). Either way, the sudden hope seems short-lived.

3:26–41 The poetic content of this section is different than the rest of Lamentations. The author makes a theological move, remembering Yahweh's justice and willingness to equalize suffering and blessing (v. 31–36), shifts to rhetorical questions magnifying God (v. 37–39), and ends by blaming his suffering on himself (v. 40). While hopeful, this section does not reach the apex of emotion that verses 22–25 do; nor does its logical treatment of affliction soothe the afflicted heart of chapters 1 and 2. But whatever reasons the author has for taking up this tune, it is insufficient to alleviate his or her pains and, again, relapses into brooding.

3:42–66 The NIV treats this section as a quote originating from the exhortation in verse 41. The Hebrew text gives no such indication, but rather the narrator returns to the poetic style of chapters 1 and 2. This time, however, the narrator portrays God not as an enemy of Israel but as the liberator who looks upon the plight of the oppressed and acts mightily on behalf of the scorned, and, in typical lament fashion, the narrator issues a call for retribution.

THE GOLD WITHOUT LUSTER · 4:1–22

After three chapters of lament, the poet has grown exhausted or perhaps uses a disjointed poetic style to create a feeling of despair (Dobbs-Allsop 130). In any case, the narrator turns back to the style of chapters 1 and 2.

4:1–16 The *how* of 1:1 is repeated. The couplets primarily function to show different ways in which Zion is depraved and thus to lead the reader to understand the depths of Israel's suffering. The infant images are abundant (vv. 2, 3, 4, 10) and are paralleled with other images of delicacy or purity (milk, snow) to contrast sharply with the mention of cannibalism in verse 10. These forms of purity in the early verses of chapter 4 also contrast with the uncleanness of the nation in verses 14–16.

4:17–20 A final voice appears in the book in verse 20, indicating the community. The first plural ("we") perspective begins here and continues for the rest of the book, except in 4:21–22. The community in its own voice, rather than the narrator's, now recounts the story of their oppression by the enemy and relives the horror of chapters 1 and 2. The reference to Yahweh's *anointed* at one level mourns the demise of the monarchy as a symbol of the nation, and phrases like *our very life breath* remind the audience of the king's crucial role as a protector. The community's wistful regret at no longer living *under his shadow* expresses a loss of hope in both human and divine kingship (compare Ps 89:20–26).

4:21–22 The poem ends with mixed words of hope and revenge. Lament psalms often emphasize poetic justice (Westermann 207). Some have thought the initial words of rejoicing to be sarcastic (Dobbs-Allsop 137). As in 3:22–26, the narrator expresses hope that all will be equalized. The narrator's future is set and the section makes clear the expectation of divine justice. The *cup* is presumably that of God's vengeance.

DOES GOD REMEMBER? · 5:1–22

This communal lament begins with a list of calamities (vv. 1–18) and ends with a sad cry to God for mercy (vv. 19–22). The people have settled into everyday hardship (Lee 192), with the siege of Jerusalem as a memory. The poem ends the book on a note of uncertainty and faint hope.

5:1–18 The list of disasters includes emotional, economic, and social elements. Verse 6 comments on public policies of the last years of Judah's independence, when its kings courted Assyria and Egypt. Verse 7 follows the basic claims of the prophets and of 1–2 Kings, which argued that the fall of the nation was a divine punishment. However, the poet turns this theological claim around by noting that the present sufferers did not commit the sins that led to the downfall. The text thus questions an easy equation between present suffering and past sin. Verse 8's *slaves rules over us* refers to the Babylonians' use of minor officials, some of them royal eunuchs, to control subject populations. The *crown* (v. 16) may be that of a king (as in 2 Sam 12:30; 1 Chron 20:2; Ezek 21:31; Song 3:11) or of partygoers (Isa 28:1, 3; Ezek 23:42). The crown can also signify honor (Job 19:9; 31:36; Prov 17:6), which Israel has lost.

5:19–22 The closing lament of the book appeals to God's pity and majesty. God's eternal splendor should lead to the healing of Israel, but the song ends not knowing whether it will.

THEOLOGICAL REFLECTIONS

As texts by and about refugees, the elegant poems of Lamentations challenge easy assumptions about divine benevolence or the correlation between sin and suffering. This text protests God's treatment of the people while still reverencing God. Living in the narrow space between blind faith in God and defiance, the poet seeks to honor human suffering without giving it the last word. Like Job, he or she seeks to vindicate both God and suffering humanity without opting for moralism or implacable anger. For that reason, Lamentations is a text for all times when people suffer.

FOR FURTHER STUDY

Linafelt, Tod. *Surviving Lamentations: Catastrophe, Lament, and Protest in the Afterlife of a Biblical Book*. Chicago: University of Chicago Press, 2000.

Perry, Robin A. *Lamentations*. Grand Rapids: Eerdmans, 2010.

WORKS CITED

Dobbs-Allsopp, F. W. *Lamentations*. Louisville: Westminster John Knox, 2002.

Garr, Randall. "The Qinah: A Study of Poetic Meter, Syntax and Style." *Zeitschrift für die alttestamentliche Wissenschaft* 95 (1983): 54–75.

House, Paul R. *Lamentations*. Nashville: Nelson, 2004.

Klein, Jacob. "Lamentation over the Destruction of Sumer and Ur." In *The Context of Scripture*. Volume 1: *Canonical Compositions from the Biblical World*, 535–39. Leiden: Brill, 1997.

Lee, Nancy C. *The Singers of Lamentations: Cities under Siege, from Ur to Jerusalem to Sarajevo* . . . . Leiden: Brill, 2002.

Renkema, Johan. *Lamentations*. Leuven: Peeters, 1998.

Westermann, Claus. *Praise and Lament in the Psalms*. Translated by Keith R. Crim and Richard N. Soulen. Atlanta: John Knox Press, 1981.

Ezekiel

Brandon L. Fredenburg

CHAPTER CONTENTS

MAPS, TABLES, & FEATURES

The images, visions, and actions of Ezekiel have always challenged audiences. Some influential Jewish teachers in the early Common Era nearly succeeded in keeping Ezekiel from being widely read, fearing it would be misunderstood. Jerome (about 340–420 CE) noted that some rabbis prohibited men under thirty from reading large sections of the work (see *Babylonian Talmud Hagigah* 13a) because of the complex and sometimes disturbing visions at the beginning and end. Contemporary interpreters, regardless of age, also find their task daunting.

Ezekiel's words and actions are intentionally hard to understand. Because his Israelite audience is exceptionally unreceptive (2:3–8), Ezekiel speaks and acts in often grotesque ways to arouse an interest in Yahweh's activity. Through Ezekiel, Yahweh tries to elicit a response—any response!—from a hard-hearted people.

Yahweh's activity through Ezekiel and other prophets is intimately bound to the covenant with Israel. Yahweh repeatedly pleads with, threatens, and disciplines Judah to get them to repent. Yet divine actions meet increasing resistance.

Yahweh sends Ezekiel not to entice with words of hope and redemption, but to announce the end of God's patience and the time for national repentance. God will soon fulfill the most painful threats of the covenant: Israel will be exiled from its land and the temple will be demolished. These calamities would surprise Ezekiel's audience.

Warning & Hope
Many prophets preceded Ezekiel with words of both warning and hope. This pattern of warning and comfort reflected the structure of the Mosaic covenant, particularly its rehearsal of blessings for loyal behavior and curses for infidelity (see Lev 26; Deut 28; see comments at 4:9).

Another surprise is that Yahweh enlists hard-hearted Ezekiel, whose name in Hebrew means "God hardens" (see 3:8–9). Ezekiel is at best reluctant and at worst, a liability in need of strong control (3:26–27). Yahweh's command that he *not rebel like that rebellious house* (2:8) and Ezekiel's admission of going into his task *in bitterness* and *anger* (3:14) signal his unruly nature. Only after Jerusalem falls does Yahweh allow Ezekiel his own voice (33:21–22). Then Ezekiel extends comfort and hope.

We know Ezekiel only from the book that bears his name. He obviously knew the oracles of Jeremiah and others (Zimmerli, *Ezekiel 1*, 42–46). Born into a priestly family (1:1), Ezekiel may have heard Jeremiah both denounce his birthright occupation as a priest and denigrate Israelite prophets (Jer 2:8; 5:31; 6:13; 8:10). Yet it is unknown whether Ezekiel ever acted as a priest. His reluctance to be a prophet may originate from familiarity with Jeremiah's career. Summoned to be a prophet of doom, Ezekiel could hardly have welcomed the same treatment from his kinsmen that Jeremiah received. This would have been especially true since, unlike Jeremiah, Ezekiel was married (24:15–27). Some scholars speculate on Ezekiel's mental health, but the text provides no certain support for their theories.

CONTEXTS

Nineteenth and twentieth century critics used methods of literary analysis to separate many supposed later additions to the book from Ezekiel's "original" material. Zimmerli's more balanced work substantially slowed this trend, and more recent commentators, influenced by newer literary approaches, usually regard the content of the book as substantially from Ezekiel.

Tribute
In the ancient Near East, a nation under threat of attack paid tribute with silver and/ or gold objects and/or treasure taken from royal or temple stocks to the nations threatening to attack it (see 1 Kgs 20:1–7; 2 Kgs 18:13–16; 2 Chron 28:16–21).

The process by which Ezekiel's words (perhaps written at various times, see 24:1–2; 37:16; compare Jer 36; Wilson, "Ezekiel," 656–57) and actions became written text is unknown. Some Jewish rabbis suggested "the men of the Great Synagogue" (in Ezra's day, about 450 BCE) collectively edited the book (*Babylonian Talmud Baba Bathra* 15a), but this assertion cannot be proved. The essential composition may be dated to about the mid fifth century BCE (see Fredenburg 24–25), but significant variations of order and content in the book's oracles appear in copies and versions through the sixth century CE.

Ezekiel was born during a tumultuous period of Israelite history. Manasseh (697–642 BCE), Amon (642–640), and Josiah (640–609) had successively been client kings of Assyria's Ashurbanipal (668–627). Their client status obligated them to promote the worship of Assyria's gods and pay tribute. Assurbanipal's death in 627 BCE sparked a power struggle among his sons that allowed Judah and other subject nations to reassert independence. Josiah did this through religious reforms designed to eradicate Judean idolatry. His initial efforts around 628 BCE coincided with Yahweh's call of Jeremiah; Josiah intensified his program in 622 BCE (2 Kgs 22–23). Ezekiel was probably born near this time.

The Babylonians also took advantage of Assyria's civil strife. In 614 BCE, Babylon allies, the Medes, conquered the Assyrian capital, Asshur; in 612 BCE, the new capital of Nineveh fell. Concerned about Babylon's growing power, the Egyptian pharaoh Neco II allied with Assyria and tried to aid them against Babylon at Harran in 609 BCE. However, Josiah engaged and delayed Neco's forces at Megiddo; Josiah died in that battle and his son, Jehoahaz, took his father's throne.

Returning through Judah from defeat at Harran, Neco took Jehoahaz to Egypt, replaced him with his pro-Egyptian brother Jehoiakim, and demanded heavy tribute. By 605 BCE, Babylonia's Nebuchadrez-zar had defeated the Assyrians and taken Palestine from Neco. Nebuchadrezzar made Jehoiakim his client and deported many leading Judeans to Babylon (see Dan 1:1–6). In 601 BCE, Jehoiakim allied with Egypt again. Nebuchadrezzar returned to Palestine to deal with Jehoiakim's rebellion in 598 BCE. Around this time, Jehoiakim died and his son Jehoiachin replaced him (Jer 22:18–23). Nebuchadrezzar besieged Jerusalem in December 598 BCE, and Jehoiachin surrendered on 16 March 597 BCE. Nebuchadrezzar again took leaders of Judah, including Ezekiel, into exile in Babylon (2 Kgs 24:14–16; Ezek 1:1–3). Nebuchadrezzar appointed Josiah's son Zedekiah as client-king over Judah. Over the next decade, Zedekiah was eventually influenced to ally with Egypt again. He did so around 588 BCE; Nebuchadrezzar responded by destroying Jerusalem in 586 BCE.

The exile raised serious theological problems for the Judeans, including Ezekiel. Those who remained

Ezekiel's Life & Times
612 *Nineveh falls to the Babylonians and Medes*
609 *The battle of Carchemish and the final fall of Assyria*
605 *Nebuchadrezzar subjects Judah to his rule*
586 *Jerusalem falls to the Babylonians, and the exile begins*

Nebuchadrezzar
This spelling of the king's name, rather than the more common Nebuchadnezzar, better reflects the Babylonian original, Nabu-kudurri-usur ("may the god Nabu guard the boundaries").

in Judah believed they were the remnant of the true Israel (11:3) and that the deportees deserved their fate. In their view, Yahweh had rejected and removed the wicked from his land. The deportees understood matters even more darkly. Fully embedded in the ancient Near Eastern view that earthly events reflect realities of the unseen realm, many exiles regarded the defeat of their nation and king as a reflection of the defeat of Yahweh by Marduk and the Babylonian pantheon. To them, their situation demonstrated the inability of Yahweh to protect his territory and people. Ezekiel and his companions, now in Babylon, lived far from the comfort of any promises made by their defeated Judean territorial god, Yahweh. Intra-Judean debates about who are Yahweh's chosen people, and interest in Yahweh's covenant blessings and curses, seemed fruitless to those who viewed Yahweh as an impotent god recently conquered.

Yahweh's invocation of the blessings and curses of the Mosaic covenant pervades Ezekiel (see Lev 26; Deut 28; see comments at 4:9). Yahweh was not defeated; the dispirited exiles had simply failed to recall the curses, chief among which was deportation and the subjugation of Jerusalem and its environs. Rather, citing the curses demonstrated the same covenant fidelity as the providing of blessings. Moreover, in Deuteronomy 30, Yahweh promises that he will once again receive the people in covenant—after the blessings and curses are fulfilled. This covenanted order—curses followed by renewed covenant blessings—forms the fundamental outline of the book.

Yahweh's actions are not limited by territorial boundaries, either. Yahweh's sovereignty over all nations appears throughout, most notably in the "oracles against the nations" (25:1–32:32). Judah's oppressive neighbors will come under Yahweh's judgment. Moreover, Yahweh's manipulation of Nebuchadrezzar's interests and armies demonstrates who the true "king of kings" is (compare 26:7). Ezekiel also shows Yahweh's control over ancient Near Eastern myths (see comments after 17:24). Ezekiel transforms several well-known polytheistic mythical symbols and narratives into oracles praising God.

Finally, the three named visions (1:4–3:15; 8:1–11:25; 40:1–48:35) show Yahweh's essential holiness. Israel and the nations around them misunderstand

The "Recognition Formula"
Not only had Yahweh's people forgotten the covenant, they had forgotten him. The phrase, "then they will know that I am Yahweh," called a "recognition formula" by scholars, occurs in the book over sixty times and reminds Ezekiel's audience that the enactment of both the covenant blessings and the curses inextricably points to Yahweh's activity. Yahweh brings the same fidelity to enact the covenanted curses as to enact the blessings. Hardly impotent, Yahweh is powerful enough to act.

Structure of Ezekiel
The book is organized in a two-part structure reflecting the coming curses and subsequent blessings. The "oracles against the nations" separate these sections. Also, several chronological notices indicate the progress of Ezekiel's ministry.

the unique nature of God. As Moses learned, "I am who I am" refuses to be pigeonholed into familiar ancient Near Eastern categories. Among the severest mistakes of Ezekiel and his companions was their settled theological notions about how their covenanted God would and could act. Their views of a domesticated Yahweh had to be shattered. Ezekiel and his audience came to experience a much more dynamic God.

COMMENTARY

SUPERSCRIPTIONS & EZEKIEL'S CONSCRIPTION · 1:1–3:15

1:1–3 The first-person autobiographical superscription is elaborated by a third-person editorial superscription that identifies the event that launches Ezekiel's career; it does not provide career dates. The *thirtieth year* may refer to Ezekiel's age, but this is uncertain. David lowered the age for priestly duty from thirty to twenty (Num 4:3; 2 Chron 23:24, 27). Thus, this reference to thirty may indicate that in the year Ezekiel would have become a priest, Yahweh called him to be a prophet instead. Boadt (310) suggests the number refers to the years since Josiah's reform. Ezekiel views himself as one of *the exiles by the Kebar River*. Geographical location here is less significant than the fact that Ezekiel is near the center of the Babylonian empire but far away from a demolished homeland and his presumably defeated patron god. Against all expectation, here *the heavens were opened and* he *saw visions of God*.

The Kebar River

The Kebar was a human-made irrigation channel near Nippur in southern Iraq.

A later editor correlates the date with *the fifth year of the exile of King Jehoiachin*. The date is 31 July 593 BCE (for dates adopted here, see Block, *Ezekiel 1–24*, 28–29). Ezekiel's visions are *the word of* Yahweh; this frequent Old Testament phrase indicates that the content is authoritative, not necessarily the medium by which the message was delivered. To underscore that Yahweh encountered Ezekiel away from Judah, the editor writes that the visions come in *the land of the Babylonians* and that *there the hand of* Yahweh *was upon him*. The contrast between Ezekiel and his fellow exiles' view of their plight and Yahweh's view is stark. Forced to march to Babylon and see the immense temples and tile relief images of Babylonian gods, the exiles assumed their God's defeat. Yet, *there*, in the land protected by powerful Babylonian deities, the *hand of* Yahweh—symbolic of overwhelming compulsion and control upon those it grasps (Deut 4:34; Ps 136:12)—presses upon Ezekiel.

1:4–3:15 Two stylistic elements stand out in this first vision (1:4–28a). First, the Hebrew has a highly energetic quality and is difficult to translate in places. The display of power and the images are unexpected and confusing. Ezekiel tries to relate the indescribable. Second, he is reduced to simile and analogy, using *looked like*, *like*, *appearance of*, and *form of* throughout.

1:4–28A The vision begins when a wall of cloud with intense *flashing lightning* comes from *the north* (Ps 18:9–14; Nah 1:3b–6). Ezekiel may have believed this cloud harbored Babylonian gods rather than Yahweh. Whether Ezekiel literally saw a storm cloud or the entire episode was a vision is unclear. In the cloud, he sees *four living creatures*, each with *four faces and four wings*. Some scholars suggest the creatures' faces generically represent humanity, wild and domesticated animals, and birds. More likely, the faces reflect composite representations of Babylonian gods similar to the tile reliefs in Babylon. Moreover, Ezekiel's focus on their wings recalls the throne-bearing cherubim of Israelite theology (Exod 25:17–22; Isa 6:2). Ancient Near Eastern deities are often depicted on thrones borne by winged creatures (Allen, *Ezekiel 1–19*, 26–33). Ironically, the Babylonian gods are portrayed as Yahweh's throne-bearers. Ezekiel also describes a war chariot/wagon with unusual *intersecting wheels* with studded rims (*full of eyes all around*). The Hebrew says the wheels were tall and fear-inspiring. When the creatures moved the wagon, which may resemble wheeled wash stands found in Cyprus as well as chariots, the noise was deafening and awe-inspiring.

On a platform above the creatures rode a *figure like that of a man* surrounded in *brilliant light* (compare Exod 40:34). Ezekiel does not claim to see Yahweh; rather, he uses *like* ten times to express separation from what he sees and its reality. He describes *the appearance of the likeness of the glory of* Yahweh, whose *radiance* reminded him of *a rainbow in the clouds on a rainy day*. This recalls Yahweh's covenant promise to Noah (Gen 9:13) after the flood to be merciful in future cataclysmic judgments.

> **The Glory of the Lord**
>
> *God's "glory" pervades creation (Ps 19:1; Isa 6:3) and dwells in the tabernacle (Exod 40:34–37), temple (Ps 76:4), Zion (Isa 60:1–2), the ark of the covenant (1 Sam 4:19–22; 1 Kgs 8:1–13; Ps 24:7–10), and God's heavenly dwelling (Jude 24–25). It defies precise definition. Psalm 145:5 speaks of* the glorious splendor of God's majesty.

This vision forms the backdrop for the rest of Ezekiel's ministry. It rejects the view that Yahweh now serves the Babylonian gods. It challenges the notion that Yahweh is constrained by territorial boundaries: both the storm cloud and war wagon easily move over the terrain. And it hints that the theophany is about Yahweh's ability to keep covenant promises even when Israel leaves the world they once knew.

1:28B–2:2   Ezekiel prostrates himself (compare Esth 4:11) and awaits his summons. The figure commands, *Son of man, stand up on your feet and I will speak to you.* Son of man (2:1) highlights Yahweh's right to command his human subjects rather than Ezekiel's mortality (against NRSV's *mortal one*). Each use of *son of man* reminds Ezekiel of his obligation to obey immediately and completely. *The Spirit* who will direct his ministry helps him to his feet (Block, *Ezekiel 1–24*, 115).

2:3–8   Like Isaiah (Isa 6:8–13), Ezekiel is sent to a *rebellious* people. So severe is Israel's faithlessness, Yahweh calls them a *goy*, an Old Testament term often used of non-Yahwistic, non-Israelite people. To this *obstinate and stubborn* people,

Ezekiel is to declare *what the Sovereign Lord says*. He is to declare Yahweh's faithfulness in fulfilling his covenant obligations to bring curses on Israel. Ezekiel, too, must now choose to rebel or to obey. Thus, Yahweh presses, *You must speak my words to them . . . listen to what I say to you. Do not rebel. . . . Open your mouth and eat what I give you.*

3:4–15 Once again, Yahweh reminds Ezekiel that his *hardened and obstinate* audience will refuse to listen. To help, Yahweh will make him *as unyielding and hardened as they are*, impervious to ridicule. Yahweh commands Ezekiel to *take to heart all the words I speak to you*, that is, to be convicted by his own ministry. This will not occur until Jerusalem falls. Yahweh commands Ezekiel to *go now to your countrymen in exile and speak to them* and removes him from the visionary throne room while "the glory of Yahweh rose from its place" (v. 12, a textual emendation). In a rare self-reference, Ezekiel admits his deep *bitterness* and *anger* at Yahweh's heavy-handedness. He is so outraged he daringly refuses to speak to his companion exiles *where they were living* at *Tel Abib* for seven days. The site must have been one of the ancient city mounds in southern Mesopotamia (Zimmerli, *Ezekiel 1*, 139), and has nothing to do with the modern city Tel Aviv.

Prophetic "Call Narratives"
Biblical *"call narratives"*—reports about the prophet's entrance into that role—often highlight the prophet's mouth (*Exod 4:10–12; Isa 6:5–8; Jer 1:6–9*). In Ezekiel's call narrative (2:9–3:3), Ezekiel must eat a scroll *with writing* on both sides *full of* lament and mourning and woe. *Yahweh has much to say; there is no room for Ezekiel's comments. Yahweh commands him four times to eat, an indication of Ezekiel's reluctance. That the woeful words* tasted as sweet as honey (*see Ps 19:7–11*) is ironic and may even be sarcastic.

EZEKIEL'S MESSAGE, PHASE I: COVENANT CURSES · 3:16–11:25

3:16–21 After seven days, Yahweh gives an ultimatum. Yahweh has *made* Ezekiel *a watchman for the house of Israel*. The task is irrevocable, and Ezekiel's life depends on his response. Echoing Jeremiah 6:17, the text presses Yahweh's demand in four scenarios: Ezekiel's warning or not warning the *wicked* and the *righteous*. The cases survey Ezekiel's choices, not responses to his message. Yahweh will *hold* Ezekiel *accountable for* the *blood* of those he does not warn and will deliver him if he does warn them.

3:22–27 After rehearsing Ezekiel's options, Yahweh gives him room to obey. Yahweh requests a rendezvous, this time without calling him "son of man." Now, without coercion, Ezekiel *got up and went to the plain* and *fell facedown* before the *glory of the Lord*. He relents to Yahweh's demand. Yahweh responds in verses 24–27 by constraining him physically and vocally—symbolic gestures that communicated to an ancient Near Eastern audience Yahweh's complete control over his prophet's actions and words (Wilson, "Dumbness").

4:1–7:27 Ezekiel begins with pantomimes (4:1–5:4) and oracles (5:5–7:27) against Jerusalem, its surrounding mountains, and the land of Judah. These

Blessings & Curses of the Mosaic Covenant

The primary task of Yahweh's prophets was to call the people back to a full, sincere observance of the Mosaic covenant. The messages of Amos, Hosea, Isaiah, and the rest are impossible to understand fully without grasping the core of the covenant restrictions and the incentives Yahweh provides for keeping them.

The heart of the Mosaic covenant is the unique, uncompromising confession of monotheism, "Yahweh is our God; Yahweh alone. You shall love Yahweh your God with all your heart, and with all your being, and with all your might. Observe these words I am commanding you today in your heart" (Deut 6:4–6).

One statement of the basic principles of the Mosaic covenant appears in Exodus 20:2–17, and Deuteronomy 5:6–21, the Ten Commandments. The first four commandments summarize Israel's obligations to Yahweh: recognize God's uniqueness, give uncompromising loyalty amid rampant polytheism, respect Yahweh's character by one's actions, and confess Yahweh as sole provider by observing Sabbath. The remaining six summarize the obligations of Israelites to one another: respect authority, life, family structures, property rights, and personal rights, and beware of temptations to undermine the community by failing to meet one's obligations (Kaufman).

Many scholars think the Mosaic covenant follows the structure of ancient Near Eastern treaties between conquering kings (suzerains) and defeated kings (vassals). These treaties ended with incentives for each party to keep its obligations to the other, known as "blessings" and "curses." Such agreements called on the gods of the conquered and conquering nations to enforce the treaty. The Mosaic list of blessings and curses appears predominantly in Leviticus 26 and Deuteronomy 28 and is enforced by Yahweh alone.

A list of blessings includes seasonal rain, crops, orchards, vineyards, herds, wives, and children that are productive, abundant food, secure personhood and property, domestic calm, no wild animal attacks, no foreign invaders, victory in battle, international prosperity, respect, acclaim, and Yahweh's presence in their midst.

Covenant curses reversed the blessings: pestilence, all kinds of diseases and maladies on people, crops, and livestock; drought, famine, military defeat, improper burial, persecution, assault, rape, destruction of property, theft, slavery, idolatry, taunts and mockings by foreigners, deportation from their land, international disdain, oppressive debt and poverty, besieged villages and cities, cannibalism, paranoia, terror, shame, and Yahweh's abandonment of his people to every physical, social, environmental, political, financial, and agricultural enemy.

The governing principle behind the blessings and curses is simple: Yahweh blesses covenant fidelity and punishes infidelity. When Israel disobeys, it faces increasingly harsh curses until it proffers fidelity once again. Reception of the blessings depends on Israel's repentance and fidelity. These fundamental promises and expectations provide the foundation for Ezekiel's message (see Stuart, xxi–xliii).

undermine the concept that Jerusalem is inviolable (compare Jer 7). The panto-mimes describe what will occur; the oracles explain why and by whom.

4:1–3 Yahweh constrains Ezekiel's actions and words through fourteen months of prophetic sign acts. These actions prob-ably occurred within a regular daily routine. In the first, Ezekiel is to *draw the city of Jerusalem* on a *clay tablet* and to *lay siege* against *it*. The Hebrew is highly repetitive: the models of *siege works*, a *ramp, camps*, and *battering rams* are to be "against" the diorama. An *iron pan* separates the "city" from Ezekiel, who plays the role of Yahweh. Ezekiel is to *turn* his *face toward it* (literally, "set your face against it" in hos-tility). Yahweh's hostility reflects Leviticus 26:14–20. This pantomime is a *sign to the house of Israel* that

> **Prophetic "Sign Acts"**
> *The prophets performed "sym-bolic acts," or "sign acts," before live audiences to arouse the curi-osity of their hearers (Ezek 37:18) and to make their messages unforgettable in the memory of those who saw them (1 Sam 15:24–28; 28:16–17).*

Yahweh will soon invoke the covenant curses. After building the diorama, Ezekiel lies near it on his *left* side 390 days, then on his *right* side 40 days, representing the years of Israel's and Judah's history of sin and punishment. These numbers in the Masoretic text and the Septuagint do not agree; thus, their precise refer-ents are uncertain (compare Num 14:33–34; Boadt 312). While lying down, Ezekiel is to "set his face against" the siege scene *and with bared arm prophesy against* it. This depicts Yahweh as a warrior ready to do battle against Jerusalem as he had done against Egypt (see Deut 5:17).

4:9–17 Daily, Ezekiel interrupts his pantomime to eat. Depicting the sever-ity of the siege (see Lev 26:26), he is to mix flour from ground *wheat and barley, beans and lentils, millet and spelt. Twenty shekels* (8 oz.) of bread and *a sixth of a hin* (11 oz.) of water are meager daily rations. Ezekiel is to cook a *barley cake* on the embers of *human excrement*. Ordinarily, one used animal dung as a fuel for cooking. This depicts both the scarcity of combustibles and the harsh, ritually unclean conditions of a siege. Ezekiel objects (compare Deut 23:12–14), and Yahweh permits him to use *cow manure* instead.

5:1–4 In carnival-like manner, Ezekiel is to *shave* his *head* and *beard* with a *sword* when his previous pantomime ends (compare Lev 21:5; 26:33). Ezekiel represents both Yahweh and the city; the *hair* is the Jerusalemites. His mangy, nicked appearance depicts a destroyed, humiliated Jerusalem. He is to weigh the hair, *divide* it into thirds, *burn* a third, *strike* out at a third, *scatter* a third, and *tuck* a few strands into his *garment*. Babylonian priests used hair to divine omens; Ezekiel's audience may (wrongly) have thought he was doing the same. Three of these four actions depict curse fulfillments (Lev 26:17, 24–25). In an unexpected mercy, Yahweh will save a small remnant (see 11:16–21).

5:5–17 In verse 5, Yahweh says the shaved hair is *Jerusalem* and indicts the disobedient city. As the *center of the nations*, Jerusalem was to lead the world by example (see Exod 19:5–6); instead, it grew worse than *the nations and countries around her*. Echoing Leviticus 26:17, Yahweh promises by his life to punish Jerusalem *in the sight of the nations*. Twenty-six times, Yahweh uses "I" and "my" to ensure Jerusalem knows whence its punishment comes. Cannibalism will occur before deportation (see Deut 28:53–57; Lam 2:20), but Yahweh will have no pity. Yahweh's patience is ended because (in a foreshadowing of chapters 8–11) the people *defiled my sanctuary* with *vile images and detestable practices*. Israel had forgotten Yahweh by engaging in illicit religious practices. Jerusalem will indeed be *the center* (of attention) *of the nations* as *a ruin, a reproach, a taunt, a warning and an object of horror to the nations* (5, 15).

6:1–14　Yahweh's judgment expands to the *mountains of Israel* surrounding Jerusalem. As announced in Leviticus 26:30, Yahweh *will destroy* Israel's idolatrous *high places*, or open-air worship places, by enforcing the covenant curses. The *altars* will be desecrated with pulverized Israelite bones (Amos 2:1–3; 2 Kgs 23:16) and corpses. In the first of thirty-eight times, Ezekiel crassly uses a mocking pun in Hebrew to call the idols Yahweh will eradicate "little dung pellet gods" (v. 4; compare Jer 8:12). These idols are as worthless as excrement, both as objects of worship and protectors of their subjects. In a note of mercy (vv. 8–10), Yahweh promises to *spare some* Judeans by deporting them. These deportees, Yahweh hopes, will recall their sins and realize their punishment comes as part of Yahweh's faithfulness to the covenant. The final section (vv. 10–14) reverts to gestures of judgment and repeats descriptions of covenant curses seen already. In verse 14, one should read "Riblah" instead of *Diblah*. Riblah is north of Israel in Syria (2 Kgs 25:20–21), while Diblah is unattested (see Blenkinsopp 43–44).

7:1–27　The three sections of chapter 7 repeatedly refer to *the day* [of Yahweh] (vv. 7, 10, 12, 19) as an approaching day of judgment. Each section ends with a variation of the recognition formula (vv. 4, 9, 27). As Wilson remarks, "Over and over the prophet repeats his devastating message until his words pound the reader like a hammer" ("Ezekiel," 666).

7:1–9　Until Amos, the phrase *the day of the Lord* evoked notions of Yahweh's protection and comfort for Israelites. Amos turned that tradition on its head (Amos 5:18, 20), and Ezekiel follows suit: Yahweh will *unleash* his *anger against* Judah, *judge* the nation *according to* its *conduct, repay* it *for all* its *detestable practices*, and *not look on* it *with pity or spare* it from Babylonian exile. This calamity will come while people's abominable idols (*detestable practices*) are present. Their dung gods cannot save Judeans from their God. The terse Hebrew of verse 5 makes Ezekiel's announcement more shrill: *Thus says the Lord God, A disaster, a singular disaster—behold! It comes!* The coming day will bring *panic, not joy, upon the mountains*. Also, the Hebrew of verses 10–12a is somewhat confusing and chaotic. Ezekiel skillfully conveys the chaos of the day he describes through his language.

7:10–22　After a reference to Korah's rebellion (Num 16–17), Ezekiel announces the suddenness of the impending calamity. *Buyers* and *sellers* will have time neither to savor their gain nor to grieve their loss. The trumpeted call to arms will come too late. In another coarse reference, Ezekiel describes the cowardly Judahite soldiers: *every hand will go limp* ("a limp hand" describes impotence or weakness) and *every knee will* flow with water (better, "men will wet themselves"; NIV needlessly adds *weak as*). Attempts to bribe soldiers with *their silver and gold* will be unsuccessful: one cannot be bribed with what one is taking anyway. Most shocking of all, Yahweh will permit the temple to be looted and desecrated.

After the Judeans are deported, the Babylonians will *take possession of their houses,* just like ancient Israelites received Canaanite homes. In exile, Yahweh will render all four kinds of leaders, *prophet, priest, elder,* and *king,* unable to function.

Shackling of Prisoners
In 7:23–27, the call to prepare chains refers to the manner of deportation. Both Assyria and Babylon shackled deportees together. Assyrians also ran chains through rings that pierced the nose, cheek, or lower lip (see 19:4; 38:4; Isa 37:29; 2 Kgs 19:28; Amos 4:2).

8:1–11:25 Chapters 8–11 comprise a single vision in five sections framed by the guiding Spirit's entrance into (8:1–4) and departure from the temple (11:22–25). The first section (8:5–18) displays Israel's idolatry in the temple; the last four (9:1–11; 10:1–22; 11:1–15; 16–21) portray Yahweh's responses. Chief among these is Yahweh's progressive exit from the temple (9:3; 10:3; 11:23).

8:1–4 On 18 September 592 BCE, while still on his side, Ezekiel hosts *the elders of Judah* in his house. Their mission is unclear; perhaps they inquire about Ezekiel's pantomimes or seek comment on news from Judah (compare Jer 27–29). Unexpectedly, the *hand of the Sovereign Lord* falls on him, and Ezekiel lapses into a vision as he did in his first vision. *The Spirit* brings Ezekiel to the temple in Jerusalem.

8:5–18 Ezekiel sees four distinct foreign worship practices, probably reflecting the successive obligations to worship foreign gods that began during Manasseh's servitude to Assyria. Manasseh had erected an *idol of jealousy* (2 Kgs 21:7), likely an Asherah pole; Josiah had removed it (2 Kgs 23:6–7), since it violated Deuteronomy 5:8 (also Deut 12:3; see Smith 111–18). Ezekiel next encounters the *seventy elders of the house of Israel* (Num 11:16–25) secretively worshiping images of creeping animals, perhaps representations of Egyptian gods. That *Jaazaniah son of Shaphan* is among them indicates the quick return to idolatry after Josiah's death (2 Kgs 22:3–14; Jer 26:24). Finally, Ezekiel sees priests *bowing down to the sun in the east,* thus turning their backsides to Yahweh. The phrase, *putting the branch to their nose* is enigmatic. Fisch (46) notes the Masoretic scribes intentionally changed its wording because it offensively referred to breaking

The God Tammuz
In some forms of Babylonian mythology, Tammuz would die (and rise) yearly in tandem with seasonal changes. In contrast to the elders' clandestine worship, Ezekiel sees the women openly lamenting a dead Babylonian god.

wind in God's nose (see Boadt 314). Yahweh decides to pursue judgment upon the guilty without mercy.

9:1–11 Yahweh summons *six* armed *men* to carry out the judgment; they are accompanied by a scribe *clothed in linen*. They approach from the location of the idol of jealousy (8:3). When they assemble for duty, *the glory of the God of Israel* moves to the *threshold of the temple* (or perhaps the podium on which it stood). Before executing judgment, Yahweh commands the scribe to mark the innocent with the Hebrew letter *taw*. The six are to spare these while slaughtering the guilty among the *old men, young men and maidens, women and children*—a foreshadowing of the slaughter to come. The first to be killed are *the elders in front of the temple* (see 1 Pet 4:17) who had insulted Yahweh. Ezekiel, deeply distressed, pleads for Yahweh to preserve a *remnant*. Yahweh does not directly answer, but instead, justifies the slaughter because of Judah's *bloodshed*. After Yahweh promises to *bring down on their own heads what they have done*, the scribe returns to report that his job is done.

10:1–22 Yahweh orders the scribe to go *among the wheels beneath the cherubim* to receive burning coals. Evidently, this is a superhuman figure able to be in the holy of holies. Unlike their purifying use in Isaiah 6, these *coals* are to be scattered over the city to foreshadow its destruction (2 Kgs 25:9). In this vision, Ezekiel notes that the cherubim have shifted to the *south side* of the holy of holies in anticipation of leaving. The scribe *stood beside a wheel* and receives the coals from the midst of the cherubim. He leaves to complete his task. The cherubim and chariot resemble those in 1:15–28 (see Block, *Ezekiel 1–24*, 314–17). In the first vision, Ezekiel describes *living creatures* and demonstrates Yahweh's power over Babylonian deities in their own territory. Here, the thronebearers conform to Israelite artistic traditions as *cherubim*. The *glory* of Yahweh turns from the entrance to the holy of holies and sits *above the cherubim* for transport out of the temple. For the first time since his presence filled the temple in Solomon's day (1 Kgs 8:10–11), Yahweh leaves. On the way out, *the glory of the God of Israel* stops at the *east gate* of the temple for one final look. When the glory is gone, the temple and the city lack their divine protector. Verses 20–22 identify the *living creatures* of the first vision with the *cherubim* of this vision. Ezekiel twice notes he had seen them before *by the Kebar River*. By paralleling the two visions, he demonstrates that Yahweh may have abandoned the city and temple but not the people themselves. The temple and city are vitally important, but they are not essential for Yahweh's presence among the people. Yahweh is not distant but is among the people in their plight.

Cherubim

In the Old Testament, the cherubim protect sacred space (Gen 3:24; Exod 25:17–22). They are fearsome creatures with both human and animal features. They stand ready to protect Yahweh's holiness by escorting God away.

11:1–15 Chapter 11 reinforces the point that Yahweh's people reside in Babylon, not Jerusalem. Before its destruction in 586 BCE, Jerusalem's leaders and people regarded the exiles as castaways and themselves as Yahweh's favored subjects (vv. 1–6). Ezekiel's reactions to the vision (9:8; 11:13) show he believed the same. The *leaders* are Zedekiah's anti-Babylonian, pro-Egyptian advisors. Their call to *build houses* may be variously translated (see NIV alternate translation). It looks forward to prosperous days under Egyptian rule. *Meat* was not a staple of ancient Near Eastern diets; the city leaders' metaphor is an arrogant claim to Yahweh's special favor. Their arrogance devalues the lives of others to the point that they commit murder. The wicked leaders' judgment will come through what they most fear: they *will fall by the sword . . . at the borders of Israel*. This is later realized when the Babylonian general Nabuzaradan takes the officials to Riblah and executes them (2 Kgs 25:10–21; Jer 52:10). In verses 13–15, *Pelatiah's* death is ironic since his name means "Yahweh delivers (a remnant)." Ezekiel is aghast; he considers the Jerusalemites, not the exiles, as the remnant. Yahweh disabuses him of this view in verse 15. He calls Ezekiel's exilic companions *the whole house of Israel*: the faithless exiles are the remnant.

11:16–21 Verse 16 shows that the Jerusalemites have arrogantly rejected the exiles as their kin and people. Ezekiel's sympathies for those who have rejected him and his companions are misplaced. This oracle of hope is a rejoinder to the Jerusalemites. Yahweh shockingly claims to be a *sanctuary for* the exiles *in the countries where they have gone*. In contrast to the Jerusalemites' claims to the land, Yahweh promises it only to the remnant-in-exile. In terms explained more fully in chapters 34–48, the exiles will return to a renewed land with *undivided hearts* and *new spirits* ready for obedience. The promise concludes with the covenant formula, *They will be my people, and I will be their God*.

11:22–25 After the *glory of* Yahweh departs from the east gate to *the mountain east* of the city (that is, the Mount of Olives), the spirit returns Ezekiel to his fellow exiles. This time, Ezekiel tells *the exiles everything* Yahweh *had shown* him.

MORE COVENANT CURSES FOR JERUSALEM & JUDAH · 12:1–24:27

Chapters 12–24 comprise one third of the book and offer extended reasons for Yahweh's judgments just announced. These oracles show why the exiles should abandon their view that Yahweh's blessings must be tied to the land and the temple. Editors arranged the oracles into six sections: 12:1–20 and 24:1–27 are sign acts about the destruction of Jerusalem that form an inclusio; 12:21–14:11 are about prophets and prophecy; 14:12–16:63 explain why Jerusalem will fall; 17:1–22:31 relate causes for Jerusalem's fall; and chapter 23 contains oracles about *Oholah* and *Oholibah*.

12:1–16 The phrase *eyes . . . hear* is common in the Bible (see also Isa 6:9–10; Jer 5:21, 23; Mark 4:9, 23). Ironically, the following pantomimes provide much to see and hear: *while they watch* appears six times in verses 3–7. Ezekiel appears to prepare for an imminent end to the exile (see Jer 27–28). *During the day*, he is to set his bags out. At twilight, he is to go into exile (the exiles do not know where he is going) after he digs through his own house wall. As he goes off into the evening, he is to *cover* his face. This sign act is an object lesson for his companions.

In a double entendre, *oracle* (Hebrew *massa'*) may be translated "burden," or "load": "The prince is the *burden* in Jerusalem and the whole house of Israel who are there." Thus, as a *sign*, Ezekiel portrays Yahweh hauling Zedekiah and his associates out of Jerusalem and *into exile as captives*. Ezekiel also plays Zedekiah (2 Kgs 24:20c–25:7). The phrases *spread my net* and *caught in my snare* are common prophetic metaphors for destruction (Hos 7:12; Isa 8:14–15; 24:17–18; Jer 48:43–44), similar to formulas in ancient Near Eastern treaty curses (Block, *Ezekiel 1–24*, 376–77 n. 66–68). This oracle ends with the recognition formula tied to enforcing the covenant curses (see Lev 26:33a).

12:17–20 This eating enactment, also about *those in Jerusalem and in the land of Israel*, is more animated than 4:9–17. It applies the covenant curse of extreme anxiety in Deuteronomy 28:65–67 to those in Judah. In Deuteronomy, the curse applies to worshipers of foreign gods on foreign land. Ezekiel's allusion implies that those in Jerusalem are foreigners. This view is supported when verse 19 calls the exiles *people of the land*, a phrase reserved for inhabitants of Judah. The preceding oracles thus dash the hopes of the exiles for a quick return

Distinguishing True from False Prophecy

The phenomenon of prophecy was widespread in the ancient Near East, finding its place in Israel and in other nations (see Nissinen, Seow, and Ritner). Because prophetic activity was widespread, it was difficult for ancient Israelites to discern true from false prophecy.

Little wonder, then, that Ezekiel's audience despairs of genuine prophetic messages. The only certain course was to reject prophets who openly encouraged the pursuit of other gods (Deut 13:1–5), but false prophets usually had more sense than to mount a direct frontal assault. Even genuine prophets could not always discern a false prophet, as the sad episode of 1 Kings 13 relates: a false prophet speaking a true message hoodwinks a true, but disobedient, man of God.

Despite these formidable obstacles, most true prophets shared three characteristics. First, they show an overwhelming compulsion to speak or enact their messages under extreme difficulty or at great personal cost (compare 1 Kgs 18:40; 19:1–2; 22:8, 27; Isa 20:2–4; Jer 12:6; 16:1–2; 38:1–28; Ezek 24:15–27; Hos 1:2). Second, they address the sins of the people rather than downplay them (Jer 23:22; Zech 1:4), whereas false prophets wink at sin (Lam 2:14). Finally, true prophets apply the covenant blessings and curses in proper order. The covenant is arranged in a blessings-curses-blessings restored sequence. The false prophets grasped this superficially, too quickly announcing coming blessing. False prophets were often guilty, not because of the hope they offered, but because of the time when they offered it. A true message spoken too soon offers false hope.

and demolish their rosy view of those left in the land. Such views had been fueled by false prophets—a subject to which Ezekiel turns next.

12:21–28   Before addressing false prophecy, Ezekiel challenges his audience's cynicism and apathy about prophets and prophecy as seen in their terse, four-word proverb: *Days amass, visions vanish!* Which prophecies are being referenced is unknown—perhaps Ezekiel's, Jeremiah's, Hananiah's, Shemaiah's, or others' (see Jer 27–28). Yahweh, weary of being charged with the inability to fulfill his words, will *put an end to this proverb* by bringing the calamities soon, *in your days*.

13:1–16   Yahweh charges false prophets of Ezekiel's day with seven offenses: they *follow their own spirit* and are not inspired by Yahweh; they have no recourse to Yahweh's heavenly council, and so they *have seen nothing* (see 1 Kgs 22:19–22; Isa 6:1–13; Jer 23:16–22); they are mercenary, *like jackals among ruins*, scavenging for believers among Israelites; they are careless—they do not *repair* the *breaks in the wall* (a metaphor for protecting against spiritual intrusions); their genuine *visions* give *false* comfort; their real *divinations* tell a *lie*; their worst offense is to claim Yahweh's approval of their deceit with "Yahweh *declares*" after their words. Therefore, Yahweh is *against them* (see Lev 26:17) and will completely exclude them from his people. They *will not belong to the council of my people*; they will be removed from the *records of the house of Israel*, losing all inheritance rights; and they will not *enter the land of Israel* upon return. The false prophets' messages are like an incompetent plaster job on an adobe house (vv. 10–16). Ezekiel puns on the word *plaster* (not NIV's *whitewash*). Instead of "plaster," Ezekiel uses "malicious folly" (Hebrew root *tafal*). The bad plaster job—that is, the malicious folly—of the false prophets will become evident when the Babylonians storm Jerusalem.

> **The "Book of Life"**
> *Several biblical texts refer to the ancient Near Eastern practice of "recording" or "enrolling" names in a scroll or book to denote people who are included in or excluded from a certain group or activity (for example, Exod 32:3; Isa 4:3; Ps 69:28; Mal 3:16; Phil 4:3; Rev 21:27).*

13:17–23   There are female false prophets, too. They use *magic charms* and *veils* to *ensnare people like birds*. The exact practices are impossible to determine with current evidence. The point is clear enough: Yahweh is deeply angered by female diviners (*witches*) who beguile the people with their magic instead of calling them to *turn from their evil ways*. Yahweh will *save* the *people* from them.

14:1–11   *Some elders* consult Ezekiel as a prophet while harboring *idols in their hearts*. Their idolatry is mental and probably includes their misguided favor of Judah and Jerusalem. To whatever inquiry they make, Yahweh *will answer . . . in keeping with* the inquirer's *great idolatry*, that is, tell the fool what he wants to hear (Prov 26:5). Yahweh wants to *recapture the hearts* (literally, "seize by the hearts") of the people and so calls them to *repent* of their duplicity. Inquirers of Yahweh's prophets are not to be double-minded. Additionally, the prophets ought not be quick with answers; they must wait on Yahweh. The problem of divine enticement is difficult, but Block (*Ezekiel 1–24*, 437) catches the sense of verses 9–10: "So-called prophets of the Lord who acquiesce before the flattery. . .of hypocritical inquirers become accomplices in their crimes and may expect the same punishment." Once duplicity and vanity are removed from Israel, *Israel will no longer stray* from Yahweh, and the covenant formula will be fulfilled.

14:12–23 Echoing the four punishments listed in the covenant curses of Leviticus 26:21–26—*famine, wild beasts, sword,* and *plague*—and reinforcing the point with the oath *as surely as I live* (vv. 16, 18, 20), Yahweh declares his policy of individual merit in bringing about deliverance. In a rejection of the earlier episode with Sodom (Gen 18:16–33), Yahweh insists that even the renowned righteousness of *Noah, Daniel, and Job* would only benefit themselves and not their children in the current situation. Noah and Job are well known, but scholars dispute the identity of *Daniel*. He is most likely not the biblical Daniel, but rather an ancient, non-Israelite (like Noah and Job) character, known also to Canaanites in the second millennium BCE, legendary for his righteousness, justice, and care of widows and orphans. Whoever *Daniel* is, the point remains: the righteousness of the fathers does not overcome the treachery of the children. Despite the totality of the hypothetical calamities, when Jerusalem is punished, some children of the exiles will unexpectedly survive, but not because of their righteousness. Instead, they will serve to vindicate Yahweh's decision: Jerusalem must be destroyed.

15:1–8 A similar viticulture metaphor appears in Psalm 80 (compare Hos 10:1; Jer 2:21). This *wood of the vine* alludes to Israel as Yahweh's vineyard (Deut 32:32; Isa 5:1–7). Grapevine wood, otherwise unusable, is useful for fuel. The metaphor turns to an analogy about *the people of Jerusalem*. Yahweh has set his face against them (Lev 26:17) and is pruning the vine and burning the branches. *Come out of the fire* refers to Nebuchadrezzar's siege of 598–597 BCE. *The fire will yet consume them* in the destruction of 586 BCE. Once again, an enforcement of a covenant curse supports the repeated recognition formula.

16:1–63 Ezekiel uses gutter language to reach his insensitive audience. So far, he has referred to idols as "little dung gods" (6:1–7), crassly described soldiers as impotent, incontinent old men (7:17), and mentioned priests "breaking wind in God's face" (8:17). Ezekiel uses no euphemism here (but English translators still do); instead, he bluntly describes Jerusalem as a whoring nymphomaniac (Hebrew *zonah*) and freely employs sexual, sometimes pornographic, images throughout. The shocking language seeks to rehabilitate Judah by alerting the people to their true state.

This oracle rounds out a series defending the justice of Yahweh's destruction of Jerusalem (14:12–16:63), and it serves as an opening frame for a series exploring its causes (17:1–22:31). The concluding frame oracle is the similarly sexually graphic chapter 23.

16:1–14 Born to *Canaanites*—an *Amorite father* and *Hittite mother*, Jerusalem begins with idolatry in her blood (Deut 7:1–5). Girls in the ancient world were often *thrown* naked *out into the open field* at birth to die. Yet Yahweh finds and adopts Israel, an unusual and negative take on Israel's election. Verse 7 parallels her infancy with puberty: she *grew up*, her *breasts were formed*; she *developed* pubic *hair*; she was completely nude (see Block, *Ezekiel 1–24*, 478), *naked and bare*. When she is *old enough* for sexual intercourse, Yahweh marries her with his *solemn oath* and *covenant* pledge (see Ruth 3:9). This practice would not have been unusual or shocking to Ezekiel's contemporaries, whatever our sensibilities. This symbolic marriage occurred when David took the city and Solomon built the temple there (2 Sam 5:6–12; 6:12–19; 7:1–17). The remaining description shows Yahweh's extravagant tenderness in providing sexual relations, clothing, and food. Jerusalem owed its life, *fame*, and *beauty* to Yahweh's affection.

16:15–22 As a betrayed husband, Yahweh indicts Jerusalem for using his gifts to buy sex with others. She used her *beauty* and *fame* to become promiscuous and *lavished* her *favors on anyone who passed by*. From her *garments*, she *made gaudy high places*; from her *gold and silver*, she made *male idols* (possibly cast metal phalluses; NJPS: *phallic images*; see Isa 57:8; Exod 32:2–4) that she adorned with clothes and provided with food. Worst of all, she sacrificed *my children to the idols* because she ungratefully forgot *the days of* her *youth* when she was rescued from death.

Ungrateful Nations

The book of Ezekiel tells stories of three ungrateful cities or nations who abused the "beauty" Yahweh had given them for selfish goals, so that Yahweh destroyed each one: Jerusalem, the beautiful bride (Ezek 16); Tyre, the beautiful ship (Ezek 27); and Egypt, the beautiful cedar (Ezek 31).

16:23–34 Verses 23–34 focus on Jerusalem's sexual partners, a metaphor for political alliances (Hos 8:9; Jer 22:20). *Woe! Woe to you* shows Yahweh's anger and condemnation. At *shrines* to foreign gods, Jerusalem *offered* her *body* (literally, "threw the legs open") to any passer-by. This lecherous behavior shows Israel's desire to achieve security through alliances with other countries rather than through fidelity to Yahweh. Alliances with *Egypt* began with Solomon's horse trading (1 Kgs 10:28–29); compare the crude, *your neighbors with the huge penises* (NIV translates it, more politely, *your lustful neighbors*; compare 23:20). Even the notoriously uncivilized *Philistines* find Jerusalem's deeds offensive. Unfulfilled by the Egyptians, she turns to the *Assyrians* (under Ahaz; 2 Kgs 16:7–18); still not sated, she engages the *Babylonians* (beginning with Hezekiah; 2 Kgs 18:5–8; Isa 39:1–8). In verse 30, Yahweh declares his fury (literally, "How incensed I am at you." NIV's *How*

Child Sacrifice

The Israelites borrowed the practice of child sacrifice from their pagan neighbors, especially in very stressful circumstances, as a desperate means of persuading Yahweh to help them (2 Kgs 16:3; 21:6; Jer 7:30–31; Mic 6:6–7).

weak-willed you are is inaccurate; see Allen, *Ezekiel 1–19*, 229 n. 30a). Jerusalem both refuses her husband and *scorned payment* for sex. Worse than other whores, she *gives payment* (that is, tribute).

16:35-43   Before sentencing, Yahweh summarizes the indictment. She *poured out* her *lust* (NIV alternate translation). Ezekiel's pornographic phrase clinically means "your genitals became lubricated." Then she *exposed* her genitals and engaged in brazen sex. Yahweh also recalls the "dung pellets of your abominations" and the murder of children.

A Husband's Wrath

As depicted in Ezekiel 16:37–40, ancient Near Eastern custom allowed a betrayed husband to publicly strip (a reversal of verses 10–13) and humiliate his wife. The community participated, sometimes throwing feces on the woman to demonstrate communal outrage (Isa 47:3; Nah 3:5–6). Ancient people believed such jealous anger to be appropriate to the marriage relationship.

41–43   Metaphor merges with the reality of 586 BCE in this description of Jerusalem's destruction. Yahweh strikes an alliance of sorts with Jerusalem's *lovers* to punish her; here, it is Babylon. When Jerusalem's death sentence is completed, Yahweh's *jealous anger will turn away*.

16:44-52   Even in *death*, Jerusalem will suffer the shame of a bad reputation (see 2 Sam 18:18; Ps 83:4) and be the butt of an unflattering *proverb*—just like her bigger (not *older*) *sister Samaria* and smaller (not *younger*) *sister Sodom*. By comparison, Jerusalem *became more depraved* than Sodom. Yahweh rehearses Sodom's sins: Sodom was *arrogant, overfed and unconcerned* about *the poor and needy*, and *did detestable things*. Note that Sodom's sins here are not primarily (if at all) sexual.

Whatever sins *Samaria* committed, she *did not commit half the sins* Jerusalem *did*. Indeed, both sisters *seem righteous* by comparison. Samaria and Sodom had been utterly destroyed for crimes less egregious than Jerusalem's; therefore, Jerusalem's punishment is just.

53–58   Yet destruction is not Jerusalem's end, because the covenant promises blessings after curses. Yahweh promises to *restore the fortunes of Sodom* and of *Samaria* when he restores Jerusalem. Justice requires that, if he restores Jerusalem to her former glory (vv. 8–14), Yahweh must also restore those whose crimes were less.

16:59-63   In another unexpected oracle of hope, Yahweh promises to *establish an everlasting covenant* with Jerusalem (compare Jer 32:40). Yahweh's graciousness will arouse shame for *all* they *have done*, and they will be unable to *open* their *mouth* in complaint at their harsh punishment.

17:1-24   Told to *riddle a riddle and allegorize an allegory*, Ezekiel presents a historical fable about two eagles and two plants. *A great eagle comes* to *Lebanon* and snaps off a *cedar shoot*. It transplants the sprig to *a city of traders*. The eagle also plants an indigenous grapevine seedling, tends it, and it grows well, spreading *toward* the great eagle. When another *eagle* comes, the grapevine alters course and grows toward it. The fable refers to the shifting reliance of Judah upon Babylon and Egypt. In a series of questions (vv. 9–10), Ezekiel asks his audience to judge the fate of the vine. Similar to Amos' rhetorical strategy (Amos 1:2–2:16), Ezekiel has his hearers deliver their verdict before they realize it is a self-judgment. They are obtuse (see 12:2–3).

The riddle allegorically rehearses Israel's recent changing allegiances and condemns Zedekiah for disloyalty to Nebuchadrezzar (vv. 11–24). The great eagle is Nebuchadrezzar, *the king of Babylon*. *Lebanon* is Jerusalem. The cedar shoot *carried off* is Jehoiachin and his advisors. Zedekiah is the *member of the royal family* with whom Nebuchadrezzar *made a treaty*. Zedekiah *rebelled* in 588 BCE *by sending his envoys to Egypt*'s Pharaoh Hophra. In a surprising turn, Yahweh holds Zedekiah accountable to his vassal obligations to Nebuchadrezzar. No doubt their treaty contained typical blessings and curses, as well as the invocation of the two parties' gods (including Yahweh) as covenant enforcers. Thus, Yahweh can call Zedekiah's oath *my oath that he despised and my covenant that he broke*. The phrase *as surely as I live* reflects Yahweh's intention to fulfill his own obligation: Zedekiah *shall die in Babylon*. Yahweh's fidelity again calls forth the recognition formula.

With Jehoiachin in Babylon and Zedekiah's death imminent, it appears Yahweh's "forever" oath to David (2 Sam 7:1–17) is ended. Recycling images from the preceding fable, Yahweh promises that, even though the covenant is suspended, it will continue. Unlike the humble vine Nebuchadrezzar planted, Yahweh's plant will *become a splendid cedar*. Yahweh underlines his fidelity to reestablish a Davidic king with *I Yahweh have spoken, and I will do it*.

18:1–32 In 14:12–20, Yahweh rejected a prior policy of delivering a sinner through the righteousness of another. In verses 1–4, he rejects the exiles' view of punishment for them because of the sins of their ancestors, voiced in their proverb, *The fathers eat sour grapes, and the children's teeth are set on edge* (but see Exod 20:5; 2 Kgs 24:3–4). Yahweh rejects such fatalism because it dismisses the value of each person (v. 4) The text then cites as its warrant Deuteronomy 24:16: *The person who sins is the one who will die*.

To persuade his audience, Ezekiel reviews the cases of three successive generations (vv. 5–9). The first, *a righteous man*, evinces qualities generally described in Deuteronomy 24:6–22 and Exodus 22:21–27. He abstains from idolatrous practices, observes sexual purity, and engages others with concern, care, and integrity. "Life" here means being delivered from a premature death in exile and a general enjoyment of tangible, material blessings. No afterlife is in view.

Then appears *a violent*, murderous *son* (vv. 10–13). Whatever his father did not do, he does. In addition, he does *detestable things*—a general charge for good measure. Ezekiel asks and immediately answers a rhetorical question about his fate: *Will such a man live? He will not!*

In the third generation (vv. 14–18), the grandson is entirely unlike his father and like his grandfather, except that *he does not . . . require a pledge* (compare v. 7). Ezekiel does not ask "Shall he die?" because this is the point at issue with his audience: *He will not die for his father's sin; he will surely live*.

Ezekiel & Ancient Near Eastern Mythology

Biblical scholars do not agree on a single definition of the term "myth" when applied to biblical literature. They do, however, agree that Ezekiel and his audience not only knew their neighbors' myths, but that many Israelites subscribed to them. This is the essence of Israelite idolatry. It is hardly surprising that Ezekiel would adapt familiar elements of polytheistic mythology to communicate his points effectively to his audience. Myths are not "false," but are stories about the deep structure of reality.

Ezekiel adapts at least five major mythological elements in his oracles. First, the throne-chariot vision in chapters 1 and 10 contains elements similar to Canaanite depictions of the storm gods Baal and El riding their chariots in pursuit of enemies. This image is widely used in the Old Testament, but biblical writers adapt it to describe Yahweh instead of Baal or El (for example, Deut 33:26; Pss 18:9; 68:4, 33; 104:3; Isa 18:1; Nah 1:3).

Second, Ezekiel also refers to the mythological symbol of the cosmic tree (17:22–24; 19:10–11; 31:1–19; compare Dan 4:10–12). Similar tree symbols appear in Akkadian, Sumerian, Babylonian, and Egyptian literature, sometimes in association with another mythological tree, the tree of life. Usually, the cosmic tree symbolized the grandeur of an empire.

Third, Ezekiel uses the cosmic, deep watery chaos prevalent in biblical references to creation (the deep in Gen 1:25; Pss 65:6–7; 89:9; 95:4–5; 124:4–5). This primeval, chaotic sea represented the initial state of all that existed; it stood against all order and harmony. From it, dry land emerged. In Ezekiel, this watery chaos swallows Tyre (26:19), the ship Tyre (27:26–27), and, in a reversed image, appears as the river of life flowing from the new temple (47:1–12).

Fourth, adaptations of the myth of the great sea monster Tiamat (or Rahab or Leviathan) appear throughout the Old Testament, especially in the Psalms (Job 3:8; 7:12; 26:12; 41:1; Pss 74:13–14; 77:16; 89:10; 104:26; Isa 27:1; 51:9; Amos 9:3). Ezekiel uses this image in oracles against Egypt's Pharaoh Hophra (29:3–5; 32:2–8). The biblical accounts of Yahweh's easy victory over this sea creature undermine some Israelites' view that everything is ulti-mately chaotic. Instead, when Yahweh is involved, matters move quickly from chaos to order.

Finally, ancient Near Eastern creation myths often describe a garden paradise of the gods. One popular Sumerian myth described this paradise, Dilmun, as a fertile, well-watered land free of all pollutants, sickness, death, and hostility among animals. Ezekiel's references to "the trees of Eden in the garden of God" (28:13; 31:8–9, 16, 18) are adaptations of the idyllic state. Ezekiel adapts various strands of ancient Near Eastern paradise myths for his own purposes and transforms them through the language of Genesis. Ezekiel's usage need not suggest that he viewed the Genesis account of the garden as fictional. Rather, he uses old images for monotheistic ends.

Ezekiel's adaptation of these and other mythical elements is part of his "by any means necessary" communication strategy to his hard-hearted and rebellious audience. His tactic also demonstrates that Yahweh is not bound to any particular means of communicating but is sovereign even over the polytheistic myths that would deny God's uniqueness.

Ezekiel next words his audience's question: *Why does the son not share the guilt of his father*? They assume their exile is the consequence of others' sins. Ezekiel rejects a corporate fatalism and insists on individual responsibility. Fishbane (141) explains the transition:

> [W]hile the first [section] argued that there was no transfer of guilt from one generation (person) to another, nothing was said about the sinner in his own lifetime. Was a (repentant) person considered guilty in later years for sins committed earlier, and vice versa?

The answer is similar in both the generational and individual cases: Yahweh deals with people in their present state. Current Israel perpetuates former Israel's sins. In their hard-heartedness, *Israel* declares Yahweh's policy absurd (NIV's *not just* is misleading). Yahweh twice hurls the charge back: *Is it not your ways that are* ridiculous?

Ezekiel's attempt to persuade fails, so he pronounces God's judgment: *I will judge you, each according to his ways* (vv. 30–32). Israel's refusal to agree with Yahweh's policy does not hinder its implementation. Yet Yahweh's judgment allows for repentance: Yahweh does not want the people to die. He commands them to *get a new heart and a new spirit*. Usually these are a divine grant (11:19; 36:26), but this oracle focuses on Israel's obligation to take responsibility for its state rather than claim to be a victim of its ancestors' sins.

19:1–14   Chapter 19 presents two allegorical, ironic laments for Judah's last four rulers. The first (vv. 1–9) uses a zoological metaphor. A *lioness* raises a *cub*. When grown, he becomes violent, is captured, and is taken to *Egypt*. The lioness rears another cub. When grown, he becomes more violent than the previous cub. He is captured and taken to the *king of Babylon*. These cubs are *princes of Israel*. The first is undoubtedly Jehoahaz (2 Kgs 23:34). The second cub probably represents Jehoiakim.

The second lament uses another viticultural simile (see chapters 15, 17). The *mother* is *like a vine in your vineyard*. It had *many and strong branches*. However, the hot *east wind* dried up the branches, and fire burned *one of its main branches*. What remains is unfit *for a ruler's scepter*. The mother is the Davidic dynasty and the branches its succession of kings. Babylon is the hot *east wind*; the *fruit* and *strong branches* are Jehoiachin, his sons, and the other deportees taken into exile *in a dry and thirsty land*. Zedekiah, deemed unfit as king by Ezekiel, is the smoldering *main branch* that remains.

20:1–44   Most of this chapter surveys Israel's history from its origin to its end in five eras. The hallmark of this historical review is Yahweh's patience. From each God requires fidelity, Israel rebels, God intends to punish it utterly, but avoids punishment to defend God's honor, and so gives limited punishment and new regulations to assist Israel's fidelity. Yet the people rebel.

On 14 August 591 BCE, *some of the elders come to inquire of* Yahweh. Yahweh emphatically swears (*as surely as I live* is an oath formula) they will receive no response. He also asks Ezekiel whether he will *judge them*. Despite Ezekiel's oracles, Yahweh realizes that he is still sympathetic to the exiles' views. Nevertheless, Ezekiel is to *confront them with the detestable practices of their fathers*. The review is unlike anything they had heard before (see Pss 78; 106).

Israel never had a golden age; the nation's idolatry began in Egypt (but see Josh 24:14–15). When Joseph comes to Egypt, he assimilates by taking the Egyptian name Zaphenath-Paneah and marrying the daughter of the high priest of On (Gen 41:44–45). Moses, reared in Pharaoh's house, is also thoroughly Egyptianized (Exod 2:19). Even his name is Egyptian. Nevertheless, Yahweh *chose Israel* (Deut 7:6–11), reaffirmed the original oath *with uplifted hand* to be their *God*, was *revealed* through Moses (Exod 6:6–9), determined to *bring them out of Egypt*, and give them a land *searched out for them*. In return, Yahweh requests singleminded loyalty (Exod 20:2–6).

> **Historical Summaries**
> *The Bible contains several "historical" summaries of Yahweh's dealings with his people, proclaiming various messages (Josh 24:2–15; Judg 11:14–28; 1 Sam 12:6–18; Neh 9:6–37; Pss 78; 105; 106).*

Predictably, *they rebelled* and did not *forsake the idols of Egypt*. Ezekiel tells what Exodus does not. While still *in Egypt*, Yahweh determines to punish them. Yet, not wanting to become a laughingstock *in the eyes of the nations they lived among*, Yahweh refrains.

Instead, God brings them to Sinai and gives *decrees, laws*, and *Sabbaths*, that is, Saturday, Sabbath years, Jubilee (compare Lev 23:24, 39). Again, they *rebelled* and *desecrated* the *Sabbaths*. Yahweh determines to *destroy them in the desert* and then relents. Moses' critical role in this goes unmentioned (but see Exod 32:7–14). Instead, Yahweh suspends the blessing of his promise (the promised land and abundant fertility) to the first generation because of their sins; he has greater hopes for their children.

Incredibly, during the wilderness wanderings, *the children rebelled*. Rather than destroy them, Yahweh disperses that generation *among the nations and scatters them through the countries* (Deut 28:64), thus anticipating the deportations of Ezekiel's own time. For them, the land will be but a temporary grant. Verses 25–26 are a difficult passage (Allen, *Ezekiel 1–19*, 11–12; Block, *Ezekiel 1–24*, 637–41; Fisch 126), but the solution is reasonably clear. A slight stylistic variation in the gender and presence of a possessive suffix ("my") for *statutes* (Hebrew *chuqqotay* in verses 11, 13, 16, 19, 21, 24 versus *chuqqim* in verse 25), usually inconsequential, signals a differentiation in this context. These statutes do not come from Yahweh (compare *the statutes of your fathers*, verse 18) because *they could not live by* them, whereas Yahweh's laws bring life (vv. 11, 13, 21; compare Ps 119:93). Verse 26 seems to explain the generalized *statutes* and *laws* of verses 18 and 25:

Yahweh allowed them to follow their own rules with the expectation that they would become horrified at their child *sacrifice*.

In verses 27–29, Ezekiel broadly describes all the generations between those Yahweh *brought into the land* and his own day. The entire sweep is characterized by idol worship: the forefathers *blaspheme* Yahweh by *forsaking* (literally "acting traitorously against") him to present idols with *sacrifices, offerings, incense*, and libations on the *high places*. Ezekiel thus dismisses all Israelite history with one rhetorical flourish. For greater nuance on this subject, see Joshua-Kings.

According to verses 30–38, The exiles are not punished for their forefathers' sins, but like them, they continue (*to this day*) to lust after and *sacrifice* their children to *all* their *idols* (also 16:36). This disqualifies them from inquiring of (that is, obtaining information from) Yahweh. Despite their desire *to be like the nations . . . who serve wood and stone*, Yahweh *will never* let them be like all others. Using the metaphor of a shepherd (seen again in chapter 34), Yahweh will *gather* his sheep *from the countries* to examine each one and *purge* the flock of rebels. These *will not enter the land of Israel*.

Go serve your idols (vv. 39–44) offers a temporary, ironic permission because judgment is set. The consequences of its future arrival will be true Yahwistic worship, a resumption of blessing of promised land to *the entire house of Israel*, a thorough repentance and a fulfillment of the recognition formula by Israel and the nations (16:59–63).

20:45–21:32 Four oracles comprise this section developed thematically around the word "sword"—a sign of Babylon's imminent invasion of the eastern Mediterranean basin and the destruction of Jerusalem. The English chapter and verse divisions diverge from the Hebrew divisions until the end of chapter 20.

The Four Oracles

The oracles show a progression: from Yahweh's decision to bring the sword upon Judah, to preparing the sword and giving it to a slayer, to the slayer making ready, to the aftermath.

20:45–21:7 The first oracle, like the one in chapter 17, is divided into metaphorical presentation and allegorical explanation. The words *south, south*, and *southland* represent different Hebrew words. The first, *teman* (literally "to the right"), refers to that side of a map when east is the orienting direction, as is common in ancient Near Eastern cartography. The second (*darom*) is the usual directional word for south. *Southland* in Hebrew is *negev* and refers to the Negev wilderness south of Jerusalem. That the Negev was never *forest*ed in historical times indicates that the oracle has other than literal meaning. In an unusual move, Ezekiel objects that his use of figures of speech brings the disdainful dismissal, *Isn't he just telling parables?* It is unclear whether Ezekiel laments his unpopularity or the use of an ineffective medium for his message.

The overall explanation is clear, however. *Jerusalem, the sanctuary*, and *the land of Israel* are the intended referents. The fire is the *sword* of Babylon; the trees are *both the righteous and the wicked*. *Cut off* may refer to deportation rather than death, although death for the wicked cannot be excluded. Ezekiel's sign act of *groan*ing focuses on the effect of the raid.

21:8–17   This sword song, spoken separately from the earlier oracle, is difficult in places. The meter is unclear, but it approaches the limping meter of a lament. Ezekiel likely brandished a sword wildly as he proclaimed this oracle. Verse 10b is hopelessly corrupt in Hebrew; it appears to rebuke the exiles for their view that Jerusalem is inviolable because of its Davidic connections. Similarly, verse 13 is incomprehensible: "Indeed, it looks like a group of words randomly thrown together, opening with an enigmatic reference to *testing*" (Block, *Ezekiel 1–24*, 679). NIV adds *Judah* to both verses without any textual support. Ezekiel is to accompany this song with actions: *wail*, *beat* his chest, *strike* his hands together three times. The threefold repetition signifies the completeness of the violence against its victims. When done, Yahweh's *wrath will subside*.

> **The Sword Song**
>
> *In this poetic form, the first line of a couplet has three stressed syllables, while the second line has two stressed syllables. Hebrew poetry rarely has regular meter or rhyme.*

21:18–27   In another sign act, Ezekiel depicts Nebuchadrezzar's decision to go to Jerusalem and destroy it rather than Rabbah. He uses three divinatory actions to receive an *omen*. Correct procedures were outlined for ancient Near Eastern diviners in omen texts. To *cast lots with arrows* simply required pulling a premarked arrow from a quiver. Scholars are uncertain about how the idols were *consult*ed. To *examine the liver* required a sheep sacrifice. The size, shape, color, density, and amount of fat around the liver all required careful interpretation to ascertain the gods' decisions. The decision, Yahweh claims, is his, not theirs. Not only will the people be deported, but also Zedekiah (*O profane and wicked prince of Israel*) will be removed for disloyalty to his vassal oath (compare 17:16–21). The NIV's *A ruin!* is better translated "Upside down!" All social structures will be inverted. Verse 27 echoes Genesis 49:10, but ironically inverts it: the reference is not to a messianic deliverer, but to Nebuchadrezzar, as the similar phrase at 23:24b confirms.

21:28–32   Verses 28–29 repeat phrases from the earlier sword song to announce the Ammonites' impending destruction. Another oracle about Ammon appears in 25:1–7. At verse 30, Yahweh addresses Babylon, telling its king, *Return the sword to its scabbard*; the executioner's task is done. Yahweh then claims to have *created* Babylon and thus to be entitled to *pour out wrath* on it. The point is the same here as in the inaugural vision: Nebuchadrezzar does Yahweh's work.

22:1–31   Three oracles asserting Jerusalem's impurity have been loosely assembled here. The first oracle (1–16) opens with a focus on Ezekiel. Just as in chapter 20, Yahweh asks whether Ezekiel *will judge this city of bloodshed*, highlighting again where his sympathies lie. Nahum (3:1) had earlier called Nineveh a *city of bloodshed*. If the parallel is intentional, Nineveh's fate forecasts Jerusalem's.

Jerusalem's sins break both segments of the Ten Commandments (to worship idols is to reject Yahweh, while bloodshed destroys community) and violate portions of the priestly legislation of Leviticus 17–26. Jerusalem has become the *infamous city*, an *object of scorn to all the nations*.

The first list (vv. 6–8) enumerates a rejection of Yahweh's values by *the princes of Israel*: parents are maligned, perhaps cursed (Exod 20:12; 21:17); *alien, fatherless*, and *widow* are exploited (see Exod 22:21–22); and *Sabbath* is violated (Num 15:32–36; Ezek 20:12–13, 16, 21, 24).

Next comes a list of sexual boundary violations (vv. 9–11). *To eat at mountain shrines* and *commit lewd acts* may refer to ritualized sexual intercourse with cult prostitutes (Num 25:1–3), but more likely simply means casual sex during community gatherings. The other matters listed are violations of purity laws found in Leviticus 18.

Finally (v. 12), the legal and economic foundations are flouted by judges who *accept bribes* (Exod 23:8; Isa 5:23; Amos 5:12) and those who charge *excessive interest* to a *neighbor*, that is, a fellow Israelite. All the sins listed are attributable to one cause: *You have forgotten me, declares the Sovereign Lord* (Deut 4:9, 23; 6:12; 8:11, 14; 26:13). Jerusalem's problems were no lapse in judgment but a wholesale defection.

Yahweh's sentence compactly rehearses the covenant curses (vv. 13–16). When they are invoked, the recognition formula will be fulfilled.

> **Metal Refining**
>
> *Refining was a two-stage process in which lead ore was melted to extract trace amounts of silver. The process also yielded copper, tin, and iron.*

22:17–22 The second oracle mentions no sins; instead, it presses a silver refining analogy, perhaps adapted from Isaiah 1:22, 25 and/or Jeremiah 6:27–30. In Ezekiel's analogy, the dross represents those left in the land after the deportations of 605 and 597 BCE; after Yahweh's fiery blast of 586 BCE, nothing salvageable remains. Bringing the *dross* into Jerusalem reflects the reality of ancient Near Eastern siege warfare. Rural Judeans would rush to fortified Jerusalem ahead of an advancing army. Jerusalem, however, became not the place of protection but a prison. This oracle also ends with the recognition formula.

22:23–31 The final oracle echoes previous indictments of Judean leaders and is addressed to the land. That the *land . . . has had no rain* [literally "deluge"] . . . *in the day of wrath* implies that on the day of wrath, it will be deluged. This echo of Genesis 6:5–7 foreshadows the cleansing rain of judgment ahead. Fishbane (461–63) suggests that the indictments against Judah's leaders echo Zephaniah 3:3–4. The *princes, priests, officials*, and *prophets* fail in their respective duties as trustees of the land and examples to the people to the point that *the people of the land* exploit the *poor, needy*, and *alien* among them. Rather than move to immediate sentencing, Yahweh mercifully searches for an intermediary *among them* and finds none. Because of the leaders' dereliction, Yahweh will *bring down on their own heads all they have done*.

23:1–49 Chapter 23 shares, multiplies, and intensifies the coarse sexual images of chapter 16 in an extended allegory of judgment against Yahweh's two "wives," Oholah and Oholibah. The allegory focuses on the alliances Israel and Judah made with Assyria and Babylon—alliances of a type strongly forbidden in the Mosaic covenant (Deut 7:1–7). The influence of Hosea 1–3 and Jeremiah 3:6–13; 5:8; and 13:27 is evident throughout.

Sensitive readers will find this section particularly vulgar. Nevertheless, Ezekiel seeks to offend his audience. As Taylor (170–71) puts it:

> Despite the distasteful theme and the indelicate language, the reader of these verses must appreciate that this is the language of unspeakable disgust and must try to recognize Ezekiel's passion for God's honour and his fury at the adulterous conduct of his covenant people. The feeling of nausea which a chapter like this arouses must not be blamed on the writer of the chapter, nor even on its contents, but on the conduct which had to be described in such revolting terms.

In verses 1–4, Ezekiel returns to a pornographic portrayal of Jerusalem's sins; Samaria is added to highlight Jerusalem's depravity by comparison. If the names *Oholah* (for Samaria/Israel) *and Oholibah* (for Jerusalem/Judah) once had significance, scholars can no longer recover it. The dalliances of the Israelites with foreigners begins in Egypt *from their youth* (compare 20:5–9). Ezekiel describes their willing participation with Egypt as *prostitution* in which *their breasts were fondled and their virgin bosoms caressed*. Hosea-like, Yahweh takes both as his wives and they bear him *sons and daughters*. Yahweh knew their character before he married them. Again, as in chapter 16, the practice of marrying two sisters did not in itself offend an ancient audience.

In verses 5–10, Ezekiel portrays Yahweh's marriage to *Oholah* (Israel) first. Oholah lusts after Assyrian men in uniform, a cipher for Jehu and Menahem of Israel currying favor with the Assyrian rulers Shalmanezer III and Tiglath-Pileser III in the ninth and eighth centuries BCE. Ezekiel describes their cravings in autoerotic terms (*defiled herself with all the idols of everyone she lusted after*). Moreover, her actions simply continued her previous whorings *in Egypt*, where she serviced men in her youth who squeezed her pubescent breasts and ejaculated on her. In return for her infidelity, Yahweh allows her *Assyrian* lovers to shame her in public, take *away her sons and daughters* for the slave trade, and *kill her with the sword*. This metaphorical description matches Israel's fate in the Assyrian deportation of 721 BCE, as well as standard treatment of women caught in adultery in the ancient Near East.

The historical recital continues in several stages (vv. 11–13). The historical referent is the alliance between Ahaz of Judah and Tiglath-Pileser III against Rezin of Aram and Pekah of Israel during the Syro-Ephraimite skirmishes against Assyria in the mid-730s BCE (compare 2 Kgs 16:5–14; Isa 7:10–16). The Assyrians, however, were conquered by the Babylonians (that is, the *Chaldeans*; verses 14–18). Oholah (Israel) had only one lover; Oholibah (Judah) will have three. Oholibah sought, but was ultimately left unsatisfied with, the Babylonians, and she *turned away from them in disgust.* This briefly alludes to the history of Judean-Babylonian relations from Hezekiah's rebellious invitation to Merodach-baladan in the late 700s BCE to Zedekiah's rebellion against Nebuchadrezzar in 588 BCE. Ezekiel saves his most graphic description for Zedekiah's alliances with Egypt in 588 (vv. 19–21). In extremely crude and graphic language that alludes to Leviticus 18:22–23, Yahweh attacks Oholibah's desire to return to the same Egypt from which he delivered her. In Egypt, she "fixated upon (becoming one of) their concubines," not NIV's *lusted after her lovers.* "Concubines" refers to women used sexually by men. Oholibah's (Judah's) desire is explained by a vulgar equine simile, possibly instigated by Jeremiah's metaphor (Jer 2:24; 5:8; see Ezek 16:26): her lovers had donkey-sized penises and profuse ejaculations. In the ancient world, such bawdy references bespoke an insatiable and debauched sexual appetite. Thus, Ezekiel combines the Mosaic prohibition against bestiality (Lev 18:23) with a culturally negative description of Egyptian lewdness. Still, Judah wanted to return to the sexual escapades of her youth in Egypt.

> **Oholibah**
>
> *"Queen Oholibah" is a character in British poet Algernon Charles Swinburne's (1837–1909) "The Masque of Queen Bersabe": "I am the Queen Oholibah:/My lips kissed dumb the word of Ah/ Sighed on strange lips grown sick thereby."*

In response (vv. 22–31), Yahweh will bring her lovers from *Pekod, Shoa,* and *Koa* to wage merciless war on her. Ezekiel likely chooses these places, not for their geographic location, but because their names have symbolic meanings: "punish," "cry for help," and "scream," respectively. The description of punishment is graphic.

Yahweh's sentence ends oddly with a drinking song (vv. 32–35). The Hebrew is incomprehensible at places, giving the impression that it is a drinking song about drinking sung by a drunk (Blenkinsopp 101). Ezekiel brilliantly mimics the complete loss of decorum to which Judah has sunk. The *cup* metaphor here represents Yahweh's full wrath (compare Isa 51:17, 22; Jer 25:15–29; 49:12–13; Ps 75:9) brought against both Oholah (Samaria) in 721 BCE and Oholibah (Jerusalem) in 586 BCE because they had *forgotten* Yahweh (8:17; 22:16).

> **Punishment of Adulteresses**
>
> *It was common ancient Near Eastern practice to disfigure adulteresses by cutting off their noses and ears. These responses metaphorically anticipate the horrors of Jerusalem's destruction.*

The chapter ends with yet more charges (vv. 36–49). Again, Yahweh calls Ezekiel to indict the sisters for sins already mentioned. To these, Yahweh adds blatant religious hypocrisy: *On the very day they sacrificed their children to their idols, they entered my sanctuary and desecrated it.* He again describes Israel's and Judah's foreign alliances in sexual terms, describing the *noise of a carefree crowd* indulging in an orgy. The sisters invite *drunkards* (NIV alternate translation) and *men from the rabble* for an exhausting round of sex. Verse 45 is an aside from Yahweh to Ezekiel and his audience, guiding them to an appropriate response: *Righteous men will sentence them* as adulteresses, rather than sympathize with their kinspersons in Jerusalem. The oracle ends with references to both the covenant curses and the recognition formula.

24:1–27 Two sections comprise this chapter, a parable song (vv. 1–14) and a parabolic drama (vv. 15–27). This is the final chapter in which the covenant curses are the primary message. Ezekiel has been prophesying for five and a half years.

Yahweh tells Ezekiel to take up, perhaps even enact, the *cooking pot* metaphor used by the Jerusalem leaders in 11:3. A celebration seems in the offing; the preparation is quite routine: a pot is filled with water, meat, and choice bones and is then set on a fire to simmer. *Woe!* is the first clue that the parable is an enacted judgment for *the city of bloodshed* (compare 22:1–12). The pot is Jerusalem, the meat is the leading Jerusalemites, the cooking is the siege of 587–586 BCE. The pot, however, had not been cleaned beforehand. Its patina (or "rust") and charred food deposits ruined the meal; the choice pieces must be removed. According to verses 7–8, the contamination is *the blood she shed in her midst*. Disregarding the purity laws for kosher preparation, the blood was not properly discarded (Lev 17:10–14); this symbolizes the improper burial rites of those unjustly slain. Their blood cries out to be requited (Gen 4:10; Job 16:18). So Yahweh stokes the fire; instructs someone to *cook the meat well* (literally, "completely"—that is, burned to a crisp). Instead of NIV's *mixing in the spices*, we should read RSV's "empty out the broth" to reduce everything to carbonized residue. Then, the *copper* pot is to be superheated to remove the residue. Verse 12, although quite difficult in Hebrew, claims that even this does not work; the pot is contaminated beyond use. Verses 13–14 sum up the point: Yahweh has tried to cleanse Jerusalem to no avail. The extreme covenant curses are being invoked.

The Seige & Fall of Jerusalem

Despite the accuracy intended by having Ezekiel record this date, this very date of Jerusalem's siege, scholars disagree on the date it represents. The Old Testament unanimously describes an eighteen-month siege before Jerusalem fell. According to 2 Kings 25:1, 3, 8 (which parallels Jer 39:1–3), Jerusalem was overrun in Zedekiah's eleventh year, which was Nebuchadrezzar's nineteenth year. By modern reckoning, this year ran from March/April 586 BCE to March/April 585 BCE. Almost all scholars agree that Jerusalem was captured in mid-July and the temple razed in mid-August 586 BCE. The siege, therefore, probably began on 5 January 587 BCE, Jerusalem fell on 17 July 586, and the temple was destroyed on 14 August 586. (Some scholars follow the chronology of Parker and Dubberstein and place the siege on 15 January 588 BCE and the fall of Jerusalem in July 587 BCE.)

As in previous sign acts, Ezekiel is to incarnate the role of Yahweh: he is not to lament, weep, cry, or perform any mourning rituals over (presumably) Jerusalem's fall (vv. 15–27). Throughout, Yahweh has said he will have no pity on Jerusalem (5:11; 8:18; 9:10). The message, however, is about more than Jerusalem; it refers to Ezekiel's wife, also. Unawares, he *spoke to the people in the morning, and in the evening* his *wife died. The next morning* he *did as he had been commanded.*

Ezekiel's audience expects the sign acts to have application for them, and they inquire what the death of Ezekiel's wife foreshadows. The significance is, Yahweh will *desecrate* his *sanctuary, the delight of* their *eyes, the object of* their *affection* (compare 7:21–22). Like Ezekiel, they are not to mourn the loss because whoring, blood-shedding Jerusalem's demise is deserved. Verses 25–27 directly address Ezekiel and form an inclusio with 3:24–27. When a Jerusalemite escapee (compare 14:22) appears with the news of Jerusalem's fall, the constraints imposed some seven years earlier will be lifted. Throughout, Ezekiel has been, and will remain, a *sign to them* of Yahweh's character as their covenant-keeping God. A further reflection on this event and its consequences appears in 33:21–22.

INTERLUDE: JUDGMENT ON JUDAH'S NEIGHBORS · 25:1–32:32

Chapters 25–32 separate the announcements of Jerusalem's siege (24:2) and fall (33:21). The oracles against Judah's neighbors serve both as a literary interlude— biding time while Jerusalem languishes in its siege—and as the beginning of hope for all who love the homeland. Those neighbors that welcomed Jerusalem's fall will fall themselves. All the undated oracles in this section assume Jerusalem has fallen and may be dated after July–August 586 BCE.

Isaiah, Jeremiah, Zephaniah, and Amos have similar collections of oracles against the nations. These oracles have been editorially arranged both geograph- ically and literarily, beginning in the northeast with Ammon and then proceeding clockwise to Moab, Edom, Philistia, Tyre, and Sidon. Finally, the seventh nation, Egypt, is decried in seven doom oracles, as is Tyre. The arrangement by sevens may be a literary figure symbolizing the totality of enemy nations and their complete punishment (compare Deut 7:2).

25:1–28:24 Five of these six neighbors gloated over the fall of Jerusalem. Yahweh had warned his own people against such arrogance: *Do not gloat when your enemy falls; when he stumbles, do not let your heart rejoice, or the Lord will see and disapprove and turn his wrath away from him* [*and toward you*] (Prov 24:17–18). Faithful to the people, Yahweh will be an enemy to their enemies.

25:1–17 The first five oracles are short and for- mulaic. After Yahweh is identified as speaker comes an indictment ("Because X did Y") and sentence

> **Israel & the Nations**
> Isaiah (15–16; 21:11–12; 14:28– 32) and Jeremiah (49:1–6; 48; 49:7–22; 47) also contain oracles concerning Ammon (in Jeremiah only), Moab, Edom, and Philistia in collections of oracles concern- ing foreign nations (Isa 13:23; Jer 46–51).

("therefore I will . . ."). The oracles criticize the nations for their war crimes. Each oracle ends with a variation of the recognition formula.

Longstanding animosity between Israel and Ammon (compare Josh 13:25; Judg 11:1–32; 2 Sam 10–12) had recently flared when the Ammonites harassed Judah around 600 BCE (2 Kgs 24:2). Most recently, Ammon gloated (*said "Aha!"*, an interjection of glee; see Ps 35:21–25) when the temple was *desecrated*, when Israel was *laid waste*, and when Judeans *went into exile*. As punishment, *the people of the East* (the Babylonians) will deport them. Nebuchadrezzar destroyed Ammon in about 570 BCE (see 21:28–32).

The *Moabites* denied the special bond between Yahweh and Israel by claiming *the house of Judah has become like all the other nations*. In one sense, this was sadly true. However, Moab took advantage of Yahweh's apparent inability to protect Judah after the exile by plundering Judean territory. Like the Ammonites, Moab, too, will belong to *the people of the East* as punishment for their treachery.

The kinship ties between Edom and Judah (Gen 25:21–34) make Edom's aid of Babylon's siege of Jerusalem in 587 BCE reprehensible, but the longstanding rivalry (Isa 34; Ps 137:7) makes it understandable. Yahweh's agent of *wrath* will, surprisingly, be *my people Israel* (see Obad 19–21) Significantly, the recognition formula has Edom coming to know *vengeance* rather than Yahweh.

The Philistines' vengeful attitude toward Judah is condemned. *Vengeance* is the key term here and the linkword to the previous oracle. They *acted in vengeance, with malice in their hearts*, and *with ancient* (better, "never ending") *hostility*. Yahweh will repay their vengeance with his own.

26:1–21 Seven well-arranged oracles against Tyre appear in 26:1–28:19. The first (26:1–7) follows the pattern of the four in chapter 25. The next three (26:7–14,

Nations of the Ancient Near East

15–18, 19–21) follow a death-mourning-burial pattern. Chapter 27 is an extended metaphor. The series ends with an irony-filled indictment and judgment (28:1–10) and a mock lament (28:11–19) against Tyre's ruler.

The Hebrew text does not preserve the correct date, but the Septuagint corrects the year number to twelve, yielding the date 3 February 585 BCE (compare Allen, *Ezekiel 20–48*, 71 n. 1a; Block, *Ezekiel 25–48*, 34–35). Tyre gloats (*Aha!*) that Jerusalem's lost commerce will now come to it. Ancient Tyre was the chief eastern Mediterranean port for trade from Egypt, Palestine, Anatolia, Arabia, and Babylonia, toward the west as far as Spain. It consisted of a mainland city and an offshore island port. In response to its glee, Yahweh will *bring many nations* against the mainland city and besiege it. The island port will also be destroyed. The oracle ends with the recognition formula.

Verses 7–14 are a detailed expansion of verses 1–6. Here, Yahweh names Nebuchadrezzar and his forces as the besieging conqueror of Tyre. The details of the siege are stereotypical. The *strong pillars* (v. 11) of Tyre's celebrated temple to Melqart (Hercules/Heracles) *will fall to the ground*. Yahweh promises that after Nebuchadrezzar's victory, Tyre *will never be rebuilt*. This promise cannot be taken literally, since the city was rebuilt.

This prophecy was not fulfilled literally. Nebuchadrezzar besieged Tyre in 585 BCE but withdrew in 572 BCE without breaching its walls. Yahweh acknowledges Nebuchadrezzar's failure in 29:17–19 and thus admits the essential failure of this prophecy. Sixty-five years later, Zechariah prophesies against Tyre (Zech 9:3–4), corroborating Nebuchadrezzar's failure. Tyre was ransacked by Alexander the Great in 332 BCE. Attempts to circumvent the clear admission of Scripture of this oracle's failure by transferring this prophecy from Nebuchadrezzar to Alexander fail the text's specific mention of Nebuchadrezzar as the conqueror, Tyre's history as a thriving commercial center into the Middle Ages, and the city's continual habitation into the present. Contemporary readers must not try to salvage this prophecy when even Yahweh admits its failure. Biblical prophecies were still under Yahweh's control and were not predictions that referred to irreversible, inevitable developments.

Verses 15–18 describe the anticipated international reaction to Tyre's destruction. The *coastlands* will *tremble* and their rulers (*princes of the coast*) will be *clothed with terror*. Tyre's fall jeopardizes these city-states' economic prosperity and signals their own vulnerability to attack. The *lament* both admits their own fear of Tyre as the *power on the seas* and their fright at having to negotiate the new situation its *collapse* brings.

Verses 19–21 are infused with ancient Near Eastern mythological views of death and the afterlife, and also assume Tyre's destruction by Nebuchadrezzar. Drawing on associations of *the ocean depths* with the primeval chaos, Yahweh will bring a cosmic tidal wave to *cover* the city to bring it *down to the pit*. Ezekiel's description of the realm of the dead (those who *dwell in the earth below*) assumes the three-tiered universe (subterranean world, earth, sky) of ancient Near Eastern thought. Tyre's consignment is permanent; it *will never again be found*.

27:1–36   Chapter 27 provides a single, extended metaphor of the trading ship *Tyre* loaded with cargo from around the known world that sinks in a storm on the open sea. The point is clear: Tyre's fall described in 26:1–14 will have a devastating impact on international trade in the ancient Mediterranean world. In verses 1–3a, Ezekiel presents this as a *lament*.

Israelites used *perfect in beauty* to describe Jerusalem (16:13–15; Lam 2:15); Ezekiel applies this description to Tyre to reflect the arrogance mentioned in 26:2. The city's fate will match Jerusalem's. Tyre (pictured here as a ship) was beautifully built and extravagantly outfitted. The craftsmen used the best local wood for its decking, mast, and oars. Its sails, banners, and awnings were of the finest *linen*. Its *veteran* crew were only the most experienced. Because of its expensive cargo, it also employed mercenary guards from *Persia, Lydia, Put, Arvad, Helech*, and *Gammad*—locations from around the known world.

The Nations Who Trade with Tyre
The number of nations mentioned here rivals the list in Genesis 10:1–30 and partly corresponds to it. Ezekiel's listing by nation has a discernible geographical order of west to east, south to north, and far northeast. Tarshish (*Tartessos in Spain*) marks the farthest western place name. Greece, Tubal, Meshech, Beth Togarmah, *and* Rhodes *are in Asia Minor and are listed among the Japhethites in Genesis 10:2–4.*

The *merchandise* that flowed through Tyre's docks was extensive. Among the goods listed are metal commodities and ores; slaves; all kinds of animals for work, wool, food, and fur; precious gemstones, ivory, and ebony; manufactured and dyed fabric goods; and consumable commodities like wheat, honey, oil, and wine. In short, the raw and manufactured wealth of the whole ancient Near East came to market in Tyre.

At verse 16, the sequence shifts from south to north, beginning with Edom (NIV alternate translation; "Aram" and "Edom" differ only in the middle letter, *resh* or *daleth*, in Hebrew; see comment at 6:14). Next are *Judah and Israel. Minnith* is directly east of Israel in Ammon. North of Israel lay *Damascus*, with *Helbon* and *Zahar* to its north. Because of another letter confusion, NIV's *Danites and Greeks from Uzal* should be "and casks of wine from Uzal." *Dedan, Arabia, Kedar, Sheba, and Raamah* are Arabian locales; *Haran, Canneh, Eden, Asshur, and Kilmad* are to the distant northeast. *Tyre's* loss would cripple the worldwide economy.

A gale, or *east wind*, clearly a cipher for Nebuchadrezzar and Babylonian armies, *will break Tyre to pieces*. All cargo and hands will be lost.

Ezekiel describes the response to Tyre's loss in stereotypical terms. Fellow sailors will mourn their lost comrades with loud wailing, *dust on their heads, rolling in ashes*, shaved heads, *sackcloth*, and lament. The lament proper in verses 32b–36 echoes 26:17–18. It rehearses Tyre's importance in international trade, bemoans

Tyre's calamitous loss, and finally admits that those who formerly reveled in associations with Tyre now find their relationship potentially problematic. Tyre's loss portended the same fate for its trading partners.

Although the oracle itself is remarkably free of references to Yahweh or to various sins, it is clear that the metaphorical *Tyre*, filled with arrogance, drowns in the watery chaos because Yahweh sends an east wind. Yahweh will ultimately destroy all forms of arrogance, Tyrian or otherwise.

28:1–10 This oracle denounces Tyre's *ruler*, Ethbaal III, for arrogance. He is portrayed as claiming to *sit on the throne of a god* in an ancient Near Eastern pantheon and thus be unassailable. Yahweh responds that he is *a man and not a god*, but with caustic, sarcastic irony, he "admits" that Tyre's king

> **Ancient Mourning Customs**
> *Putting dust on the head, rolling in ashes, shaving the head, tearing one's garment, wearing sackcloth, and loud wailing were all cultural means of expressing grief in Israel and the ancient Near East (see Amos 8:10; Isa 15:2–3; Mic 1:8, 16; Jer 25:34; 49:13).*

is wiser than *Daniel* (NIV's rhetorical questions in verse 3 are better read as ironic assertions; see RSV). The figure may refer to the Canaanite sage (compare 14:14) or to the biblical prophet *Daniel* who refuses to use his powers for gain (Dan 5:13–17). Verses 6–8 reflect the same punishment seen in earlier oracles against Tyre. In verse 9, with grotesque humor, Ezekiel portrays the defiant "god" Ethbaal informing his attackers (literally, "his desecrators") of his divine invulnerability. He will be as shocked at his fatal wound as his executioners will be delighted. Finally, in a sneering insult, Yahweh consigns Tyre's ruler to *the death of the uncircumcised* (Tyrians practiced circumcision). Once again, Ezekiel uses an offensive sexual term, much like some contemporary slurs question the marital status of one's parents.

28:11–19 Because this oracle lacks standard features of a *lament* and its description *concerning the king of Tyre* unmistakably reflects elements found in Genesis 1–3, it is best read as a satire of Ethbaal: if he is divine, he should be addressed and treated as such. Interpretations that perceive in this oracle the fall of Satan, as Calvin remarks on Isaiah 14:12, arise "from very gross ignorance, . . . these inventions have no probability whatever, let us pass by them as useless fables." The phrases *model of perfection, full of wisdom*, and *perfect in beauty* begin the extravagant satire. The remaining description weaves together elements of ancient Near Eastern mythology, Genesis 1–3, and prophetic denouncement (see comments on 17:24). The imagery and meaning are complex, but the lesson is not. The arrogance of Tyre, especially its *dishonest trade*, must be punished in a manner befitting its own grandiose view of itself.

28:20–24 This oracle against Sidon contains no specific charges. It ends in verse 23 with the standard recognition formula. Yahweh's purpose in punishment is simply to *gain glory*. Verse 24 rounds out the oracles against Judah's six closest neighbors by describing them as *painful briers and sharp thorns* (compare Num 33:55) and again closes with the recognition formula.

28:25-26 This brief announcement of blessing comes midway among the oracles against the nations and reiterates Yahweh's intent to bless his people after the covenant curses have been expended (compare Deut 30:1-10). *My servant Jacob* implicitly recalls the condition of blessing: Jacob/Israel will serve God in the manner they were created to do. Their regathering is not simply for their own sake, but so that Yahweh may appear *holy among them in the sight of the nations* (Exod 19:6). The promise of restoration ends with the recognition formula mixed with a shortened covenant formula.

29:1-32:32 As with the previous ones against Tyre, the seven oracles against Egypt follow no obvious sequence.

29:1-6A Ezekiel received this first oracle on 7 January 587 BCE, a few days after Jerusalem fell under siege. It is against both *Pharaoh* and *all Egypt*; as goes Pharaoh, so goes the nation. For Pharoah to claim *I made* the Nile *for myself* supplants Yahweh's role in creation. Yahweh, in the image of a crocodile hunter, will capture the beast and fling it into the desert to die. Its carcass will be *food* for *the beasts of the earth and the birds of the air*, a common ancient Near Eastern description of a shameful death without burial (Deut 28:16; 1 Sam 17:44, 46; 1 Kgs 14:11).

> **Pharaoh as Monster**
> *Pharaoh is described as an arrogant mythical* great monster lying among your streams, *that is, the crocodile, an oft-used symbol of the pharaoh.*

29:6B-12 Shifting metaphors, Yahweh calls Pharaoh a *staff of reed* (compare Isa 36:6). In 587 BCE, Hophra proved to be an insufficient military ally to Zedekiah during Jerusalem's siege (Jer 37:1-10). Although Yahweh forbade Israel to make military alliances with Egypt, he still holds Hophra accountable for his failure (17:18). Yahweh's punishment will encompass all Egypt *from Migdol to Aswan as far as the border of Cush*, that is, from the northern frontier in the Sinai to the southern border in northern Sudan. *Forty years* is a stereotypical, not literal, number that occurs throughout the Old Testament in similar contexts (for example, Num 14:33-35; 32:13).

29:13-16 Unexpectedly, Yahweh promises a diminished restoration for Egypt after its punishment (compare Isa 19:16-25). Unlike the other nations that are erased entirely, perhaps Egypt is spared because it did not gloat over Jerusalem's demise and attempted aid. This oracle contains three recognition formulas.

29:17-21 Ezekiel learns on 26 April (New Year's Day) 571 BCE that Nebuchadrezzar's forces made an unsuccessful thirteen-year attempt to starve and overrun Tyre. *Every head was rubbed bare and every shoulder made raw* from carrying dirt and fill for siege ramps in baskets atop the head or next to the head on the shoulders. Since the Babylonians *got no reward* from Tyre, Yahweh transfers the fulfillment of 26:7-14 to Egypt as a consolation prize. Yahweh also promises that, when Nebuchadrezzar conquers Egypt (*on that day*), the news will give Israel confidence that its restoration is near (*a horn* will *grow for the house of Israel*), and they will happily acknowledge that Ezekiel was right after all (*open your mouth among them*). Nebuchadrezzar invaded Egypt in 568 or 567 BCE; no extrabiblical records indicate the extent of his success.

30:1–26 This unit contains two oracles. The first is undated, but its opening lines connect to *on that day* in 29:21. It describes Nebuchadrezzar's defeat of Egypt and its allies *Cush, Put, Lydia, all the rabble, Libya, and the people of the covenant land.* Cush and Put lie in modern Sudan, and Lydia is in southwestern Asia Minor. The several uses of *that day, the day, the day of* Yahweh, and *a day of clouds* recall similar terms in 7:7, 10–12 (also Joel 2:1–2; Zeph 1:15). Egypt's destruction will come from both Nebuchadrezzar and Yahweh (vv. 9–19). Nebuchadrezzar and his army will *destroy the land* and *fill the land with the slain.* Yahweh will bring drought (v. 12) and fire (v. 16). The major urban centers *Memphis, Zoan, Thebes* (see Nah 3:8–10), *Pelusium, Heliopolis, Bubastis,* and *Tahpanhes* (most in northern Egypt) will be destroyed. All these sites were major centers of Egyptian worship. As with the ten plagues, Yahweh's actions will demonstrate sovereignty over the gods of Egypt (Exod 12:12). *Memphis,* the principal city and capital during most of Egypt's history, was associated with the god Ptah. Both Ptah and Pharaoh (*prince of Egypt*) will be removed. *Thebes,* in the south, was the center of Amun worship. *Pelusium* was an important eastern fortress; it would have been an initial casualty of Nebuchadrezzar's invasion. *Heliopolis* (On; 20:5–9) was the center of sun worship; *Bubastis* served as the center of feline worship. *Tahpanhes,* like Pelusium, was a northeastern fortress city. The terms *dark* and *clouds* may refer to the smoke of its destruction; more likely, this is apocalyptic imagery (32:7–8; Isa 13).

30:20–26 This oracle, received on 29 April 586 BCE, reflects Hophra's defeat by the Babylonians

> **God & the Gods**
> *The Bible frequently affirms that battles which "seem" to be taking place on earth among human beings are actually taking place in heaven between Yahweh and other gods or heavenly beings (see Exod 18:8–12; Judg 16:23–30; 1 Sam 5:4–7; 17:43–47; 2 Kgs 19:14–19).*

when he tried to aid Zedekiah (compare Jer 37:1–11). Ezekiel uses *arm* as a theme in a deliberate, ironic attack on Hophra's self-given pharaonic title, "Strong Arm." Babylon's victory against part of Hophra's army broke an arm of "Strong Arm." The broken arm symbolizes a severely crippled army division unable any longer to *hold a sword.* The oracle also suggests Babylonian troops will receive reinforcements against Egypt. The oracle applies two recognition formulas to Egypt.

31:1–18 Ezekiel speaks this three-part, single-chapter oracle on 21 June 586 BCE. The oracle begins and ends with a reference to *Pharaoh and his hordes.* "Hordes" (literally, "abundance") has a double meaning, referring to Pharaoh's armies and to his arrogance. Verse 2b asks Pharaoh to identify a peer in greatness; verses 3–8 present Ezekiel's hyberbolic portrayal of Pharaoh's "answer." Drawing from the ancient Near Eastern myths of the cosmic tree and the garden of the gods, "Pharaoh" allegorically compares his empire with Assyria. This tall "cedar" was well-watered by the heavy tribute from its vassal kingdoms. Assyria was a ruthless collector of *all the great nations*. Verse 7 summarizes; verse 8 makes an even more grandiose claim: *no tree in the garden of God could match its beauty* (compare 28:12–15). Yahweh interrupts to take credit for Assyria's might in verse 9.

The comparison is double-edged (vv. 10–14). If Egypt is equal in Assyria's grandeur, it must also be equal in its downfall. Assyria is judged *because it was proud of its height*. Its demise, here allegorically described as the felling of the cosmic tree, came when Nebuchadrezzar defeated Assyria at Harran in 609 BCE and at Carchemish in 605 BCE.

The *grave* (Hebrew *sheol*) welcomes all equally. Assyria's subjects, allies, rivals, and conquerors all become equal in the *pit* (vv. 15–18). For all its hubris, Pharaoh's Egypt will meet the same fate as the once great Assyria and also *the uncircumcised* (Egyptians practiced circumcision; Jer 9:25–26). Yahweh's last word against arrogance is the silence of a common grave of nations and people.

32:1–16 This sixth oracle occurs on 3 March 585 BCE. NIV misses the contrast of the opening lines; it is "You seemed like a lion . . .; instead, you are (merely) a monster in the seas" (compare NRSV). Instead of a *lion*, Egypt is more like a crocodile constrained by its habitat (29:3). The description of the captured crocodile left in the open to bloat, burst, rot, and be eaten by scavengers parallels gruesome Assyrian descriptions of discarding enemies' bodies (Greenberg 656). Egypt's destruction is described in apocalyptic terms similar to Isaiah's oracle of Babylon's fall (see Isa 13:1–14:27). The thorough darkness described is a lampoon of Egypt's chief deity, Ra the sun god (compare Exod 10:21–23).

32:17–32 The final oracle lacks a month in the date notice; it is probably 18 March 585 BCE. The force of this oracle is the same as chapter 31: both the great and the ignominious *go down to the pit*. NIV adds *say to them* in verse 19 without warrant. Egypt is addressed, not by Ezekiel, but by *the mighty leaders from within the grave*, a "Sheol welcoming committee." With a series of frequently repeated phrases, Ezekiel describes the rogue's gallery of dead nations where Egypt will take its place. Each nation, regardless of its earthly prestige, meets an identical fate: its demise occurs through shameful military defeat (compare Isa 14:3–21). These defeats are presumably handed out by Yahweh for each one's contribution to general chaos and terror. Boadt (324) may be correct that the quality of "sleeping arrangements" corresponds to one's honor in life.

The "Day of the Lord"

The language of darkened sun, moon, and stars appropriately describes a "day of the Lord" (Joel 2:2, 10, 31; 3:15; Amos 5:18–20; Zeph 1:15) and demonstrates how language that seems to describe the historical end of the world does not necessarily do so. As verses 9–10 demonstrate, the apocalyptic terms merely describe a calamitous international political, military, economic, and culture-shaping event. Its fulfillment is described in more common terms in verses 11–15: Babylon's destruction of Egypt.

Significantly, after Egypt arrives, seven nations inhabit this netherworld. The nations are listed by decreasing geographical distance from Egypt: *Assyria, Elam, Meshech and Tubal, Edom, all the princes of the north and the Sidonians* (that is, Phoenicians), and *Pharaoh*. Verse 27 in NIV reverses the point by making the first sentence into a question; it should read "They do not lie. . . ." Also, *punishment for their sins* should read "shields" (so NRSV, JB, REB).

EZEKIEL'S MESSAGE, PHASE II: COVENANT BLESSINGS · 33:1–48:35

Chapters 33–48 recognize that Jerusalem has fallen (see 33:21); Ezekiel's doom oracles are fulfilled. While Jerusalem's fall vindicates Ezekiel's early ministry, it drives the exiles to greater despair (33:10; 37:11). If they had suspected Yahweh was impotent because of their exile, Jerusalem's demise cemented the notion. However, Yahweh's enforcement of the covenant curses was the necessary prelude to recreating a full relationship with Israel (Lev 26:40–45). Ezekiel's later ministry is even more difficult than before. It will be hard to convince his companions in exile that Yahweh can now fulfill the covenant blessings.

33:1–33 This chapter has two purposes. First, it serves to renew Ezekiel's call. With Jerusalem's fall, Ezekiel's doom oracles are not only vindicated, but he is now permitted to tell of coming glory days. Yet the oracles of blessings do not assume unilateral action by Yahweh; the exiles must respond obediently. Preceding the oracles of blessing, this chapter lays the foundation for understanding them properly. Just as the covenant curses were not imposed apart from Israel's faithlessness, so the blessings will not be accomplished without Israel's future obedience. Israel's repentance is the necessary condition to enjoy these proferred blessings.

Verses 1–20 rework themes from 3:16–21 and allegorize Ezekiel's own ministry among the exiles. He indeed has been a faithful *watchman*. But the point now is not about Ezekiel's faithfulness. It is about his hearers' response: will they *take warning* or not?

> **Oracles of Blessing**
>
> *The oracles of blessing generally reverse the doom oracles, though not in a simple way. These oracles of blessing contain trans-historical and apocalyptic elements, along with heightened symbolism. Scholars disagree on the manner of fulfillment of these oracles.*

In verses 10–20, Ezekiel voices the exiles' despair and remorse. Their complaint echoes the final curse named in Leviticus 26:39. Ironically, Leviticus 26:40–41 announces the conditions of national restoration: the people must confess their sins and humble themselves. Yahweh's answer consistently repeats the call in 18:21–32: *Turn! Turn from your evil ways!* (see 18:30). Their national death will not please Yahweh, but, just as the watchman's warning could not make one respond (vv. 4–5), so Yahweh cannot force *the house of Israel* to turn.

Out of proportion to its importance, the announcement that vindicates Ezekiel's doom oracles and lays the groundwork for the blessing oracles is composed merely of two Hebrew words that mean "the city is struck." The report arrives on 8 January 585 BCE, almost five months after the temple was razed on 14 August 586 BCE. The night before, Yahweh *opened* Ezekiel's *mouth and* he *was no longer silent* (see 24:25–27). Ezekiel's silence had kept him from announcing blessings before their time. This announcement does little to change Ezekiel's audience.

Old attitudes die hard. Both those left in Judah (vv. 23–26) and those in exile (vv. 30–36) maintain views that prevent them from experiencing blessing. Nebuchadrezzar's forces do not deport everyone in Judah. The poorest are left to tend the fields (Jer 39:10). Yet even these *people living in those ruins in the land of Israel* still maintain the same arrogant attitude as their now-dead leaders. Their expectation to possess the land as Abraham's descendants fails to recall that Abraham's claim was a divine grant related to his fidelity to Yahweh. Ezekiel lists at least six different ways these inhabitants fail in their covenant commitments. For them, Yahweh invokes the covenant curses again to cleanse the land. After they are removed, Israel's only hope will be among the exiles. As verses 30–33 emphasize, many in exile are also faithless, coming to Ezekiel only to hear his erotic *songs*. They feign sincerity, but they come under no conviction. As Ezekiel had already recognized (20:49), his medium hampered his message. The reference to *all this* in verse 33 is unclear; whatever *it* is will vindicate Ezekiel. The chapter, strategically placed to guide the reading of the prophecies of blessing that follow, offers no real optimism that the exiles will return in heart to Yahweh.

34:1–39:29 In the following blessings, Yahweh frees Ezekiel to announce a period of unity, prosperity, security, and relationship with God. These oracles fall into three sections: oracles about Yahweh's sheep (34:1–31), about mountains (35:1–36:15), and about the land of Israel (36:16–39:29). The unexpressed purpose

---

The Fulfillment of Ezekiel's Promises of Blessing

Although modern interpreters sometimes argue over possible future fulfillment of Ezekiel's prophecies, his exilic audience would have expected the blessings to be fulfilled in as tangible, material, and literal a way as the curses, for both curses and blessings are announced in the same covenant and do not await Ezekiel's distant future (12:25–28; 36:8).

Biblical prophecy has within it the seeds of its own nonfulfillment. Jeremiah 18:7–10 articulates the principle of conditional prophecy: all prophecy regarding a people's well-being or woe has an inherent element of conditionality in it. For example, the Ninevites repented and were spared even though Jonah offered no conditions of reprieve (Jonah 3:6–10), as Jeremiah 18:7–8 allows. Ezekiel's exilic audience's situation confirms Jeremiah 18:9–10: the blessings were not fulfilled, presumably because they did not obey.

The category of unfulfilled prophecy recognizes that Yahweh's promises of blessing extend genuine offers to Israel that give tangible expressions to God's ultimate desires for them, but that such offers must be received in faithful obedience as the covenant relationship demands (Lev 26:40–45).

is to call the exiles to obedience by showing them what is in store if they obey. By once again extending the covenant blessings to exiled Israel, Yahweh demonstrates a readiness to act on "behalf of his holy name" by keeping covenant. Each section begins with Yahweh's determination to remove the defilements that make obedience difficult.

34:1–31   Ezekiel recycles and expands the oracle in Jeremiah 23:1–8. Both assume the Davidic covenant language of 2 Samuel 7. Verses 1–10 are indistinguishable from a doom oracle. *Shepherds* assumes the common ancient Near Eastern theme of a king as a shepherd over his people. The plural suggests that all leaders are in view. They are guilty of selfishness, seen in both passive neglect and active oppression, leaving the flock effectively with *no shepherd*. Fisch (229) suggests this neglect applies most pointedly to the most vulnerable in Israelite society, the widow, orphan, and alien. Yahweh, then, claims them as *my sheep*. The scattering here reflects the Assyrian and Babylonian deportations, and *wild animals* is a cipher for their deporters. It was customary to hold shepherds accountable for lost sheep. They either had to pay for those lost or bring a piece of a mangled sheep to the owner (Exod 22:13; Amos 3:12). Here, Yahweh *removes them*.

> **The Tasks of Shepherds**
>
> *Ezekiel 34:4, 16 delineates seven tasks of shepherds: seek lost sheep; bring back the strayed; bind up the injured; strengthen the weak; heal the sick; remove or destroy belligerent sheep that harm the peaceful; and treat the sheep gently, not harshly. The New Testament describes the responsibilities of elders in similar language (Acts 20:17; 28:30; 1 Pet 5:1–4).*

Yahweh, the primary actor in the remainder of the chapter, will regather his flock and protect it from external threats. *Scattered on a day of clouds and darkness* refers to the deportations that came with the falls of Samaria and Jerusalem (32:7–8). Yahweh's care is portrayed in idyllic fashion, and the justice lacking earlier will be abundant. In addition to scrutinizing the shepherds, Yahweh will also cull the sheep (vv. 10–17). This section suggests that Israel's leaders were not the only problem. Some among the exiles made life difficult for others. As in 20:37–38, the *rams and goats* are the oppressing upper classes that victimize those weaker among them. By removing the *shepherds of Israel*, however, Yahweh appears to cancel the Davidic covenant, particularly for a Davidide to be Israel's king perpetually. Verses 23–24 reaffirm Yahweh's pledge to be *their God*. Also, his *servant David will be prince among them*. This promise is irrevocable, but it is not unconditional (see Waltke 130–32).

Yahweh's blessings include more than a new leader; they will inaugurate a new phase of relationship with his people, a *covenant of peace* (compare especially Isa 54:7–10). *Peace* (Hebrew *shalom*) conveys many meanings here: harmony between Yahweh and the people, between Yahweh and nature, between oppressive and oppressed people, and between people and nature. The *wild beasts* could either be literal or refer to Nebuchadrezzar's armies or to the bad leaders. Verses 27–30 offer curse reversals to prove to *the house of Israel* that the faithful Judeans have Yahweh among them, even without a temple. Verse 31 echoes the covenant formula ("They will be my people, and I will be their God").

35:1–15 Having removed Israel's bad leaders and people and promised its ideal ruler, Yahweh addresses the external obstacles to Israel's coming prosperity. The oracle begins with the need to remove Edom (35:1–15) before the restoration of the mountains of Israel (36:1–15). The oracle against *Mount Seir* (a metonymy for Edom) is punctuated with four recognition formulas, a clear indication of Yahweh's severe hostility. The opening segment announces the outcome twice, *you will be desolate*. Yahweh will destroy Edom because it willingly assisted the Babylonians against Israel during Jerusalem's siege and afterward (Obad 11–14; Ps 137:7). This betrayal was the culmination of *an ancient* (better, "enduring") *hostility* going back to Jacob and Esau. Verse 6 mentions blood (Hebrew *dam*) four times in a veiled wordplay on Edom (Hebrew *'edom*). The latter part is better rendered, "Surely, it was bloodshed borne of hatred, and the blood avenger will pursue you." Edom will also fall because it annexed parts of Judah after it helped deport Judah's population. Like other nations, Edom *boasted against* Yahweh; like them, it will fall. The oracle ends with another twofold reference to *desola*tion. Yahweh has not deserted the land; he still guards *the inheritance of the house of Israel*.

36:1–15 Verses 1–15 are spoken to the *mountains of Israel* and assume the oracles against *the rest of the nations, and against all Edom*. Zimmerli (*Ezekiel 2*, 231–32) suggests this oracle is an editorially manufactured composite, evident from the sevenfold repetition of *This is what the Sovereign Lord says*. On the other hand, the repetition supplies strong reinforcement to Yahweh's claim to be able to act. It also reverses the curses of chapter 6. The initial section (vv. 1–7) responds to the enemies' gloating over the land's depopulation. In *typical fashion*, the nations uttered *gossip, slander, insults*, and *disgrace* against God's vanquished people (vv. 3, 15). In an application of *lex talionis* ("an eye for an eye"), the *scorn of the nations* against *the land of Israel* will return to the nations who gave it. Yahweh had always intended the land of Israel to be the site of blessing for his people (vv. 8–15). Landedness was an essential element of the promise to Abraham (Gen 12:6–7; 13:14–18; 35:11–13). Yahweh promises to make the land fertile (compare Lev 26:1–13) and to bring the exiles home (compare 11:7). Ezekiel's words clearly limit this promise to the exiles in Ezekiel's day. In retrospect, they did not return soon, and the land did not literally become all that was described for it here. The reason lay in the dispirited exiles' failure to repent.

Landedness was but one leg of a three-sided relationship (deity-people-land) assumed across many ancient Near Eastern theologies (see Block, *Gods*, 21–153). So interconnected were these concepts that, when a nation's land suffered natural calamities, or when a nation's people were massacred or deported, other nations assumed the defeat or impotence of that nation's gods. Thus, by invoking the covenant curses, Yahweh created a bad reputation for himself in the eyes of the nations. The remaining oracles through chapter 39 address these problems. Yahweh rehearses why the deportation was necessary (36:16–21), he reasserts the people's purpose to be a witness to the surrounding nations (36:22–38), and promises to reenliven the demoralized exiles so that they will reinhabit the land with joy, hope, and unity (37:1–28). Finally, events will confirm both Yahweh's power toward the nations and concern for the people and land when defeating Israel's enemies (38:1–39:29).

36:16–38 With a revolting simile, Yahweh explains Israel's deportation. Like blood in a menstruant's rag, the Israelites had saturated the land with defilement. Of necessity they were *scattered through the countries*. Significantly, in Leviticus, exile is among the last curses threatened. While Yahweh's people are off their land, it can *rest and enjoy its sabbaths* (Lev 26:34). Israel's exile, however, had the unwelcome effect of bringing Yahweh's ability and reputation into disrepute (*they profaned my holy name*). In response, Yahweh determines that divine honor is too important to allow the profanation to continue. In a replay of the exodus, Yahweh will reestablish the people-land relationship by bringing Israel *back into your own land* (see "my land," verse 5). In a reenactment of the covenant ceremony at Sinai (Exod 24:1–11), God will *sprinkle clean water on* them. The cleansing theme recalls the menstruant's responsibilities before reestablishing social contact (Block, *Ezekiel 25–48*, 347). In addition, God will supply them with a *new spirit*. This is not the in-dwelling Holy Spirit but the renewed national spirit described in 37:1–14. The reestablished deity-people-land relationship will be complete: *You will live in the land I gave your forefathers; you will be my people and I will be your God.* Wilson ("Ezekiel," 690) fails to see the conceptual parallels with Deuteronomy 30:1–10 and so wrongly asserts that Israel will return while still wicked. Verses 29–38 are typical expansions of previous language, with one surprise. Whereas before Yahweh refused to hear Israel's pleas (8:18; 14:3; 20:3, 31), he will *once again yield* to their cries (v. 37).

> **God & People**
>
> *"I am [will be] your God and you are [will be] my people"* occurs frequently throughout the Bible to denote the intimate mutual commitment of God and his people to each other (for example, *Deut 29:13; Hos 2:23; Jer 7:23; 11:4; 24:7; 2 Cor 6:16; Rev 21:3*).

37:1–28 The two oracles of chapter 37 continue to describe Israel's restoration. The elements of the vision of verses 1–14 arise from the exiles' despairing complaint in verse 11: *Our bones are dried up and our hope is gone; we are cut off.* This description is a metaphor for Yahweh's ability to inspire the dispirited exiles to renewed hope, obedience, and trust in his power to revivify them nationally. The envisioned bones are remains of bodies left unburied (29:5; 32:4–6). When asked, *Can these bones live?* Ezekiel defers answering, finally appearing to comprehend that Israel's fortunes lie with Yahweh's power. The *wind/breath/spirit* (Hebrew *ruach*) wordplay throughout echoes Yahweh's giving life to Adam in Genesis 2:7. The "resurrection" here is metaphorical, echoing a new exodus motif. NIV misleadingly capitalizes *Spirit*, wrongly implying fulfillment in the Christian era.

The exiles are at their lowest point, so low that the dead-in-the-grave metaphor is apt (vv. 15–28). To motivate them, Yahweh offers like terms of Israel's zenith: the peaceful days of the undivided kingdom under David and Solomon. In this final sign act, Ezekiel is to *join* sticks representing Judah and Ephraim (Israel) in his hand. The ancient rivalries will be more than permanently undone, as the thematic words *one/single* (Hebrew *'echad*) and *forever/everlasting* (Hebrew *'olam*) demonstrate. The promises repeat earlier ones. Since Yahweh is one (Deut 6:4), so Israel must be one. This intention will be realized most fully in their future combined worship in Yahweh's abiding *sanctuary*.

Reuniting Israel & Judah

Hezekiah (2 Chron 30), Josiah (2 Chron 35:1–19), Jeremiah (Jer 30:1–11; 31:1–9, 15–20), and Ezekiel (Ezek 37:15–28) championed a reunification of all Israel, which had been divided since the split under Jeroboam I and Rehoboam (1 Kgs 12:1–19).

38:1–39:29 The oracles against Gog and his allies continue Yahweh's promises of a bright future for the dispirited exiles. Modern readers, eager to discover the identity of an end time antagonist to God's people, wholly miss the point. While the language echoes ancient Near Eastern myths, contains apocalyptic symbolism, and groups a variety of elements by sevens, the audience is *my people Israel* (that is, the exiles), portrayed as having returned to *the mountains of Israel*. Given the exiles' present location and despairing attitude, Yahweh's promise once again addresses their deepest psychological fears, namely, that after their hoped-for return, Yahweh will summon the worst enemy imaginable to invade Israel, only to have it meet catastrophic and final defeat by Yahweh himself. In short, after Israel's future return, there will never again arise an enemy like Babylon.

Apocalyptic Language

The answer to the question in 38:17 is, "No, not literally, but yes, typologically." Apocalyptic language pervades verses 19–22. A literal fulfillment would bring untold destruction on the very land Yahweh is protecting! Here, the earthquake symbolizes Yahweh's direct intervention to change spiritual realities (compare Exod 19:18; Ps 97:4–5; Isa 24:18–20; Zech 14:4–5; Matt 27:51–53). The symbolic seven weapons Yahweh uses against Gog recall Yahweh's actions against Canaan (Deut 7:17–24).

38:1–9 All attempts to identify *Gog of the land of Magog* are speculative. Although some claim Gog refers to Gyges of Lydia, or stands as a cipher for Babylon, Gog and his seven allies simply personify the exiles' deepest fears that their ruinous experiences with Assyria and Babylon will be repeated in the future when they least expect it. The image of unfortified villages assumes that the covenant of peace (34:25–31) is in force. Three new allies join, bringing the number to ten, symbolically representing all of Israel's enemies. Just as he had previously used a willing Nebuchadrezzar for his purposes, Yahweh will now *show* himself *holy through* Gog *before* everyone's *eyes*.

39:1–16   Ezekiel farcically describes Yahweh's dispatch of Gog and his allies. Like a puppeteer, Yahweh twirls, drags, brings, and flings Gog *against the mountains of Israel*. Upon arrival, the ominous, menacing Gog, leader of the world's best-equipped armies, face-to-face with Yahweh, has his weapons knocked from his hands and drops dead before firing an arrow. Yahweh abandons the enemy to the *carrion birds and to the wild animals*—an image expanded upon in verses 17–20. After watching Yahweh defeat Gog from the sidelines, Israel collects seven types of arms to burn for *seven years*: *weapons, small and large shields, bows and arrows, war clubs and spears*. Gog and his allies will eventually be buried; it will take *seven months* to do so. The repetition of *seven* represents the finality of Yahweh's action. Removing all traces of Gog will finally *cleanse the land*. Ezekiel serves up humorously grotesque fare in this out-of-sequence expansion of verse 4. It is not hard to imagine a banquet hall, scavengers seated in an orderly fashion, garnished platters of dismembered body parts on the tables, and goblets filled with blood raised in toast to Yahweh's victory. Surprisingly, Yahweh serves the sacrificial meal of human flesh. Verses 21–24 summarize the negative themes of the book. Verses 25–29 summarize the essence of chapters 34–39. The final verse reasserts Yahweh's intention to revitalize the nation, seen in 37:1–14.

40:1–48:35   For ancient Hebrew readers, the details of chapters 40–48 provided the climactic end of Ezekiel's book. For contemporary readers, these same details seem almost insurmountably ancient and beyond our ability to grasp. Perhaps more than any other section of the Old Testament, these details remind us that this vision was not written to us; it was preserved for us. Earlier readers struggled, too, as Fisch (265) notes:

> The Rabbis of the Talmud (Men. 45a) remarked that only the prophet Elijah, who will herald the ultimate redemption, will elucidate these chapters. They added the observation that had it not been for Rabbi Chanina ben Hezekiah, who explained several of these difficulties, the Book of Ezekiel would have been excluded from the Scriptural canon.

Many contemporary interpreters hold that these chapters are best understood eschatologically (see Wilson, "Ezekiel," 693). While this view has a long history, it is fundamentally flawed. This vision represents Yahweh reaching out to his people in Babylonian exile. Despite the exiles' idolatrous attachment to Solomon's temple, Yahweh here amazingly offers to build another at which they can worship and offer atoning sacrifices (compare 45:13–46:15). These chapters provide for the returning exiles what the Mosaic instructions provided for the first generation of Israelites. As a vision preserved for us (not written to us) that was not and will not be fulfilled, these words still offer a glimpse into Yahweh's heart for Israel.

After a brief introduction (40:1–4), the vision falls into four large sections: the description of a new temple (40:5–43:11), its regulations for operation (43:12–46:24), its geographical setting (47:1–48:29), and the new city of Yahweh's people (48:30–35). In some sections, a large number of unique words and technical architectural terms make understanding precise details difficult.

40:1–4   Ezekiel saw this vision on 28 April 573 BCE, the second latest date notice in the book. The typical elements of a transport vision are present: the *hand of* Yahweh, the relocation to Israel, and the guide. The preponderance of multiples of five and twenty-five (for example, 40:7, 13, 15, 19, 21, 30, 47; 41:9, 14; 42:2, 16–20; 45:1–6; 48:8–22, 30–35) leads scholars to discern allusions to the Jubilee Year (Lev 25:8–38).

> **Enthronement Vision**
>
> *Some scholars have suggested that the vision of Yahweh's reenthronement, recounted in Ezekiel 40:1–4, occurred just days before Babylonians celebrated an annual ritual to enthrone their chief god, Marduk. Ezekiel must freely tell the* house of Israel everything he sees.

40:5–43:11   The guide takes Ezekiel through the visionary temple complex, meticulously measuring every area outside and inside. In all these, only one vertical measurement is taken (40:5). The temple's *outer wall*, too thin and short to be a fortification wall, marks boundaries and controls access.

The *burnt offerings, sin offerings,* and *guilt offerings* (40:39) mean the same things they did in Solomon's temple and in the tabernacle. Ezekiel also provides for the organization of temple space for priests and underscores the holiness of the entire building complex.

43:1–11   The meticulous measuring of the temple and its perimeter structures demonstrates to Ezekiel and his audience its perfect suitability for its

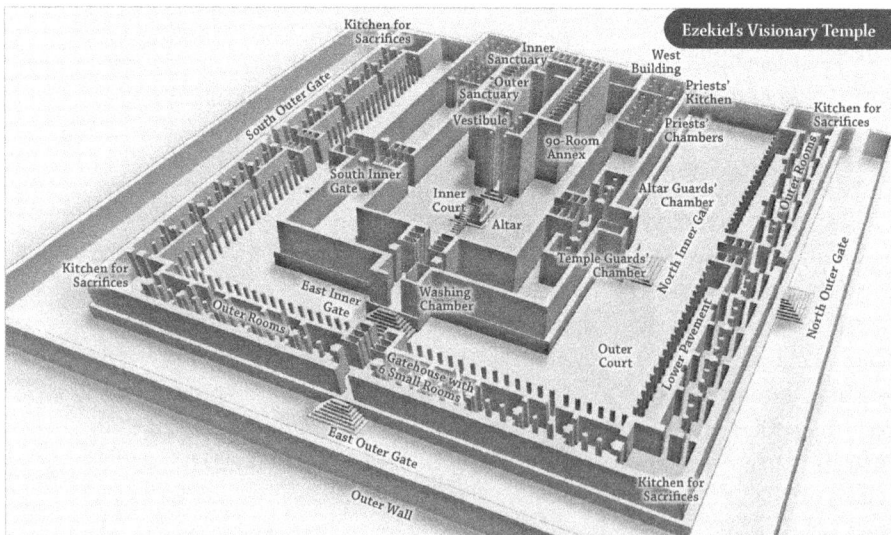

Ezekiel's Visionary Temple

divine inhabitant, who now returns. Ezekiel describes *the glory of the God of Israel* in terms similar to his earlier visions, but without mentioning the cherubim, previously protectors of Yahweh's holiness. Yahweh declares the temple to be *where I will live among the Israelites forever* (see 37:26–28). This indwelling, however, is conditioned upon Israel's renewed fidelity (v. 9). Ezekiel's audience would have been overwhelmed at the size and detail with which the new temple was constructed. The symmetrical perfection of the structures and Yahweh's meticulous attention to order demonstrate a deep desire to woo the people back.

43:12–46:24 With a new relationship between Yahweh and Israel, and a new temple in which to maintain it, comes the need for a new sacrificial system, administrators, and regulations. In this new environment, Ezekiel is cast as a new Moses, a new lawgiver. These new instructions (Hebrew *torah*) address many different issues. The new torah begins with the consecration of the new altar so that the relationship between Yahweh and the returned exiles can continue. In another clue that this vision offered a potential future to the exiles, Yahweh commands Ezekiel himself to be the inaugural priest at the altar (43:18–27; compare Lev 1–7). Ezekiel also receives *torah* for the Levites and Zadokites, the prince, the new tribal land allotments, and the ritual calendar. The exclusion of foreigners in 44:9 differs from the rule in Isaiah 56:1–8. Ezekiel 44:10–16 explains the postexilic distinction between priests and Levites, which does not seem to have been so hard and fast in the preexilic era. On the festival rules in 45:18–46:2, compare the somewhat different instructions in Leviticus 23 and Numbers 28–29. Again, Ezekiel's rules never went into effect, but they do show a powerful insight into the prophet's concern to express the beauties of Yahweh's renewed presence with Israel.

47:1–48:29 As noted earlier, a harmonious deity-people-land relationship was crucial for any ancient Near Easterner. So far in this vision, Yahweh has returned to his temple and has provided instruction to his people about how to maintain their renewed relationship through careful observance of sacrificial ritual. It remains for the final leg of the stool to be repaired. Yahweh's sanctification of the land comes by means of a *river* that inexplicably deepens without tributaries, flows over and through hills, makes fresh the most salty water on earth, and causes trees perpetually to produce fruit. But, in a vision, anything can happen. The near-mythical claims reinforce Yahweh's magnanimous offer. Life on their land, with Yahweh and the temple in its midst and as its life-giving source, would be indescribably and unimaginably wonderful . . . when they returned. Ezekiel 47:13–48:29 instructs Israel on how to parcel their property properly. This passage calls to mind Joshua 13–19.

48:30–35 In a wordplay, the former capital, the "City of Peace" (Hebrew *yerushalayim*) is replaced with "Yahweh is There" (Hebrew *Yahweh-shammah*). In keeping his promises to Jerusalem (16:53, 55), Yahweh reconstructs and renames the city.

This vision addresses the exiles' concern over the severed deity-people-land relationship. Their deportation had broken the people-land leg of that theological triad. The invasion of Judah had broken the deity-people leg, at least in the dispirited exiles' minds. The destruction of the temple had broken the third leg. But Ezekiel's visions assert Yahweh's faithfulness. God had reestablished the temple with exquisite care, then reinhabited it. God had destroyed Israel's enemies in the guise of Gog. One more leg was left to mend: the people must return from exile, both physically and spiritually. Yet, Yahweh cannot coerce this most important move. The exiles' return must be their own doing.

THEOLOGICAL REFLECTIONS

That Yahweh would use Ezekiel seems remarkable. Throughout, we get hints that Ezekiel was hardly a willing prophet. The few times he speaks directly to Yahweh, he shows ignorance, recalcitrance, or irritation. His sympathies lay with Jerusalem and its leadership rather than Yahweh. One wonders whether Ezekiel's vulgar language was given by Yahweh, or whether Yahweh used a priest already practiced in coarse speech. The latter view should not surprise; Yahweh seems to delight in choosing the problematic and unpolished to speak for him, as the choices of Moses, Balaam's ass, Micaiah ben Imlah, Amos, Jeremiah, and Jonah make clear. These choices show that Yahweh is prone to act through difficult and unlikely means. His primary covenant partner Abraham was a polytheist (Josh 24:14), prone to half-truths and stubbornness. The nation descended from him was barely worth notice from the start, and had adopted Egypt's religious views as its own. Its second king, a "man after God's own heart," was arguably a rapist, certainly a murderer, and a negligent father. Israel's third king was the very model of inconstancy: he built Yahweh's temple but married the daughters of the nations.

Yet remarkably Yahweh persists in working through all these and others like them. That Yahweh chooses to use imperfect spokespersons to declare faithless, despairing Israelites in exile his "remnant" should give his imperfect, sometimes doubting servants of today hope.

Many view Ezekiel's repetitious use of the recognition formula "Then they will know that I am the Lord" as a claim that Yahweh is in omnipotent control. Perhaps more than any other Old Testament book except Psalms, Ezekiel proclaims Yahweh's sovereignty over history. Or so it seems. Most often the formula functions to assert that, when the covenant curses come to fruition, both the exiles and those remaining in Judah will perceive the calamities as intentional invocations of the curses by Yahweh (Ezek 6:7, 10). The realization that Yahweh faithfully executed the covenant curses will permit Israel to anticipate his faithful orchestration of the covenant blessings. The exiles had experienced the curses: they had survived Jerusalem's siege in 597 BCE, witnessed the deaths of friends in that event, and suffered deportation. Nevertheless, Ezekiel's companion exiles never turned their minds to the covenant. Instead, they despaired at Yahweh's inability to protect them and sneered at prophetic pronouncements. That the blessings were not materially fulfilled to them suggests that most never came to recognize Yahweh's invocation of the curses as the prelude to the certainty of his blessings. The restored blessings-curses-blessings sequence of the covenant was not realized as Yahweh hoped.

What, then, is one to make of Ezekiel's portrayal of Yahweh's sovereignty? Contemporary readers who assign all events to Yahweh's omnipotent, omniscient control are rightly caught short by Yahweh's unrealized plans and prophecies. Fundamentally, the conditions for Yahweh to enact blessings are limited by the same covenant condition that assigns the curses (see 18:30–32; 33:10–20). The essential nature of the relationship between Yahweh, intoned by the covenant formula, "I will be their God and they will be my people," requires reciprocal fidelity. Yahweh self-limits sovereignty to allow room for free, genuine response. Despite Yahweh's intense desire for Israel's happiness, and equally intense dislike for sin, Yahweh awaits Israel's genuine repentance (Lev 26:40–46; Deut 30). To act unilaterally after invoking the curses, apart from Israel's return, would undermine the very faithfulness the recognition formula communicates. Yahweh faithfully waits for Israel to turn. Until then, self-imposed covenant limitations only permit Yahweh to plead for Israel's return.

FOR FURTHER STUDY

Kutsko, John. *Between Heaven and Earth: Divine Presence and Absence in the Book of Ezekiel*. Winona Lake, IN: Eisenbrauns, 1999.
Launderville, Dale F. *Spirit & Reason: The Embodied Character of Ezekiel's Symbolic Thinking*. Waco, TX: Baylor University Press, 2007.

WORKS CITED

Allen, Leslie C. *Ezekiel 1–19*. Dallas: Word, 1994.
———. *Ezekiel 20–48*. Dallas: Word, 1990.
Blenkinsopp, Joseph. *Ezekiel*. Louisville: John Knox, 1990.
Block, Daniel I. *Ezekiel 1–24*. Grand Rapids: Eerdmans, 1997.
———. *Ezekiel 25–48*. Grand Rapids: Eerdmans, 1998.
———. *The Gods of the Nations: Studies in Ancient Near Eastern National Theology*. 2nd ed. Grand Rapids: Baker, 2000.
Boadt, Lawrence. "Ezekiel." In *The New Jerome Biblical Commentary*, edited by Raymond Brown et al., 305–28. Englewood Cliffs, NJ: Prentice-Hall, 1990.
Calvin, John. *Commentary on the Book of the Prophet Isaiah*. Translated by W. Pringle. 4 vols. Grand Rapids: Christian Classics Ethereal Library, 1999.
Fisch, Solomon. *Ezekiel*. London: Soncino, 1960.
Fishbane, Michael. *Biblical Interpretation in Ancient Israel*. Oxford: Clarendon, 1985.
Fredenburg, Brandon L. *Ezekiel*. Joplin, MO: College Press, 2002.
Goldingay, John. *Models for Interpretation of Scripture*. Grand Rapids: Eerdmans, 1995.

Greenberg, Moshe. *Ezekiel 21–37*. Garden City, NY: Doubleday, 1997.

Kaufman, Stephen A. "The Structure of the Deuteronomic Law." *Maarav* 1, no. 2 (1978–79): 105–58.

Lust, Johan. "Ezekiel 36–40 in the Oldest Greek Manuscript." *Catholic Biblical Quarterly* 43 (1981): 517–33.

Nissinen, Marti, C. L. Seow, and Robert K. Ritner. *Prophets and Prophecy in the Ancient Near East*. Atlanta: Society of Biblical Literature, 2003.

Smith, Mark S. *The Early History of God*. 2nd ed. Grand Rapids: Eerdmans, 2002.

Stuart, Douglas. *Hosea–Jonah*. Waco, TX: Word, 1987.

Taylor, John B. *Ezekiel*. Downers Grove, IL: InterVarsity Press, 1969.

Tov, Emanuel. "Recensional Differences between the MT and LXX of Ezekiel." *Ephemerides theologicae Lovanienses* 62 (1986): 89–101.

Waltke, Bruce K. "The Phenomenon of Conditionality within Unconditional Covenants." In *Israel's Apostasy and Restoration: Essays in Honor of Roland K. Harrison*, edited by Avraham Gileadi, 123–39. Grand Rapids: Baker, 1988.

Wilson, Robert R. "Ezekiel." In *Harper's Bible Commentary*, edited by James L. Mays: 652–94. San Francisco: HarperSanFrancisco/Society of Biblical Literature, 1988.

———. "Interpretation of Ezekiel's Dumbness." *Vetus Testamentum* 22 (1972): 91–104.

Zimmerli, Walther. *Ezekiel 1*. Translated by Ronald E. Clements. Philadelphia: Fortress, 1979.

———. *Ezekiel 2*. Translated by James D. Martin. Philadelphia: Fortress, 1983.

Daniel

Mark W. Hamilton

CHAPTER CONTENTS

MAPS, TABLES, & FEATURES

The book of Daniel has long inspired Jews and Christians with its lessons of faithfulness in adversity. In reading this story of people who remained faithful to God even when great powers threatened their existence, it is important to keep a few things in mind.

CONTEXTS

Daniel is really two books in one. Chapters 1–6 contain a series of stories about wise Jews at the royal court. Chapters 7–12 contain several visions about a future resolution of the conflict between good and evil. Also, the book is written in two different languages: 1:1–2:4a and 8:1–12:13 are in Hebrew, while 2:4b–7:28 are in Aramaic. Originally, the court stories in the book circulated orally apart from the apocalyptic section at the end. By combining these differing materials, the author of Daniel captures a flavor of foreignness and alienation.

The two parts of the book are nevertheless interlinked, not only because they are about the same person, but also because they consider the same problem—how to be God's people under foreign rule. Literarily, chapters 2–7 are arranged in a ring structure: 2 and 7 report visions of the coming divine kingdom; 3 and 6 discuss potential martyrdom of Jews who worship God alone; and 4 and 5 expose

Events in the Book of Daniel

(all dates below are BCE)

605 *Nebuchadnezzar of Babylon makes Judah a vassal state*

586 *Nebuchadnezzar destroys Jerusalem and ends the state of Judah*

539 *Babylon's last king, Nabonidus, and his son Belshazzar lose their kingdom to the Persian emperor Cyrus*

322 *Alexander the Great, king of Macedonia, destroys the Persian empire*

301 *Alexander's successor divides his empire; Palestine comes under the rule of Ptolemy, now king of Egypt*

200 *Palestine passes to the Seleucid dynasty, rulers of Syria and Mesopotamia*

167 *Antiochus Epiphanes, king of Syria, tries to impose the worship of Greek gods on the Jewish population, which in turn revolts*

164 *Antiochus dies; there are no later events referred to in the visions of Daniel*

arrogant kings. This careful arrangement, with chapter 7 as a bridge between the book's two parts, creates an overarching unity.

The book covers events over a period of several centuries. The stories describe the Jews' exile under the Babylonians in the 500s BCE, while the visions concern mostly events from Alexander the Great down to the Jewish revolt of the 160s BCE. Whatever the time period, however, the major theological issues are the same.

The first half of the book concerns the era of the Neo-Babylonian and early Persian empires. Here we see life at court, as a courtier like Daniel tries to live faithfully to God and loyally to his king, despite the fact that some of his royal masters are less than sensible. Here the book echoes a theme that is widespread in Jewish literature of the Second Temple period, the foolishness of the Gentile king. Compare the drunken, out-of-control Ahasuerus in the book of Esther or dismissive statements about kings in Ecclesiastes. Jews took a dim view of foreign royalty. In this they share the attitudes of other people subject to the great empires. Greek texts also portray Persian kings as drunken tyrants, much as Esther does, for example.

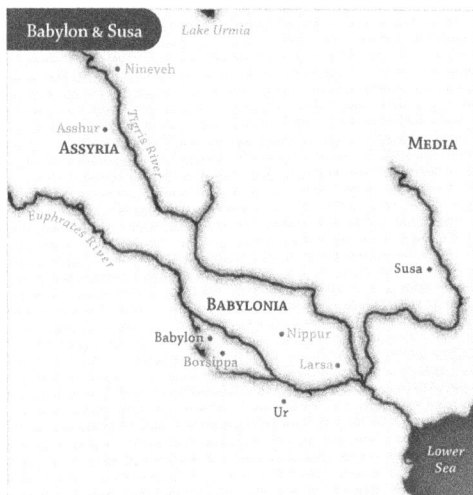

Babylon & Susa

These chapters do, however, believe that faithful people can survive in the dominant system. By attending to prayer and food laws and by avoiding idolatry and acts of injustice, the good

Jew can excel, even at court. Indeed, such a person's success can be a sign of God's protection of the chosen people.

The second half of the book takes a different view. Here events have darkened the picture. No longer can Jews survive under the present conditions of empire. And so God will intervene to rectify the situation and bring in the eternal kingdom. The shift is understandable in the light of the changing conditions of the second century BCE, as Jews came under increasing pressure to assimilate to Hellenistic (Greek) ways of life.

The hero of these stories is God, who speaks to the powerful through Daniel. God's words of judgment and hope inspire the book's readers with the knowledge that the powers that be do not survive forever and that present adversity will soon give way to a time of triumph.

The book's human heroes, Daniel and his three friends, must make tough decisions about how to live faithfully in a foreign land. These stories must have inspired Jews living under similar constraints.

The visions of the last half of the book do not describe a far distant future. Rather, they describe a time in real history, the early second century BCE, when Jews in Palestine had to fight for the very survival of their faith and their people. The visions do not merely recount history. They offer hope.

Finally, the book of Daniel provided visionary language for later prophets to use in interpreting their own times. The most obvious example of this process is the book of Revelation, which applies Daniel's language to the Roman Empire of the first century. Whenever religious people live under duress, such language helps express hope and trust in God. However, Daniel and Revelation do not refer to the same historical events, but only parallel ones.

COMMENTARY

LIFE AT COURT · 1:1–6:28

The stories in chapters 1–6 portray life at the royal courts in Babylon and Susa, not in a systematic way but from the point of view of a Jewish community struggling to maintain its existence under foreign control. The stories identify major boundary markers of Jewish identity, especially diet, avoidance of idolatry, and prayer to Yahweh. Other possible markers, such as names or careers, appear less important, and indeed Daniel and his friends take Babylonian names and work in the royal bureaucracy. Thus the stories do not value separation from the pagan society but rather steady application to ways of life that will succeed within it while still remaining loyal to the faith of Israel. The stories also address the crucial theological question of how Yahweh rules over the nations when Israel no longer experiences political independence (Albertz 20).

1:1–21 The opening story connects Daniel's life with the end of the kingdom of Judah, though with a problematic dating of his deportation to the third year of Jehoiakim (606 BCE). Jeremiah 25:1 dates Nebuchadnezzar's invasion to the

Additions to Daniel

The text of Daniel differs extensively between the Hebrew/Aramaic version and the Greek translation (the Septuagint). The latter includes three significant additions, all predating the time of Jesus. Between 3:23 and 3:24 the revisers of the book inserted the "Prayer of Azariah and the Song of the Three Young Men," a poem that is 68 verses long and that combines lament and praise. After chapter 12, they inserted two detective stories, "Bel and the Dragon" and "Susanna." In the first, Daniel proves that the Babylonian god Marduk does not eat the sacrifices that people give him; the priests of Marduk do. In the second, Daniel defends a wrongly accused Jewish woman from lecherous old men she has spurned. All the stories pick up themes seen elsewhere in the book, especially the dangers of living under pagan rule and the need to honor God in spite of adversity. Most editions of the Apocrypha print these additions separately from the biblical book, often under the label "Additions to Daniel," even though no ancient text transmits them separately from the rest of the book.

following year at the earliest, while Babylonian records indicate a date of about 598 BCE for the first siege of Jerusalem (see Collins 130–31). However one resolves the problem, the book aims to portray Daniel and his friends as typical of all Jews (though extraordinarily talented) living in the Diaspora.

Verses 3–7 describe a process of recruiting and training potential leaders in the Babylonian government. Such a practice did occur in the ancient empires, and some evidence exists for Assyrian, Babylonian, and Persian bureaucrats who were members of subject peoples, even if such persons rarely rose to the top of the political structure. Verses 3–4 describe qualifications of ideal leaders, at least according to ancient thinking: descent from leaders, physical excellence, and intelligence. The NIV's *language and literature of the Babylonians* should be translated more literally "the book and language of the Chaldeans." That is, the boys learn to write Akkadian cuneiform (on clay tablets), especially texts related to telling the future (divination). Thousands of such texts exist from ancient Mesopotamia.

The Diaspora

After the destruction of Jerusalem in 586 BCE, Jewish communities sprang up all over the Near Eastern and Mediterranean worlds. The resulting Diaspora, or "dispersion," remains a major factor in Jewish history until the present day. Until the twentieth century, Jerusalem remained only one center of Jewish life, and life outside the promised land became a standing issue for Jewish thinkers and leaders.

Changing the names of the captives (v. 7) integrates them to some extent into Babylonian society. Like many ancient names, some of theirs constitute sentences making explicitly theological statements. Thus Belteshazzar means "protect the king's life," and Abednego is a distortion of "servant of Nabu" (a major Babylonian deity). The other two names' meanings are less clear (Collins 141). Jews in the sixth through the third centuries BCE often used Babylonian or Persian names (for example Esther equals "Ishtar" and Mordecai equals "Marduka"). However, such names did not indicate unfaithfulness to Judaism, a point this book emphasizes in the following stories.

The test of Daniel's resolve (vv. 8–16) involves food. No specific law in the Pentateuch forbids consuming Gentile food or wine, but Daniel opts for a vegetarian diet in order to avoid eating non-kosher meat. Later Jewish law forbade the eating of Gentile food for the same reason. The head eunuch (NIV *chief official*) allows a ten-day test, which results in Daniel's success. The eunuch's fear for his *head* (v. 10) is surely a figure of speech calculated to intimidate Daniel into eating. Daniel makes a counteroffer, however. The story reminds ancient readers of the importance of observing the food laws and of negotiating openly with Gentiles in order to live an observant Jewish life. It assumes that such a diet will prove its superiority so that no one need worry about further concessions.

Verse 17 summarizes the boys' early career in a way reminiscent of 1 Samuel 2:26 (compare Luke 2:52). Their accomplishments, all gifts from God, include a high level of literacy ("understanding in every book"). Scribes in antiquity specialized in certain kinds of documents, though the most highly skilled ones could produce everything from literary texts to royal inscriptions to letters to transcripts of rituals. Daniel, apparently unlike the other boys, could interpret dreams and thus gain access to the ultimate source of knowledge, heaven.

2:1–49 Daniel 2 describes a dream of Nebuchadnezzar's. The text contrasts the Babylonian diviners, who have no access to divine insight, with Daniel, who does. Thus the contrast works on two levels: Daniel versus the pagan soothsayers, and Yahweh versus the idols. Even more importantly, the dream sets up a contrast between God's eternal kingdom and those transient human kingdoms that dominate Israel.

> **Divination & Magic**
> *Ancient readers assumed that these practices had some validity. They worked. However, they involve danger, and so many parts of the Bible severely restrict them (for example Lev 19:26; Deut 18:9–13). Yet Joseph (Gen 44:5) as well as Daniel and his associates tell the future and excel others in doing so.*

Verse 4 marks the transition from Hebrew to Aramaic as the language of the text. This shift heightens the exotic nature of the following stories of life at court.

While some Christian readers continue to identify the kingdoms mentioned in chapter two with whatever empire dominates their own time, scholars have fallen into two basic camps. Conservative scholars have identified them as Babylon, Persia, the Hellenistic kingdoms, and Rome. This typology rests on the assumption that the kingdoms of Daniel coincide exactly with those of the book of Revelation. Christian readers historically have understood the text in this way and have seen the triumphant kingdom of 2:34, 45 as the church. Most scholars, however, understand the kingdoms to be Babylon, Media, Persia, and the Hellenistic realms. The second interpretation rests on two facts: the visions of chapters 7–12 concern the Hellenistic kingdoms and nothing later (Rome is mentioned only as the Kittim in 11:30; they are not yet a dominant empire); and Greek ideas about four successive kingdoms, dating to the centuries just before and after the life of Jesus, identify Babylon, Media, Persia, and Greece as a series. On the other hand, the fact that Media never dominated Israel presents a problem for this interpretation.

Although the second interpretation is more probable, either view yields the same theological point: God will intervene in the affairs of the oppressive dominant powers in order to vindicate truth and right. The kingdoms of the world will give way to the kingdom of God.

Daniel 2 shares basic elements with Genesis 41: a king has a dream that no diviner can interpret; an Israelite in God's name offers the correct understanding; and the king rewards the Israelite. Daniel's story adds a level of challenge in that Nebuchadnezzar demands that his diviners guess the dream itself. Perhaps this element illustrates his basically tyrannical nature (v. 15), but it especially highlights Daniel's (and thus Yahweh's) superiority to the Babylonians. Daniel's foreign colleagues argue that Nebuchadnezzar's request is unprecedented, thus implying that, since kings should rule according to ancient custom (as the Babylonians certainly believed), his request lacks merit. They also argue that only the gods can do what he asks (v. 11). For the author of Daniel, this is the critical point. Only the hero Daniel has access to divine knowledge.

> **The Kingdom of God**
>
> *The term "the kingdom of God" is rare in the Old Testament, but it appears in 1 Chronicles 28:5 and 2 Chronicles 13:8. God is often called king. But the kingdom does not equal Israel, nor is it necessarily something lying far in the future. "Kingdom" is a metaphor for the perfect reign of God, which is breaking into the world. And so it is in Daniel.*

Verses 20–23 contain an eloquent prayer for help by Daniel. He seeks not to impress Nebuchadnezzar, but to survive the test. The opening in verse 20 offers phrases typical of psalms of praise (for example, Pss 113; 134; 135; compare Ps 122). Verse 21 in this context pointedly criticizes the Gentile kings, noting their subjection to the God of Israel. Verse 22 alludes to an idea of God as the knower and revealer of secrets (see Job 28; Prov 25:2). The specific secret now revealed concerns Nebuchadnezzar's dream (v. 23).

The audience with the king, like Joseph's (Gen 41:15–36), focuses attention on Yahweh. Daniel agrees with the Babylonian diviners that no human being can both tell and interpret the king's dream, but this impossibility becomes further proof of the might of the God of Israel (v. 28).

The description of the dream (vv. 31–46) maps out the history of Jewish subjection prior to the Maccabean revolt (Collins 166–68). The metals become progressively stronger and less valuable, indicating the decreasing status of Jews under foreign rule. The division of the fourth kingdom symbolizes the breakup of Alexander's empire into several major powers. Two of them, Egypt under the

Ptolemies and Syria-Mesopotamia under the Seleucids, fought over Palestine, which lay at the border of their realms.

The theological climax of the vision comes in verses 44–45, which expects God's decisive intervention in human history. The *rock cut out of a mountain* refers to the chosen people of Israel, as in Isaiah 51:1–2 (Seow 47). God will not abandon Israel even when Gentile kingdoms seem most powerful. The vision closes with a notice of the elevated status of Daniel and his colleagues (vv. 48–49).

3:1–30   The text opens and closes with the actions of Nebuchadnezzar, indicating the degree to which faithfulness is a matter of response to the decisions of others. The three Hebrew men, now provincial governors, fall victim to slander by opportunistic opponents, who charge them with not worshiping the king's gods and thus of being disloyal. According to the slanderers, true worship shows disloyalty to the dominant system. The chapter follows a seven-part narrative flow: an introduction (vv. 1–7); an accusation (vv. 8–12); the confrontation with the king (vv. 13–18); the king's condemnation of the Jews (vv. 19–23); the king's astonishment (vv. 24–25); God's deliverance (vv. 26–27); and the king's proclamation (vv. 28–30). The proclamation of tolerance in verses 28–29 makes the story's main point. Since only Yahweh can save in such a dramatic fashion, ridiculing either Jews or their faith makes no sense. A sensible ruler, even if a pagan, should honor Israel and its God, and the state has an interest in insuring religious tolerance of the Jews. The story thus, ultimately, makes the same point as the book of Esther.

Although enforced idolatry was rare in antiquity, Jews undoubtedly experienced the pressure to conform as they engaged in business dealings and other kinds of relationships with their polytheistic neighbors. Also, martyrdom was uncommon, though it did happen. Stories about martyrdom—or as here, the divine rescue from impending martyrdom—encouraged Jews to be faithful even under the most extreme circumstances.

Gigantic statues (v. 1) did exist in antiquity (Collins 180). This one may have been overlaid in gold (compare Isa 40:19). Its odd dimensions (a height ten times its width) would have made it unstable. Possibly, the author is satirizing the Babylonians' lack of realism (compare Haman's 75-foot-high gallows [Esth 5:14]), a level of stupidity finding its fullest expression in their idolatry.

Verse 2 lists officials in the Babylonian empire (though the titles actually come from Persian administration). The list highlights the bravery of the three Jews, who resist such a large crowd. The story does not mention Daniel, probably because

What Did the Men Pray?
At Daniel 3:24, the Septuagint adds the "Prayer of Azariah and the Song of the Three Jews," a beautiful hymn of praise (vv. 1–22), description of the Babylonians' troubles in intensifying the fire (vv. 23–27), and a second prayer of praise (vv. 28–68). The first part of this addition, the "Prayer of Azariah," highlights the loss of the temple and true worship and the resulting emotional trauma that Jews experienced.

the author wishes to portray the bravery of a wider assortment of Jews, not just of one man.

Several verses focus on idolatry as a theme. Verse 12 contrasts the worship of the king's gods with the Jews' behavior. Failure to worship equaled disloyalty to the state, according to the magicians. Verse 15's *what God could deliver you from me?* changes the story to one of direct challenge to Yahweh (like Pharaoh's role in Exod 1–14).

The major transition of the story takes place at verse 24. Nebuchadnezzar's question about the number of men in the furnace draws attention to the miracle of God's deliverance of the three Jews. The *one like a son of the gods* must be an angel. Some early Christian interpreters thought that Nebuchadnezzar saw Jesus, but this is unlikely for many historical and theological reasons.

4:1–37 This text, framed as a first-person narrative by Nebuchadnezzar himself, begins with a dream in which the mighty tree is leveled. Then Daniel interprets the dream as a divine judgment on the king for his arrogance. Curiously (given the events of the previous chapter), Daniel mourns the message of the dream, Nebuchadnezzar's impending punishment.

There is a significant historical problem regarding this text. The Dead Sea Scrolls contain a similar story (see Flint 332–38), but with Nebuchadnezzar's successor Nabonidus as the absentee king. In fact, we know that Nabonidus abandoned Babylon for several years in order to live in Teima, in what is now Saudi Arabia. Some scholars suggest, therefore, that this move serves as the basis of the story, which then gets transferred to Nebuchadnezzar, the better-known king.

In the book of Daniel, however, the story functions as a morality tale about the arrogance of power (see Henze). Note verse 27, the king's analysis of his own actions (*I built . . . my power, my glory*). Failure to give glory to God (in contrast with 3:29) provokes divine punishment.

The chapter's six parts (vv. 1–3; 4–8; 9–18; 19–27; 28–33; and 34–37) move from a royal decree in the first person ("I") to a third-person ("he") narration. (The Old Greek translation of the chapter significantly reorganizes it, indicating that the story remained unfixed early on.) Hebrew verse numbers differ from those in English; this commentary follows the latter.

1 Enoch

The First book of Enoch *is a collection of teachings and visions written between 350 BCE and 1 CE. Chapters 72–82 come from the Persian period and describe heavenly beings. Chapters 1–36 date to the second century BCE and resemble Daniel 7–12.*

Like chapter 2, the story begins with a royal dream. The "tree in the middle of the earth" (better than NIV's *land*) symbolizes the universe itself; like Pharaoh in Ezekiel 31, Nebuchadnezzar claims universal rule (compare 4:1). The *watcher* (see NIV footnote) is a type of angel, also discussed in *1 Enoch* and *Jubilees*, Jewish books from the third and second centuries BCE. This being conveys God's decree of judgment (the cutting of the tree symbolizing Nebuchadnezzar).

Verses 19–27, like 2:36–45, interpret the dream in a robustly theological way. The dream emphasizes God's rule over human kingdoms. The *seven times* (vv. 16, 23, and 32; compare 7:25) equals seven years. No Babylonian evidence exists for an interruption in Nebuchadnezzar's reign, and Nabonidus' trip to Teima lasted ten years. The number seven is thus symbolic, not historical. It symbolizes a complete cessation of royal rule and thus a complete testimony to the power of God.

Verses 34–35 offer the main theological claims of the chapter. The prayer of a pagan king, lately a dumb animal, attests to the sovereignty of Israel's God and the truth of Israel's faith. God is the *Most High*, who reigns over an eternal kingdom, ordering human kingdoms in whatever way ensures the greatest possible degree of justice. Verse 34 alludes to Psalm 145:13 and verse 35 to Isaiah 40:17, with its claim that the nations ultimately fail (compare Isa 24:21; 34:4). Given the ability of the powerful to act arrogantly to claim an ever greater share of power, status, and wealth, God's pursuit of justice leads inevitably to a disruption of the status quo.

5:1–31 Chapter 5 contains a story of royal extravagance, a popular theme in postexilic Jewish literature (compare Esther), as well as in contemporary Greek stories about the Persian court. The royal court serves as a moral universe counter to the one in which faithful Jews should live (see Mills). Belshazzar, the son and viceroy of Nabonidus, the last Babylonian king, throws a party using the vessels from the Jerusalem temple while Babylon lies under siege by the Persian armies. He thus combines sacrilege with obliviousness. The chapter consists of four sections: the introduction (vv. 1–6); the failure of the diviners (vv. 7–12); Daniel's audience with Belshazzar (vv. 13–28); and the conclusion (vv. 29–30). Earlier themes of the book appear here: the superior insight of Daniel and thus the superior wisdom of God, the lack of awareness of the king, revelation through dreams, contempt for luxury and privilege (v. 17), and the importance of submission to God on the part of the king, since the king should model moral behavior for his subjects.

Nebuchadnezzar had taken the temple's metal kitchenware as booty (2 Kgs 25:13–15). Since only the priests could use them, their use by Belshazzar's *concubines* (vv. 2–3) only adds to the offense. Verse 3's reference to Babylonian deities as mere statues underscores the folly of the king's party. Jewish texts of the Diaspora highlight their dismay at idolatry.

The story portrays the king's weakness and folly in several ways. He loses control of his limbs (and possibly his bowels; see Seow 79) and *cried out* (NIV *called out* does not capture his fear). Unlike Nebuchadnezzar, he cannot command himself. His promise to make the interpreter of the words on the wall *third highest ruler* (v. 7) need not be taken literally (Collins 247). The title refers only to a very high rank.

In contrast to the king, the *queen* (probably the queen mother since she knows more than he) calmly plans a solution. She calls for Daniel. Unlike his polite response to Nebuchadnezzar's praise of him (2:27–45), Daniel brushes off Belshazzar's promises (v. 17). His answer reports past history for a present purpose, to remind the king of the price of arrogance. His condemnation of the king (v. 22) is reminiscent of the prophets.

The Aramaic words in verses 25–28 present several problems. First, it is hard to understand why no Babylonians can read the words, since some of them must have read Aramaic. Thus the problem was not one of reading but of interpretation. Second, the words at first appear to be nouns and possibly the names of weights (see Collins 251–52; Seow 82–83). If the words refer to weights, then the first two minas (*mene, mene*) might indicate the superiority of the early Babylonian rulers to the last ones, who were a mere shekel (*tekel* being the Aramaic equivalent of the Hebrew *sheqel*). Third, however, verses 26–28 interpret the first words as verbs, all referring to Belshazzar and his rule, and the last as a pun on "Persia" (*peres* is the singular form of *parsin*). The chapter, like the older biblical prophetic books, pronounces God's judgment on foreign powers that behave arrogantly (see for example Isa 13–23; Jer 46–51; Ezek 26–32; Amos 1–2; Obadiah; Nahum).

Queen Mothers

Stories of remarkable queen mothers survive from ancient Mesopotamia. For example, the mother of Nabonidus (and thus grandmother of Belshazzar), Adad-guppi, left an important inscription commemorating her worship of the moon-god Sin. In the late ninth century, the queen mother Shammuramat ruled Assyria. She may be the basis of the many later legends of an Assyrian queen Semiramis. Those legends circulated among the Greeks and Armenians for many centuries.

The text also emphasizes the importance of memory. Belshazzar's courtiers remember the aged Daniel, who reminds the king of Nebuchadnezzar's rise and fall, which he interprets theologically in light of Israel's central ideas about the nature of God and God's actions in the world. The record of the past becomes a moral example for the present. Remembering the past is important because it helps us avoid mistakes through self-understanding and self-examination.

6:1–28 As in chapter 3, slanderers again blame a potential Jewish martyr for not praying to idols. Again, the story ends with divine rescue and the king's worship of God. The king's confession in verse 27 acknowledges (as before) God's eternal reign and, by implication, the temporariness of the king's own.

Ancient Weights

The value of ancient weights fluctuated in antiquity. A talent varied from 45 to 90 pounds. A mina was usually $1/60$ of a talent, and a shekel was $1/60$ of a mina.

Chapter 6 adds a new ingredient, the emphasis on prayer. Daniel's faithfulness is marked by the thrice daily practice of prayer toward Jerusalem. Prayer thus moves in several directions: upward to God; outward to Jerusalem; and inward to the faithful person's soul. Daniel prays in the direction of Jerusalem to illustrate the Jews' reverence for that city as the location of God's saving actions.

The chapter consists of six parts: an introduction (vv. 1–3); the plot (vv. 4–9); Daniel's "crime" and sentence (vv. 10–18); his deliverance (vv. 19–24); the royal proclamation (vv. 25–27); and the conclusion (v. 28). The story's structure closely resembles that of chapter 3.

Verse 1 offers several historical problems. First, the identity of *Darius* remains difficult. Babylonia fell to Cyrus the Great, and the three kings named Darius all lived after any historical figure named Daniel. Attempts to connect Darius to the governor of Babylonia named Gubaru are extremely speculative. Second, the Persian empire never had *120 satraps*; the number usually ran around two dozen. Apparently Daniel uses the title loosely to include lower ranking officials (such as Nehemiah), as also some Greek writers did (see Collins 264). Third, the Persian government normally had seven cabinet officials, not three (see Ezra 7:14; Esth 1:14). The number must thus be symbolic, not literal.

The conspirators against Daniel appeal to the king's vanity (v. 7). Ancient monarchs did not think of themselves as gods (except in Egypt), but the elaborate royal protocol of the Persians did bother the Greeks, and it may lie behind the idea that a king would demand worship.

The text portrays the king as regretting his decree and fretting for Daniel's safety. Even the king must obey the law. His inability to save Daniel, however, only highlights the power of Yahweh. Again the story climaxes when a foreign king praises Israel's God (vv. 16, 26–27; compare 2:47; 3:28–29; and 4:34–37).

Verse 17 describes a practice for sealing rooms. The king and nobles stamp their rings into clay or wax placed on the edge of the stone. Such *signet rings*, often of semiprecious stones, were common for ancient persons of means as ways of attesting to documents.

> **The Law of the Medes & the Persians**
> *The idea that no one could repeal the laws of the Medes and Persians also appears in Esther 8:8. However, no evidence for this legal practice exists from Persia itself. In Esther such an approach to jurisprudence highlights the folly of the Persian regime, since the irrevocability of the law leads to street violence.*

The decree in verses 26–27 does not call for an end to polytheism, but merely respect for Jewish religion. The theology of the decree draws heavily on Exodus, Psalms, and other biblical texts in portraying God as a rescuer and wonderworker (see Pss 78; 105).

VISIONS OF THE FUTURE · 7:1–9:27

While chapters 1–6 portray survivable dangers for Jews in the Diaspora, chapters 7–12 reflect an uglier reality. Jews in these visions do not flourish and so must await God's coming deliverance.

7:1–28 The chapter repeats much of the material of chapter 2, with a similar notion of a succession of kingdoms. The narrative contains five sections: an introduction in the third person (vv. 1–2a); the vision proper (vv. 2b–14);

interpretation of the dream (vv. 15–18); a clarification regarding the fourth beast (vv. 19–27); and the conclusion (v. 28).

The story begins in a flashback. The *four beasts* come from the cardinal directions. The story vaguely resembles the Babylonian creation story in that creatures from the sea fight against the main deity, but Daniel differs significantly from the older story (Lacocque; Collins 286). Daniel may draw the species of beast from Hosea 13:7–8 (Collins 295), but sculptures of beasts of mixed species (especially winged lions) appeared throughout the ancient Near East. The monsters equal kingdoms who devour prey (hence the bear's *three ribs* from its prey). They may or may not equal the four kingdoms of chapter 2.

The fourth beast, because of its ferocity, receives extended comment in the text. Coins from Alexander the Great and his immediate successors portrayed a ruler wearing a horned crown, and such an image may have triggered the author's imagination here. On the other hand, horned gods and kings figured in Near Eastern art much earlier, as well. Speechmaking was an important role for monarchs, but to speak *boastfully* (v. 8) marked a king as an opponent of God (see Isa 37:23; more generally Ps 12:2–3).

The vision of God's throne (vv. 9–10; compare 1 *Enoch* 14), portrays the victor over the evil beasts/kingdoms. The *Ancient of Days*, namely God, sits amid a vast staff of angels. The throne consists of fiery wheels (see Ezek 1:15–21). The idea of the opened *books* echoes the ancient Near Eastern image of the "tablets of destiny," documents recording in advance all human and divine activities. Here, however, the books fall under the control of the victorious God. The figure of the *one like a son of man* (or "human being"; verse 13), like the image of God as an aged person, receives no explanation here. Traditional Christian readers read verse 13 as a reference to Jesus, but the text does not make this figure messianic or even human. It may be an angel, perhaps Michael (Collins 310; Seow 108). The vagueness of the reference did, however, warrant the later Christian interpretation. In any case, God's kingdom endures forever, in contrast to the human kingdoms that dominate Israel in Daniel's dream.

The Ten Kings

Various theories exist for how to account for the ten kings of Daniel 7. They seem to include the first seven Seleucid rulers, possibly Alexander the Great, and probably Seleucid rulers down to Antiochus IV. However, the number ten may be a symbolic round number.

Verses 15–24 begin an extended analysis of the dream, focusing especially on the fourth kingdom. The "three and half times" of verse 24 equals three and a half years, half of seven years, and roughly the lapse between the desecration of the temple by Antiochus IV Epiphanes and its cleansing by the Maccabees (167–164 BCE). More importantly, the *time* of trouble contrasts with the *everlasting kingdom* soon to replace it (v. 27; Seow 112–13).

The climax of the crisis comes in verses 25–27, which envision the Syrian persecution of Jews. Daniel announces the divine decision to bring an end to the persecution. The text also tries to set this persecution in the context of the era's rapid political and social changes, over which Jews had no control. Such rapid change could suggest either that the world is so unstable we can be confident in nothing; or that the world's instability is proof momentary evils will pass away because underneath the instability is a calm stability anchored in the steadfastness of God. The writer wants us to elect the second conclusion.

8:1–27 The text depicts the rise and fall of Alexander the Great. The description of him as a he-goat probably comes from the fact that his coins portray him with horns, because he sought to present himself as the offspring of the Egyptian chief god, Ammon, who was a ram. Alexander invaded the vast Persian empire in 334 BCE and gradually destroyed it. He died at age 33, master of the known world. Jews in Jerusalem welcomed Alexander and generally got on well with his successors for the next century. But the instability following his invasion and death, and then the struggle for domination among his generals, inevitably created uncertainty for everyone in the region, including Jews.

The chapter consists of four parts: an introduction (vv. 1–2); a vision report (vv. 3–14); the interpretation of the vision (vv. 15–26); and the conclusion (v. 27). The vision takes place in Susa, a city in present-day Iran not part of the Neo-Babylonian Empire but one of the capitals of the Persian Empire (see Neh 1:1; Esth 1:2), apparently as a result of visionary transportation to the site (compare Ezek 8:3; 11:24; 40:2; see Collins 329). The *Ulai Canal*, a human-made irrigation work, has the same name in Greek sources.

The *ram* of verse 3 signifies the Persian Empire, which fell to the *goat* from the west (Alexander the Great from Macedonia; v. 7). The *four prominent horns* (v. 8) signify the breakup of Alexander's empire after his death, when his generals partitioned the region. The little horn of verses 9–12 is, again, Antiochus Epiphanes, who defiled the temple in the *Beautiful Land* (v. 9; that is, the land of Israel) and claimed semidivine status. The *Prince of the host* must be God. As in the previous chapter, the audience must recognize that even the gravest threats to their faith cannot separate them from God.

Verses 11–14 focus on the defilement of the temple by Antiochus Epiphanes. The end of sacrifice could conceivably mean that Israel's sins were not atoned for and thus that God might not protect the people, but the text reminds its readers that such a conclusion is unwarranted. The angelic speaker (*a holy one*) presents this conclusion as beyond dispute, since only an arrogant Gentile king would argue with a heavenly being! Atonement does not depend on human actions alone, but on the sovereign choice of God, who hears a contrite people crying out for relief, and who will restore the sacrifices after *2,300 evenings and mornings*. Since the priests in Jerusalem sacrificed each evening and morning (at the beginning and midpoint of each day), verse 14 envisions a break in the temple worship lasting 1,150 days, or about three and a half years (compare 7:25). Again, the text speaks of the crisis under Antiochus Epiphanes.

Verses 15–25 give the foregoing interpretation of the vision. The vision ends with a notice that Daniel must keep the vision a secret though it overwhelms him emotionally (the same themes appear in 7:28). Obviously, the vision did not remain secret since it appears in this book. Secrecy functions as a literary device—a fiction—emphasizing the importance of the vision as a way of encouraging a Jewish audience to persist against persecution by reminding them that God knew all along what would befall them.

9:1–27 This chapter reflects on the nature of divine revelation, particularly as it relates to human activity in the present. The chapter includes three parts: an introduction (vv. 1–2); a prayer of repentance (vv. 3–19); and an answer promising deliverance (vv. 20–27).

Verses 1–2 introduce *Darius* as the son of *Ahasuerus* the Median, both otherwise unknown characters, and portray Daniel contemplating Jeremiah's prediction of exile (Jer 25:11, 12; 29:10). *Seventy years* is a round number, but Daniel's vision roughly corresponds with the time preceding the prophecies of Haggai and Zechariah, whose work led to the rebuilding of the Jerusalem temple. Verse 3 introduces the prayer itself by noting Daniel's discipline of his body in preparation for confronting God. Sackcloth and ashes symbolized mourning (see Isa 58:5; Lam 2:10; compare Seow 140).

The prayer of verses 4–19 resembles the penitential prayer of Nehemiah 9:5b–37 (compare Pss 78; 79; Lam 2). Daniel's prayer alternates praise to God and blame for himself and his people. Verses 11–14 recall the covenant curses of Deuteronomy 28, though with the expectation that God will eventually relent from punishing Israel when they repent (as in 1 Kgs 8:35–40, 46–51). Verses 15–18 center God's (and the reader's) attention on the distress in Jerusalem and Judah. Restoration of the temple equals restoration of the nation. Such a request thus functions at several literary levels: in the world of the story set in the sixth century BCE, Daniel prays for the restoration of the temple under Zerubbabel; while in the world of the ancient reader of Daniel, the prayer both anticipates the cleansing following Antiochus' desecration and reminds Jews that God has done such a thing before. Thus Daniel's prayer, though on the surface sounding desperate, invites the one praying to hope.

The Prayer of Daniel

Three major theological moves occur in the prayer. First, verses 10–11 call God (and implicitly the prayer's Israelite audience) to reflect on the promises and laws of the ancient Scriptures (Law and Prophets) and thus on human sinfulness and redemption, the need for ethical behavior on the part of humans, and the reality of steadfast love and graciousness on the part of God. Second, the prayer of Daniel seeks to understand the disaster that has befallen the nation as earned punishment for sin, specifically for idolatry and social injustice (the paired sins prevalent throughout the prophetic books). Third, the return to the promised land, actually fulfilled in the late sixth century, is a prominent theme. God will restart the clock on the covenant people (see also Jer 31) and thus bless all humankind (see Isa 49; 56).

Verses 20–27 explicitly address the problem of the meaning of Jeremiah's prophecy. Since restoration should not give way to further devastation, any Jewish interpreter of history must try to connect experiences of the second century with the words of the already ancient book of Jeremiah. Daniel denies that the rebuilding of the temple under Zerubbabel completely fulfills Jeremiah's prophecy. His *seventy sevens* (v. 24) would equal 490 years, but the number is probably symbolic (since it does not correspond to any known sequence of events in the first millennium BCE). Daniel merely states that the final fulfillment of Jeremiah's prophecy will come when the Jews purge the temple after Antiochus' desecration. Verse 24 envisions a probationary period when God's people will put an end to sin and fulfill Daniel's prophecies and perhaps others (*seal up vision and prophecy*; see Collins 354; Seow 148). The consecration of the *most holy* (Hebrew *qodesh qodashim*, a name for the innermost part of the temple [1 Kgs 6:16; 7:50; 8:6; 2 Chron 3:8, 10; 4:22; 5:7; Ezek 41:4]) refers to the cleansing of the temple and thus the institution of regular sacrifice.

> ### Daniel & Jesus' Apocalyptic Visions
>
> *Mark 13 (which parallels Matt 24 and Luke 21:5–28) employs much of the language of Daniel. It is a mistake, however, to assume that they refer to the same historical events. Indeed, they cannot possibly do so without serious rearrangements of early Christian history and even understandings of Jesus. Rather, Mark recycles the images of Daniel to describe a parallel event, the destruction of Jerusalem by the Romans in 70 CE and to offer hope of God's ultimate restoration of all things in Christ. The powerful images of Daniel thus serve a new purpose in a new situation.*

The *Anointed One* of verse 26 refers to Onias III, murdered in 171 BCE (*2 Maccabees* 4:23–28). This beginning to a turbulent period climaxes in the erection of the *abomination that causes desolation*, almost certainly the altar to Zeus that Antiochus erected in the Jerusalem temple. Chapter 9 ends without a resolution of the conflict, but that will come in the conclusion of the book.

A FINAL VISION · 10:1–12:13

Chapters 10 through 12 form a continuous vision, the longest in the book. The chapters consist of five sections: an introduction (10:1); report of an angelic vision (10:2–9); conversation with an angel (10:10–11:1); the angel's historical discourse (11:2–12:4); and a final conversation and revelation (12:5–13). Chapters 10–11 repeat much of the previous visions. Again we read a lesson on Hellenistic history, particularly as it affected Jews in Palestine. Alexander's empire broke into several parts. The Seleucids in Syria and the Ptolemies in Egypt fought over Palestine, with the Seleucids eventually prevailing. The Seleucid monarch Antiochus Epiphanes sought to destroy Jewish religion. The text responds to this by indicating God's ultimate ability to overcome even the most terrible evil.

The angelic vision in 10:2–9 begins with Daniel fasting to prepare himself for his encounter with the divine realm. Since the vision occurred in the first month, he must have fasted through Passover, indicating the seriousness of the events that the vision recounts (see Seow 155–56; but Collins 373). Daniel refrains from the celebration of the happiest time of the Jewish year in order to highlight the terrible times awaiting the book's readers.

The figure appearing in 10:4–6 resembles that in Ezekiel 9–10; the angel may be Gabriel as in chapters 8–9. *Chrysolite* (a semiprecious mineral, often greenish, of magnesium iron silicate) and other aspects of his appearance resemble the elements of the throne of God in Ezekiel 1. Since the vision terrifies Daniel, the angel assures the prophet that he is *highly esteemed* and therefore that no harm will befall him (v. 10; for the comforting of an anxious prophet, see Isa 6:7; Jer 1:9).

The conversation with the angel in 10:10–11:1 portrays Daniel's humility and relentless search for truth (v. 12) to benefit his people. The prince of Persia (apparently the angel in charge of Persia) resisted the angel of the vision for *twenty-one days* (v. 13), the duration of Daniel's fast (Collins 375). After explaining his delay in appearing, the angel again comforts Daniel (10:18–19), states the key point of his vision (10:20), and explains that the angel Michael will also help him.

The vision proper (11:2–12:4) describes the conflict between the Seleucid rulers of Syria and the Ptolemaic rulers of Egypt, who fought over Palestine throughout the late third and early second centuries BCE. It also mentions the marriage alliance between Berenike of Egypt and Antiochus II of Syria (11:6), the rise of Ptolemy III, Berenike's brother (11:7), the changes of military fortunes under Seleucus III and Antiochus III of Syria (11:8–13), the conflicts in Judea between supporters of Syria and Egypt (11:14–19), and the rise of Antiochus IV, the great foe of the Jewish people (11:20–12:4).

Antiochus comes in for severe criticism, not only for his arrogance, but for his mad attitude toward the God of Israel, and even his own gods (11:36–39; compare 1 *Maccabees* 1:41–50). Antiochus emphasizes the worship of Olympian Zeus, even, says Daniel, to the detriment of other gods. The *one desired by women* (v. 37) was the god Tammuz/Adonis, who died and rose from the dead and whose worship especially drew women. Despite initial successes, however, Antiochus' actions lead to his downfall and thus to the deliverance of the faithful among the Jews.

Daniel ends with a reflection on the differences between the faithful and the unfaithful. The former have their names *written in the book* (12:2), that is, the book of life (related to other books in Dan 7:10; 10:21; compare the so-called *Book of the Heavenly Luminaries* from the Dead Sea Scrolls). The righteous dead experience resurrection. Again, Daniel 12 is the only text in the Old Testament that unequivocally expects a resurrection of the dead, though it does not explicitly describe their subsequent state, nor does it mention the fate of the wicked dead.

According to 12:7, the crisis under Antiochus Epiphanes would last three and a half *times* (or years). By emphasizing its relative brevity, the vision encourages readers to persevere until the resurrection. As a time of trial, it can only lead to the refinement of the saints. Daniel 12:11 describes the gap in sacrifice between the desecration of the temple by Antiochus and its cleansing by the Maccabees, an event now commemorated in the Feast of Hanukkah.

Like the New Testament, Daniel does not try to explain the precise timing of the resurrection, the nature of the resurrected human body, the specifics of the life of the blessed with God, or other questions that we as readers (and believers!) naturally ask. The focus is exclusively upon the divine promise that we will someday be saved, and evil will no longer threaten in any way. In the meantime, we persevere.

Daniel & Resurrection
Daniel 12 is the only text in the Old Testament that clearly talks about a resurrection from the dead, which will result from God's decisive saving action. Like Jesus in Matthew 24, Daniel merges the saving events of a particular time (here the second century BCE) into the final time of salvation, in which the dead are really raised. Timing is not the text's particular concern. The ultimate destiny of God's people is.

THEOLOGICAL REFLECTIONS

The theology of Daniel takes the shape of stories and visions, not systematic treatises. Still, several major themes emerge. First, Yahweh, the God of Israel, is in fact the only God. God reveals the future to whomever he wishes. God judges kingdoms and rulers on the basis of their behavior, particularly as regards their treatment of the poor and vulnerable. Second, God ensures the continuity of the story of Israel. Even in exile, under the most terrible conditions, God redeems the chosen people and provides for them. Since many Jews never returned to the land of Israel but continued to live in the Diaspora, such a vision of the universality of God was extremely important. Third, Israel thus does not exist as a group of people by virtue of their location in a given locale, even a land "flowing with milk and honey" promised to the ancestors (as Deuteronomy emphasizes), but because of their commitment to the basic norms of the law. Daniel especially emphasizes observance of the food laws (chapter 1), avoidance of idolatry, and prayer toward Jerusalem. These boundary issues make a person a Jew, and thus a faithful person. Fourth, prayer in this view is an act of radical orientation to the ultimate reality. Prayer brings the faithful person into contact with both God and other people at prayer, and thus with the Jewish people throughout the ages. Fifth, Israel lives in a hostile world (especially in chapters 7–12) in which the powerful both worship false gods and live by false mores. The visions of the crisis of the second century in particular wish to portray the fragility of the seemingly invincible evil empires. They fall under God's judgment because of their unethical behavior.

FOR FURTHER STUDY

Bauckham, Richard, James Davila, and Alexander Panayotov. *Old Testament Pseudepigrapha*. Grand Rapids: Eerdmans, 2013.

Gowan, Donald E. *Daniel*. Nashville: Abingdon, 2001.

Henze, Matthias. *Mind the Gap: How the Jewish Writings Between the Old and New Testament Help Us Understand Jesus*. Minneapolis: Fortress, 2017.

Theodoret of Cyrus. *Commentary on Daniel*. Translated by Robert C. Hill. Atlanta: Society of Biblical Literature, 2006.

WORKS CITED

Albertz, Rainer. *Israel in Exile: The History and Literature of the Sixth Century BCE*. Atlanta: Scholars Press, 2003.

Collins, John. *Daniel*. Minneapolis: Fortress, 1993.

Flint, Peter W. "The Daniel Tradition at Qumran." In *The Book of Daniel: Composition and Reception*, edited by John J. Collins and Peter W. Flint, 2:328–67. Leiden: Brill, 2001.

Henze, Matthias. *The Madness of King Nebuchadnezzar*. Leiden: Brill, 1999.

Lacocque, André. "Allusions to Creation in Daniel 7." In *The Book of Daniel: Composition and Reception*, edited by John J. Collins and Peter W. Flint, 1:114–31. Leiden: Brill, 2001.

Meadowcroft, Tim. "Exploring the Dismal Swamp: The Identity of the Anointed One in Daniel 9:24–27." *Journal of Biblical Literature* 120 (2001): 429–49.

Mills, Mary. "Household and Table: Diasporic Boundaries in Daniel and Esther." *Catholic Biblical Quarterly* 68 (2006): 408–20.

Rappaport, Uriel. "Maccabean Revolt." In *The Anchor Bible Dictionary*, 4:433–39. New Haven: Yale University Press, 1992.

Seow, C. L. *Daniel*. Louisville: Westminster John Knox, 2003.

Hosea

Philip G. Camp

CHAPTER CONTENTS

MAP

The Book of Hosea presents God as one who longs for Israel and desires their wholehearted devotion, but Israel refuses such a relationship with God by trusting in idols and foreign alliances. Therefore, Hosea announces both the judgment of God on his people and God's desire to restore them. The primary audience is the northern kingdom, Israel, though some oracles also address Judah (1:7, 11; 4:15; 5:5, 10–15; 6:4, 11; 8:14; 10:11; 11:12; 12:2).

CONTEXTS

Little is known about the prophet Hosea. He is the *son of Beeri* (1:1), who is otherwise unknown, the husband of *Gomer* (1:2–3), and the father of at least three children (1:3–9). According to the superscription (1:1), Hosea's activity extends from sometime in the reign of King Jeroboam II of Israel (786–746 BCE) to sometime in the reign of King Hezekiah of Judah (715–687 BCE), a minimum of about thirty years.

Hosea witnessed one of the most turbulent times in the histories of Israel and Judah. His career began as an era of peace and prosperity for Israel and Judah, during the reign of Jeroboam II, was coming to a close. Following Jeroboam's death, Israel experienced a period of turmoil that lasted until the kingdom's end in 721 BCE. The final twenty-five years saw six kings take the throne of Israel, usually through violence (see 2 Kgs 15:8–31). Beginning around 734 BCE, the Assyrians asserted control over Syria-Palestine, and eventually both Israel and Judah became Assyrian vassals. In 734 BCE, kings Pekah of Israel and Rezin of Aram allied to oppose Assyria. When Jotham of Judah and his son, Ahaz, refused to join them, the allied kings attacked Judah with the intent of replacing the king, the so-called Syro-Ephraimite War. Ahaz appealed to the Assyrian king Tiglath-Piliser III for help, and he responded by wiping out Aram and subduing Israel, which was spared only because Hoshea seized the throne and surrendered (2 Kgs 15:37–16:9; Isa 7:1–9). When Hoshea later rebelled against Assyrian rule, the Assyrians brought the northern Israelite kingdom to an end (2 Kgs 17:3–6).

The book of Hosea presents at least three noteworthy critical issues. First, the bulk of the book is essentially from Hosea, but the superscription and the biographical account in chapter 1 indicate that the book was edited, probably after Hosea's death and probably in Judah. Second, the references to Judah and the predominance of Judean kings in the superscription (1:1) have led some scholars to conclude that the book was not only edited but also updated after the fall of Israel in order to address Judah. While possible, such a conclusion is not necessary. A prophet in Israel could have addressed Judah at times, as well. Third, the text of Hosea has been poorly preserved in ancient manuscripts, leading to notorious translation problems in places. However, the general message of the prophet remains clear.

The contents of the book of Hosea fall into two major divisions. Chapters 1–3 draw parallels between the prophet's relationship to his wife and children and Yahweh's relationship with Israel. Chapters 4–14 contain a collection of oracles, most announcing judgment on Israel for various transgressions but others extending hope of restoration after the judgment.

COMMENTARY

The content of the book of Hosea is *the word of the Lord*, and the prophet *Hosea* is merely the messenger. The references to the *kings of Judah* draw Judah into a message primarily aimed at Israel and serve as a warning to Judah. The only king of Israel mentioned is *Jeroboam son of Jehoash*, though six kings would follow him during Hosea's career. Perhaps the omission of their names implies that the "glory days" of Israel ended with Jeroboam.

HOSEA'S WIFE & CHILDREN · 1:2–2:1

1:2 God commands Hosea to take *an adulterous wife and children of unfaithfulness*, which serves as a symbol of the relationship between God and his people. *Adulterous* and "unfaithfulness" are the same word in Hebrew. The root (*zanah*) often refers to prostitution in the Old Testament and is better understood that way here. While the root can refer to literal prostitution (for example, Gen 38:24; Lev 19:29; 1 Kgs 3:16), it often indicates spiritual prostitution, selling oneself to other gods or foreign nations, in exchange for what they seem to offer (compare 2:12a; 4:10–15; 9:1; Exod 34:15–16; Deut 31:16). Scholars debate whether *Gomer* is a prostitute prior to the marriage (see McComiskey 11–17), but the parallels drawn in the next chapter suggest her prostitution begins after their marriage (see Anderson and Freedman 116).

1:3–9 She gives birth to three *children of unfaithfulness* (or "prostitution"), which means that the children are born to a prostitute. The text specifies that she *bore him* (Hosea) a child only with respect to the firstborn (1:3; compare verses 6, 8), leaving the paternity of the other two a question (2:4–5). Each child's name anticipates judgment. *Jezreel* refers to the judgment coming upon the *house of Jehu for the massacre at Jezreel* (compare 2 Kgs 9–10). This word is fulfilled with the overthrow of Jeroboam II's son, Zechariah (2 Kgs 15:10). *Lo-Ruhamah* means "no mercy," and *Lo-Ammi* means "not my people," both signaling God's rejection of Israel. God will *no longer show love* (better translated "mercy") to Israel, though he will be merciful to Judah and *save them.* The fulfillment comes when Assyria destroys northern Israel (2 Kgs 17:3–23).

Jehu's Punishment

Curiously, God punishes the dynasty of Jehu for a coup d'état commanded by one of God's own prophets (2 Kgs 9:6–10). This is not a case of inherited guilt, but rather of poetic justice. Since Jehu's family practiced the same sins as Ahab's, they will meet the same fate (see Anderson and Freedman 180).

1:10–2:1 Then God announces an amazing reversal. Recalling the promise to Abraham (Gen 22:17), the Israelites *will be like the sand on the seashore.* The judgments signified by the children's names will be reversed, and a reunited

Israel and Judah will *come up out of the land*, which is language of sprouting and a play on the meaning of *Jezreel* ("God sows"; 2:21–23).

THE MARRIAGE ANALOGY APPLIED TO GOD & ISRAEL · 2:2–23

2:2–4   The *mother* symbolizes God's estranged "wife" Israel (collectively), who has destroyed the covenantal bond. The word translated *rebuke* sometimes functions in prophetic texts to indicate that God is putting his people on trial (4:1; 12:2; Isa 3:13–14; Jer 2:9; Mic 6:1–2). God warns Israel to stop playing the whore with other gods, or she will be humiliated and her *children* (individual Israelites) shown no mercy.

2:5–13   Israel has pursued idols, including *Baal*, thinking they provide her with the necessities of life. Because Israel has not *acknowledged* the true origin of these gifts, God withholds them, proving that her *lovers* cannot *pay* what they promise.

2:14–23   God intends to return to the "honeymoon" era with Israel in the *desert* following the exodus *out of Egypt*. Given the volatile nature of Israel's relationship with God in the wilderness, such an idealization of the past seems strange. However, in the wilderness Yahweh provided food and drink for Israel (Exod 16:1–17:7; Num 11), things Israel now attributes to *Baals*, that is, local versions of the Canaanite storm and fertility god. In this way, God will *remove the names of the Baals from her lips* because she will no longer see a need for them. Israel will no longer even utter a common designation for a husband: *my master* (*ba'al*). *In that day*, an unspecified future time, God will reestablish the covenantal bond, rooted in the very qualities of God, *righteousness*, *justice*, *love*, *compassion*, and *faithfulness*. When Israel *will acknowledge* God's overtures, they will receive the things they need. The reversal of Hosea's children's names in verse 23 symbolizes the healing of the relationship with God.

RECONCILIATION ILLUSTRATED · 3:1–5

To illustrate his ultimate intention to restore Israel, God commands Hosea to *show love* again to his *wife*, despite her unfaithfulness. Some scholars argue that the woman here is not Gomer but a second wife, but the parallels with chapter 2 indicate that Hosea reclaims Gomer with the condition that she remain faithful from now on.

Prophets & Symbolic Actions

God often commanded his prophets to perform symbolic actions, some of which involved personal pain and humiliation (Isa 20:1–5; Jer 16:2; Ezek 4:4–6). The command for Hosea to marry a woman of prostitution falls into this category. Such prophetic acts created vivid, memorable illustrations of the prophets' messages and underscored the depth of both God's love and the people's estrangement. While difficult for the individual prophets, these acts served God's larger loving intention of calling the people to account in order to redeem them. So the dignity of the individual is sacrificed for the greater good of the whole community (compare Luke 23:11; 35–39; 1 Cor 4:9–13).

Like Gomer, Israel must experience separation prior to reconciliation. Verse 4 describes the key institutions of a well-functioning ancient society. Their absence highlights the impending desperate plight of Israel.

ISRAEL ON TRIAL · 4:1–19

4:1–10A   God again brings *a charge* (2:4) against the *Israelites*, who show *no faithfulness*, *no love*, and *no acknowledgement of God*. The absence of these qualities leads to breakdown within the community: *cursing, lying, murder, stealing, adultery* (see also Exod 20:13–17; Deut 5:17–21). The people's sinfulness derives in part from the malfeasance of the *priests* and *prophets*, who have failed in their duty to teach the people covenant faithfulness. Therefore, God will *punish* them through deprivation of food and offspring (Deut 28:17–18).

4:10B–19   The *prostitution* discussed in these verses may not be simply figurative. The Israelite women may have become cult prostitutes at the shrines of their gods and are patronized by the men of Israel. *Judah* is warned not to patronize such cults at *Gilgal* and *Beth Aven*, the latter being a pun of the name *Bethel* ("house of God" versus *Beth Aven*, "house of iniquity"). Because Israel is *stubborn* in their idolatry, God's judgment will *sweep them away*. Beginning here in the book (except for 13:1), *Ephraim*, the main northern tribe and after the Syro-Ephraimitic War the only remaining dependent territory, indicates the whole northern kingdom of Israel.

"Prostitution" in Canaanite Religion

Earlier scholars believed Canaanite religion to include cult or sacral prostitution, in which a female worshiper of the god would offer sexual services to men. According to this view, males could also serve as cult prostitutes, likewise offering their services to men (Deut 23:18). The term translated shrine prostitute *in 4:14 has been particularly associated with cult prostitution (Gen 38:21–22; Deut 23:17–18; 2 Kgs 23:7). More recent research, however, has cast considerable doubt on this interpretation. More likely, Hosea uses the sexual language here as a graphic metaphor, perhaps reflecting the excesses of some festival-goers, but more generally playing off the key metaphor of God's "marriage" to Israel (see Ackerman).*

JUDGMENT ON THE BRAZEN PROSTITUTE · 5:1–7

This oracle continues the theme of Israel's prostitution. The *judgment* against Israel is inclusive. The *priests* and the *royal house* may have led Israel into apostasy, but the *Israelites* are guilty for following. Theoretically, they could repent, but their *spirit of prostitution* is so ingrained in their *heart* that they cannot *return to their God*. When they do *seek the Lord, they will not find him* because they continue to be *unfaithful*. *Mizpah* and *Tabor* may have been worship sites, but this is unclear.

AN INEFFECTIVE CURE · 5:8–15

5:8–12   The context for this oracle is the Syro-Ephraimite War (Achtemeier 47). The comparison of *Judah's leaders* to *those who move boundary stones* (see Deut

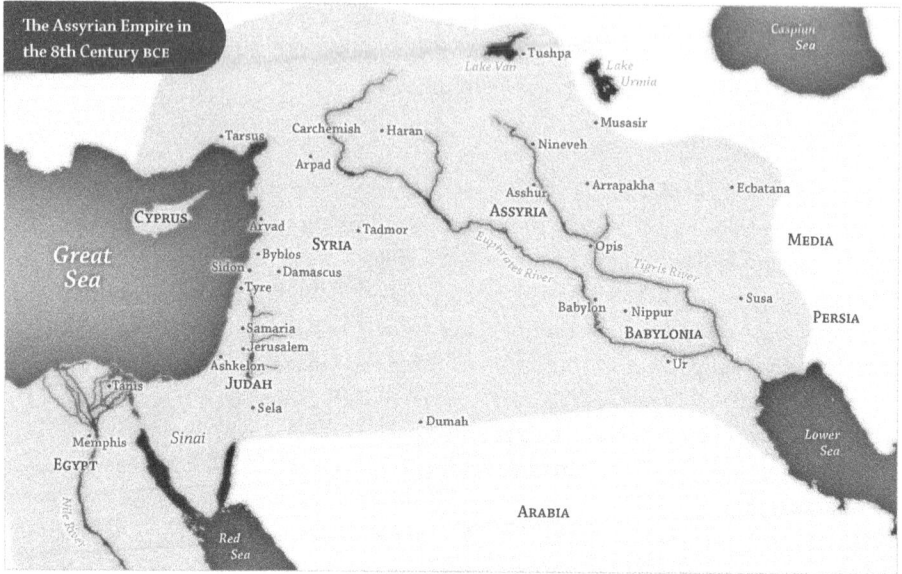

19:14; 27:17; Prov 23:10) points to Judah's takeover of territory to the north of Jerusalem (*Gibeah, Ramah,* and *Bethel*) outside Judah's territorial boundaries, probably after Israel withdrew from attacking Judah in order to meet the approaching Assyrians. God had set the tribal boundaries, and Judah had no right to violate them (Stuart 104). Even in warfare, nations must observe humanitarian limits.

5:13–15   Both Israel (2 Kgs 15:19–20) and *Judah* (2 Kgs 16:7–9) had turned to *Assyria* for security. Their vulnerability to the nations was their *sickness,* and this superpower seemed the obvious *cure.* They do not see that they are vulnerable precisely because they have failed to trust God for their security, and he will show them the futility of relying on Assyria. He will attack Israel, ironically through Assyria, who will wipe out Israel and nearly destroy Judah (see 2 Kgs 18:13). Only then will the people *admit their* guilt and seek God.

AN EXHORTATION TO RETURN TO GOD · 6:1–3

Hosea calls on his people to *return to the Lord.* Drawing on the language of the previous oracle, Hosea says that, though *Yahweh* inflicted injury on Israel, he will *heal* them. However, the people must first *acknowledge the Lord* (2:8; 4:1; 5:4). The result will be God's assured presence, which will be an ongoing blessing like *winter rains* and *spring rains.* Most rain falls in Palestine between November and January, with annual totals ranging from about four inches in the Negev (southern desert region) to 25–30 inches in northern Galilee. The NIV distinction between winter and spring rains is misleading; verse 3 refers to the rains of October and March beginning and ending the season. Rainfall was essential to Israel's agricultural productivity, and the symbolism reminds Israel that God alone is the source of rain.

GOD LONGS FOR HIS CHILDREN · 6:4–11A

Like a parent pleading with a child, God asks both *Israel* and *Judah*, *"What can I do with you?"* Their *love* for God is fleeting, like the *morning mist* and *dew*. Therefore, through the *prophets*, he announces and executes *judgments* against his people. Their attempts to appease God through *sacrifices* and *burnt offerings* are meaningless because they think they can divorce worship from *mercy* toward others and *acknowledgement of God* (Matt 9:13; 12:7). They sacrifice in an attempt to pacify or manipulate God, yet they remain violent and *defiled*.

A SELF-DESTRUCTIVE NATION · 6:11B–7:16

6:11B–7:2 This passage again displays God's desire to *restore* and *heal* his people, but they make it impossible. They think they have hidden their *sins*, but their transgressions *are always before* God. The prophet's extreme language, again, aims at healing Israel, not merely indicting it.

7:3–16 Three additional problems, all political, illustrate the degeneration of Israel. First, Israel's *king* is pleased with their *wickedness* and *lies* and even *joins hands* with drunken revelers (contrast Ps 101). Second, the Israelites *devour their rulers* through repeated violent *coups d'état*. Third, the Israelites flit back and forth between *Egypt* and *Assyria*, the two superpowers of the time, in search of security, but these nations *sap Israel's strength* (for example, resources and manpower). Israel slides closer to death but *does not notice*. In *arrogance*, Israel thinks it can manage its own security, but God sees this as a rejection of him as Israel's true protector. Thus, God will not protect Israel, and, ironically, Israel *will be ridiculed* by those they thought would protect them. The prophet thus comments on the politics of small states like Israel as they seek to play the great power games. Without justice and piety, they will be pawns in a game whose rules they cannot control.

ILLEGITIMATE KINGS & GODS · 8:1–6

The prophet warns that *an eagle* (Assyria) will carry out God's judgment on Israel for breaking God's *covenant* (Deut 28:49). God sees through Israel's *cries* of desperation, knowing they have *rejected what is good*, God himself. The oracle specifies two offenses. First, they *set up kings* without God's consent. Choosing kings was God's prerogative (Deut 17:15; compare 1 Sam 8–12), and in the past God designated Israel's kings through prophets (1 Sam 9:15–10:7; 16:1–13; 1 Kgs 11:29–39; 2 Kgs 9:1–10; 10:30). The second offense is idolatry. The *calf-idol of Samaria* refers to the image set up in Bethel by Jeroboam I (1 Kgs 12:26–33), and the reference to *Samaria* is a case of synecdoche, a literary device in which a part (in this case the capital city) represents the whole (Israel).

The Transforming Word

REAPING THE WHIRLWIND · 8:7–10

For Israel to *sow the wind and reap the whirlwind* means they invest themselves in what is useless, and the return is disastrous. Israel thinks their security rests in *Assyria* or other *nations*. They fail to see God as the source of their security. Instead of providing safety, the Assyrians will *swallow* the productivity of Israel, and Israel *will* suffer *oppression* under Assyrian rule.

DISPLEASING SACRIFICES & MISPLACED TRUST · 8:11–14

Israel's worship rituals are useless. From God's perspective, the very *altars* that are intended for atonement from sin have become *altars for sinning*. Israel disregards God's *law*, so to appeal to him for forgiveness through sacrifice is useless and even blasphemous. The same is true of fellowship offerings, after which Israel would *eat* a portion of *the meat* symbolizing a fellowship meal with God (Lev 7:11–18; Deut 16:2–4; 27:7). Since they have broken that fellowship, God is *not pleased* with such offerings. God's judgment will reverse the exodus: *They will return to Egypt*, that is, to captivity (compare Amos 9:7–10).

> **The "Sin Offering"**
> The *"sin offering"* (Lev 4:1–5:12; Num 15:22–31) served not to remove an individual's sin but to purify the sanctuary from human impurity. Thus, Hosea is saying that Israel's worship does not work anymore.

Israel *has forgotten* the one who made them, as illustrated by their trust in their kings (signified by *royal palaces*), and so has Judah, who trusts in their *fortified . . . towns*. God's *fire* of judgment will demonstrate that their trust is misplaced.

THE RETURN TO CAPTIVITY · 9:1–6

In Israel, harvest time was supposed to be characterized by joy and thanksgiving to God (Deut 16:9–15), but Hosea instructs the people not to *rejoice*, because they are *unfaithful to God*. The *threshing floor* may have served as a location for worshiping non-Israelite gods—or treating Yahweh like one of those gods, through cult prostitution (Achetmeier 72–73; Stuart 142). Thus, the reference to Israel's prostitution here may be both symbolic and literal. In any case, the produce of these *threshing floors* and of the *winepresses* will *fail* to meet the people's needs (Deut 28:38–39). Israel will also be exiled and will eat *unclean food*, which will make them unclean and no longer holy to God (see Lev 11:1–47; Deut 14:3–21). Furthermore, *their sacrifices* in exile will not *please* God because he will consider them like food used in mourning rituals, which was unacceptable as an offering to God (Deut 26:14). Finally, Israel should not view Egypt as a place to *escape from destruction*, because those who go there will die there (see Jer 41:16–44:30).

THE PROPHET: WATCHMAN OR MADMAN? · 9:7–9

God graciously sends his *prophet* to act as a *watchman* to warn *Israel* that their *punishment* is *at hand*. But the people consider *the prophet a maniac* (2 Kgs 9:11;

Jer 29:26) and do not heed his warning. The depth of Israel's corruption is here compared to *the days of Gibeah*, when that town's violence and corruption led to civil war in Israel (Judg 19–21).

BEREAVED OF CHILDREN · 9:10–17

9:10–13 This passage compares Israel's *fathers* in the wilderness generation to the Israelites in Hosea's day. The ancestors were initially pleasing and promising in God's eyes, but they continually broke faith with him, as evidenced in their participation in idolatry at *Baal Peor* (Num 25:1–10). The implication is that not much has changed. The hyperbolic language of verses 11–13 points to the end of Israel because its offspring are cut off in one way or another.

> **Hosea & Tradition**
> *Hosea cites many older stories of the Exodus, wandering, and the period of the so-called judges. Presumably, Israel knew and treasured these stories, and Hosea can appeal to a common stock of ideas and beliefs in order to rehabilitate Israel's relationship to God. Conspicuously absent is any reference to southern traditions about David.*

9:14–17 Hosea and God engage in dialogue. Hosea beseeches God to exact vengeance on the wicked, invoking God's judgment on Israel in the form of *wombs that miscarry* (Deut 28:18). To say God *hated them* refers to the intensity of God's rejection and his plan to *drive them out* into exile. *Gilgal* was once a site for sacrifices to God (1 Sam 10:8; 15:21), but it also served as a place for problematic worship (Judg 3:19; Hos 4:15; 12:11; Amos 4:4; 5:5).

THE BEGINNING & END OF ISRAEL'S IDOLATRY · 10:1–8

Like a fruitful *vine* (compare Isa 5:1–7; Jer 2:21), Israel *prospered*, but their apostasy grew in proportion to their prosperity (Deut 8:10–20), as evidenced in their multiplication of *altars* and *sacred stones* (Deut 16:22). Despite the announcement that God will *demolish* these sacred objects and will take away their *king*, Israel's concern is for the *calf-idol* of Bethel (see 8:5–6). Verse 4 describes abuses in the court system (compare Deut 17:8–13). The idol, like their king, who may be God's patron, is powerless to save even itself. *Assyria* will take both away along with the people of *Samaria*. The cry for the *mountains* to *cover* them indicates great despair (see Luke 23:30; Rev 6:16).

BREAKING NEW GROUND · 10:9–15

The sinfulness at *Gibeah* in the days of the judges (Judg 19–21) has characterized God's people from that time to Hosea's day. Therefore, God will place the *yoke* of Assyrian domination on both Israelite nations (Deut 28:48; Isa 14:25). God intends this judgment to be ultimately redemptive, but Israel and Judah must begin anew. They must *break* new *ground* by suffering through judgment until they *seek the Lord*. This judgment will clear away those things in which Israel misplaces trust: its *own strength* and *fortresses*, idols like the one at *Bethel*, and its *king*. The identity of *Shalman* (for suggestions, see Stuart 171–72) and the location of *Beth Arbel* are uncertain, but the Israelites well remember his brutality there. The prophets, like Deuteronomy, have strong ethical scruples against war crimes, even those involving the victimization of non-Israelites (Deut 20; Amos 2:1–3).

GOD'S PARENTAL LOVE FOR ISRAEL · 11:1–11

This passage depicts God as the devoted parent of a rebellious child. God brought the *son*, Israel (Exod 4:22), up *out of Egypt* (Matt 2:15) in the exodus and lovingly taught Israel *to walk* and *healed them* (On childbearing as a symbol of God's care and provision for Israel, see also Deut 1:31). But Israel did not return God's love, worshiping instead *Baals* and other *images*.

> **Matthew's Use of Hosea**
>
> *Matthew reuses this verse, not to claim that Hosea somehow predicted Jesus' flight to Egypt, but to help construct an artistic picture of Jesus as living out Israel's early life, this time in perfect obedience to God. Thus Matthew 1–4 portrays Jesus as hunted like Israel by an evil king, as moving to Egypt, as living in the wilderness, and so on.*

In light of Israel's rebellion, God exercises "tough love," giving them over to foreign nations. But because of his deep affection for his people, God cannot *give* them *up* to the fate of *Admah* and *Zeboiim*, cities that fell along with Sodom and Gomorrah (Deut 29:23; see also Gen 19). God's *compassion* leads him to new plans for Israel. However, that redemption comes through judgment because Israel must first return to God.

PAST EXAMPLES, PRESENT EVIL · 11:12–12:14

This passage indicts Israel and *Judah* for a variety of transgressions, centering primarily on *deceit* (Wolff 207–8).

11:12–12:6   Israel is duplicitous in its foreign policy. While allied to *Assyria* through *treaty*, Israel attempts to woo *Egypt* with bribes. Such machinations lead the Assyrians to destroy Israel (2 Kgs 17:3–6). Thus, as Israel's *lies* multiply, so does *violence*. Israel's ancestor *Jacob* was notorious for his deceitfulness (Gen 27:5–36), and his descendants follow in his footsteps. Again, the ancient stories give the prophet a way of talking about current realities. The differences are that Jacob *begged for* the *favor* of God's *angel* (Gen 32:22–32) and that he *found* God at *Bethel* (28:10–19; 35:1–15). Likewise, Israel *must return* to the God of Jacob.

12:7–8   The Old Testament repeatedly condemns *dishonest scales* (for example, Deut 25:13–16; Amos 8:5; Mic 6:11; Prov 11:1; 20:23). Those who are *very rich*, presumably because of such unscrupulous business practices, believe that no one will find them guilty of *iniquity or sin*. Such *boasts* are likely rooted in the corruption of the judicial system through bribery and favoritism toward the wealthy, which the Old Testament also repeatedly condemns (for example, Exod 23:8; Deut 16:19; Prov 17:23; Isa 1:23; 5:22–23; Amos 5:12).

12:9–10   These verses point to the wilderness period (see also 2:14–15; Amos 5:25), a time when all Israelites were equally dependent on God. The reference to the prophets reminds the reader of God's mercy in sending prophets to warn Israel, which also leaves Israel without excuse.

12:11–14 Hosea contrasts Israel with Jacob and Moses. On *Gilead*, see 6:8, and on *Gilgal* see the discussion on 9:14–16 above. Jacob's duplicity led him to be "exiled" from his home and to suffer equivalent justice of a sort when he *served to get a wife* from a duplicitous Laban (Gen 29:1–30). Yet, he eventually turned to God and was restored (see above on verse 4). Also, God used the faithful *prophet* Moses (Deut 18:15, 18; 34:9–10) to deliver *Israel* from *Egypt* and to *care* for Israel in the wilderness. But Israel shows neither the faith of Moses nor the proper response to God's commands in Moses' law or from subsequent prophets. Therefore, God will *repay* Israel for such *contempt*.

A MATTER OF LIFE & DEATH · 13:1–16

13:1–3 Life and blessing for Israel naturally flow from being faithful to the covenant relationship with God (Deut 5:32–33; 30:15–20), but Israel is unfaithful and so invites death. The phrase *Ephraim . . . was exalted in Israel* suggests that here *Ephraim* means the tribe rather than the whole northern kingdom. This tribe was prominent and powerful within Israel, and it was also the tribe of the northern kingdom's first king, Jeroboam I (1 Kgs 11:26). Following his rise to the throne, Israel rapidly fell into idolatry, particularly *Baal worship* and worship of Jeroboam's *calf-idols*. A translation problem makes it uncertain whether Israel really was practicing *human sacrifice* (see the NIV note on v. 2), but such a meaning here is certainly possible (see 2 Kgs 17:17). Israel's idolatry means they will soon vanish.

13:4–8 Verse 4 echoes of the first commandment (Exod 20:3; Deut 5:7), reminding that God demands exclusive loyalty from Israel. He has the right to do so because he delivered them from *Egypt*, *cared for* them *in the desert*, and also *fed them* in the land. But they have forgotten he is the one who provides (Deut 8:10–20). Therefore, in a vivid image of judgment, God will attack and destroy them like a predator attacks its prey.

Human Sacrifice in Pagan Worship

Human sacrifice occurred in the ancient world, especially at times of crisis (see Judg 11; 2 Kings 3:27; Mic 6:7). The Greeks told the story of Agamemnon's sacrifice of his daughter Iphigeneia during the Trojan War, and the Carthaginians, who were descendants of Phoenician colonists, sacrificed huge numbers of children and buried them in a special cemetery, the Tophet. The Bible condemns this practice.

13:9–11 These verses allude to the stories of Samuel and Saul. God was Israel's *helper* (*'ezer*), the one who delivered them in their battle with the Philistines at Ebenezer ("stone of help"; 1 Sam 7:12). Yet Israel demanded *a king* to lead them in battle (1 Sam 8:20), indicating a lack of trust in God. He granted their request, anointing Saul then later rejecting him for disobedience (1 Sam 9–15). Until Hosea's day, Israel has continued this pattern of rejecting God's help and installing kings who disobey. But these kings are powerless to *save*, and, thus, Israel is *destroyed*.

13:12–16 God knows well the sins of Israel, and, thus, Israel will "die," like a stillborn child, when Assyria destroys the nation. The meaning of verse 14a–d is debated (see 1 Cor 15:55). If one follows the NIV's translation, the first two lines are assertions—God will *ransom* and *redeem* Israel *from* death—and the next two lines taunt *death*. On this reading, there is hope that restoration will follow judgment. Such an abrupt shift from judgment is not unprecedented in Hosea (for example, 2:14–23; 11:8–9; McComiskey 223–24). However, many commentators and several translations (NASB 95, NRSV, NLT) understand the first two lines as questions: *Shall I ransom them from the power of Sheol? Shall I redeem them from Death?* (NRSV). On this reading, the answers to the first two questions are no, and the third and fourth questions are God's invitation to "death and Sheol . . . to loose all their pestilent powers from the underworld upon this faithless people" (Achtemeier 107). The latter view fits better contextually. Verses 14e–16 continue the images of death. The scorching *east wind* from the *desert* represents the Assyrians, who will sweep into Israel and kill violently and indiscriminately.

AN INVITATION TO RETURN · 14:1–9

14:1–3 The prophet summons the people to *return* to their *God*, even providing *words* of confession to *take* with them. They are to ask God to *forgive all* their *sins*, and they must acknowledge they have misplaced their trust. Neither *Assyria*, nor their own military might (symbolized by *war horses*), nor their *gods* can *save* them.

14:4–8 God offers to *heal* and *love* Israel in response to such a confession. He must *heal* them because they cannot do it for themselves (Hos 7:1; Jer 30:17; 33:6). Israel will again grow and prosper (2:21–23). When they sincerely call on God rather than *idols*, he will then *answer* and *care* for them.

14:9 This wisdom statement addresses the reader of the book. The *wise* person is the one who takes to heart *these things*, that is, what this book has said. The reader is left with a choice: to walk in God's *ways* as *the righteous do* or to be like *rebellious* Israel and *stumble* (Ps 1; Prov 4:18–19).

THEOLOGICAL REFLECTIONS

With images of God as a husband and father, Hosea gives us glimpses into the heart of God, who loves the covenant people. Like the husband of an unfaithful wife, God's heart is broken by idolatry or unwise political alliances. Like the loving parent of a rebellious child, God longs for Israel to realize the error of their ways and come home. God takes the covenant seriously, even when Israel does not.

Because of this love, God is willing to send judgment on them to ultimately restore them (see also Lev 26; Deut 27–28). In this light, the frequent caricature of the Old Testament's God as one of anger and wrath falls flat. Certainly, God's anger and wrath appear in Hosea, but God's judgment comes because of Israel's sin and rebellion, and it serves a loving and merciful intention to eradicate injustice and idolatry within Israel so as to bring life (compare Deut 30:11–20). Such judgment is a last resort. God graciously sent prophets to warn the people, but they refused to listen.

Israel's God is also not impotent like the gods and nations to whom Israel turned. God has repeatedly demonstrated his ability to protect the people (Exod 14–15; 17:8–16; Judg 4–5; 7) and provide for them (Exod 16:1–17:7). In Hosea, God intends to demonstrate his power and the powerlessness of those whom Israel pursues by withholding the security and provision Israel seeks from them. When they realize the futility of their pursuit and turn again to God, they will receive restoration and blessing again (Deut 30:1–10).

Following Hosea, the New Testament characterizes the church as the bride of Christ (2 Cor 11:2; Rev 19:7) and its members as God's children (Gal 3:26; 1 John 3:1). Hosea's words warn us against entrusting and devoting ourselves to anything other than God for provision and security. Yet when we do prostitute ourselves to such impotent "gods," Hosea reminds us that God will pursue us, discipline us, and, if we turn back to him wholeheartedly, graciously restore us.

FOR FURTHER STUDY

Birch, Bruce. *Let Justice Roll Down: The Old Testament, Ethics, and Christian Life.* Louisville: Westminster John Knox, 1991.

Nardoni, Enrique. *Rise Up, O Judge: A Study in Justice in the Biblical World.* Peabody, MA: Hendrickson, 2004.

WORKS CITED

Achtemeier, Elizabeth. *Minor Prophets I.* Peabody, MA: Henrickson, 1996.

Ackerman, Susan. "Cultic Prostitution." In *Eerdman's Dictionary of the Bible* (2000): 300.

Anderson, Francis I., and David N. Freedman. *Hosea.* Garden City, NY: Doubleday, 1980.

McComiskey, Thomas E. "Hosea." In *The Minor Prophets: An Exegetical and Expository Commentary*, edited by Thomas E. McComiskey, 1:1–237. Grand Rapids: Baker, 1992.

Stuart, Douglas. *Hosea-Jonah.* Waco, TX: Word, 1987.

Wolff, Hans Walter. *Hosea.* Translated by Gary Stansell. Philadelphia: Fortress, 1974.

Joel

John T. Willis

CHAPTER CONTENTS

Scholars debate Joel's structure. Prinsloo describes eight units, each one intensifying the preceding unit. Wolff claims that Joel contains two parts, arranged in reversed chiasm, but this view requires rearranging and omitting several verses. A productive way to view Joel's structure is to divide it into two sections, the first describing doom and demanding repentance; the second announcing hope and enemies' destruction. Joel and his audience would have been familiar with several such organizational Old Testament traditions (Gray 208–225; Crenshaw 27–28).

Chiasm or *Chiasmus*

A way of arranging parts of a text in a repetitive pattern in which the first part parallels the last, the second part the next to last, and so on (A B C C'B'A'). Chiasmus appears frequently in the Bible.

CONTEXTS

The book of Joel originated about 400–350 BCE. We know this because the Babylonian exile is spoken of in the past tense (3:1–3, 17), and the community leaders are elders (1:2, 14) and priests (1:9, 13; 2:17), not kings. Since the temple (1:13–14, 16; 2:17) and the city wall of Jerusalem (2:7, 9) exist in this book, a date of composition sometime after 445 BCE is necessary. Chapter 3:4–6 mentions that the Phoenicians and Philistines have confiscated Judah's riches and sold Judean slaves to Greeks, *far from their homeland*, therefore indicating that the text precedes Alexander the Great's defeat of Tyre in 332 BCE. If these events had occurred after the conquest of Tyre, slaves sold to the Greeks would not necessarily have been sent far from Israel.

All but verses 1:1 and 2:30–3:8 are in poetry. From the 1870s to the 1960s, most scholars believed Joel to consist of two originally independent works (1:1–2:17 and 2:18–3:21), or an expansion of an earlier work. Most current scholars, however, think it is essentially a unity.

COMMENTARY

SUPERSCRIPTION · 1:1

Joel son of Pethuel appears only here in the Old Testament. In prophetic books, it is often difficult to distinguish between Yahweh's and the prophets' words. Joel 1:1 designates Yahweh as the source of Joel's message but does not specify how Yahweh communicated it.

LOCUST PLAGUE & DROUGHT; CALL TO REPENTANCE · 1:2–2:17

1:2–20   Joel names five groups that locusts and drought have harmed: elders and people (vv. 2, 14); drunkards (v. 5); priests (vv. 9, 13); farmers and vinedressers (v. 11); and animals (vv. 18, 20). In verses 2–3, *Hear* and *Give ear* elicit audience attention (Hos 5:1). *Elders* are civil leaders (see Ruth 4:4) or older people (see Psalm 37:25) who can testify that no locust plague or drought like this has occurred in decades (Exod 10:6, 14). Each generation of Israelite parents would *tell* their children about the community's problems and needs, and how Yahweh had overcome them (Deut 6:6–7; Ps 78:1–8). In verse 4, the four locust groups (compare 2:25) are not symbols for nations, as some have claimed, but possibly reflect stages of locust development: larva, pupa, young locust, and mature locust; or, more probably, they refer to different types of locusts.

> **Locust Swarms**
>
> *Locust swarms may cover many square miles and include trillions of insects. Their devastating passage leads to human famine and disease.*

Locusts devour grapevines and fig trees so that *drunkards* lack wine. Locusts are innumerable and irrepressible, like an attacking *nation* (2:4–9). According to verses 8–10, cultic officiants cannot function, because sacrifices require *grain*, *wine*, and *oil* (Hos 2:8–9). Ancient Near Easterners wore *sackcloth* (v. 8) for mourning (Lam 2:8–11) or repentance (Isa 32:9–15). The trauma gripping priests is like that of a young widow bemoaning her husband's death.

Owing to the locust plague, farmers have no grains to harvest; vinedressers, no fruits to glean (11–12). These verses list all the main agricultural products of the land of Israel. Joel thus envisions the total devastation of the land. In verses 13–14, Joel charges priests to assemble elders and people to *the temple* (mentioned in verse 16). *A fast* demonstrated sadness (Neh 1:4) or repentance (Isa 58:1–12). In verses 15–17, locusts and drought signal *the day of the Lord*, which in the Old Testament refers to Yahweh's intervening to punish or bless his people or their enemies. Joel 1:15; 2:1–2, 11 denote God's judgment on Judah (Isa 2:10–17; Zeph 1:7); and 2:31; 3:14, the overthrow of nations and the deliverance of Judah. Verse 1:15 recalls Isaiah 13:6. *Almighty* translates the Hebrew name *Shaddai* (Exod 6:3). Verses 16–17 reiterate verses 4–13. In 18–20, locusts and drought harm fodder crops, causing animals to starve. In verses 19–20, Joel begs Yahweh to remove the devastation (compare Amos 7:1–6). *Fire* and *flames* accompany drought (Amos 7:4), which verses 10, 12, and 17 imply.

2:1–11   Verses 1–11 do not envision an "apocalyptic army" (Wolff 39–43) or Yahweh's earthly army (Crenshaw 116–32), but actual locusts, as the words *appearance* (v. 4) and *like* (vv. 5, 7) show. Joel 1:2–20 describes locusts in the country, and 2:1–11 announces the advance of locusts into Jerusalem. Joel's comrades must proclaim calamity: *the day of Yahweh* is near, and Yahweh's locust *army* (vv. 2, 5, 11, 25) threatens Zion (vv. 4–5, 7). In the first two verses, a trumpet blast means an enemy army approaches (v. 1; Hos 5:8). Ironically, the warning achieves nothing. *Darkness* signifies God's punishment (Amos 5:18– 20; Zeph 1:15). The plague has no precedent. In verses 3–11, Joel proclaims the locusts' advance into and through Jerusalem. These verses graphically describe the sound and movements of the enormous locust swarms, which may include billions of insects. Their whirring wings are like *rumbling of chariots and crackling of. . .fire* (v. 5). The hyperbolical comparison *like the garden of Eden* (Gen 2:8–14) contrasts with *a desolate wilderness* (v. 3). Devouring fire precedes Yahweh (Psalms 50:3; 97:3). Fear overwhelms the people (vv. 6, 11).

2:12–17   Yahweh does not wish to annihilate Judah but to deliver it. God addresses first the people (vv. 12–14), then the priests (vv. 15–17). The people should *return* (Hebrew *shuv*; verses 12, 13) so that Yahweh might *turn* (Hebrew *shuv*) away punishment and bless them (v. 14; Mal 3:7). Genuine *return* begins in the heart and produces appropriate external actions (v. 12; Jer 24:7). External actions include *fasting, weeping, mourning* (v. 12; see Esth 4:3). The text states two motivations for repentance: Yahweh is *gracious and merciful*, a stereotyped portrayal (Exod 34:6); and Yahweh may yet *relent and leave a blessing* (v. 14). God is free even to avert promised destruction (Ps 115:3). Often Yahweh *relents*, changing plans (Jer 18:7–10; Jonah 3:4, 6–10). The *blessing* is grain, wine, and oil for sacrifices (1:9–10, 13; compare 1:13–14). Yahweh charges the priests to assemble Judah for repentance. Verse 15a repeats verse 1a; verse 15b repeats 1:14a. Since locusts and drought devastated all, all must come to the temple. The priests must *lament* over sins—that is, they must lead the people in praying in the manner of the psalms of lament. As Yahweh's *heritage* (or private possession; see Exod 19:5–6), Israel must escape destruction so nations cannot mock them. When God's people suffer economic setbacks or military defeats, nations ask scornfully, *Where is their God?* (v. 17; Ps 79:10).

> **To "Rend Garments"**
> *Rending clothing (v. 13) signifies displeasure (2 Kgs 5:7–8), mourning (2 Sam 3:31), shame (2 Sam 13:19), or repentance (1 Kgs 21:27). It did not prove genuine repentance.*

RESTORATION OF THE PENITENT & THEIR ENEMIES' DEFEAT · 2:18–3:21

2:18–32   Joel addresses a changed audience. Between 2:17 and 2:18, the hearers repented, following the pattern of the psalms of lament. Like a husband (Prov 6:34), Yahweh *became jealous* for the devastated land; like a father (Ps 103:13), he *had pity on his people*. The paternal imagery here parallels other instances of its use in the Old Testament (for example, Deut 11:31). *The eastern sea* equals the Dead Sea, and the *western sea* is the Mediterranean. Pastures will flourish (v. 22; 1:10, 18–20), fig trees and grapevines bear fruit (v. 22; 1:5, 7, 12), rain pour (v. 23; 1:10, 12, 18–20), grain, wine, oil (v. 24; 1:10), and food abound (v. 26; 1:16), and Yahweh will remove the people's shame (vv. 26–27; 2:17). Again, the text lists the major agricultural crops and thinks of national distress as a matter of honor and shame. Joel discourages fear (vv. 21–22; 2:6) and encourages joy (vv. 21, 23; 1:5, 8, 11–13, 16) and praise (v. 26).

3:1–15 Yahweh will punish the nations who afflicted Israel. Verse 1b recalls Jeremiah 29:14. Yahweh will gather all nations to *the valley of Jehoshaphat* (a symbolic name; verses 2, 12) for punishment. This may be a literal valley lying near Jerusalem, or it may refer to the fact that Jehoshaphat of Judah defeated the Moabites, Ammonites, and Meunites in the valley of Beracah (2 Chron 20:20–26). Joel announces that Yahweh will act similarly now in punishing Israel's foes. Verses 2e–3 enumerate crimes the nations committed that warrant Yahweh's punishment. Invaders *cast lots* to determine ownership of captives (Obad 11). In verses 4–8, Yahweh specifies Phoenicia and Philistia, asking what prompted them to oppress the Israelites. They stored Judah's wealth in their temples (a common practice in antiquity) and sold Judeans to Greeks. Were these retaliations for Judah's crimes? Yahweh summons *the nations* for judgment (v. 12), mockingly charging them to make weapons, deliberately reversing the language of Isaiah 2:4 (v. 10); Yahweh's *warriors* will fight them (vv. 11–12). Yahweh will destroy the nations like harvesting grain (Isa 17:5) or treading grapes (Isa 63:1–6). Verse 15 reiterates 2:10.

> **The Divine Spirit**
> *Yahweh will heal Judah's spiritual despondency (1:12; 2:6), pouring out the divine spirit (a life-giving force, according to Zech 4:6) on all flesh, that is, the survivors of locusts and drought (v. 32). Peter quotes 2:28–32 in Acts 2:17–21, applying it to his context and message.*

Joel 3:16–21 highlights Yahweh's presence in Judah, which is like a roaring lion (v. 16; Amos 1:2), striking fear in the nation's enemies (Amos 3:4, 8) but protecting God's people (Hos 11:10–11). *The Lord dwells in Zion* (vv. 17, 21) evokes a centuries-old understanding of the temple and Jerusalem as being under God's protection (Pss 2, 84; but see Jer 7). Verse 18d recalls Ezekiel 47:1–12.

THEOLOGICAL REFLECTIONS

Joel is an encouragement to penitent believers. It affirms Yahweh's presence and sovereignty over nature and nations. Locusts and drought punish God's people for sins by removing essentials for physical life and worship. Sin is serious to the holy God. Like a mighty warrior, Yahweh leads a locust "army" across the countryside and into the city. The ultimate intention is not to destroy but to save the penitent. When they recognize their destitute circumstances, God calls them to genuine repentance, not to mere external actions. Gracious and merciful,

God may relent, and knowledge of this possibility leads the people to repent. God will then punish their enemies and restore their losses, making Jerusalem a "refuge" and "stronghold."

FOR FURTHER STUDY

Matthews, Victor H. *The Hebrew Prophets and Their Social World*. Grand Rapids: Baker Academic, 2012.
Nogalski, James D. *The Book of the Twelve and Beyond*. Atlanta: SBL, 2017.

WORKS CITED

Crenshaw, James L. *Joel*. New York: Doubleday, 1995.
Gray, George Buchanan. "The Parallel Passages in 'Joel' and Their Bearing on the Question of Date." *Expository Times* 8 (1893): 208–25.
Prinsloo, W. S. *The Theology of the Book of Joel*. Berlin: de Gruyter, 1985.
Wolff, Hans Walter. *Joel and Amos*. Philadelphia: Fortress, 1977.

Amos

Philip G. Camp

CHAPTER CONTENTS

FEATURE

The book of Amos announces God's judgment on the northern kingdom of Israel, especially for the injustices perpetrated by the wealthy and powerful on the poor and weak.

CONTEXTS

Amos' oracles address Israel in a period of national expansion and prosperity sometime during the first half of the eighth century BCE. The long, stable reigns of Israel's King Jeroboam II (786–746 BCE) and Judah's King Uzziah (1:1), the peace between their nations, and their secure borders allowed for such conditions. However, the influx of wealth did not benefit the entire nation. The rich got richer through the manipulation and exploitation of the poor.

Amos was a *shepherd* from *Tekoa* who also *took care of sycamore-fig trees* (1:1; 7:14). God called him to prophesy to the northern kingdom, Israel. The reference to Amos in the third person in the superscription (1:1) and the narrative in 7:10–15 suggest that someone other than Amos edited the book. However, there is no scholarly consensus on the nature and extent of the editing process (see Paul 16–27; Stuart 294–95).

COMMENTARY

SUPERSCRIPTION · 1:1–2

In addition to the information covered in the "Introduction," the superscription also says that Amos *saw* (compare Isa 1:1; 2:1; Mic 1:1) these things *two years before the earthquake* (see Zech 14:5). The date of this event is uncertain (Paul 35), but it would have been fresh in the mind of Amos' audience.

Verse 2 sets the stage for the rest of the book. God's judgment booms with devastating effect from *Zion/Jerusalem* (see Jer 25:30; Joel 3:16), the site of his holy temple. Note that a lion *roars* after it has caught its prey (see 3:4), indicating that, while judgment is still to come, Israel is as good as dead.

ORACLES AGAINST THE NATIONS · 1:3–2:16

Oracles against nations usually announce God's sovereignty over and judgment on foreign nations (Isa 13–23; Jer 46–51; Ezek 25–32), but Amos also uses the genre to lump *Israel* (and *Judah*) in with all the other neighboring nations, implying there is no real distinction. The oracles in 1:3–2:16 share several common features. First, the N, N+1 pattern, *for three sins . . . even for four* (1:3, 6, 9, 11, 13; 2:1, 4, 6), is a literary device that sometimes specifies an exact number (as in Prov 30:15–31), but here it indicates the totality of these nations' sins (Paul 27–30). Thus, with the exceptions of *Judah* and *Israel*, each oracle specifies only one sin that characterizes the general wickedness of that nation. Second, with the exception of *Israel*, God says he will send *fire* that will *consume* the *fortresses* of these nations (1:4, 7, 10, 12, 14; 2:2, 5). That is, the nations' defenses will not withstand the judgment of God. Third, the agent of God's judgment is not specified, but historically conquests by Assyria and later Babylon accomplish these judgments.

1:1–5 *Damascus* is the capital of *Aram* (Syria). The *house of Hazael* refers to the line of a usurper who murdered his predecessor (2 Kgs 8:7–15), and *Ben-Hadad* is Hazael's son (2 Kgs 13:3, 24). Both violently oppressed Israel, including attacks on *Gilead*, in the late ninth and early eighth centuries BCE (2 Kgs 8:28–29; 9:14–15; 10:32–33; 13:22–25). God will "reverse Aram's history" (Achtemeier 180) by sending them back to *Kir*, the place of their origin (9:7).

1:6–8 *Gaza, Ashdod, Ashkelon*, and *Ekron* are four of the five city-states of the Philistine Pentapolis (Gath is the fifth; see 6:2). Selling captives as slaves was not an unusual practice in ancient warfare, but this reference suggests the *Philistines* raided *communities* expressly for the purpose of capturing people to sell into slavery (compare Exod 21:16; Joel 3:4–6).

The Philistines

Derived from the Hebrew plishtim, *the Philistines were a people who inhabited the southern coast of Canaan during Old Testament times, but who had probably migrated there in the twelfth century BCE from Crete.*

1:9–10 *Tyre* is also charged with selling *captives to Edom*, which is seen as a violation of *a treaty of brotherhood*. If Israel is the treaty partner, then this refers to David's and later Solomon's cordial relationship with King Hiram of Tyre (1 Kgs 5:1, 12).

1:11–12 *Edom* is Israel's *brother* nation because the Edomites descend from Esau, the brother of Jacob (Gen 25:30; 36:1). Since Edom has taken up the *sword* against Israel, God's judgment is coming (as in Obad 1–21). *Teman* and *Bozrah* are principle cities of Edom.

1:13–15 *Ammon*, whose capital is *Rabbah*, is charged with massacring *pregnant women of Gilead* (2 Kgs 8:12; 15:16; Hos 13:16). This practice was rare in ancient warfare and was considered especially brutal. This reference probably represents a wide range of similarly heinous acts by the Ammonites (Cogan 755–57).

2:1–3 *Moab* is charged with burning *the bones of Edom's king*, namely the desecration of his tomb. In the ancient Near East, not respecting a burial was a great disgrace. *Kerioth* is the site of a sanctuary for Moab's chief god, Chemosh.

2:4–5 Pointing out the impending judgment of *Judah*, Israel's sister nation, for violating God's *law*, including following *false gods*, should open Israel's eyes to their own precarious situation (Jer 3:6–11).

2:6–16 The oracle against *Israel* expands on the pattern of the previous seven oracles. Amos names several *sins*, all examples of oppression and injustice. Human life is devalued as people are sold into slavery for insignificant amounts, probably to pay off their loans. The powerful abuse those unable to defend themselves and *deny* them *justice* (Exod 23:2–3, 6; Lev 19:15; Deut 16:19–20). *Father and son* disgracefully use the same *girl*, probably a slave, for sexual gratification (see Gen 35:22; 49:3–4; Lev 18:8, 15). Furthermore, the worship of *their god* takes place alongside the use of clothing as collateral, in violation of Israelite law (see Exod 22:26–27; Deut 24:12–13, 17) and levying undeserved *fines*.

> **Gilead**
>
> *The area northwest of the Dead Sea. Israel, Ammon, and Moab each ruled the area at different times. A recently discovered Moabite text records the capture of Ammonite settlers in this area and their deportation to Moabite work projects. An earlier Moabite text, the Mesha Stele from the ninth century BCE, records the massacre of Israelites in the same general area.*

By reciting God's gracious deeds on Israel's behalf, Amos places responsibility for the coming judgment squarely on Israel. God also raised up *prophets* (Deut 18:15–22; 2 Kgs 17:13, 23) and *Nazirites* (Num 6:1–21) for the benefit of Israel, but Israel turned against both. Therefore, severe judgment is coming upon them.

ORACLES OF JUDGMENT AGAINST ISRAEL · 3:1–6:14

3:1–2 Chapter 3 contains three judgment oracles. The first oracle couches the judgment of Israel in the context of its special relationship with God, based on the election of the Israelites from among *all the families of the earth* and their deliverance from *Egypt*. God's intention was to bless the Israelites and, through them, the nations (compare Gen 12:3; 18:18–19; Deut 4:5–8). Their refusal to live up to their calling, as evidenced in their idolatry and treatment of the poor, jeopardizes God's intentions for them and the world. Thus, their election will not insulate them from God's judgment (Paul 101).

3:3–8 This oracle begins with seven rhetorical questions. The obvious answers of the first six lead the audience to the obvious answer of the seventh question: Of course, *disaster* does not *come to a city* unless *the Lord has caused* *it*. The larger context of Amos indicates that cities deserving of God's judgment are in view here (as in 1:3, 5, 6–10, 12, 14; 2.5; 3:14; 5:5–6) and not every city that experiences a tragedy. However, God mercifully does not send judgment without first warning the people through *prophets* (see Gen 18:16–33; 2 Kgs 17:13, 23), and Israel should take Amos' message as just such a warning.

3:9–12   God calls both Philistines and Egyptians to *assemble* in order to witness the *unrest* and *oppression* in Israel and to witness the resulting judgment, implying that Israel is worse than these nations that the Israelites would consider the epitome of oppressors (Exod 1:11–12; 3:9; Judg 10:7–8; 31:1). The image of the rescued bits of a sheep indicates the totality of the judgment.

3:13–4:13   This long oracle announces God's judgment on the wealthy and idolatrous oppressors of Israel. The opening verses connect idolatry and injustice by announcing judgment on symbols of each one: *altars* and *houses* of the wealthy, respectively. The two offenses are linked because forsaking God for idols means forsaking divine standards in all matters, including justice. The *altars of Bethel* include Jeroboam I's altar at the shrine of his calf image (1 Kgs 12:26–13:5) and may include unauthorized altars for God, as well.

In 4:1–3, the prophet then addresses the rich *women*, who stand for all those who *oppress the poor*. Amos derogatorily compares them to *cows* fattened for the slaughter. They will be dragged through breaches in the city wall, tethered by *hooks*, an image of defeat and humiliation (see 2 Kgs 19:28; 2 Chron 33:11; Ezek 38:4; Hab 1:15). The meaning and location of *Harmon* is uncertain (Stuart 333; Paul 135–36).

The call to *sin* at *Bethel* and *Gilgal* (4:4–5; compare Hos 4:15; 9:15) is ironic. If the wealthy Israelites continue to live as they do now, no amount of *sacrifices* or *offerings* can save them. True worship and ethical living are inextricably intertwined.

In keeping with the curses in the law (Lev 26:14–26; Deut 28:15–48), God sent judgments of increasing severity upon the people, even completely destroying *some* in the manner of *Sodom and Gomorrah* (4:6–12; compare Gen 19:1–29). However, to this point, God has been unwilling to destroy everyone (2 Kgs 13:23). The goal of such judgments is corrective and redemptive, intending to lead the people back to God, as indicated by the refrain *yet you have not returned to me* (vv. 6, 8, 9, 10, 11; see Lev 26:18, 21, 23, 27, 40).

Alternative Sanctuaries
In ancient Israel, temples or open-air sacred spaces existed at several locales. Bethel and Dan, the border cities of the northern kingdom of Israel, were the largest and best known. Gilgal had been in use since the earliest days of Israelite life in Palestine. Amos does not condemn the sanctuaries per se, but rather the actions that occurred within them and the worshipers' neglect of ethical living.

Because the wealthy refuse to respond to such correction, Amos warns them to *prepare to meet* their awesome *God*. The word *this* in verse 12 probably refers back to destruction and exile predicted in 3:13–4:3. Exile is the final and most severe of the curses of the law (Lev 26:27–35; Deut 28:49–68).

Justice & Righteousness

Justice and righteousness are central to the character and action of God (Pss 33:5; 36:6; 37:6; 89:14; Jer 9:24; Hos 2:19), whom Israel should imitate. These concepts are related, and, thus, they are often paired in the Old Testament. Justice (Hebrew mishpat*) derives from the root* shaphat, *"to judge," which indicates the restoration of harmony and wholeness (Hebrew* shalom) *between individuals or within a community. A disruption of that wholeness can occur when two parties have a dispute or when one party wrongs another. A third party (for example, a judge, the king, or God) intervenes to restore* shalom, *and justice (*mishpat) *is the act and result of this intervention (hence* mishpat *is also often translated "judgment"). Thus, justice is active. The term frequently applies to a legal setting, as is often the case in Amos, but it is not limited to this setting (Liedke 1392–99; Birch 155–56, 259). Righteousness (Hebrew* tsedaqah *or* tsedeq) *is a relational term that entails both the act and results of faithfully maintaining the integrity of the relationship so that both parties enjoy the benefits of the relationship. Thus God delivers and preserves Israel, and Israel keeps God's commands, most of which focus on how humans treat each other (see Birch 153–55, 259–60; Koch 1046–62; von Rad 370–83).*

Injustice, violence, and oppression are antithetical to justice and righteousness because they disrupt the harmony and wholeness of the community and violate the relationships between God and Israel and between fellow Israelites (see Isa 1:21; 5:7; Jer 22:3; Ezek 45:9). Once Israel becomes unfaithful to its covenant relationship with God, love of neighbor also disappears, and violence and oppression erupt. God sends prophets like Amos to warn the people to restore justice and righteousness, but, when they refuse, God intervenes to save the oppressed and to judge and punish the oppressors (Ps 103:6, 17–18).

5:1–17 God, who takes no pleasure in bringing judgment, laments the impending "death" of *Israel* (vv. 1–3). In verses 4–6, God's intention is to bring the people to repentance. Therefore, Amos calls on them to *seek* him and *live* (Deut 30:15–20) instead of turning to the idolatrous shrines of *Bethel, Gilgal,* or *Beersheba* (8:14), which will all perish in the coming judgment.

Verses 7–13 draw a fearful picture of a God who will not allow injustice to continue unpunished in the land. *Justice* and *righteousness* should characterize the people of God, as they characterize God himself, but Israel has undermined both. They *hate* those who testify truthfully in *court* (literally "gate," where legal matters were handled; also in verses 12, 15) and use bribery to corrupt the system in their favor (Exod 20:16; 23:1, 8; Deut 16:19). They grow wealthy on the backs of the *poor* by coercing them *to give* over their livelihood, perhaps by manipulating the courts against them (Stuart 348), or through excessive taxation (Paul 172–73), or through making debt repayment impossible. But God assures the rich that they will not long enjoy the fruits of their corruption (see Deut 28:30). The *prudent man* here could refer to those who simply remain quiet in order to avoid being crushed by the corrupt system, or it could refer to the unjust, who should resist any attempt to justify themselves before God.

Verses 14–15 again call Israel to repent, particularly by ensuring *justice in the courts*. The use of *perhaps* (v. 15) indicates that the extension of God's *mercy* to Israel is not guaranteed. Israel has violated the covenant, so restoration can occur only because of God's mercy. However, if things continue as they are, God's judgment will result in great *wailing* as God *passes through* their midst, a scene reminiscent of the plague on the firstborn of Egypt (vv. 16–17; Exod 11:4–6; 12:29–30).

5:18–27 The *day of the Lord* refers to a time when God will decisively intervene in history to judge and to save. Israel mistakenly expects that such a day will benefit them because they think their religious exercises appease or manipulate God. But God hates their worship and refuses to *accept* their *offerings* because they have subverted *justice* and *righteousness* (compare Isa 1:10–15), both of which should flourish in Israel. Furthermore, their worship of God is only half-hearted because they also worship *idols*.

The question in verse 25 is curious. In light of verses 21–23, the expected answer is no, but several passages indicate that *Israel*, in fact, made *sacrifices and offerings* during the wilderness period (for example, Exod 24:5; Lev 9:8–22; Num 7:87–88). The complete sacrificial system, however, came into force only after Israel settled in the land (Deut 12). Faithfulness, rather than performing rituals, is the central element of a proper relationship with God (Stuart 355; Achtemeier 212; Paul 193–94).

6:1–14 The rich are *complacent* and *feel secure* because their wealth continues to increase and their borders are safe. In their own eyes, they are indeed *notable men of the foremost nation* and are better than *Calneh*, *Hamath*, or *Gath*, states neighboring Israel or Judah. These cities fell under Assyrian control around Amos' time. Israel's wealth does not indicate God's favor. They sin not simply by enjoying luxuries but by ignoring the *ruin* of their fellow Israelites, whom they oppress to obtain those luxuries.

God reveals deep disgust for Israel's misplaced *pride*. Past military victories at *Lo Debar* and *Karnaim* should not make them confident in their own strength or in God's favor upon them. Because they pervert *justice* and *righteousness*, God will *deliver up* Israel to foreigners who will leave nothing but *bodies* behind. Any survivor will not want *the name of the Lord* mentioned, lest he draw God's attention and die too. The geographical range from *Lebo Hamath* (in the gap between the Lebanon and Antilebanon mountain ranges) to *the valley of*

Prophetic Intercession

In the Old Testament, three great prophets succeed in changing God's mind regarding the destruction of a people: Abraham for the number of citizens of Sodom required to save the city, Moses after the golden calf episode, and Amos here. The Bible does not portray God as an inflexible manipulator of human actions.

the Arabah (the rift valley south of the Dead Sea) represents the northernmost and southernmost conquests of Jeroboam II (2 Kgs 14:25).

7:1–9   Three visions of God's judgment arouse Amos' compassion for his people so that he intercedes on their behalf (like Moses in Exod 32:11–14). Twice God *relented* because of his compassion for Israel (2 Kgs 13:23), but Israel cannot presume upon God's mercy, since God is also just and righteous (Jer 7:16; 11:14). The first vision is of a devastating plague of *locusts* (vv. 1–3; compare Joel 1:2–12; 2:1–11). The second vision (vv. 4–6), *judgment by fire*, may symbolize severe judgment in general or may hyperbolically picture a terrible drought (see. 4:7–8). The third vision (vv. 7–9) is of a *plumb line*, a tool that provides a standard for making sure that walls are straight or *true*. God finds that his people are not *true* to his calling for them (compare 2 Kgs 21:13; Isa 28:17; 34:11). Another possible translation for the word translated *plumb line* (Hebrew *'anak*) is "tin." If this translation is correct, it may be an auditory wordplay on similar sounding Hebrew words (see 8:1–2) for groaning or moaning (*'anach* or *'anaq*), or it may be an image of a tin wall, which would be weak and offer little protection for Israel (see Holladay 492–94; Stuart 373; Paul 233–35). Whatever the correct translation, the point of the oracle is clear: God will no longer withhold judgment against Israel's *sanctuaries* and the royal family (see 2 Kgs 15:8–12).

7:10–17   The encounter between Amaziah the priest and Amos interrupts the series of vision reports, but it explains Amos' words against the house of Jeroboam (7:9). Amaziah accuses Amos of treason. Since Amos never specifically predicts the death of Jeroboam, this accusation probably reflects Amaziah's own interpretation of Amos' prophecy in verse 9. Amaziah sees Amos as a prophet-for-hire (as in 1 Kgs 22:6; Mic 3:5) and orders him to return to Judah and earn his living there. Amos denies that he is the kind of prophet Amaziah has in mind. He is neither a professional prophet nor a disciple of a prophet (*a prophet's son*). Rather, God *took* him and sent him to prophesy (see Deut 18:15, 18). Amos then announces degradation and death for Amaziah's family and exile for Amaziah.

8:1–3   This vision report involves a wordplay between two similar sounding Hebrew words, "ripe fruit" (*qayits*) and "end" (*qets*), which the NIV translates the "time is ripe," preserving the sense of the wordplay. The picture of that day of God's judgment is mayhem followed by desolation.

8:4–14   This extended oracle reviews the sins of Israel before giving several pictures of the day of God's judgment on them. According to verses 4–6, the oracle addresses those who gain wealth by cheating *the poor* through deceptive business

Amos & Foreign Cultures
Amos and other biblical writers knew a great deal about the geography, patterns of life, and even religious traditions of neighboring cultures. The active trading culture of the time would have made such broad knowledge possible.

practices (Lev 19:36; Deut 25:13–16; Prov 11:1; 20:23) and by treating their lives as cheap commodities (see above on 2.6). The rich formally observe the *Sabbath* but forget its significance as a reminder that God is the creator and sustainer of all (Exod 20:8–11) and that God delivered all Israel from slavery (Deut 5:12–15). Sabbath observance was to serve as the great equalizer in the Israelite community, reminding Israel that they all benefited from God's care and thus should show each other similar care and compassion. However, God is well aware of their practices and will soon respond by convulsing Israel like the rising and falling of the *Nile* in its annual flood cycle (vv. 7–8).

Three descriptions of *that day* of God's judgment then follow. First, the images of the cosmos darkening (Amos 5:18, 20; Isa 13:10; Jer 4:28; Ezek 32:7–8; Joel 2:10; 2:31; 3:15; compare Matt 24:29) and of celebration turned to *mourning* (Isa 24:6–13; Jer 16:8–9; Hos 2:11; Rev 18:21–22) are common images of severe judgment. Second, there will be a *famine* of God's *words* (11–12). Israel had already rejected God's word in the Law, which was to truly sustain them (Deut 6:1–2; 8:3), and now God will withhold the prophetic word. When God no longer sends prophets, Israel will face judgment (1 Sam 3:1; 28:6; Lam 2:9; Ezek 7:26). Third, the judgment will be so severe that even the most vigorous will *faint* and not be revived.

9:1–6   Amos sees the image of God striking a temple, probably the Bethel sanctuary, so that it collapses on the worshipers within. Any survivors are *killed with the* sword, which illustrates the point of this oracle: *none* of those under God's judgment *will escape*. No place is low enough, high enough, or far enough to *hide* from God (Rom 8:38–39) who intends *evil*, that is, harm, for them rather than *good*.

9:7–10   With this final oracle of judgment, the book of Amos comes full circle, again proclaiming God's sovereignty over all nations and again lumping Israel among the nations (Amos 1:3–2:16). God brought both *Israel* into its land, and other nations into theirs (Deut 2:2–23; 32:8). However, God promises not to *totally destroy* Israel but rather to scatter *Israel among the nations*, but *the sinners*, those who arrogantly believe they will not *meet* judgment, *will die*.

9:11–15   Following the judgment, God announces another *day* for the pitching again of *David's fallen tent*, which anticipates the restoration of all Israel. Territorial expansion, rebuilding, replanting, and abundance will mark this restoration. God will *plant* Israel so that it will never be *uprooted* (Jer 31:27–28; 32:41; Hos 2:21–23). Thus, God's ultimate goal is to restore and bless the people.

THEOLOGICAL REFLECTIONS

Does the book of Amos present good news or bad news? For those who gain and maintain wealth through the oppression of the poor and corruption, it is bad news. It is bad news for those who divide their loyalties between God and idols. Whatever they think, abundance does not prove that they have pleased, appeased, or manipulated God.

However, for those among the poor and oppressed, Amos' words are good news. God is indeed aware of their plight and will act on their behalf. Within the Law, God has repeatedly expressed a concern for the weakest of society and an intention to intervene on their behalf (see Exod 22:21–24; Lev 19:33–34; Deut 10:17–19; 15:1–11). Through the prophets, like Amos, God announces that such intervention is at hand because Israel refuses to maintain justice and righteousness, especially for the poor and weak (compare Isa 1:10–20; Jer 22:1–9; Mic 3:1–4, 9–12; Hab 1:1–11).

Even to those under God's judgment, however, Amos reveals that God's mercy and compassion are at work. First, God sends prophets like Amos to warn the people to repent, and judgment comes only after they reject the prophet's message (2:11–12; 3:17). Second, God delays judgment repeatedly and refrains from executing it totally (4:11; 7:3, 6). Third, God announces a plan to restore and bless the people (9:11–15).

Amos' words are a timely warning for the American church today, especially in light of our great wealth compared to the world at large and to fellow Christians abroad. Amos warns us against acquiring our wealth, directly or indirectly, through the oppression of the poor and weak. He further warns us against manipulating the system against the weak by favoring the rich over the poor or by denying the poor access to the same level of justice we enjoy. Amos reminds us that we, as the people of God, are responsible to care for fellow Christians in need, wherever they are, to ensure there is no favoritism toward the wealthy or powerful in our churches, and to fulfill our calling by living as people of justice and righteousness in this world. Jesus came to proclaim release for the oppressed (Luke 4:18), and we must join him on the side of the oppressed.

FOR FURTHER STUDY

King, Philip J. *Amos, Hosea, Micah: An Archaeological Commentary*. Philadelphia: Westminster, 1988.

Nardoni, Enrique. *Rise Up, O Judge: A Study in Justice in the Biblical World*. Peabody, MA: Hendrickson, 2004.

WORKS CITED

Achtemeier, Elizabeth. *Minor Prophets I*. Peabody, MA: Hendrickson, 1996.

Birch, Bruce C. *Let Justice Roll Down: The Old Testament, Ethics and the Christian Life*. Louisville: Westminster John Knox, 1991.

Cogan, Mordecai. "'Ripping Open Pregnant Women' in Light of an Assyrian Analog." *Journal of the American Oriental Society* 103 (1983): 755–57.

Holladay, William L. "Once More, *'anak* = 'tin.' Amos 7:7–8." *Vetus Testamentum* 20 (1970): 492–94.

Koch, Klaus. "*sdq*." *Theological Lexicon of the Old Testament* 2 (1997): 1,046–62.

Liedke, Gerhard. "*špt*." *Theological Lexicon of the Old Testament* 3 (1997): 1,392–99.

Paul, Shalom M. *Amos*. Minneapolis: Fortress, 1991.

Stuart, Douglas. *Hosea-Jonah*. Waco, TX: Word, 1987.

von Rad, Gerhard. *Old Testament Theology*. Translated by D. M. G. Stalker. 2 vols. San Francisco: Harper San Francisco, 1962.

Obadiah

Mark W. Hamilton

CHAPTER CONTENTS

The book of Obadiah has the twin distinctions of being both the shortest book in the Old Testament and the only one that substantially duplicates part of another book. At twenty-one verses, it is only 1.7 percent as long as Jeremiah, the longest prophetic work, and it extensively parallels Jeremiah 49.

Importantly, Obadiah offers a powerful reflection on the morality of world politics, as God perceives it. In addressing the question of God's interest in Israel's enemies, it also complements Jonah's gracious universality with a realistic perception of the complexities of international affairs and the true effects of war on conquered peoples.

CONTEXTS

The date, career, and background of the prophet Obadiah remain obscure. Scholars have dated his work anywhere between 900 and 450 BCE, although his reference to Edomite betrayal of Judah makes best sense in the context of events surrounding Nebuchadnezzar's destruction of Jerusalem in 586 BCE (see Ps 137; Lam 21:22; Ezek 25:12–14). Raabe and Wolff have proposed, plausibly, that Obadiah's prophecy may come from a service of lamentation at the location of the destroyed temple in Jerusalem during the years immediately preceding its rebuilding at the end of the sixth century BCE (Wolff 20–21; Raabe 55–56). See also Psalm 74.

While scholars have offered various scenarios by which originally separate, brief oracles could have coalesced in this single book, the more recent trend has been to try to understand the book as a coherent

"Book of the Twelve"
"Book of the Twelve" is a Hebrew term for the twelve minor prophets in the Old Testament canon.

unit originating probably in one situation. (However, the opening words *the vision of Obadiah* (1a) probably come from the editor of the Book of the Twelve.) Since verses 1b–18 are poetry, and 19–21 are prose, the end of the book may stem from a separate occasion in the prophet's life, but even this hypothesis remains unproven. As they stand, verses 19–21 explicate the previous lines, explaining concretely what the generalized talk of Israel's restoration in verses 17–18 will mean. Admittedly, the book does seem to jump from metaphor to metaphor in a slightly bewildering way, but this can be explained by its origins in oral performance (as was true of most prophetic oracles), and in its rich use of wordplays and a kaleidoscope of images to carry its message.

One of the simplest, yet still powerful, examples of wordplay revolves around a series of puns in Hebrew. For example, verse 12 mentions the *day of their destruction* (Hebrew *yom 'avedam*), which sounds like verse 13's *day of their disaster* (*yom 'eydom*), which in turns sounds like "day of Edom." Whenever the hearer of Obadiah's oracle thinks of Edom, he or she also thinks of disaster. A second series of wordplays centers around the name of the Edomite capital Bozrah (*Botsrah*). For example, verse 12 refers to Edom's behavior in Judah's *day of trouble* (*beyom tsarah*), and verse 5 uses the word for *grape pickers* (*botserim*). The fondness for wordplay is common in Hebrew poetry, and skill at such punning must have marked the successful poet. Since this poetry was probably originally oral, the punning also allows easy memorization of the words.

Yahweh's Servant
Obadiah places his great poetic gifts in the service of the theological proclamation of the absolute sovereignty of Israel's God.

As one expects from Hebrew poetry, the lines of Obadiah consist of strings of couplets linked by numerous wordplays and chains of imagery. For example, verses 3–4 open with a reference to the mountainous home of the Edomites (*you who live in the clefts of the rocks*), then refer to something that also nests among the mountains (*the eagle*), then imagines such birds nesting higher still, among the stars, and finally concludes by reversing the boast of verse 3 (*Who can bring me down to the ground?*) with God's taunt in verse 4 (*I will bring you down*).

COMMENTARY

The book consists of two large intertwined blocks of material, plus a superscription and concluding tag line.

THE SUPERSCRIPTION · 1A

Befitting the brevity of the book, *The vision of Obadiah* is the shortest superscription in the prophetic works. Typically, the superscription locates a prophet in time and space by naming his father or birthplace and dating the prophetic words to a king's reign. For example, Micah 1:1 introduces: *The word of the Lord that came to Micah of Moresheth during the reigns of Jotham, Ahaz, and Hezekiah, kings of Judah*. . . . The terseness of the heading of the book of Obadiah allows the editor who combined it with other parts of the Book of the Twelve to connect its reference to the day of Yahweh with prior discussions of that theme in Joel and Amos. We hardly notice that one book has ended and another has begun.

YAHWEH'S INDICTMENT OF EDOM · 1B–14, 15B

1B   Opening with the typical prophetic style of introduction, the messenger formula *This is what the Sovereign Lord says*, the oracle immediately shifts to a different point of view, *We have heard*. The *We* may include other prophets, or the divine council, or simply Obadiah's hearers, as well as the prophet himself. The rest of the verse calls someone, probably foreign nations though possibly Israel, to battle.

2–4   After the call to battle, God taunts Edom, referring to its mountainous terrain. While the Edomites think of this territory as impregnable, Yahweh knows better. The metaphor of rising to the *stars* typically symbolizes the arrogance of political leaders, notably the king of Babylon in Isaiah 14:12–14 (see also Gen 11:1–9). Numbers 24:21 describes the nomadic tribe of the Kenites nesting in the strongholds of the mountain. *Declares the Lord* marks the end of the first paragraph of the oracle.

5–7   The second paragraph emphasizes the Edomites' vulnerability. *Grape pickers* alludes to the extensive grape production around the capital, Bozrah (see LaBianca and Younker 403). Even those who should enhance Edom's economic prosperity become potential enemies. Verse 7 makes the threat concrete: *All your allies* will abandon you. Obadiah faults Edom's choice of *allies*, which led to its betrayal of its natural partner, Judah. How ironic, then, that these very allies should now abandon Edom! *Allies* translates the Hebrew "men of your covenant." A "covenant" here means a political agreement—that is, a treaty. Often in the Bible, the term designates God's agreement with Israel.

8–10   These verses describe the *day* of the Lord, a recurring theme in the prophets. The day may not appear on any calendar. Rather, it marks any moment of decisive divine intervention. While Edom may not have enjoyed more *wise men* than other nations (though Job hailed from the region), their demise meant the loss of practical skills and of social memory. *Teman* is a town in northwest Saudi Arabia (for its link to Edom,

Edom

The land of Edom lies south and east of the Dead Sea in what is today Jordan and northern Saudi Arabia. An arid region that receives 4–8 inches of rain per year, Edom relied on herding and limited agriculture to make a living. After the Babylonian conquest of Judah, Edomites gradually moved west into southern Judah. The region became known as Idumaea (the Greek form of "Edom").

Egyptian sources mention the region as early as the reign of Ramesses II (1304–1237 BCE). However, extensive settlement of the area dates only to the centuries after 1000 BCE (see MacDonald; LaBianca and Younker).

see Amos 1:12). Curiously, the last Neo-Babylonian king, Nabonidus, spent most of his reign in *Teman* pursuing religious enlightenment. So his contemporary Obadiah may envision here the destruction both of Edom and of the geopolitical system into which it has placed itself.

11–14 Obadiah uses the Hebrew imperfect verb in verses 12–14 to make the terrible events surrounding the sack of Jerusalem seem more real, more current. For an even more graphic description of the city's fall, see the book of Lamentations. *Gates* symbolizes the entire fortification system of a city (13). The breach of a city's gates by enemy armies spells doom for its inhabitants.

15B The conclusion of Yahweh's indictment refers to the *lex talionis*: *As you have done, it will be done to you*. Leviticus 24:17–21 establishes a basic principle of Israelite justice: punishment fits the crime. Punishment should not be excessive, arbitrary, or prejudiced. Since Edom has betrayed its friends and participated in ethnic cleansing, it must suffer the consequences. The final line, *your deeds will return upon your head*, reflects a slightly different idea, namely, that actions have consequences irrespective of the intervention of others (including God).

> **Lex Talionis**
> *The legal principle of exact reciprocity, or "mirror punishment," sometimes called "eye for an eye" justice, which was common in ancient legal systems.*

YAHWEH'S DELIVERANCE OF ZION · 15A, 16–21A

15A This verse links the two major sections of the book, the indictment of Edom and the deliverance of Zion. The prophet describes both events, which are ultimately one event, as *the day of the Lord* (see Joel 3:14; Zeph 3:14–16). As in Psalm 2, Yahweh saves Jerusalem from foreign powers threatening it.

16–18 Scholars debate the identity of the subject of *you drank*. Since drinking can sometimes in the Bible symbolize suffering and calamity (for example, Ps 75:8; Isa 51:17–23; Hab 2:16), some argue that *you drank* must refer to Israel, the group that has suffered *on my holy hill*, which is to say, Jerusalem (Raabe 203). On the other hand, since Edom has been the addressee so far in the book, others argue that it must be so here, as well (Wolff 64). This would mean that *drink* in 16a means "to drink in celebration," while in 16b it means "to drink in suffering." This more poetically elegant double entendre, probably the better interpretation of the verse, would emphasize the reversal of fortune awaiting Edom. NIV's rendering *they will drink and drink* obscures the change of verb in the Hebrew text: "they will drink and guzzle" would capture the original text's intensification better.

The promise of deliverance, paralleled in roughly contemporaneous texts such as Isa 40–55 and Jer 31, extends to all Israelites. *House of Jacob* and *house of Joseph* must include even those deportees from the northern kingdom of Israel. All will return to *Mount Zion*, meaning that all the people will once again worship Yahweh in one place as one people. In some unspecified way, their relocation around Jerusalem will involve the destruction of Edom, like *stubble* burned in *fire* (an image readily understandable to dwellers in arid regions like Edom).

19–21A   The author describes the various parts of the land of Israel. The Negev in the south, the *foothills* (*Shephelah*) separating Judah from the Coastal Plain, the plain itself (*land of the Philistines*), the *fields* (fertile hills) *of Ephraim and Samaria, Gilead* (in modern Jordan), and south-ern Lebanon (*Zarephath*)—all these regions will once again fall under Israelite control. In other words, the nation will recover all the territory it has ever occupied. Moreover, deportees from as far away as Sardis in Asia Minor (*Sepharad*) will resettle in the land. *Deliverers*, presumably Israelites who work to free their people from foreign domination,

> **The Negev**
>
> *The Negev is a rocky desert region of southern Israel. The word "negev" derives from a Hebrew word that denotes both "dry" as well as "south."*

will also *govern* Mount Esau. NIV's *govern* translates the Hebrew word *shaphat*, "to rule as judge," the word normally associated with the premonarchic chieftains in the book of Judges. Obadiah thus does not envision the restoration of an earthly king, but of a looser kind of organization, directed by God. NIV's *mountains of Esau* would be better translated "Mount Esau." Obadiah coined this term to parallel *Mount Zion*: God will rule over both Israelites and Edomites.

CONCLUSION · 21B

And this is, of course, the point. Yahweh, not the Babylonian superpower, not the pesky Edomites, will rule: *the kingdom*, or better, "kingship," belongs to God. See Psalm 22:27–28.

THEOLOGICAL REFLECTIONS

Obadiah's fierce denunciation of Edom challenges the comfortable notions of divine love to which Christians in the prosperous West often subscribe. We ask, can God truly seek the destruction of a whole people, as this book envisions? Nor is Obadiah alone, for extended oracles against Edom appear also in Isaiah 34 and 63; Jeremiah 9, 27, and 49; Ezekiel 25 and 35; and Amos 1. (Shorter oracles appear elsewhere.) Indeed, the prophets frequently denounce foreign nations, not only for their mistreatment of Israel, but for their abuse of each other (see Amos 2:1).

The criticism of foreign powers reflects Israel's understanding of God as a God of justice who becomes involved in the messiness of history. Since politics and warfare inevitably involve injustice, a God who is concerned with the real-ities of human existence must work within their parameters. Edom, Obadiah charges, has betrayed its "brother" Jacob (note the stories in Gen 27 and 32–33 that serve as a background of this book) by allying itself with foreign, oppressive powers. Babylonia cut a swathe of destruction across the whole of southwest Asia, destroying cities of every nation and slaughtering or enslaving numerous populations. Most of Palestine lay underpopulated throughout their rule. To conspire with such a power, as Edom did, is to commit a range of injustice (see vv. 11–13 for the catalogue) that a just God cannot overlook. This belief inspires Obadiah's seemingly hate-filled speech.

In reading this book, we become keenly aware of the injustices that humans can inflict on each other. Like the author of Jonah, the next book in the canon, we question to what degree violence can ever compensate for previous violence. Since the last verse of Obadiah envisions Yahweh's rule over both Israel and Edom, the prophet himself, ever the political realist, may have understood the punishment of the latter to be merely a prelude to a glorious time of international harmony and piety. Still, we ask what oracles like those of Obadiah tell us about the nature of God. If the book leaves us with more questions than answers, we nevertheless find in it a keen sense of hope. If the desperate refugees from Jerusalem can find their way home and can live anew as God intended them to do, perhaps we may also hope for something better.

FOR FURTHER STUDY

Brown, William P. *Obadiah through Malachi*. Louisville: Westminster John Knox, 1996.

Sharp, Carolyn. *The Prophetic Literature*. Nashville: Abingdon, 2019.

WORKS CITED

Bartlett, John. *Edom and the Edomites*. JSOT Supplement 77. Sheffield: Sheffield Academic Press, 1989.

LaBianca, Øystein, and Randall Younker. "The Kingdoms of Ammon, Moab and Edom: The Archaeology of Society in Late Bronze/Iron Age Transjordan (ca. 1400–500 BCE)." In *The Archaeology of Society in the Holy Land*, edited by Thomas Levy, 399–413. New York: Facts on File, 1995.

MacDonald, Burton. "Early Edom: The Relation between the Literary and Archaeological Evidence." In *Scripture and Other Artifacts*, edited by Michael Coogan, J. Cheryl Exum, and Lawrence Stager, 230–46. Louisville: Westminster John Knox, 1994.

Raabe, Paul R. *Obadiah*. Volume 24D of *The Anchor Bible Commentary*. New York: Doubleday, 1996.

Wolff, Hans Walter. *Obadiah and Jonah*. Translated by Margaret Kohl. Minneapolis: Augsburg, 1986.

Jonah

John T. Willis

CHAPTER CONTENTS

V arious scholars have thought of Jonah as a historical account, legend, fable, novella, allegory, parable, satire, narrative, midrash, or didactic story. It is probably a religious drama, meant to be memorized and performed or recited before God's people. One of the purposes of this book is to challenge the audience's assumption that God loves only them. The book of Jonah was most likely written to Jews in Judah who had returned from Babylonian exile in the sixth through the fourth centuries BCE, as Persian customs, Aramaisms, themes of God's justice and the possibility of repentance are evident in the book.

> **Midrash**
> *An ancient approach to biblical texts, the midrash sought not to explain the texts so much as to use them to illuminate current issues.*

CONTEXTS

To facilitate memorization and performance, Jonah uses striking rhetorical and literary strategies, such as:

Contrast · Jonah contrasts actions and attitudes of God and Jonah, Jonah and the sailors, and Jonah and the Ninevites.

Intensification · Jonah progressively "moves downward" (1:3–5; 2:6), metaphorically indicating spiritual decline. For example, the storm worsens (1:4, 11, 13); the sailors' fear increases (1:5, 10, 16).

> **Aramaisms**
> *Although written in Hebrew, Jonah uses words and expressions borrowed from the closely related language Aramaic. This familiarity with Aramaic suggests a postexilic date for the book.*

Repetition · The word *great* occurs 15 times (1:2, 4, 10, 12, 16, 17; 3:2, 3, 5, 7; 4:1, 6, 10, 11). *Evil*, with various nuances, occurs nine times (1:2, 7, 8; 3:8, 10 [where it occurs twice]; 4:1, 2, 6); and Yahweh *provides* four times (1:17; 4:6, 7, 8).

Questions · Jonah contains thirteen questions (1:6, 8 [where we find five questions], 10, 11; 3:9; 4:2, 4, 9, 11), each playing an important role in the message.

STRUCTURE & MESSAGE

James Limburg (*Hosea–Micah* 137) identifies five sections of the book: "Israel," which explores the relationship between Yahweh and Jonah (1:1–3); "Sea," which examines Jonah and the sailors (1:4–16); "Fish" which shows Yahweh and Jonah (1:17–2:10); "Nineveh" which shows the interplay between Yahweh, Jonah, and the Ninevites (3); and "Outside Nineveh," which again portrays the relationship between Yahweh and Jonah (4). Another possible structure has been developed by Leslie C. Allen (181, 200), who proposes two basic sections of Jonah: "Hebrew Sinner Saved" (1–2); and "Heathen Sinners Saved" (3–4). Either of these organizational templates makes sense, but this commentary proposes a third way to view the structure of the book of Jonah (1–3, 4).

COMMENTARY

JONAH'S ACTIONS · 1:1–3:10

1:1–3 That Yahweh charges *Jonah* to preach to the great city of *Nineveh* shows confidence in Jonah, but more importantly, it emphasizes that Yahweh is a universal ruler, dedicated to saving all people. Nineveh's *wickedness* is *violence* (3:8) and oppression (Nah 2:11–12; 3:19). Jonah betrays Yahweh by fleeing (v. 10). Yahweh tells Jonah to go east to Nineveh, but instead, Jonah flees west to *Tarshish*, probably Tartessos in southern Spain. Gradually he *went down*, away from the will of God.

1:4–16 This section emphasizes Jonah's flight from Yahweh. Yahweh *sent a violent storm* to intercept Jonah. The harder the sailors work, the rougher the storm becomes (1:11, 13), threatening to wreck the ship and provoking the sailors to pray, in startling contrast to Jonah's indifference. To save their lives, the sailors risk economic ruin by jettisoning their cargo. The *captain* urges Jonah to pray, recognizing Yahweh's sovereign freedom to respond as he wills (v. 14). Again, the pagan sailor's piety contrasts with Jonah's impiety. Lot casting was a legitimate means of determining a guilty party in ancient times (Josh 7:14–18). The sailors' questions expose Jonah. *Who is responsible*? Jonah is, for striving to avoid doing Yahweh's commission. *What do you do*? Jonah is Yahweh's messenger. *From what people are you*? Jonah is an Israelite charged to "bless" the nations (Gen 22:18) by Yahweh's message (Isa 49:1–6). Jonah's reply *terrified* the sailors (v. 5). The question *What*

> **Merchant Ships & Their Cargo**
> *The cargo of ships in the ancient Mediterranean often consisted of large copper ingots or large storage jars full of wine or oil.*

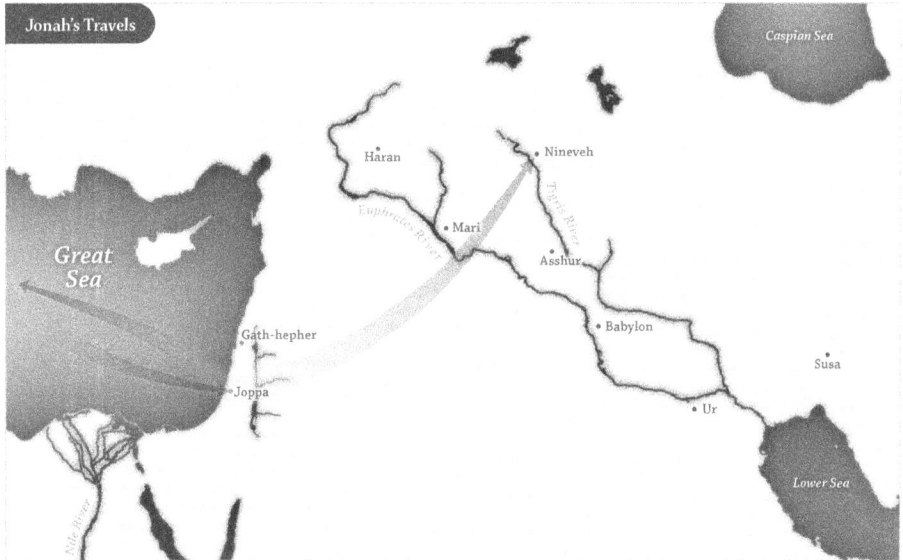

Jonah's Travels

Caspian Sea

Haran • Nineveh

Euphrates River • Mari

Great
Sea

Asshur

Gath-hepher • Babylon

Susa

•Joppa • Ur

Lower Sea

Nile River

have you done? is intended to force Johah to admit the seriousness of his actions (Gen 3:13; Jer 8:6). Jonah tells the sailors to throw him overboard to calm the storm, since Yahweh has sent it to punish him. Jonah had rather die than preach to Nineveh. Jonah tries everything to avoid preaching to Nineveh, while the sailors try everything to save the ship and passengers. The sailors' prayer, rooted in their desire to preserve life, evinces great hesitation to throw Jonah overboard and contrasts sharply with Jonah's preference for death. However, in desperation, they eventually acquiesce. Immediately the sea grows calm. The sailors, again unlike Jonah, worship Yahweh with gratitude.

1:17–2:10 Yahweh provides a fish to save Jonah from drowning, and Jonah, evincing a change of heart, thanks Yahweh for deliverance. As is often the case for those praying during times of great distress, Jonah's prayer (2:2–9) is composed largely of quotations, particularly from psalms (Sasson 159–215; Limburg, *Jonah*, 63–71). The fish carries Jonah for *three days and three nights* before bringing him back to dry land, giving him much time to pray. In the book of Jonah, the three-day duration of Jonah's ordeal has no obvious significance, although, of course, in the New Testament Jesus uses it to describe the time he will spend in the tomb (Matt 12:39).

Following his liberation from the fish, Jonah thanks Yahweh for saving him from drowning (vv. 3–7). Jonah deserved to die, but Yahweh has

> **Jonah's Prayer**
> *In his prayer inside the fish, Jonah uses the traditional language and structural formula of "thanksgiving psalms": a summary of experience (v. 2; Pss 31:22; 120:1); a description of peril (vv. 3–6b; Pss 31:22; 42:7; 69:1; 102:10); deliverance (v. 6cd; Ps 103:4); a summary of experience (v. 7; Pss 102:1; 142:3; 143:5); and a message to the congregation (vv. 8–9; Pss 3:8; 31:6; 116:17–18).*

been gracious. The storyteller here takes center stage (2:8–9) to contrast the *pagans'* trust in *worthless idols* and Jonah's (the believer's) thanksgiving for deliverance. Verses 5–6 portray an ancient view of the structure of the world, with mountains resting upon deep waters (see Pss 24:2; 148:4, 7, 9).

3:1–10   Jonah is now safe at home, but Yahweh repeats his earlier instructions to go to Nineveh, and this time, having experienced Yahweh's wrath, Jonah obeys. His message is: *Forty more days and Nineveh will be destroyed* (v. 4), indicating Yahweh's seriousness yet leaving open the possibility of forgiveness. A condition is understood (Jer 18:7–10): the fulfillment of Old Testament predictions and prophecies depends on the hearers' response. In this case, the Ninevites repent, using the traditional symbols of fasting (Joel 2:12), wearing sackcloth, and sitting in dust or ashes (Dan 9:3). Their hope is that *God may yet relent*. As Jonah has feared (4:2), Yahweh *changed his mind* (see also Exod 32:11–14); Yahweh's *compassion* extends to the penitent nation.

Jonah & Assyria

Given Assyria's historical role in the destruction of the Israelite monarchy and annexation of the land, the story of Jonah must have seemed daring to ancient Israelites. The repentance even of the Assyrian animals (3:7–8) both signals the comedic side of the book of Jonah and paints a serious picture of the possibilities of human repentance and God's forgiveness.

JONAH'S ATTITUDE · 4:1–11

4:1–8   Jonah 1–3 seem complete, yet the drama continues as the author, reflecting God's point of view, seeks to change the attitude both of Jonah and of the Jewish audience, who presumably agrees with Jonah about the repentance of the Ninevites. Yahweh turns from his *fierce anger* (3:9), but Jonah, in turn, now becomes *angry*. Here he reveals his motivation for running from God's command in chapter 1: he did not go to Nineveh at first (1:3) because he knew that Yahweh would be merciful even to pagans of the cruelest type. Jonah is upset when Yahweh forgives the penitent sinners of Nineveh, presumably because they are "pagan." When God confronts Jonah about his attitude, Jonah stalks off, unwilling even to answer. The death of the plant reveals Jonah's selfishness and failure to understand Yahweh's graciousness. Jonah complains that he is miserable and wants to die (v. 3). Jonah chooses death in protest if Yahweh saves people or destroys plants.

4:9–11   The storyteller takes center stage again (2:8–9) with Yahweh's question: Should one be like Jonah, who loves a plant that has no eternal destiny? Or should one be like Yahweh, *concerned* with *people* whose lives have their own integrity?

THEOLOGICAL REFLECTIONS

Jonah is written for people convinced that they alone are saved and all others are doomed. Against such arrogance, it proclaims that Yahweh is creator of everything (1:9), not merely of the chosen people, who have the task of proclaiming God's message to all nations to save them (Isa 49:1–6). Jonah represents the chosen people. The audience shares his attitude and must decide how to respond. The Ninevites are lost but will listen to Yahweh's messengers. Yahweh loves all peoples and desires their salvation.

FOR FURTHER STUDY

Ben Zvi, Ehud. *Signs of Jonah*. Sheffield: Sheffield Academic Press, 2003.
Havea, Jione. *Jonah: An Earth Commentary*. New York: Bloomsbury, 2020.
Simon, Uriel. *Jonah*. Philadelphia: Jewish Publication Society, 1999.

WORKS CITED

Allen, Leslie C. *The Books of Joel, Obadiah, Jonah, and Micah*. Grand Rapids: Eerdmans, 1976.
Limburg, James. *Hosea–Micah*. Atlanta: John Knox, 1988.
———. *Jonah*. Louisville: Westminster John Knox, 1993.
Sasson, Jack M. *Jonah*. New York: Doubleday, 1990.

Micah

John T. Willis

CHAPTER CONTENTS

M aterial in the book of Micah dates from before the fall of Samaria in 724–721 BCE (1:5–7) to near the return from Babylon in 536 BCE (2:12–13; 4:6–10). Micah addressed Israel (1:5–7) and Judah (3:9–12) in about 725–700 BCE. Those passing on Micah's words (see Jer 26:17–19) assembled the book in about 536 BCE.

CONTEXTS

Recurring themes in Micah include the notion that punishment must fit the crime, calls for justice, and the importance of a restored remnant. Similarly, a number of images recur in the book: a shepherd and sheep, Zion, and the Davidic dynasty. Micah's reproof of Israel's and Judah's leaders is contrasted with the image of Yahweh's just and righteous leadership. The book thus demonstrates an overall coherence. Wordplays abound, and it appears that Micah's composers arranged the book for oral reading or dramatic performance before religious assemblies.

English versification from 5:1–15 (adopted here) equals the Hebrew versification of 4:14–5:14.

COMMENTARY

SUPERSCRIPTION · 1:1

Micah 1:1 affirms that the source of Micah's message is Yahweh. Micah's hometown was *Moresheth-gath* (1:14), twenty-five miles southwest of Jerusalem. Micah preached to *Samaria* and *Jerusalem* during the reigns of *Jotham* (742–735 BCE), *Ahaz* (735–715 BCE), and *Hezekiah* (715–687 BCE).

PUNISHMENT & RESTORATION: ISRAEL & JUDAH · 1:2–2:13

Prophets & Lament
Prophets lamented disasters and sins (compare Amos 5:1–3), expressing grief traditionally by loud weeping (Jer 9:17–20), going barefoot and naked (Isa 20:2–4), howling like jackals, moaning like owls or ostriches (Job 30:29–31), and shaving their heads bald (Amos 8:10). Simundson observes: "The message was contained both in the words and in the acting out of the lament" (Simundson 546).

1:2–7 This passage portrays a "covenant lawsuit." Yahweh is the plaintiff; the prophet, the plaintiff's lawyer; Israel and Judah, the defendants; and the peoples and earth, witnesses that Yahweh's charges are valid. Micah summons the *peoples* and *earth* to learn from Yahweh's response to the people (Amos 3:9). Yahweh *comes down* from *his holy temple*, heaven (Gen 11:5–8), dissolving mountains and valleys. This language is common in poetic descriptions of God's appearances.

Yahweh will punish *Israel*'s and *Judah*'s sins, which are radiating from *Samaria* and *Jerusalem*. Israel's sins infect Judah; Yahweh's punishments follow (1:9, 13). Yahweh will make Samaria and Jerusalem a *heap of rubble* (1:6; 3:12). Invaders will destroy Samaria's walls and idols (1:6–7). The translation of verse 7d–e is debatable. Samaria prospered by allying with foreign nations (see Hos 8:8–10), so the nation will lose its prosperity to foreign nations. The oracle anticipates the Assyrians' destruction of the northern kingdom.

1:8–16 This section reflects Sennacherib's invasion in 701 BCE (2 Kgs 18–19; Pritchard 287–88). The towns in 1:10–15 lie between Lachish—Sennacherib's headquarters near the Mediterranean (2 Kgs 19:8)—and Jerusalem. The Assyrians destroyed them while approaching Jerusalem. Because Micah 1:10–15 does not proceed in geographical order west to east (compare Isa 10:27c–32), it presents translational difficulties. Experts have proposed various explanations for these problems, including the possibility that the beginning of each line was damaged, so that parallelism, wordplays, ancient versions, and "educated guesses" must be used to restore the text (Andersen and Freedman 253).

Places & Wordplay in Micah
Several place names here form word plays: Beth Ophrah sounds like the word for dust; Zaanan, like come out; Lachish, like the Hebrew for team; Achzib, like the word for deceptive; Mareshah, like conqueror.

Her *wound* in verses 6–7 refers to Samaria's devastation in 721 BCE, which *has come to Judah* by Sennacherib's invasion. The *gate of my people* is Jerusalem (Obad 13). The verse begins with a pun: Hebrew *taggidu* (*tell*) sounds like the word for *Gath. Tell it not in Gath* (2 Sam 1:20) implies that Philistines will plunder or gloat over Israel if they discover Israel's defeat. Verbs in verse 16 are feminine singular, thus referring to Jerusalem; *the children* in whom Jerusalem delights are Judah's fortified cities. *They who go into exile* are the 200,150 Judeans Sennacherib carried into exile, according to his Annals.

2:1–11 Micah 2:1–11 explains why the Assyrians devastate Judah. Because powerful Judeans seize inheritances of the poor, Yahweh sends the Assyrians to seize and divide their land. This woe oracle might have ended at verse 5, but prophetic opponents challenged Micah (vv. 6–7). Micah insists his charges are true and his opponents are liars and deceivers (vv. 8–11).

I am planning disaster (v. 3) counters *those who plan . . . evil* (v. 1) with just retribution (see Gal 6:7–8). Sin begins within, then erupts externally (v. 1). Oppressors *covet* others' possessions, then *seize* them (v. 2; see Amos 5:11–12), violating the tenth commandment (Exod 20:17). Yahweh's punishment is threefold: he crushes the oppressors' pride (v. 3b); enemies remove them from the land (v. 4); and invaders seize the possessions that the oppressors had previously claimed, ridiculing their impotence (vv. 4–5).

Verses 6–11 are difficult. In verses 6–7, Micah relates prophetic opposition to his message in verses 1–5: these so-called prophets claim they will not experience *disgrace* (v. 4); they say that Yahweh does not unleash anger against the people (v. 3), for he is *slow to anger* (Exod 34:6–7); and they argue that, because Yahweh blesses the *upright*, and God's people are prospering, therefore the people are upright.

Verses 8–11 contain Micah's response to these false prophets' rebuttal in verses 6–7. Verse 8a in the NRSV indicates certain prophets who rose up against defenseless Judeans as an enemy, while the NIV points to wealthy, powerful Judeans (vv. 1–2) rather than to prophets. Whether prophets or the wealthy, these miscreants stole travelers' outer garments (Job 22:6), or kept garments taken in pledge (Deut 24:10–13), and drove women from their homes, leaving their children without an inheritance. Micah encourages the oppressed to flee, calling his opponents liars and deceivers. He satirizes his opponents for selling out for alcohol.

2:12–13 Here, the mood, setting, and message change, and a different performer speaks. His hearers are in Babylonian exile (compare 4:9–10). He summarizes major themes of other Mican hope oracles: that Yahweh, as Judah's *king*, will *gather* the exiles; and that he will *bring* together the remnant of Israel (in Jerusalem) as a shepherd assembles his *flock*.

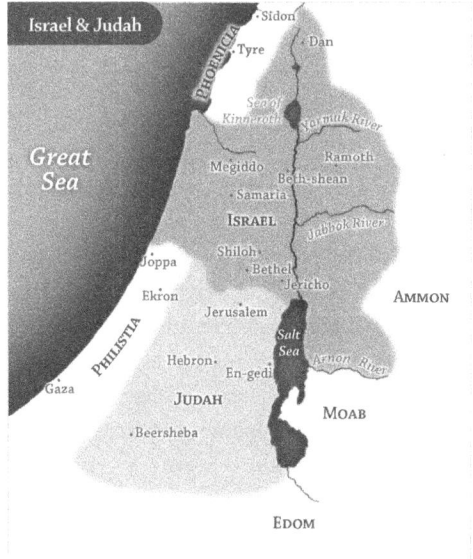

DENUNCIATION OF INJUSTICE & RESTORATION: JUDAH · 3:1–5:15

The first part of this section balances a denunciation of injustice in Judah with a vision of the restoration of the righteous remnant.

3:1–8 Micah reproves Judah's *leaders*, responsible for maintaining *justice*, for oppressing the defenseless in the same way that cannibals flay and consume victims, demonstrating they *hate good and love evil*. This gory image works rhetorically to gain the audience's attention. According to verse 4, Yahweh's punishment fits the crime (2:1–3). Oppressors will suffer oppression and *cry out to the Lord*; yet God will not play the role of deliverer (Ps 27:7–9).

The second person plural "you" (v. 6a) indicates that Micah addresses his prophetic opponents' criticism (v. 8). Micah censures the other prophets for preaching to please powerful rulers, who reward them liberally.

God's punishment of *prophets*, *seers*, *diviners* (three synonyms for technicians who seek to understand the divine will for the future) fits the crime. They proclaim peace; Yahweh sends the Assyrians to punish Judah (night and darkness represent such punishment; Amos 5:18–20), publicly disgracing them. *Cover the lips* (NRSV) signifies disgrace (Ezek 24:17, 22). Micah affirms that he is *filled with power*, the *spirit* (or presence) of Yahweh (compare Ps 51:11), *justice* and *might*, proclaiming Yahweh's displeasure with Judah's *sin*.

The Will of the Gods

Ancient peoples went to great lengths to discern the will of the gods. They studied the entrails of sacrificed animals, the movement of the stars (astrology), and unusual events. They collected and systematized omens so as to create a body of precedents for predicting the future. The Bible forbids many, but not all, such practices (Lev 19:31; Deut 18:9–13).

3:9–12 Micah denounces Judah's *leaders*, *priests*, and *prophets* for oppressing the helpless (2:2, 8–9), accumulating wealth, and assuming exemption from *disaster* (see 2:3) no matter how they live. Again, as in verses 6–7, Micah refers to a triad of leaders.

Yahweh says he will devastate Jerusalem, as he did Samaria (1:6–7), and destroy the temple. This does not happen immediately, because Hezekiah and Judah repent (Jer 26:17–19). Although doom oracles sound superficially as if they allow no alteration of God's will, in fact they function as calls to repentance. They are revocable.

The prophet borrows from a Song of Zion (see Isa 2:2–4), affirming Zion's elevation of status and the pilgrimage of all nations to it. He adds a description of peace, using traditional metaphors (v. 4), then states this peace will occur when Israel follows Yahweh's ethical standards (v. 5). Verses 1–5 contain five contrasts to 3:9–12: a description of an elevated (4:1) versus ruined Temple Mount (3:12); Yahweh's empowering (4:2) versus the priests' debasing teaching (3:11); Yahweh's equitable (4:3) versus the leaders' unjust judging (3:9, 11); *Zion*, or Jerusalem, characterized by Yahweh's instruction (4:2) versus the leaders' wickedness (3:10); and divine peace (4:3–4) versus human chaos (3:9–10).

4:1–5 The word *for* in verse 2f (NRSV) is crucial to understanding the sequence. First, Yahweh will exalt the Temple Mount (v. 1a–c). Second, Yahweh's messengers (prophets or priests) will carry teachings from Zion to the nations (v. 2f–g). Third, receptive nations will stream to Zion to receive Yahweh's further instruction (vv. 1d–2e). The NRSV's *in days to come* and *instruction* are preferable to the NIV's *In the last days* and *law*.

Yahweh decides disputes between nations; they assent and live at peace (1 Kgs 4:25). Far from being merely the god of a small kingdom, Yahweh is actually the sovereign of the universe.

The prophet and his associates resolve to *walk in the name of the Lord* as they carry Yahweh's message to the nations (v. 2f–g), so the hopes of verses 1–4 may become reality.

4:6–7 Verses 6–7 (compare 2:12–13) assume that God's people are in Babylonian exile. Yahweh *afflicted* (NRSV) them (v. 6d) through the Babylonians (Jer 25:8–11). Yet Yahweh will next reassemble the deportees, transform them into a *remnant* (compare Isa 10:20–23) and *a strong nation*, and reconstitute them as a political entity on *Mount Zion*.

4:8–11 The verses from 4:8 to 5:2 contain the chiastic, or sandwiching, word-play: *we 'attah* ("and you") (4:8); *'attah* ("now") (4:9); *we 'attah* ("and now") (4:11); *'attah* ("now") (5:1); and *we 'attah* ("and you") (5:2). The punning focuses on the hearers' deep involvement in the crisis of national destruction. Micah 4:9–10 assumes Jews are in Babylonian exile but will soon return to Jerusalem (550–538 BCE), depicting the fate of *daughter Zion* (NRSV) in four stages: distress due to *enemies*; the rigors of deportation (*camp in the open field*); travel to *Babylon*, and a final hopeful word concerning Yahweh's rescue.

The *king and counselor* may be Zedekiah, the last king of Judah, who failed in his plot to throw off Babylonian rule (2 Kgs 25:1–21). *A woman in labor* is a metaphor for terror during military attack (see Jer 4:31). To *redeem* (Hebrew *ga'al*; Isa 44:22–24) is the task of the avenger of blood (Hebrew *go'el*; Deut 19:6, 12), a term which is sometimes used to describe Yahweh delivering Israel from Egypt (Exod 6:6).

Many nations gather to destroy Jerusalem (see Psalm 2), yet Yahweh gathers them *like sheaves to the threshing floor* (Isa 21:10) to pulverize them. The use of farming imagery to describe military action occurs elsewhere in the Bible (for example, see Amos 1:3). The word *devote* is a technical term for giving spoils of holy war to God (see Josh 6:17–19).

Sennacherib & Hezekiah

Sennacherib (who reigned 705–689 BCE) wrote about his siege of Lachish and Jerusalem:

"As for Hezekiah, the Judean, I besieged 46 of his walled cities. . . . Using packed down ramps and applying battering rams, infantry attacks by mines, breeches, and siege machines, I conquered them. . . . [As for Hezekiah] I locked him up within Jerusalem, his royal city, like a bird in a cage."

(translation by Mordechai Cogan, in Hallo and Younger, Contexts of Scripture, 2: 303).

5:1–6 *Now* (NRSV) in verse 5:1 begins a new oracle. This oracle comprises verses 1–6, and its setting was Sennacherib's invasion in 701 BCE. *Israel's ruler* is Hezekiah. The blow *on the cheek with a rod* symbolizes the destruction of most of his kingdom because he used human strategies, such as tribute to Sennacherib (2 Kgs 18:13–16) and alliance with Egypt (Isa 31:1–3). The ruler from Bethlehem (v. 2) refers to Hezekiah when he trusts in Yahweh after Sennacherib sends a letter demanding Judah's surrender. Victory over the Assyrians (vv. 5b–6) refers to the angel of Yahweh smiting 185,000 Assyrians and the rest of the army returning to Nineveh (2 Kgs 19:35–36). Verse 1 is best translated by the NRSV: *Now you are walled around with a wall.* In verse 2, as David's descendant, the king is from *Bethlehem* (1 Sam 16:1–13). *From of old* parallels *former dominion* in 4:8 and thus David's dynasty.

Israel [Judah] is *abandoned* by Yahweh until *she who is in labor* (Jerusalem, 4:9–10) *gives birth* (that is, produces a righteous king). The *rest of his brothers* are those in Assyrian exile, who will return to help the besieged in Jerusalem.

Feminine Imagery for Jerusalem

In Hebrew, all place names are feminine nouns. The prophets very often, therefore, use female metaphors such as birthing, nursing, and childbearing to describe the actions of the nations of Israel and Judah and their capitals.

A transformed Hezekiah will *shepherd his flock* (Judah) in the *strength of the Lord.* "Shepherd" is one biblical term for "king" (for example, 2 Sam 5:2). Yahweh's people "living securely" parallels 4:4. *He* (Hezekiah transformed) *shall be the one of peace* (NRSV); through him, Yahweh will expel the Assyrian invaders. Verses 5b–c and 6d–e form an *inclusio.* When the Assyrians invade, the Judeans will raise against them *seven shepherds, even eight leaders of men.* This number pattern (similar to the one in Amos 1–2) simply implies that there will be adequate leadership (*the ruler* of 5:2d), not literally fifteen leaders (compare Prov 30:15–31).

5:7–15 According to verses 7–8, depending on the nations' actions, the *remnant* will bless them *like dew* and *showers* nourish grass (4:1–3), or crush them *like a lion* mauls sheep (4:11–13). As Yahweh's spokesman (v. 9), the prophet assures the remnant that it will triumph.

Yahweh's threat, *I will cut off* (NRSV), makes verses 10–14 cohere, denouncing Judah's objects of trust (Isa 2:6–8), such as military armaments (vv. 10–11) and idolatrous paraphernalia (vv. 12–14). Such punishments should refine Yahweh's people (Isa 1:21–28). Verses 12–14 list several idolatrous practices aimed at providing national security without loyalty to Israel's God.

PUNISHMENT & RESTORATION: SAMARIA & JERUSALEM · 6:1–7:20

This section contains three parts: Yahweh reproves Judah for infidelity due to ingratitude for Yahweh's blessings (vv. 1–5); a hearer asks what Yahweh wants, according to the prophet (vv. 6–7); and the prophet declares that Yahweh wants fidelity and care for others (v. 8). In verse 1, the prophet summons his audience to heed (imperative plural) Yahweh's instructions to announce the case against Israel. The *mountains* and *hills* serve as witnesses to the case because they have been around long enough to judge Israel's conduct. Mountains and hills witness to Yahweh's covenant with Israel at Sinai, as do the heavens and earth (Deut 32:1), and thus can vouch for Yahweh's integrity in his lawsuit.

6:1–5 Micah reports Yahweh's accusations against Israel. Yahweh speaks as defendant, asking for the people's grounds for their infidelity. The proof of Yahweh's fidelity comes from the ancient story of the exodus and deliverance in the desert (see Num 22–24; Josh 3–4).

6:6–7 An imagined hearer sarcastically asks what Yahweh desires. The list of possible religious acts, up to and including human sacrifice, serves rhetorically to contrast Israel's actions with God's desires.

6:8 The prophet responds with three teachings of Yahweh's law: *do justice* (NRSV) rather than enact oppression (2:1–11; 3:1–4, 9–12); love steadfast love, not fickle or hypocritical love; and *walk humbly with your God*, not arrogantly.

6:9–16 These verses may resume Yahweh's lawsuit (vv. 1–5) following the interruption (vv. 6–7), or verses 9–16 may be a separate announcement of Yahweh's judgment. *The city* mentioned here may be Samaria (1:5–7), Jerusalem (3:9–12), or both, since Micah closely connects Samaria's and Jerusalem's sins and punishment (1:5–7, 9, 13). Yahweh reproves merchants for using a substandard *ephah* (a vessel for measuring grain), *dishonest scales*, and *bag[s] of false* (irregular-sized stone) *weights* to weigh commodities, thus gaining wealth unethically (Deut 25:13–16; Amos 8:5).

Dishonest Scales

In the absence of governmentally standardized weights and measures, customers were often at the mercy of unscrupulous merchants. Basic ethics dictated the use of fair measures and weights on scales. Buyers often paid in silver chunks (before the invention of coinage).

In verses 13–15, Yahweh will send unspecified armies to divest oppressors of their objectives (Lev 26:26; Deut 28:38–41).

Verse 16a–c summarizes verses 10–12; and verse 16d–f, verses 13–15. Since oppressors mimic the injustices of *Omri* and *Ahab* (for example, 1 Kgs 21), kings of the century before Micah, Yahweh will destroy them.

7:1–6 The prophet laments that Judah's corruption (vv. 1–4b, 5–6) requires Yahweh's punishment (v. 4c–e). First, the prophet bemoans the oppression and dishonesty of Judah's leaders (3:9–12). The search for honest leaders proves disappointing, like a hungry person seeking grapes or figs on already gleaned plants (v. 1). Leaders hunt the defenseless, giving and accepting *bribes* to favor the rich in lawsuits, and *they all conspire together*.

Second, the prophet deplores untrustworthiness of *neighbor*, *friend*, spouse, and other family members (compare Matt 10:21; Luke 12:51–53).

7:7–20 These verses form a four-part liturgy (vv. 7–10, 11–13, 14–17, 18–20), composed for oral reading (Neh 8:1–9; 1 Tim 4:13) or dramatic performance.

Personified Jerusalem (*I*) addresses her mockers (see Ps 115:2; 137:7–8), who say: *Where is the Lord your God?* (v. 10), implying that Yahweh is weak or indifferent. This liturgy dates from the late exilic or early postexilic period. The former inhabitants of Jerusalem (v. 8) acknowledge their sins as the cause of their downfall (Lam 1:1–14), but they are confident that Yahweh will deliver them.

A priest, prophet, or messenger promises Jerusalem (*your . . . you* is feminine singular in Hebrew) that her exiles will return from captivity and rebuild the city's fortification (Neh 6:15–16).

Jewish exiles in Babylon (the NRSV's *us* in verse 15; NIV's *our* in verse 17) beseech Yahweh to carry out a new exodus and *shepherd* them like a *flock*. Nations will *be ashamed* for mocking Yahweh and the people and will acknowledge Yahweh alone as God (4:1–3; compare Isa 56).

Jewish exiles in Babylon (*remnant*, verse 18; *us, our*, verses 19–20) declare Yahweh to be incomparable (Exod 15:11) for forgiving their sins out of *steadfast love* (vv. 19–20) and *compassion*, anticipating return to Jerusalem. In *anger* (NRSV), Yahweh sent the Babylonians to devastate Judah, but that anger is temporary (v. 9; Ps 30:5); Yahweh's steadfast love prevails. The phrases *Tread . . . iniquities under foot* and *hurl . . . sins into the depths of the sea* (NRSV; echoing Exod 15:4–5) denote complete forgiveness.

THEOLOGICAL REFLECTIONS

Micah's message is not new but is based on the law and earlier prophets. Deliberate, prolonged sin in Israel and Judah brings Yahweh's wrath through the Assyrians and Babylonians. Sin is self-centeredness, manifested in arrogant rebellion against Yahweh and oppression of others in government, economic life, and religion. However, Yahweh's punishment is redemptive. There is hope for the penitent remnant, Yahweh's flock, to return to Jerusalem, enjoy protection, rebuild ruins, reestablish the Davidic dynasty, and be Yahweh's witness to the nations.

FOR FURTHER STUDY

Jensen, Joseph. *Ethical Dimensions of the Prophets*. Collegeville, MN: Liturgical Press, 2006.

McKane, William. *Micah: Introduction and Commentary*. Edinburgh: T & T Clark, 1998.

WORKS CITED

Andersen, Francis I., and David Noel Freedman. *Micah*. New York: Doubleday, 2000.

Hallo, William, and K. Lawson Yonger, eds. *The Context of Scripture*. Volume 1: *Canonical Composition from the Biblical World*. Leiden: Brill, 1997.

Pritchard, James B., ed. *Ancient Near Eastern Texts Relating to the Old Testament*. 3rd ed. with supplement. Princeton: Princeton University Press, 1969.

Simundson, Daniel J. "The Book of Micah: Introduction, Commentary, and Reflections." In *The New Interpreter's Bible*, 7:533–89. Nashville: Abingdon, 1996.

Nahum

John T. Willis

CHAPTER CONTENTS

The book of Nahum dates from between the Assyrian king Assurbanipal's sack of Egypt's capital, Thebes (also called No-Amon), in 663 BCE (3:8–10), and Babylon's overthrow of Nineveh in 612 BCE (2:1–13).

CONTEXTS

Chapters 2–3 expect imminent attack, dating the book to about 612 BCE. Recurring expressions, similes and metaphors, water imagery, and the focus on Nineveh's fall create the book's cohesion. The book is designed for oral reading or dramatic performance before worshiping communities.

COMMENTARY

SUPERSCRIPTION · 1:1

Nahum 1:1 calls the book *an oracle* (Hebrew *massa'*, which also means "burden" [as in Isa 13:1; Hab 1:1]), a genre generally employed in responding to community questions about Yahweh's intentions regarding some situation. This *oracle* concerns *Nineveh*, Assyria's capital (2:8; 3:7; NIV unjustifiably adds Nineveh in 1:8, 11, 14; and 2:1). Verse 1 calls Nahum the *book of the vision* (compare Isa 1:1; Hab 2:2), affirming that Yahweh answers community questions. No information exists about either the man *Nahum* or the location of *Elkosh*.

POEM PRAISING YAHWEH · 1:2–8

This text constitutes a broken acrostic, with each verse beginning with a different letter of the Hebrew alphabet halfway through (see also Pss 34, 119). It praises Yahweh, the mighty warrior, for overthrowing enemies and protecting followers.

Yahweh is *slow to anger* (v. 3) *but* (not *and* as the NIV translates it in verse 3) *great in power*. He is *good*, a *stronghold* (v. 7 NRSV); but *jealous, avenging, wrathful* (vv. 2, 3, 6), punishing enemies (vv. 2, 3, 6). *Jealous* on Israel's behalf (Ezek 38:18–23), God takes vengeance on Nineveh for cruelty. Yahweh's fearsome appearance brings whirlwind, storm, dark clouds, the evaporation of the sea and rivers, withering foliage on mountains and hills, quaking mountains, melting hills, and trembling of the earth and all its inhabitants (compare Mic 1:3–4; Hab 3:3–15; Ps 18:7–15). Such language speaks to the overwhelming nature of any appearance or action by God. Yahweh's opponents cannot endure his *indignation, anger,* and *wrath*. The phrase *even in a rushing flood* (v. 8a in NRSV, which completes verse 7 rather than contrasting with it, as indicated in the NIV) echoes a favorite Assyrian image for destruction. In verse 8b, Hebrew reads *her place*, the NIV reads *Nineveh*, and the NRSV reads *his adversaries*. All these interpretations are possible, but a preferable reading is "he will put an end to opposition [Hebrew *mequmah*]."

A Hymn to Yahweh

Nahum opens with a hymn to Yahweh. Its literary strategy of setting up a series of contrasting attributes was not unusual in the ancient world. For example, the Babylonian wisdom text called "I Will Praise the Lord of Wisdom" (Ludlul bel nemeqi) opens with a hymn to the god Marduk, "whose anger is like a raging tempest, but whose breeze is sweet as the morning's breath." For Nahum, the sovereign God is not that of the Mesopotamian oppressors but of the now liberated Israelites (Hallo and Younger).

ADDRESSES TO NINEVEH & JUDAH · 1:9–15

The prophet next addresses Assyrians (vv. 9–11, 14) and Judeans (vv. 12–13, 15). Baselessly, NIV inserts *Nineveh* twice (vv. 11, 14), and *Judah* once (v. 12). *Judah* is in verse 15. Context suggests *you* (plural, v. 9, as in the NRSV; not *they* as in the NIV) are Assyrians who oppress Yahweh's people. Yahweh's onslaught demolishes all foes, leaving them *entangled thorns, drunkards* (NRSV), and *dry stubble* (v. 10; Isa 28:7–8; 33:11–12). *You* (v. 11) is feminine singular, referring to Nineveh/Assyria. The *one who has come forth* from her and *plots evil against the Lord* is probably Sennacherib, who besieged Jerusalem in 701 BCE (Isa 36–37). *Wickedness* (Hebrew *beliya'al;* also verse 15), comes from the verb meaning "to swallow," suggesting the image of the god of death swallowing his victims (Isa 5:14; Hab 2:5).

Nahum & the Assyrian Empire

Nahum celebrates the collapse of the Assyrian Empire in the 610s BCE, hoping for the end to oppression in the Near East. The Assyrians practiced widespread deportations of populations in an effort to reorganize their world in a way fitting the alleged decrees of the gods.

The messenger formula *thus says Yahweh* (v. 12a) introduces encouraging words from God (*I*) to Judeans (*you* [vv. 12–13] is feminine singular, referring to Jerusalem/Judah) *afflicted* by Assyria. Although enemies have maximum strength, Yahweh will defeat them, and although Yahweh has used Assyria to *afflict* sinful

Judah (compare Isa 10:5–6), Yahweh will *break his* [that is, *Assyria's king's* as in NRSV not *their* as in the NIV] *yoke* (slave collar) and *shackles* from Judah's *neck* (see Isa 58:6, 9; Jer 28:10, 12). Assyria has served its purpose and now must pay for oppressing others excessively.

Assyria's destruction is *Judah's good news*. The messenger formula (v. 14a) introduces Yahweh's intention to vanquish Assyria's king (*you, your*; the pronouns are masculine singular and cannot refer to *Nineveh*, as the NIV suggests): the punishments meted out to Assyria are harsh: the king *will have no descendants*; Yahweh *will destroy* Assyria's *carved images* and *cast idols* (of Ashur, Bel, Marduk, Ishtar, etc.), whom the king sponsored to legitimate his rule; and Yahweh will assign him (the king) a despicable *grave* (v. 14). Suddenly, the *feet* (symbolizing the entire person) of a *good news* messenger (perhaps God) appear *on the mountains* (see also Isa 52:7; Rom 10:15) to announce the end of foreign domination. *Wicked* again translates the Hebrew word *beliya'al*, as in verse 11. Israel can begin its religious life anew in its own land.

DESCRIPTION OF NINEVEH'S IMMINENT DESTRUCTION · 2:1–3:19

2:1–13 The prophet graphically depicts a battle between invading Babylonians, Medes, and Scythians and the invaded Assyrians, portraying the attackers as charging Nineveh (*"you,"* feminine singular) to prepare for battle (v. 1). He assures both north Israel and Judah (*Jacob* and *Israel*) that, by overthrowing Assyria, Yahweh will restore the *splendor* that Assyria removed from them when it defeated Samaria (722 BCE; 2 Kgs 17:1–6) and besieged Jerusalem (701 BCE; Isa 36–37) like thieves strip grapes from *vines* (v. 2). The prophet also describes terrifying attacking *warriors* bearing blood-stained (*red*) armor, driving technologically advanced *chariots* and sacking a city (the graphic depiction of a battle sounds like an eyewitness account) (vv. 3–6). He depicts capture and *exile* of some and flight of others, amid commands (*Stop! Stop!*) as useless as a leaky *pool* (vv. 7–8). He portrays invaders inciting each other to *plunder* Nineveh's vast *treasures* (v. 9). And he summarizes widespread fear in Nineveh: *Devastation, desolation, and destruction!* (v. 10 NRSV).

The prophet taunts demolished Nineveh, formerly a *lions' den* where Assyrian soldiers felt confident bringing captives and spoils of war to benefit the city (Isa 5:29). He reports a message from *the Lord of* [*the heavenly*] *hosts* [not the *Lord Almighty*, as the NIV translates it]: *I am against* you (feminine singular, referring to Nineveh; 3:5); Nineveh will fall (vv. 11–13).

The *city* is interpreted in verse 7 (in the Masoretic Text) as *she*. Some propose that the "she" refers to Nineveh's *mistress* (see the RSV translation)—that is, the city's queen, or goddess, Ishtar. It was common in ancient Assyrian and Babylonian warfare to remove

The Fall of Nineveh
British Museum text 21901 gives Babylon's account of Nineveh's fall in the fourteenth year of Nabopolassar, king of Babylon (Pritchard 304–5).

images from a defeated enemy's temple. Wall reliefs from Assurbanipal's palace at Nineveh depict the king ritually hunting lions. He imported lions from Syria for hunts and was proud of his accomplishments as a lion hunter. Verses 11–13 report the end of such imperial boasting.

3:1–19 The prophet utters *woe* against Nineveh, *city of bloodshed* (v. 1 NRSV), whose sophisticated army exploited helpless victims, murdering ruthlessly with *swords* and *spears*, leaving *piles of dead bodies* (vv. 2–3), practicing deceitful diplomacy (Isa 36:16–17) like a *harlot* using *sorcery* (v. 4 NRSV). Yahweh reacts: *I am against you, says the LORD of hosts* (v. 5 NRSV, 2:13). Since place names in Hebrew are feminine, Nahum (like other prophets) can use female imagery for Nineveh. He chooses images of gradation. God will punish her: exposing her shame to the nations (v. 5), *treating* her *with contempt, making* her *a spectacle* so onlookers will *flee* from her, leaving none to *mourn* for or *comfort* her (vv. 6–7).

Ironically, Nineveh will suffer like its former victim *Thebes* (Jer 46:25; Ezek 30:14–16). *Ethiopia* (NRSV), *Put, and Libya* were African areas whose peoples suffered Assyrian brutality under Assurbanipal in the 660s, fifty years earlier than Nahum. The succeeding images graphically describe such destruction. Some images also appear elsewhere: *first ripe figs* that *fall* from the tree into the *eater's mouth* (compare Isa 28:1–4), female soldiers (Isa 19:16; 50:37; 51:30), *wide open gates*, and burned *bars* for the gates (vv. 8–13).

Thebes
Located in upper Egypt about 440 miles south of Memphis, Thebes was the capital of Egypt under Ethiopian kings during Egypt's Twenty-fifth Dynasty (716–663 BCE).

Satirically, the prophet summons Assyria/Nineveh (feminine singular imperatives and pronouns) to prepare for attack. *Fire* and *sword* will *devour* Nineveh like *locusts* (NRSV) devour vegetation (vv. 14–15c). Three *locust* metaphors describe Nineveh's desperate situation: rapid numerical growth cannot thwart overthrow; Assyrian and foreign *merchants* will abandon the city, leaving unattended shops like *locusts shed* their *skins* (NRSV; not *strip the land* as in the NIV), and *fly away; guards* and omen interpreters appointed to advise the king freeze before invaders *on fences* (NRSV; not *in the walls* as in the NIV) who *fly away* at sunrise (vv. 15d–17 NRSV).

The prophet reprimands the *king of Assyria* because his *shepherds* (leaders) or *nobles* provide no guidance for their *people* (1 Kgs 22:17). The king's *wound is fatal. All who hear* will *clap their hands* (approvingly; see Lam 2:15), because Assyria inflicted *endless cruelty* on defenseless peoples (vv. 18–19).

THEOLOGICAL REFLECTIONS

Learning, power, and wealth stoked Assyria's pride. It had no qualms of conscience about practicing cruelty. Extended domination reinforced her atrocities. But eventually Yahweh intervened, declaring: *I am against you!* Though *slow to anger*, God releases his wrath against persistent sin through Babylon to destroy

Assyria. Such prophetic messages are not nationalistic. Amos and others proclaim similar messages against God's chosen people, as well. Sin is serious; God deals with it accordingly. God comforts the oppressed and punishes oppressors (Exod 22:21–24; Luke 16:19–31).

FOR FURTHER STUDY

Christensen, Duane L. *Nahum*. New Haven: Yale University Press, 2009.

García-Treto, Francisco O. "The Book of Nahum." In *The New Interpreters' Bible*, edited by Leander Keck, 7:593–619. Nashville: Abingdon, 1996.

O'Brien, Julia Myers. *Nahum*. London: Continuum, 2002.

WORKS CITED

Hallo, William, and K. Lawson Yonger, eds. *The Context of Scripture*. Volume 1: *Canonical Composition from the Biblical World*. Leiden: Brill, 1997.

Pritchard, James B., ed. *Ancient Near Eastern Texts Relating to the Old Testament*. 3rd ed. Princeton: Princeton University Press, 1969.

Habakkuk

John T. Willis

CHAPTER CONTENTS

MAP

Habakkuk's flow of thought and structure demonstrates coherence. The book is designed for dramatic performance or oral presentation before worshiping assemblies.

CONTEXTS

References to Babylon's rise (1:6) and overthrow of small nations (2:5–17) suggest 612–587 BCE as Habakkuk's historical setting. The psalm in Habakkuk 3, with its superscription *on* (according to) *Shigionoth* (v. 1 is similar to the superscription of Psalm 7), *selah* (vv. 3, 9, 13), and subscription *to the leader, with stringed instruments* (v. 19; see Ps 4:6 superscription), indicates that Habakkuk borrows structure, terminology, and theology from the worship at the temple.

COMMENTARY

SUPERSCRIPTION · 1:1

Habakkuk declares he *saw* (NRSV) the *oracle* (which is the same as the Hebrew word for "burden"). The use of the word "burden" in this context suggests a response to doubt about Yahweh's intentions.

DIALOGUE BETWEEN HABAKKUK & YAHWEH · 1:2–2:4

1:2–4   Habakkuk complains because Jehoiakim and his associates abuse their power against defenseless victims (see Jer 22:13–19), but when Habakkuk *cries out* to Yahweh to redress this, Yahweh does not *listen* and *save*. Cries of *how long?* (Ps 13:1–2) and *Why?* (Ps 22:1–2) seek to persuade Yahweh to act, just as in the Psalms. Again, Habakkuk draws on the language of the temple's worship.

Jehoiakim

Jehoiakim, king of Judah from 609–598 BCE, was the son of Josiah by Zebidah, daughter of Pedaiah of Rumah. He married Nehushta and fathered King Jehoiachin. His name means, "he whom Yahweh has set up."

1:5–11 Yahweh addresses all Judah (using masculine plural imperatives and pronouns *you, your* [v. 5]), promising to use the *Babylonians* to punish Judah for injustices (vv. 5–6). This is probably immediately after Babylon defeated Assyria and Egypt at Carchemish (605 BCE; Jer 46:2–12). Babylonians are *ruthless*, *violent*, arrogant warriors, *sweeping* swiftly *across the whole earth like a desert wind* to *seize* others' *dwelling places*. The images of speed emphasize their skill as warriors and thus the depth of the danger to Judah. They *gather prisoners like sand* and besiege *fortified cities*, *building* massive *earthen ramps* to scale walls and *capture* inhabitants. Siege technology had advanced a great deal by this period. They boast *they are a law to themselves* and claim their *own strength* as *their god* (Amos 6:13).

1:12–2:1 Yahweh's announcement that he is *raising up the Babylonians* (1:6) to punish Judah perturbs Habakkuk: How can the *everlasting* (translated literally *You [Yahweh] shall not die*, v. 12c NRSV), *holy*, invincible (literally *Rock*, v. 12e; compare Deut 32:30–31; Ps 18:2), *pure* God use a foreign nation to destroy *those more righteous than themselves* (v. 13d–e)? Babylon purposes to *destroy*, not merely punish, *nations*, using massive military machinery, like fishers use *hooks* and *nets* to *catch fish*, unconcerned about human dignity and value (vv. 14–15).

The Babylonian Empire

Babylonians worship instruments that increase their wealth and power (v. 16). Will Yahweh tolerate such cruel oppression forever (v. 17)? Habakkuk *stations* himself on Jerusalem's *ramparts*, eagerly awaiting Yahweh's *answer* to his *complaint* (2:1).

2:2–4   Unlike 1:5–11, here Habakkuk's composer introduces Yahweh as speaker (v. 2a). Yahweh charges Habakkuk to *write plainly on tablets* the *vision* (NRSV) Yahweh is giving him so *that a herald* (that is, Habakkuk himself) proclaims it to Judean audiences (v. 2b–d; compare Jer 23:21); to *wait* patiently for Yahweh to restore justice, guaranteed by the written record of the *vision* (v. 3; Isa 30:8); and to be faithful to Yahweh and endure steadfastly (v. 4).

Scholars interpret verse 4 variously. In verse 4a, one should probably emend the Hebrew for "swollen" (NIV, *puffed up*; NRSV, *proud*) to more directly contrast with *the righteous* in 4c. Thus, unlike the righteous, this "swollen" person will not walk in the vision's message. Further, the Hebrew word *'emunah* in verse 4c does not mean "faith" as acceptance of doctrine or as an inner attitude toward God, but rather as steadfast endurance, or "faithfulness."

> **The Babylonian Empire**
>
> *After the collapse of Assyria in 612 BCE, most of its empire fell to Babylon. Its great ruler Nebuchadnezzar (sometimes spelled Nebuchadrezzar) ruled 605–562 BCE and was a brilliant general. Judah was a Babylonian vassal state from 605–586 BCE, after which the Babylonians utterly destroyed the little kingdom, deporting most of its population.*

Interpreters have often understood Paul (Rom 1:16–17; Gal 3:10–11) and the author of Hebrews (10:32–39) as reading the Septuagint's rendition of "faith" in the former sense rather than the latter in 4c, although there is some reason to question this reading of the New Testament texts.

WOE ORACLES AGAINST BABYLON · 2:5–20

Verses 5–6a introduce five *woes* against Babylon (vv. 6b–20), returning to the theme of 1:5–17. The addressee is in the third person masculine singular (*he, him*), referring to Babylon collectively. The proclaimers of the *woes* are all *nations* whom Babylon had *taken captive*. They cry *woe*, a funeral lament (similar to the one in Jer 22:18–19), to mock Babylon for excessive atrocities. The prophet indicates that all nations, not just Israel, have a stake in Babylon's downfall and thus the end of oppression.

The first *woe* (2:6b–8) denounces Babylon for accumulating wealth from plunder, exacting *goods taken in pledge* (NRSV; compare verse 17). Babylon's *debtors* will *suddenly arise*, make it *their victim*, and *plunder* it. Babylon reaps what it sowed (Gal 6:7).

The second *woe* (vv. 9–11) reprimands Babylon for striving to make itself impregnable by amassing *unjust gain* to build the royal palace, like an eagle *setting his nest on high* (Obad 4). The very materials Babylon collected to build the royal palace *will cry out* in protest against Babylon's cruelty and ask for punishment.

The prophet uses images of invulnerability to emphasize the futility of Babylon's relentless pursuit of power.

The third woe reproves Babylon for killing and subjugating nonsupporters and opponents (compare Mic 3:9–10). Yahweh thwarts the unjust use of *labor*, particularly by Babylon. Babylon's policy of forced resettlement, well-known from the Babylonian sources themselves, comes under scrutiny here (Floyd 143). Verse 14 echoes Isaiah 11:9, where the image of flooding waters comes ultimately from the royal propaganda of the Mesopotamian empires.

The fourth woe reproaches Babylon for making his *neighbors drunk* to *gaze on their naked bodies* (compare Gen 9:20–25), using sexual imagery to trigger disgust at their behavior. *Violence done to Lebanon* refers to indiscriminate tree felling for building, etc. (Isa 14:8) and random *destruction of animals* for sport or to hector enemies, both of which were activities for displaying royal power. Retributively, Yahweh will *fill* Babylon with *shame* and force it to *drink the cup* of Yahweh's wrath (compare Jer 25:15–29) to *expose* its own nakedness.

The fifth woe ridicules Babylon for idolatry, labeling their gods as human *creations* (Ps 135:15–18). Idol makers control images they make and so determine their own theology and lifestyle. By contrast, Yahweh creates and sustains humanity. In verse 20, God's *temple* equals heaven (see Ps 11:4); *silence* does not mean absence of sound, but humility and trust (as in Zech 2:13).

PRAYER EXTOLLING YAHWEH AS VICTORIOUS WARRIOR · 3:1–19

Habakkuk 3 relates a prayer of Habakkuk (3:2, 16–19) responding to an ancient vision (perhaps referred to in 2:2) of Yahweh's appearance, or "theophany," to overthrow enemies (vv. 3–15), thus restoring order to creation. The song itself may be much more ancient than Habakkuk (Hiebert; but see Floyd 147–48), and it has elements of both a psalm of praise and one of complaint. The prophet functions here as a temple singer (Floyd 157–58). After the superscription (3:1), the chapter contains three parts, arranged chiastically:

A Prayer (3:2)
B Description of Yahweh's coming & victory (3:3–15)
A' Prayer (3:16–19)

The superscription calls this poem a *prayer of Habakkuk. On shigionoth* indicates it was composed for singing. Habakkuk first acknowledges God's deeds, drawing on the ancient language of theophany (vv. 3–15), afterwards resuming his prayer with: *I hear* (v. 16). He petitions Yahweh to *renew* deeds of *mercy* for Israel. Yahweh approaches from *Teman* (northwest Edom) and *Mount Paran* (hills west of the Gulf of Aqaba) (as in Deut 33:2; Judg 5:4–5), producing *glory* and *splendor*. God walks with an entourage—*plague* and *pestilence*—as would a mighty warrior approaching his enemies. God traverses the sky in *chariots* (see

Pss 18:9–10; 68:32–33), shoots *arrows*, and brandishes a *spear*. The poem thus draws on one of Israel's oldest metaphors for God, the divine warrior.

Yahweh stupefied his enemies in nature and history, combating nature by inflicting cataclysmic upheavals on *earth, mountains, waterways, sun*, and *moon*. When battling human foes, Yahweh *made the nations tremble, crushed the leader of the land of wickedness, and pierced his head* when his warriors *came like a whirlwind* (NRSV) to scatter Yahweh's people. *Anointed one* refers to the Davidic king in Jerusalem. This vision does not refer to specific historical events, though in the context of the book, the fall of Babylon must be in view.

Rehearsal of Yahweh's appearance terrified Habakkuk. Like lamenters in the Psalms, he experiences bodily dislocation. He imagines massive failures of crops and herds. Yet he resolves to *wait patiently* for Yahweh to overthrow Babylon and to rejoice in Yahweh as his strength, indicating acceptance of Yahweh's assurance in 2:4.

THEOLOGICAL REFLECTIONS

Habakkuk struggles with how a just and loving God could permit personal, political or social, and international injustice to rule in the world. Yahweh does not resolve this by restoring justice in Habakkuk's day but by challenging him to trust in Yahweh's eventual intervention to punish the wicked and vindicate the righteous.

FOR FURTHER STUDY

Achtemeier, Elizabeth. *Nahum–Malachi*. Louisville: Westminster John Knox, 1986.
Dempsey, Carol J. *Amos, Hosea, Micah, Nahum, Zephaniah, Habakkuk*. Collegeville, MN: Liturgical Press, 2013.
Szeles, Maria Eszenyei. *Wrath and Mercy: A Commentary on Habakkuk and Zephaniah*. Grand Rapids: Eerdmans, 1987.

WORKS CITED

Floyd, Michael H. *Minor Prophets Part 2*. Grand Rapids: Eerdmans, 2000.
Hiebert, Theodore. *God of My Victory*. Atlanta: Scholars Press, 1986.

Zephaniah

John T. Willis

CHAPTER CONTENTS

Apparently, Zephaniah was a great-great-grandson of King Hezekiah of Judah, who reigned 715–687 BCE (1:1). Zephaniah prophesied during the reign of Josiah (640–609 BCE). Hilkiah discovered the book of the law, on which Josiah based his reforms (2 Kgs 22:3–23:25), in the temple during its repairs (621 BCE).

CONTEXTS

The setting explains Zephaniah's condemnation of idolatry and child sacrifice (Zeph 1:4–9, 11–12; 3:1–4; 2 Kgs 23:4–15), which Manasseh brought into Judah (2 Kgs 21:2–9, 16) and which Josiah removed. Philistines, Moabites, and Ammonites taunted Judah (2:4–11); Cushites (that is, inhabitants of Sudan who then ruled Egypt) seemed weak but threatening (2:12); Babylon had not yet destroyed Nineveh (2:13–15). These facts indicate the book dates from between 621 and 612 BCE. Zephaniah and Jeremiah, the first prophetic voices since Isaiah and Micah roughly 75 years previously, likely helped initiate and encourage Josiah's reform. Zephaniah's familiarity with Jerusalem (1:10–13), its officials (1:8–9; 3:3–4), and sacrifices at the temple (1:7–8), as well as his insights into the attitudes and circumstances of Jerusalem's residents (1:12–13; 3:7), and his joy anticipating Yahweh's deliverance of a faithful remnant (3:14, 17) suggest he was a Jerusalemite who frequented the temple and knew people in the city personally, including officials. The book's structure and content indicate it was composed for oral reading or dramatic performance at a major pilgrim festival at the Jerusalem temple, probably the Feast of Booths, also called Tabernacles or Ingathering (see Exod 23:16–17; Lev 23:33–44; Num 29:12–40; Deut 16:13–17).

COMMENTARY

Zephaniah 1:1 declares that Zephaniah's message *came* from Yahweh, that Zephaniah was the descendant of king *Hezekiah*, and that he prophesied *during the reign of Josiah*.

THE DAY OF YAHWEH'S WRATH AGAINST JUDAH · 1:2–2:4

Declares the Lord (1:2, 3, 10) is a version of the "messenger formula" that ancient heralds used to proclaim the sender of their message. As a royal messenger, the prophet relates Yahweh's announcement to all nations (1:2–3, 18; 2:4), especially Judah (1:4, 10–12; 2:1), using the first person singular pronoun "I" and the third person singular "Yahweh" to emphasize the speaker's significance. Yahweh announces the nearness of the *great day of the Lord* (1:7, 14). As in Amos 5:18–20, the intended day of national deliverance will bring instead national judgment. It will be a *day* of *sweep*ing *away* (1:2, 3, 4; 2:2; as in Noah's flood, Gen 6:7), of a *sacrifice* of apostate Judean officials (1:7–9), of Yahweh's *punishment* (1:8, 9, 12) and *wrath* (1:15, 18; 2:2, 3), as well as a series of graphic signs of destruction (1:15–17). Zephaniah portrays his audience as people practicing idolatry (1:4) and foreign religious rites (1:5, 8, 9), abandoning Yahweh (1:6), and full of *violence* (1:9), smugness (1:12), and dependence on their riches. Their silver and gold (1:11, 13, 18) provoke this punishment. The effect will be extensive destruction of humans and all the surrounding ecosystem (1:2, 3, 17, 18), of physical property (1:13), and of *fortified cities* (1:16; 2:4), with *cry*ing and *wailing* (1:10, 11, 14). Whereas many citizens of Judah saw the collapse of the Assyrian Empire as a chance for independence, Zephaniah correctly foresaw only anarchy.

1:2–6   Under Manasseh and Amon, many Judeans worshiped at the same time *Baal*, the Canaanite deity of fertility and battle (compare Hos 2:2–20); the *starry host* (sun, moon, and stars) (Deut 4:19); *Molech* (NIV), or *Milcom* (NRSV), perhaps an Ammonite deity or one to whom they sacrificed babies (Lev 18:21; 1 Kgs 11:5, 7; Jer 32:35); as well as Yahweh (1:4–6). For ancient persons, this mixture of religious elements (or syncretism) would have seemed perfectly normal.

1:7–9   *Leaping over the threshold* (v. 9 NRSV) of a temple was a superstitious act of Philistine

---

Molech

Phoenician texts, especially from Carthage in North Africa, a Phoenician colony, speak of a mulk sacrifice—a lamb offered along with a child sacrifice or perhaps sometimes in substitution for it. "Molech" is not ordinarily a god. The better reading of verse 5, in any case is "their king," with no god's name present at all (Sweeney 71).

Dagon

Dagon was a god of grain and agriculture worshiped by the early Amorites and popular in the ancient cities of Ugarit and Ebla. Dagon is mentioned in extrabiblical sources as early as 2300 BCE.

religionists of the deity Dagon (1 Sam 5:5), perhaps indicating fear of demons or of terrifying consequences.

1:10–13   Invaders will attack Jerusalem from the north, the direction of the road from Mesopotamia. The places in verses 10–11 mostly lie in the western part of the city. Yahweh, using assailants, will search every inch of *Jerusalem with lamps* (v. 12a; see Ps 139:12); none will escape (Amos 9:1–4). Many Judeans are complacent, *like wine left on its dregs* (as in Jer 48:11). Numerous Jerusalemites settled into a spiritually and morally deteriorating, indolent lifestyle, assuming *the Lord will do nothing, either good* (blessing) *or bad* (punishing) (v. 12b–e; Jer 5:12; 23:17; Amos 9:10; Mic 3:11). When the Israelites settled Canaan, they lived in houses they did not build and drank wine from vineyards they did not plant (see Deut 6:10; Josh 24:13), but Yahweh will reverse this: Babylonian invaders will dwell in houses Israelites built and drink wine of vineyards Israelites planted (v. 13), as the law threatened if Israel forsook Yahweh (Deut 28:30).

> **New Wine & Dregs**
> *To give wine strength and flavor, vintners let new wine stand with grapes' sediment ("dregs") temporarily, straining it through a cloth before drinking.*

1:14–18   As a mighty *warrior*, Yahweh will lead Babylon's army (1:14d; Jer 25:8–11). Judah's citizens' blood and *flesh* (NRSV) will cover the ground *like dust* and *dung* (1:17d–e; compare NRSV; Jer 8:2; 9:22). Assailants will refuse exorbitant bribes from victims to cease attacking (v. 18a–c).

2:1–4   Even while announcing Judah's severe mass destruction, Yahweh contemplates deliverance. There is time for repentance as the phrases in verse 3 indicate. *The humble* accept Yahweh's instruction, leadership, and teaching (see Mic 6:8; Ps 25:8–9). *For* (v. 4a NRSV) joins verse 4 to verses 1–3; verse 4 describes impenitent Judah's fate through previous Philistine devastation. This verse names four of five Philistine cities (omitting Gath, as does Amos 1:6–8; compare 1 Sam 6:17), using metaphors of a woman jilted before marriage, abandoned by her husband, divorced, or rendered barren to depict pain of enemy atrocities.

THE DAY OF YAHWEH'S WRATH AGAINST THE NATIONS · 2:5–3:8

Woe (2:5; repeated for emphasis in 3:1) begins a new section, which again heralds Yahweh's punishment of *the nations* (3:6, 8) or the *whole world* (3:8), including Judah (3:1–5, 7), but now especially other nations. The prophet names the nations by their position relative to Judah: *Kerethites* or *Philistines* westward by the sea (2:5–7; Ezek 25:15–16); *Ammon* and *Moab* eastward (vv. 8–11; Jer 48:1–49:6); *Ethiopians* (NRSV) southward (12; Isa 18:1); *Assyria* northward (13–15; Nah 1:12–3:7); and finally Judah (3:1–5, 7). Yahweh

> **"There is none besides me . . ."**
> *The nations ignore their dependence on God, boasting superiority to Yahweh, who alone claims dominance successfully (as in Isa 45:5–6, 18). Judah falls under the same judgment.*

will punish the nations for oppressing Judah (2:8, 10) and for *pride* (2:10). The warrant for this divine punishment comes in 2:15: *I am, and there is none besides me* (2:15; Isa 47:8, 10; Ezek 28:2). The following verses lay out the abuses of power by leaders (compare Ezek 22:23–19), the priests' defilement of the temple, and the idolatrous attitudes of the people.

Yahweh's intention in *dispensing justice* (3:5c) through severe retribution is to refine and redeem. The soaring language of the text glorifies Yahweh, who works to transform human hearts and bring justice among individuals and nations. Ultimately, Yahweh blesses the people in several ways: Philistine territory *will belong to Judah* for pasturage, indicating economic recovery for Judah (vv. 6–7d); Yahweh *will care* for Israel (v. 7e–f; 3:20; Jer 30:18; 33:26); Yahweh's *people* will occupy Moab and Ammon (v. 9g–h). In short, a restored Israel will occupy the entire region. Yahweh also blesses the nations and destroys their gods. The restoration of Israel has implications for everyone else. The idea that other gods will fall under Yahweh's overarching rule also appears elsewhere (Exod 12:12; 18:11; Ps 82:6–7).

2:5–7   Yahweh, hence Yahweh's *word*, opposes evildoers (v. 5c; 2 Sam 12:9–10).

2:8–11   Moab's and Ammon's destruction resemble that of *Sodom* and *Gomorrah* (v. 9c–d; Gen 19:24–29; Isa 13:19; Jer 49:18).

Cush & Tirhakah

Cush (or Kush), an ancient civilization in Nubia (now northern Sudan), was one of the earliest Nile civilizations. Tirhakah (or Taharqa), an Ethiopian king during the time of Hezekiah, fought against Sennacharib in 701 BCE, preventing the latter from conquering Jerusalem and deporting its citizens.

2:12   Yahweh's sword in the hands of human soldiers (compare Ezek 21:1–23) will kill Judah's former allies against Assyria, the *Cushites* under Tirhakah (Isa 37:9).

13–15   The prophet describes *Nineveh*'s total desolation (612 BCE): this previously large, powerful, bustling city is now a ruin and the habitation of frightening animals (Isa 13:19–22; 34:8–15; compare Rev 18:2). The political revolution of the late seventh century came, says the prophet, because of Yahweh's search for human justice.

3:1–5   Jerusalem's wicked officials prowl against defenseless victims at night, leaving *nothing for the morning* (v. 3). By contrast, Yahweh appears *morning by morning*, as regular and dependable as the sunrise, to punish oppressors and deliver the oppressed (v. 5).

3:6–8   Since all the *nations*, including Judah, refuse to *fear* (that is, stand in awe of, reverence, honor) Yahweh, they will experience divine punishment (Mic 4:11–13).

THE DAY OF YAHWEH'S SALVATION OF THE NATIONS & JUDAH · 3:9–20

Yahweh's will is to heal wounds as well as inflict them (Isa 30:26). Deliverance follows punishment. Zephaniah's theme continues to be *at that time* (3:9 NRSV;

3:11, 14), the Day of Yahweh, now *a day of festival* (3:18a NRSV), probably equaling the Feast of Tabernacles. Yahweh will *change the speech of the peoples to a pure speech* (v. 9a NRSV) so they may join in prayer to God (v. 9b; Joel 2:32) and *serve* God *with one accord* (v. 9c NRSV), reversing the confusion of tongues at Babel (Gen 11:1–9). Yahweh's *worshipers*, those *scattered* from all nations who will be converted to him, will *bring his offering* (NRSV) in adoration and praise (v. 10; 2:11).

Further, Yahweh will remove from Judah the proud oppressors of the defenseless, leaving behind only the pious (vv. 11–13, 19). In a series of images reminiscent of Isaiah 54–55 and 60–62, Zephaniah describes the glorious renewal of the nation. Hearers of the prophets *should be glad and rejoice* (v. 14), avoid *fear* (vv. 13, 15, 16), and quit being terrified by enemies or circumstances (v. 16c; Isa 13:7; Jer 6:24; Heb 12:12), because Yahweh, the *King of Israel*, is *mighty to save* (vv. 15, 17). God will not *shame* them (vv. 11, 19) but will *give them praise and honor* (vv. 19–20); they will be secure in their land (v. 13); Yahweh himself will *take great delight in* them, *renew* them *in his love* (NRSV), rejoice over them *with singing* (v. 17), and *restore* their *fortunes* (v. 20; 2:7). These climactic verses turn the book's message into one of hope. The word of condemnation in chapter 1 gives way to a love song in the finale.

THEOLOGICAL REFLECTIONS
Yahweh, creator of all humanity, is deeply concerned about and cares for all peoples, including the people chosen to bring blessing to all nations and all nations to God. Yahweh has a "Day of Wrath" for all peoples, since all persist in sinning. Since sin is very serious and debilitating, God deals with it severely, yet not to annihilate, but to cleanse and redeem. Thus, beyond punishment, Yahweh has a "Day of Deliverance" (or salvation) for all peoples, on which all false gods perish, and meek, humble, and faithful people throughout the world convert to worshiping and serving God in *pure speech* and *with one accord*.

FOR FURTHER STUDY
Achtemeier, Elizabeth. *Nahum–Malachi*. Louisville: Westminster John Knox, 1986.
Dempsey, Carol J. *Amos, Hosea, Micah, Nahum, Zephaniah, Habakkuk*. Collegeville, MN: Liturgical Press, 2013.
Szeles, Maria Eszenyei. *Wrath and Mercy: A Commentary on Habakkuk and Zephaniah*. Grand Rapids: Eerdmans, 1987.

WORKS CITED
Floyd, Michael H. *Minor Prophets Part 2*. Grand Rapids: Eerdmans, 2000.
Sweeney, Marvin. *Zephaniah*. Minneapolis, MN: Fortress, 2003.

Haggai

Paul L. Watson

CHAPTER CONTENTS

Haggai is unique in the prophetic canon of the Old Testament. Whereas other prophets critique the worship of the people of Israel (Amos 5:21–24; Isa 1:10–17) and their uncritical loyalty to the temple (Jer 7:1–4), Haggai urges the reconstruction of the temple and a renewal of temple worship. Because of this, many readers have depreciated his message, feeling it has little current relevance. However, an understanding of Haggai's historical context and a close reading of his oracles affirm the validity of his prophecy.

CONTEXTS

All five of Haggai's oracles date to 520 BCE, the third year of the reign of the Persian king Darius the Great (522–486 BCE). While it was a time "of [the] beginnings of regional autonomy" (Peterson 27), Judah was still a subprovince of the new Persian Empire. Moreover, it was a time of land redistribution and of economic decline (March 709–10).

Such was the situation Haggai faced as he joined a contingent of exiles returning from Babylon to Jerusalem and Judah (Ezra 3:1–13; 5:1–2; 6:13–15). Haggai saw that such an impoverished, unfocused community could not survive without having a center—God—and a common commitment to worship and service. In this context, the message of Haggai makes sense.

"Beyond the River"

The Persian Empire was organized into several satrapies, or regions. The satrapy "Beyond the River" included most of today's Syria, Lebanon, Israel, Palestine, and Jordan. Judah, or Yehud, was a small division of this larger satrapy, as was Samaria.

Of Haggai the messenger we know very little. His name comes from the Hebrew word meaning "observe a pilgrimage feast." The book is written in a third-person, narrative style, suggesting that a disciple of Haggai composed it shortly after Haggai's ministry.

COMMENTARY

IS IT A TIME FOR YOURSELVES? · 1:1–11

Haggai's first oracle, dated 29 August 520 BCE, is explicitly addressed to *Zerubbabel, son of Shealtiel, governor of Judah, and to Joshua, son of Jehozadak the high priest* (1:1), and implicitly to all the residents of Jerusalem and Judah (1:5–6). The people are experiencing crop failure, scarcity of goods, and inflation (1:6). But the heart of their problem lies in their priorities: *These people say, The time has not yet come for the Lord's house to be built* (1:2). The people intend to rebuild God's temple—some day. But, for now, their primary attention is on themselves. So God puts this penetrating question to them: *Is it a time for you yourselves to be living in your paneled* [or, "finished"] *houses, while this house* [God's temple] *remains a ruin?* (1:4).

All this amounts to a violation of their covenant with God. By enacting the covenant-curses of Leviticus 26 and Deuteronomy 27–28, God reminds his people "that not foreigner nor fate nor workings of nature control the Judeans' lives, but God" (Achtemeier 99). Even the date of this first oracle is significant. Apparently, it is a feast day, connected with the Sabbath (2 Chron 31:3; Amos 8:5)—one they cannot observe "because of the lack of both altar and sanctuary" (Peterson 44).

Therefore, God says, *Give careful thought* [literally "set your heart"] *to your ways* (1:7). By shifting their focus from themselves to their relationship with God, they will in fact secure the prosperity they currently seek in vain.

I AM WITH YOU · 1:12–15

About three weeks later, on 21 September 520 BCE, Haggai delivers this message of divine approval. Leaders and people alike have *obeyed the voice of the Lord their God* (1:12). In response, God says, *I am with you* (1:13)—well before the temple was rebuilt—and God *stirred up the spirit* of all to carry out his will (1:14).

HOW DOES IT LOOK TO YOU NOW? · 2:1–9

Almost a month later—at the end of the Feast of Tabernacles (or *Sukkoth*, 17 October 520 BCE)—Haggai speaks again. Based on the recollections of the oldest members of the community (2:3a), it is clear that this will be "a half-baked building compared with the old temple that Solomon built" (Craigie 145).

God's response to the people's disappointment is twofold. First, *Be strong . . . for I am with you* (2:4–5). The size and beauty of the temple are not important; God's presence is. Second, God gives them a greater vision of the future that includes *all nations*, when God will *fill this house with glory* and will *grant peace* (2:6–9).

FROM THIS DAY ON, I WILL BLESS YOU · 2:10–19

"The ultimate danger of temple building, and indeed of all works of religion, is the temptation to become self-righteous" (Achtemeier 102). That temptation apparently lies behind this oracle, dated 18 December 520 BCE. God warns the community that holiness is not contagious (2:11–12), but corruption is (2:13–14). God then urges the community to *give careful thought* to how it has been—empty silos and wine vats, unproductive labor (2:16–17)—compared with how it can be: *From this day on I will bless you* (2:18–19). Here holiness refers to the ritual purity of objects, but Haggai expands a technical argument among priests into a discussion with wider implications.

"Give careful thought ..."
Although their forefathers had believed that technically correct worship was all that God required (Mic 6:1–8), Haggai warns that this generation needs to beware of that trap.

I HAVE CHOSEN YOU · 2:20–23

Haggai's final oracle, also delivered on 18 December 520 BCE, is God's personal promise to Zerubbabel to honor his commitment to the house of David (2 Sam 7:11b–16). In a reversal of Jeremiah 22:24, God will empower Zerubbabel—*make you like my signet ring*—for *I have chosen you* (2:23).

Signet Rings
A signet ring served ancient tradespeople and rulers as a tool for certifying documents.

THEOLOGICAL REFLECTIONS

The message of Haggai, which at first glance seems to contradict that of the rest of the prophets, turns out to be one with theirs. God yearns to be present with Israel and to give them peace. But God will not do so unless they become persons of faith (Exod 20:1–3; Deut 6:4–6). The size and splendor of their accomplishments are not important to God; their wholehearted dedication to him is.

FOR FURTHER STUDY

Brown, William P. *Obadiah through Malachi*. Louisville: Westminster John Knox, 1996.
Collins, John J. *Joel, Obadiah, Haggai, Zechariah, Malachi*. Collegeville, MN: Liturgical Press, 2013.

WORKS CITED

Achtemeier, Elizabeth. *Nahum–Malachi*. Atlanta: John Knox, 1986.
Craigie, Peter. *Twelve Prophets*. Volume 2: *Micah, Nahum, Habakkuk, Zephaniah, Haggai, Zechariah, and Malachi*. Louisville: Westminster John Knox, 1985.
March, W. Eugene. *Haggai*. Nashville: Abingdon, 1996.
Peterson, David L. *Haggai and Zechariah 1–8*. Philadelphia: Westminster, 1984.

Zechariah

Tim Sensing

CHAPTER CONTENTS

Zechariah, which means "Yahweh remembers," is the name of twenty-nine biblical characters. The Zechariah of this book is a prophet (Zech 1:1, 7), and he responds as a prophet to the delegation's question in Zechariah 7–8. He may be the priest referred to in Nehemiah 12:16. This Zechariah was a contemporary of Haggai, and both prophesied in Jerusalem after the return from Babylonian exile sometime after 539 BCE. The edict of Cyrus (Ezra 6:3–5) allowed them to rebuild the temple. Ezra 5:1, 6:14, and Nehemiah 12:16 mention the career of both prophets, as well. Zechariah's first prophecy follows Haggai's by two months (Zech 1:1), and his work continued until 518 BCE, *the fourth year of King Darius* (Zech 7:1). Both Haggai and Zechariah advocated the completion of the temple.

Eschatology in Zechariah

Many of Zechariah's themes are eschatological in nature, describing Yahweh as the lord of the whole earth (4:14) who rules from Zion over all the nations (compare Psalm 2). Peace and justice will characterize God's reign, which completely depends on God's action and will be a reversal of the devastation of Judah in former times. Although Zechariah's vision of God's recreated future seems utopian, it still expects conflict and death.

CONTEXTS

Differences in literary style between Zechariah 1–8 and 9–14 have led many scholars to attribute the two sections to different authors. For example, chapters 9–14 contain no visions and no historic references to the restoration of Jerusalem, the temple, or the reign of Darius, while chapters 1–8 strongly emphasize those elements. Similarly, chapters 9–14 make no mention of Zechariah, Joshua, and Zerubbabel, who are so prominent in chapters 1–8. Chapters 9–14 also demonstrate considerable differences in vocabulary and other literary features (Coggins 61–62).

Yet certain themes appear in both sections: the prominence of the Zion tradition, the stress on the cleansing of the community, universalistic tendencies, the appeal to earlier prophecy, and the role of proper leadership as a sign of the new age. Such similarities suggest some historical relationship between the two parts of the book.

Dating of chapters 9–14 becomes problematic since there are no concrete references to people or events. The reference to *Greece* in 9:13 may represent a later time period for these oracles. Scholars tend to date 9–14 later than 1–8 due to the differences in literary style. Yet it is more helpful to try to understand the entire book as a single work, with historical setting of chapters 1–8 leading into a more generalized vision of the world later in the book. The emphasis on divine judgment throughout the book can certainly refer to many historical periods. On the other hand, chapters 1–8 more often envision the restoration as a present reality, whereas chapters 9–14 depict the restoration as an eschatological hope still in the future (see Conrad).

> **Yehud in the Persian Empire**
> *The district around Jerusalem, called Yehud (a short form of Yehudah, or Judah), was part of the larger Persian satrapy "Beyond the River," which covered modern Syria, Lebanon, Jordan, Israel, and the Palestinian Authority. The high priest of Jerusalem functioned as a local leader subject to the imperial Persian government. Coins from Yehud often bear the names of these high priests.*

COMMENTARY

INTRODUCTION · 1:1–6

Zechariah has long stymied interpreters. It stands between the utopian picture of the future represented in Isaiah 40–55 and the hard realities of postexilic Palestine. Much of the apocalyptic language defies concrete historical connections. However, in association with Haggai, Zechariah gives readers a rare glimpse into the state of affairs in postexilic Jerusalem.

Zechariah, *son of Berekiah, the son of Iddo*, joined with Yahweh in forming a new community fit for the new age promised by the earlier prophets. Zechariah reiterates the message of the *former prophets*, calling the community to *return* to God. Even his name reminds the community to remember God's past action and promise. The people during Zechariah's day, unlike their ancestors, repented of their sins (6b). Zechariah believed the return from exile and the rebuilding of the temple would inaugurate God's eschatological future. Zechariah looks back at an earlier era, the time of the *former prophets* (Zech 1:2–6; 7:4–14; 8:9), those like Amos or Jeremiah, and understands the exile to have been the fulfillment of their words. He declares that he and his fellow Jews now stand at the threshold of the new era.

Much of the imagery in the night visions describes common sights in Jerusalem during the rebuilding of the temple. The visions are arranged in a chiastic (A B B'A') fashion and consistently depict Yahweh's return to Zion. The first and last visions encompass the whole world. The second and seventh visions narrow the focus to Judah. The third and sixth visions focus on Jerusalem. The fourth and fifth visions examine the roles of Joshua and Zerubbabel. Fishbane (448) notes a pattern of each vision except the fourth: Zechariah reports a vision: "I saw. . ."; he describes a sign: "and there before me was/were. . ."; he asks: "What is this/are these?"; the angel identifies the sign: "This is/these are. . ."; the angel interprets the sign.

A major feature of each oracle is the prophetic introduction: the messenger formula *thus says Yahweh*, the oracle formula *says Yahweh*, and the revelation formula *the word of Yahweh came to. . . .*

Hanson observes that the structural arrangement of the visions focuses on the temple as the center of a symbolic universe (see also Halpern). Yet the visions themselves do not directly mention the temple reconstruction. No matter how the visions are numbered, the two visions of chapters 3 and 4, which focus on the political power of Joshua and Zerubbabel in the temple, are the centerpiece of the entire section.

1:7-7 Soon after the initial prophecy, while the temple is being reconstructed, Zechariah receives night visions full of hope concerning what God has already begun to do in the new age (Zech 1:11b, 16; 2:4–5, 10). The first night vision raises the question of the delay of the promise that underlies Haggai's work, by referring to *seventy years* (v. 12) of punishment, perhaps an echo of the equal time span predicated by Jeremiah (Jer 25:11; 29:10). The world Zechariah envisions does not correspond to the reality the people experienced.

1:18-21 The *four craftsmen*, divine agents of God, will destroy the *four horns*, representing the oppressive nations that *scattered Israel, Judah, and*

Zechariah's Visions
Meyers and Meyers (Zechariah 1–8, 179, 213–15) *exclude 3:1–10 from the list of visions and renumber 5–8 as 4–7. Chapter 3 does break from the pattern of the other visions by lacking the interpreting angel and Zechariah's subsequent answer, the naming of a historical person, and the mention of the* satan. *Someone else shows Zechariah the vision. I have followed here the more usual arrangement of the visions, however.*

Apocalypse in Zechariah
These chapters contain an early form of apocalyptic literature. John Collins says that it is
"a genre of revelatory literature with a narrative framework, in which a revelation is mediated by an otherworldly being to a human recipient, disclosing a transcendent reality which is both temporal, insofar as it involves another, supernatural world, intended for a group in crisis with the purpose of exhortation and/or consolation by means of divine authority" (Collins 9).
These visions work by piling up images that collectively evoke certain responses.

Jerusalem. The horns symbolize military powers, and the number four represents the four corners of the world and thus its totality. God will accomplish the promised restoration by crushing the oppressive powers.

2:1–13 Jerusalem is being measured as a symbol of its restoration. It will be *without walls*, not because foreign armies have destroyed them, but because the population of returnees grows too large. People will again dwell there in prosperity and God's *glory* will fortify the city. The oracle that follows, 2:6–13, interprets the first three night visions by affirming the restoration of Judah and Jerusalem as God's holy dwelling, ensuring the destruction of the oppressive nations, and envisioning prosperity in the future. The phrase *Holy Land* (2:12) occurs only here in the Old Testament.

3:1–10 Joshua served as the first high priest after the exile (Ezra 2:2; 3:2; see also 2 Kings 25:18; 1 Chron 6:15; Jer 52:24; Zech 4; 6:9–15). He helped build the altar and the temple, and he offered sacrifices (Ezra 3:1–13; 5:1–2). By omitting the name of the governor, Zerubbabel, this vision emphasizes the central role of the high priest in postexilic Judaism.

> **"The Satan"**
> The satan, *with the definite article, occurs in the Bible elsewhere only in Job 1–2 and 1 Chronicles 21:1, where it names a member of the divine council, not a demonic figure.*

Verses 1–5 describe the heavenly courtroom where *the satan* accuses Joshua. The Lord rebukes the satan for undercutting Joshua. The angel orders the cleaning of Joshua's priestly garments (see Exod 28:31–38), signifying the cleansing of sin and the restoration of relationship between Yahweh and his people.

Verse 6 introduces an oracle from the Lord describing the duties or privileges of Joshua. Subsequently, the future ruler from David's line, the *Branch* (see Jer 23:5–6; 33:14–15), will remove the sin from all the people in the land. Zerubbabel may be the Branch (see Hag 2:23), since 6:12–13 designates the figure as the one to build the temple, while 4:7–10 presents Zerubbabel as the one to do so. However, the prophet also presents the Branch as a future messiah who will demonstrate the inclusive nature of God's protection among the nations.

4:1–14 The central feature of this vision is the *lamp stand* symbolizing God's presence in the temple and in Jerusalem. If chapter 3 is a later addition, then the lamp stand representing God's presence sits at the center of all the visions and coincides theologically with the first and last.

> **Apocalyptic Vision**
> *In Revelation 5:6, the eyes of the Lamb take over the function of Yahweh's eyes in Zechariah 4:10b.*

Verses 8–14 describe Zerubbabel's reconstruction of the temple. The *plumb line* of verse 10 links the prophecy to Amos 7:7–9: the new prophecy reverses the doom oracle of Amos. The *two who are anointed* are Joshua and Zerubbabel.

5:1–4 The *flying scroll* symbolizes the word of God going forth among the people, cursing violators of the Mosaic law, especially the eighth and ninth commandments. The *curse* consumes those who are an internal threat to the community and thus preserves the people as a whole. Like all the night visions, this one lodges no judgment against the community as a whole. The scope of God's restoration begins to expand here to include the whole earth, a move climaxing in the final vision.

5:5–11 The theme of protecting the community from internal threat continues in the seventh and most complex of the visions. The *basket* of *iniquity* goes to *Babylonia*. The sin of the people has been removed.

6:1–8 The eighth vision structurally parallels the first in setting and theme, emphasizing God's presence. The horses represent God spreading his reign throughout the world with an emphasis on the *north country*, the land of exile, where God's *Spirit* is at *rest* and the cosmos is now ordered. The inclusive nature of God's future reign encompasses the east and west in 8:7–8 and the south in 9:14.

6:9–15 Mason (197) observes that the last oracle has little literary connection with the final vision but may serve as an "appendix" to the whole series. The central feature of the section is the crowning of Joshua and the building of the temple. Though Joshua is the true representative of God, he also functions as a sign of the unnamed "Branch" and an unspecified future to come.

SERMONIC RESPONSE TO THE PRESENT SITUATION · 7:1–8:23

7:1–3 A two-year gap occurs between the dating of the night visions and the arrival of a delegation from Bethel. According to 2 Kings 25:8–9, Jerusalem fell in the fifth month. For decades, the lamentations and fasting have beseeched the throne of God on behalf of the land, Jerusalem, and the people. And during their exile, the prophets proclaimed a coming age of grace, a time when a remnant of the people would return to the land. Now, with the return of the prophets Haggai and Zechariah, the temple itself was being reconstructed. In the second year of that reconstruction process, about halfway through, a delegation came asking whether the mourning remained appropriate in light of new circumstances.

7:4–8:23 The remainder of this section consists of a series of oracles responding to the question of 7:3 (7:4–7; 7:8–14; 8:1–8; 8:9–13; 8:14–17; 8:18–19; and 8:20–23). The oracles begin in the same way and weave together images of restoration (often drawn from earlier prophets) and call for ethical living. Nineteen times throughout the sermon in chapters 7 and 8, either the messenger formula (*thus says Yahweh of hosts*), the revelation formula (*the word of Yahweh came to*), or the oracle formula (*Says Yahweh*) constitutes Zechariah's understanding of the continuation and authority of the prophetic tradition to interpret the present in light of the past, in order to reorient the future. Mason (224) notes, "Such a homiletical practice serves at least three purposes. It explains why the promises of the prophets have not yet been fully experienced; it puts the stress on moral regeneration which is where the preacher believed it must be; and it serves to keep hope and faith alive in face of any temptation to despair and disillusion."

These oracles of Zechariah refer repeatedly to the "former" or "earlier" prophets. Mason (203) states, "It is interesting that the prophetic word is now becoming regarded as authoritative teaching on a par with Torah, for that is what the paralleling of the legal terms *statutes* with *my words* must imply." He also identifies (218) in chapter 7 allusions and images from the former prophets (for example, Deut 29:25; 32:17; 2 Chron 29:8; 30:7; Isa 29:6; Jer 3:19; 19:4; 23:19; 25:32; 44:3; Ezek 32:9; Amos 1:14; Hos 13:3).

> **Tradition**
>
> *For Zechariah, the tradition acted as testimony to faith and practice that allowed the emergence of a new understanding in his own context. He proclaims the former words as his word in order to reshape his community. Even though Zechariah's and the former prophets' message was the same, the contexts, intents, and responses were different. The former prophets' words brought devastation, Zechariah's hope.*

The delegation's question in 7:3 afforded Zechariah the opportunity to interpret the past, present, and future of God's intent for his people. Verses 9–10 state the core ethical practices of Israel. However, the people did not listen in those former days. The God of the past, who had brought prosperity, also brought judgment. Consequently, the land of prosperity became desolate (Zech 7:11–14).

Ollenburger sees the structure of the unit 7:7–14 as comprising an introduction (7:7), a summary of the words of the former prophets (7:9–10), a report of the people's response (7:11–12a), and the consequences of their response (12b-14). Zechariah refers to the adversity in the past as the reversal of an earlier prosperity due to the people's rejection of the former prophets. The scope of restoration will be broad, extending from Babylonia to the Mediterranean (8:7). It will even encompass foreigners (compare Isa 2:55).

Finally comes the answer to the question asked by the delegation (Zech 8:14). Zechariah calls his people *to be strong and not afraid* and not to interrupt the rebuilding of the temple but to continue to strive to join with God's salvation (Zech 8:10, 13c). Fast days of mourning will become seasons of celebration (8:4–5, 18–19). In the past, God's word involved a reversal from prosperity to adversity, but now the future involves a reversal from fasts to feasts. God's return to Jerusalem inaugurates the beginning of the future now (Zech 8:20–23).

THE RESTORATION OF JUDAH & ISRAEL · 9:1–11:17

The eschatological oracles of Zechariah 9–14 do not forecast international history but create a vision of the future by reenvisioning the past. The need to see the future in more distant terms was a response to the failure of the return to the land under Persian rule to produce the utopia envisioned by earlier eschatological expectations (see Isa 40–55). The oracles in Zechariah 9–14 address the disparity between present realities and unfulfilled hopes (for example, Zech 4:10). The shepherds have failed to tend the flock of God, and the flock of God has detested the shepherds. The mastery of the Lord over the whole earth is therefore called into question (chapters 9–11). Chapters 12–14 look to the future, *on that day*, when God's reign over the whole earth commences.

The promises of restoration awaited fulfillment. Four passages (9:1–17; 10:3b–12; 12:1–13:6; 14:1–21) present a bright and glorious future hope that includes a Davidic king and a reunited kingdom. This future will involve conflict, war, and death, but God will purge Jerusalem and protect Judah. Uniting these four passages are three sections (10:1–3a; 11:1–17; 13:7–9) describing the failures of the shepherds that ultimately led to the unrealized hope for king and kingdom and the intermingled texts of war against Jerusalem.

9:1–8 The divine warrior, Yahweh, sweeps across Syria-Palestine north to south toward Jerusalem on his march to restore the land. After his victory, all the people *rejoice* because their king is arriving at the temple, victorious and in peace (9:9–10). The list of nations includes Jerusalem's nearest foreign neighbors. The connection between conquest and temple building goes back before the Israelites and underlies many biblical texts (for example, Exod 15).

9:9–17 This section begins with a call to praise (vv. 9–10) and continues with a word of deliverance and encouragement (vv. 11–17). As such, these verses resemble a psalm of praise. The restored people of Israel return to the land once the future king has come in victory and sealed their relationship by *the blood of my covenant*. Although there is peace, not all is well. There is an announcement of war, for some people remain prisoners in faraway lands. The Lord desires a full return and restoration of Israel. The reference to *Greece* (v. 13) may echo the conflict between Persia and Greece in the fifth century BCE (Meyers and Meyers, *Zechariah 9–14*, 148) or date the oracle to the Maccabean struggle in the 160s, depending on one's view of the entire book.

10:1–12 The promising vision of God's restoration continues in chapter 10 with only a hint of trouble in 10:2 that anticipates the internal collapse in chapter 11 (Ollenburger 802). Other than Isaiah 57, Zechariah 10:2 and 13:2 are the only mentions of *idols* in postexilic writings. Chapter 10 parallels and extends the vision of restoration found in chapter 9. God, as the creator and sustainer of life, directs his anger toward the shepherds to bring about the future restoration of all the scattered people and a son of David of the house of Judah who will again sit on the throne of a united kingdom.

11:1–17 Chapter 11 calls into question the vision of chapters 9–10 by using a parable, or allegory, describing the symbolic act of the prophet becoming a shepherd in a tenuous relationship with the people (11:4–17). The oracle uses a first person report, or prophetic autobiography, to communicate

Corrupt Leadership
The postexilic community must see the corruption of its leadership depicted by the prophet, for this precludes the coming of God's mercy. Numerous attempts to identify the shepherds with historical figures pervade the literature, but with no satisfying consensus.

the failure of the shepherd. The shepherd breaks a staff, symbolic of a covenant, draws his wages, and hurls the money into the temple. He breaks a second staff, symbolic of the union between Israel and Judah. The breaking of this staff is a reversal of the symbolic act of Ezekiel 37:15–23. The prophet then becomes the foolish shepherd who abuses the people of God.

The reference to the *thirty shekels* of 11:13 possibly alludes to the same amount paid to a slave owner as compensation when an ox gores a slave (Exod 21:32). The passage concludes with a woe oracle directed against the worthless shepherd who neglects the flock. The shepherd usually refers to a king but in this context may include other religious leaders. The solution envisions a restored Davidic throne. The woe of 11:17 anticipates the description of the purging of Jerusalem in 12:10–13:6.

GOD'S WAR TO PURIFY ISRAEL · 12:1–14:21

12:1–14 This section depicts a war by the nations against Judah, with God bringing Judah to victory. The cryptic text defies identifying the circumstances described with any particular international setting. The future orientation of these oracles of promise (12:1–14:21) and thematic unity of God's victory as divine warrior is heightened by the repeated use of eschatological scenarios of what will transpire *on that day* (12:3, 4, 6, 8, 9, 11; 13:1, 2, 4; 14:4, 6, 8, 9, 13, 20, 21—17 times total).

The God of creation (12:1) declares that, as the nations gather to attack Jerusalem, they will be frustrated (12:2–9). The encouraged people recognize that *the Lord Almighty is their God* (12:5). Verse 10 suggests various echoes used in the New Testament (Matt 3:17; Luke 2:7, 9:35; John 1:18, 19:37; Rom 8:29; Col 1:15). Mourning and supplication will follow God's victory as the people realize their salvation has come through God's intervention (12:10–14).

13:1–9 This unit describes the cleansing that follows God's victory and the elimination of idols, prophets, and prophecy (13:2–6). Prophets come under such disdain that even their parents will slay them. Even the language of Amos 7:14, *I am not a prophet*, plays against the prophets. Finally, even a good shepherd of the people is slain, scattering two-thirds of the people; however, a third of the people will be purified and remain in the land. Thus this chapter picks up the ancient ideas of the remnant.

14:1–21 The war imagery of chapter 12 is repeated in chapter 14, with the latter making no mention of prophets, shepherds, or a Davidic house. Both chapters affirm the theology of Zion prevalent in Isaiah. In 14:1–2, the nations are gathered to fight against Jerusalem (compare Psalm 2). In 14:3, God will fight for the people and the nations will be defeated. God alone will be king (14:9, 16, 17). And after Jerusalem is purged, it will be the center of God's universal reign and recreative order. Survivors from all nations will come to celebrate the Feast of Tabernacles (see Exod 23:16; Neh 8:18). Zechariah concludes with his final word about the temple (14:20–21). *On that day*, the day of God's consummate victory in the age to come, the temple will finally be fit for worship for the whole world. The inclusive vision of the nations gathering in Jerusalem characterizes the endings of both parts of the book (8:20–23; 14:20–21).

THEOLOGICAL REFLECTIONS

Zechariah must find a way to make the words of the older prophets relevant to a new day. The book bearing his name deals with specific problems such as the rebuilding of the temple, the relationship of Jews to their Gentile rulers, and especially the meaning of Israel's preexilic history. It addresses these problems by reclaiming the hopeful language and high ethical standards of the past as it seeks to rebuild Israel as a fit location for the residence of the God of all the earth.

FOR FURTHER STUDY

Boda, Mark J., ed. *Exploring Zechariah*. 2 vols. Atlanta: SBL, 2017.

Collins, John J. *Joel, Obadiah, Haggai, Zechariah, Malachi*. Collegeville, MN: Liturgical Press, 2013.

WORKS CITED

Coggins, R. J. *Haggai, Zechariah, Malachi*. Sheffield: JSOT Press, 1987.

Collins, John. "Introduction: Toward the Morphology of a Genre." *Semeia* 14 (1979): 1–20.

Conrad, E. W. *Zechariah*. Sheffield: Sheffield Academic Press, 1999.

Fishbane, Michael. *Biblical Interpretation in Ancient Israel*. Oxford: Clarendon, 1985.

Halpern, Baruch. "The Ritual Background of Zechariah's Temple Song." *Catholic Biblical Quarterly* 40 (1978): 167–90.

Hanson, Paul. "In Defiance of Death: Zechariah's Symbolic Universe." In *Love and Death in the Ancient Near East*, edited by J. H. Marks and R. M. Good, 176–77. Guilford: Four Quarters, 1987.

Mason, Rex. *Preaching the Tradition: Homily and Hermeneutics after the Exile*. Cambridge, UK: Cambridge University Press, 1990.

Meyers, C. L., and Eric M. Meyers. *Haggai and Zechariah 1–8*. New York: Doubleday, 1987.

——— . *Zechariah 9–14*. New York: Doubleday, 1993.

Ollenburger, B. C. *New Interpreters Bible*. Volume 7: *The Book of Zechariah*. Nashville: Abingdon, 1996.

Petersen, David. *Haggai and Zechariah 1–8*. Louisville: Westminster John Knox, 1984.

——— . *Zechariah 9–14 and Malachi*. Louisville: Westminster John Knox, 1995.

Malachi

Paul L. Watson

CHAPTER CONTENTS

The book of Malachi provides a fitting conclusion to the "Book of the Twelve" (that is, the Minor Prophets). Malachi sets forth many great themes of the biblical witness: the universal rule of God; the steadfast love of God for Israel, in spite of their sins; the absolute necessity of covenant keeping from the heart; and the certainty of divine judgment, tempered with mercy.

CONTEXTS

We know virtually nothing about Malachi. In fact, "Malachi" may be his actual name or simply his title—"my [God's] messenger" (see 3:1). His messages address the restored Jewish community in Palestine during the postexilic (Persian) period. It was "a small and relatively poor community, without solid economic resources or great hopes" (Schuller 848), with the population of Judah numbering at most a few thousand. Most scholars date that community to a few decades after the rebuilding of the Jerusalem temple in 520 BCE (see Haggai and Zech 1–8), but before the time of Nehemiah and Ezra.

The Persian Empire
The Persian Empire extended from present-day Afghanistan to Greece and existed from 539–334 BCE before falling to Alexander the Great. Darius the Great came to the throne of Persia in 522 BCE after a brief civil war. He was a junior member of the royal family.

Between a brief introduction (1:1) and an epilogue (4:4–6), the book of Malachi has six distinct units. Each unit typically includes an accusatory statement and/or question by God (for example, 2:17a); a response from Israel that deflects the accusation, often by asking a counterquestion (2:17b); and God's rebuttal, often cast as a summary statement or question (2:17c), which is then expounded upon (3:1–5). This format has been labeled a disputation, a dialogue (Schuller 850), a priestly trial (Achtemeier 172), and a diatribe (Petersen 31). Whatever the book's form, the function is clear: to urge the people to recognize and repent of their sins before it is too late.

COMMENTARY

INTRODUCTION · 1:1
Oracle is a technical term used to designate prophetic speech (see Isa 13:1; Nah 1:1; Hab 1:1). In the introduction, *Israel* expresses God's inclusive view of his people (see 4:4 and Deut 1:1).

I HAVE LOVED YOU, SAYS THE LORD · 1:2–5
This is the topic sentence of Malachi. It conveys both God's feelings for Israel and a covenant commitment to them (see Deut 7:7–9; Hos 11:1). The community's response, *How have you loved us?* (1:2b), challenges that commitment.

God responds, somewhat surprisingly, by reminding Israel of its "half-brother," Esau/Edom. Even though Esau was the firstborn twin, God chose to love Jacob/Israel (Gen 25:23; 28:13–15). Edom subsequently became Israel's implacable enemy (Obad 1–21; Jer 49:7–22). *Great is the Lord—even beyond the borders of Israel* (1:5) is Malachi's first reminder of God's worldwide sovereignty and honor (see 1:11, 14; 3:12).

IF I AM A FATHER, WHERE IS THE HONOR DUE ME? · 1:6–2:9
This unit illustrates the people's contempt for God. God has loved them (1:2); but in return they have dishonored him with their *defiled* offerings—*blind, crippled, diseased* (1:8), and *injured* (1:13) animals—contrary to the explicit instructions of Leviticus 1:3; 22:17–25, and Deuteronomy 15:21. Even offering the culls from their herds is a *burden; and [they] sniff at it* (NIV; NRSV, *me*) in contempt (1:13). To God, absence of worship is preferable to disrespectful worship (1:10; see Amos 5:21–24; Isa 1:12–14), particularly since *my name will be great among the nations*, that is, honored by others worldwide (1:11).

The last half of the unit (2:1–9) is directed to Israel's priests. It may be that *two* groups of priests are involved—the Aaronic priests, who are condemned (2:2–3), and the Levitical priests, whose covenant with God is salvageable (2:4–5; see Deut 33:8–11 and Jer 33:19–22; see Petersen 189–90). The priestly blessings of unfaithful priests will become a curse (2:2; see Num 6:22–27). Priests who offer *defiled* sacrifices (1:7, 12) will themselves be defiled by having the excrement of the sacrificial animals spread over their own faces (2:3), thus disqualifying them from serving at God's altar.

HAVE WE NOT ALL ONE FATHER? · 2:10–16

At stake in this unit is the integrity of the community. By *breaking faith with one another*, the people are also breaking faith with their forefathers and with God (2:10). Some are marrying outside the covenant community (2:11–12; see Solomon in 1 Kgs 11:1–6). Others are abandoning their longtime mates—*your partner, the wife of your marriage covenant* (2:13–14). God himself has made them one (2:15a; see Gen 2:24 and Mark 10:6–9), and he expects *godly offspring* from such unions (2:15b; see Gen 1:27–28). The faithless behavior of Israelite husbands *in flesh and spirit* (2:15) has made that impossible. No wonder God says, *I hate divorce* (2:16): "The ruined lives, the collapse of hopes, and the loss of faithfulness make it a hateful practice" (Craigie 238).

WHERE IS THE GOD OF JUSTICE? · 2:17–3:5

The dialogue now turns to Israel's accusation that Yahweh is not just and fair because God accepts evildoers as good and because there is no justice in God's world (2:17).

The *wearied* Lord replies that his justice will surely become evident, first through *my messenger, who will prepare the way before me*, then by his own arrival at his temple (3:1). Verse 5 cites six specific examples of covenant-breaking and spells out the nature of God's coming—*for judgment*, on all who have rejected the messenger.

> **The Role of God's Messenger**
> *The messenger's role is elaborated upon in 3:2–4. His will be a ministry of refining and purifying God's people, in preparation for the Lord's arrival (see Matt 3:1–12 and 11:7–15, where Jesus quotes Mal 3:1).*

I THE LORD DO NOT CHANGE · 3:6–12

The next issue in the dispute is unfaithful stewardship. God begins the dialogue by reminding Israel of his consistency (3:6a). Far from being unjust (2:17), God rightly could have *destroyed* the *descendants of Jacob* (3:6b). Instead, God urges the audience to *Return to me, and I will return to you* (3:7b). Their return, however, must be in deed as well as in word. They must produce "fruit in keeping with repentance" (see Matt 3:8), specifically the *tithes and offerings* (3:8c) that they owe to God.

Such *tithes* (given to support the Levites; Num 18:21–24) and *offerings* (one-tenth of the tithe, given by the Levites to God; Num 18:25–32) are not gifts but are God's due (Lev 27:30–33). To withhold them is truly to *rob God* (3:8). Conversely, to *bring the whole tithe* (3:10) will lead to God abundantly blessing them (3:10–11). While it is more common for God to test people, here God audaciously invites his people to *test me in this* (3:10b). The results will be *a delightful land* for them, and worldwide commendation for them and their God (3:12).

IT IS FUTILE TO SERVE GOD · 3:13–4:3

In this summary debate, the recalcitrant members of the community expand their complaint against God. Having previously asked, *Where is the God of justice?* (2:17), they now assert, *It is futile to serve God. What did we gain by carrying out his requirements?* . . . *[E]vildoers prosper, and even those who challenge God escape* (3:14–15).

Interestingly enough, God does not respond immediately to their charges. Instead, *those who feared the Lord* (3:16) talk things over among themselves and conclude that God *is* right. God *listened and heard* them, records their faithfulness and promises to *spare them* and make them his *treasured possession* (3:16b–18; see Exod 19:3–6).

Then God reveals the future: *Surely the day is coming* . . . (4:1a; see Amos 5:18–20, 8:11; Isa 2:12). It will be a day of disaster for *all the arrogant and every evildoer* (4:1), but a day of deliverance for *you who revere my name* (4:2a). Like *calves released from the stall*, the faithful will *leap* in the warm sunlight (4:2b) and *trample* the *ashes* of the wicked (4:3a) who have already met their fate (4:1).

EPILOGUE · 4:4–6

These last three verses of Malachi are a divine admonition (4:4) and a divine promise (4:5–6). The admonition is to *remember the law* (teaching, NRSV; Hebrew *torah*) *of my servant Moses* (see Deut 8:1–2, 10–18). The promise is *I will send you the prophet Elijah* (4:5), whose mission will be one of reconciliation and preparation for the Lord's own coming (4:6).

THEOLOGICAL REFLECTIONS

For such a short and relatively unfamiliar biblical book, Malachi is theologically full and rich. Themes that merit further reflection include the primacy of God's love (1:2; John 3:16), worship (1:6–14; Mark 11:15–17), ministry (2:1–9; 2 Cor 4:1–2), marriage and divorce (2:10–16; Mark 10:1–12), and stewardship (3:6–12; 2 Cor 8:1–7). The theme of God's justice—present and future—rounds out the book (2:17–3:5; 3:13–4:3), leaving its readers with both an admonition and a promise (4:4–6; 2 Pet 3:10–13).

FOR FURTHER STUDY

Brown, William P. *Obadiah through Malachi*. Louisville: Westminster John Knox, 1996.
Davis, Stacy. *Haggai and Malachi*. Collegeville, MN: Liturgical Press, 2015.

WORKS CITED

Achtemeier, Elizabeth. *Nahum–Malachi*. Atlanta: John Knox, 1986.
Craigie, Peter. *Twelve Prophets*. Volume 2: *Micah, Nahum, Habakkuk, Zephaniah, Haggai, Zechariah, and Malachi*. Louisville: Westminster John Knox, 1985.
Petersen, David L. *Zechariah 9–14 and Malachi*. Louisville: Westminster John Knox, 1995.
Schuller, Eileen M. "The Book of Malachi." In *The New Interpreters' Bible*, edited by Leander Keck, 7:841–77. Nashville: Abingdon, 1996.